Back Stages

performance works

SERIES EDITORS
Patrick Anderson and
Nicholas Ridout
This series publishes books in theater and performance studies, focused in particular on the material conditions in which performance acts are staged, and to which performance itself might contribute. We define "performance" in the broadest sense, including traditional theatrical productions and performance art, but also cultural ritual, political demonstration, social practice, and other forms of interpersonal, social, and political interaction that may fruitfully be understood in terms of performance.

Back Stages

Essays across Art, Performance, and Public Life

✦

Shannon Jackson

NORTHWESTERN UNIVERSITY PRESS
EVANSTON, ILLINOIS

Northwestern University Press
www.nupress.northwestern.edu

Printed in the United States of America

10 9 8 7 6 5 4 3 2 1

Library of Congress Cataloging-in-Publication Data

Names: Jackson, Shannon, 1967– author.
Title: Back stages : essays across art, performance, and public life / Shannon
    Jackson.
Other titles: Performance works.
Description: Evanston, Illinoia : Northwestern University Press, 2022. |
    Series: Performance works | Includes bibliographical references and index.
Identifiers: LCCN 2021062396 | ISBN 9780810144842 (paperback) |
    ISBN 9780810144859 (cloth) | ISBN 9780810144866 (ebook)
Subjects: LCSH: Performing arts—Social aspects—United States. |
    Performing arts—United States. | Arts and society. | BISAC:
    PERFORMING ARTS / Theater / History & Criticism
Classification: LCC PN1590.S6 J33 2022 | DDC 791.0973—dc23/
    eng/20220105
LC record available at https://lccn.loc.gov/2021062396

For my students

CONTENTS

ACKNOWLEDGMENTS

This reader tracks more than twenty-five years of thinking and writing. As such, it is indebted to a wide network of universities, journals, presses, museums, theaters, biennials, and public art organizations who involved me in their work throughout my career. The collection is also indebted to the people at each of these spaces—whether scholars, curators, editors, artists, or students. Indeed, I want to thank the many teams of people whose invitations prompted me to think and write in the first place. Of course, I also want to thank all of the publication outlets and photographers who allowed me to reprint this work.

I am honored and grateful to be included in a series coedited by Nicholas Ridout and by my former student, Patrick Anderson, one that is published by the press associated with my graduate alma mater, Northwestern University. I have perpetual gratitude for my research assistants who tracked down material for this publication, beginning with Megan Hoeteger and Sophia Sobko, and concluding with the incredibly responsive and expert support of K. C. Forcier. Thanks are also due to Paris Cotz and Soomin Suh—my administrative staff at UC Berkeley who allowed me to focus on this project alongside our campus duties. The assembly of this collection coincided with an intense period of administrative service at the University of California, Berkeley, as well as an unfathomable global pandemic. It also coincided with a time of significant personal challenge in my life. Hence, more thanks go to my most devoted friends—Joan, Kang, Rob, Joyce, Ann, Shawn, Gina, Gail, Benjamin, Antonia, Michael T., Berit, Karen, Sarah, Jessica, Bruno, Daphne M., and Nader—for being by my side while I rekindled both brain and heart. I am grateful as always to my family—my children, Daphne and Jack, and my mother, Jacqueline Jackson—for their good humor and their tolerance of my working life.

As my dedication acknowledges, the last expression of gratitude goes to my first interlocutors, my students. I have always tuned my writing to their ears, hoping that my thinking could be, in some way, adequate to their own committed thinking and their voracious desire to learn. If there is anything worth reading in what follows, it is indebted to them.

Back Stages

INTRODUCTION

Starting: Attendance

It will be another performance where I have to sit on the floor. This piece is sited in a theater—not a gallery, museum atrium, or outdoor plaza. It's a *theater*, so seats should be part of the hospitality. But no. As we walk in, we are told to sit on the floor. Audience members should take their shoes off. They (we) can sit wherever we would like on the floor. We can sit as close or as far from the stage as we like, or rather, we can sit on the stage as close or as far from the platform—the plinth—set atop that stage, around which we gather . . . bemusedly, expectantly. I walk to the stage and sit, lowering torso to ground. I cross my legs under me. I straighten my back. I recross my legs the other way. I (we) are here to witness Faye Driscoll's *Thank You for Coming: Attendance* (2012–20), a piece that requires its receivers to decide what it means to attend—to show up, to bear witness, to sit at attention—from the get-go.

At some point, I realize that performers—dancers? artists? bodies?—are coming up behind us, crawling from the back of the stage, or rather, the back of the theater, on the stage toward the platform, slinking their way around the bodies seated cross-legged on the ground. I am still bemused, still expectant, as clearly something is starting to happen. I hear the rustle of the dancers' crawling; one is nearer to me, coming from behind. "Hi, Shannon." It's a whisper in my ear. I startle. "It's Sean," he still whispers. He winks at me while crawling past me. "From the Builders," he moves along. Sean Donovan is a performer—a dancer, artist, body—I know. He's a performer who gets "cast in" theater that I see. Who "dances for" choreographers I know. Who is hired to be a performing body in artworks that I like to experience. He is what in the performing arts world is called a triple threat—he acts, he sings, he dances. In the adventurous world of contemporary art and performance, he's a quadruple threat, because he also has the conceptual tendencies—the cognitive virtuosities—to want to be a collaborator in the experimental performances that I like to see. In addressing me, he forced me to attend to my attendance. He winked to show he knew who I was: the critic in the room, the critic on the floor. I was outed. No anonymous audience experience here. No way to take even mental notes without someone wondering whether I'm going to write about this show.

So here I am, writing.

3

Yes, here I am writing in 2021 about this show, writing about attendance after a year when I have not been able to attend any performances in person. I experienced *Thank You for Coming: Attendance* in Paris as part of Festival d'Automne a few years before. Those who follow contemporary performance know that this festival occurs every year to frame a semicoordinated array of events in established and less-established theatrical venues around the city. (Those in the artworld who do not follow contemporary performance might wonder if it is kind of like a biennial.) The festival and the venues are part of a global circuit of parallel festivals and venues who support the touring schedules of experimental performing artists like Driscoll. They appear in London, in Athens, in Adelaide, in New York, in Brussels, and more; but no, these festivals are not quite biennials. That said, such festivals are like biennials in that they draw thousands of bodies to experience art together in the same time and place; as such, festivals and biennials are gatherings imperiled by global pandemics that restrict bodily gathering. Meanwhile, before 2020, Driscoll was one of a cluster of experimental choreographers who enjoyed an inter-arts career, presented and touring among notable performing sites (e.g., The Kitchen, Brooklyn Academy of Music, and Walker), as well as well as within "visual art" world curation—at New Museum and Museum of Arts and Design (MAD) Biennial. Hence, a piece like *Thank You for Coming* might be productively placed within the network of experimental performance genealogies. Like many artists of her generation, Driscoll's career and her transit among different types of venues coincided with an accelerating interest in theater, dance, and performance among visual art spaces, part of the interart acceleration that has been preoccupying me and many others for the last decade. By thematizing "Attendance" and the hospitable exchange among participants, Driscoll arguably rides a social turn as well, where the act of showing up as a participatory infrastructure is itself the object of investigation. Those in the artworld who don't follow contemporary performance might wonder if this is relational aesthetics.

Let's see.

The piece's signature image transpires early in the performance. On that raised platform—that plinth—five bodies assemble and lean on each other, precariously, dynamically. The arm of one dancer leans on the shoulder of another, but a leg from elsewhere alights there too. A head lowers onto someone's back, and falls when that back leans forward. These bodies, propelled and propelling, suspended and suspending, compose a precious structure, a sentient collective form. As limbs release and torsos fall, dancers catch a different head or different limb, propping and being propped by new extensions, releasing in boredom or excitement to new arrangements. We can hear them breathing. If you are an audience member like me, you think you feel a vicarious connection to those connected to each other. You think you feel that discomfort as bodies grow weary or bored of the obligation to hold up the limbs of another. You feel them responding to each other—connecting, grasping, straining. Whether or not *Thank You for Coming* is relational aesthetics, it is relationality. Whether I, you, or these performers will ever be able to luxuriate in postpandemic proximity again is another question, a question for readers to answer again and again as the years ahead unfold.

Starting Again: Arts, Context, Politics

This collection of essays explores a range of disciplinary, institutional, and political puzzles that impinge on the social and aesthetic practice of performance. It begins by dialing backward, recalling some of my earliest thinking about how the framework of performance might offer alternate methodologies for understanding the social life of bodies, past and present. That thinking is indebted to the history of social reform in Chicago, as well as to my experience at Northwestern University whose press is (poignantly for me) publishing this reader. In many ways, an immersion in the methods of performance historiography stayed with me, even when I began to work with the ultracontemporary. That orientation can be found in new form as the collection of essays proceeds, analyzing disciplinary debates in the theoretical and practical elaboration of performance in higher education, including its fraught and allied relationship to literary studies, visual culture, theater, and critical theory. At a time of increased aesthetic experimentation and political debate in the artworld, this assembly goes on to alight on key artists, artist groups, and cultural organizations whose new experiments have challenged conventions of sociality, curation, and critique. Undergirding all the above, each essay navigates the political ambivalences of performance, whether those found in a late-nineteenth-century industrial economy or those coinciding with an experiential turn in a twenty-first-century postindustrial economy. *Back Stages* brings together over twenty of my essays, most of them previously published in academic journals, art catalogues, and edited collections. While each text originally addressed a differently situated audience in theater, US history, art history, visual culture, performance studies, dance, and the world of socially engaged art, the process of compilation has surfaced unexpected disciplinary connections. My hope is that—bound together—this collection of essays will provide new opportunities for mutual engagement within and across a varied network of educational, artistic, and civic sectors.

As my title and subtitle suggest, these essays are unified by their relation to performance, art, and the social—a relation that (for me) means redefining the backgrounded backstage. I offer these essays as someone who started life in drama, literature, and the performing arts and gradually began to think about performance as an anthropological ritual and sociological event. As my career proceeded, I returned to aesthetic questions but to different forms, tracking an interarts conversation across the performing arts, visual arts, video, and ever-new new media. That pursuit coincided with another abiding interest—the connection between aesthetic form and political reform, between art and social change, or within what the artworld began to call social practice. Such a tendency can be placed within a long and venerable genealogy that aligns art and performance with political action—whether in the ancient *theatron* that offered citizens a "place for viewing" or in a modern political *theatron* where Arendtian interlocutors elevate the political possibilities of performing artists and their actions. That tradition also includes another of my favorite feminist philosophers, Jane Addams, a reformer who understood the political and social potential of play. Of course, in a more recent context, some of those performative or participatory turns are about "being social" in a more mundane sense, about enabling or enforcing participation with the artwork, or about using participation and performance to activate the social scene of the artworld. I might also note that this is where the interarts conversation often becomes tangled in its own politics, its own institutional questions about which artistic forms find themselves where—on stages? In galleries? Inside or outside museums? In atriums, plazas, and biennials? Spectators to these forms adjust as well—sitting, standing, walking, interacting, sometimes in seats, but often on the floor. What does it mean that performance is finding its way, forcing its way, or being forced on the way, as a variety of art and cultural organizations seek "performative" engagement? How, moreover, has that engagement changed in a (post-)COVID world, one that elevates the screen as a delivery system for the arts, one that has given "outdoor" art or environmental art a new primacy as well? For some in the artworld, performance is and has been in the process of insidious takeover. The interarts domain thus turns out to be political in different terms, largely because the so-called turn to performance within visual arts, as well as the working conditions of contemporary performance generally, are seen to be disconcertingly symptomatic of a late capitalist shift in the coordination of immaterial service labor. Never mind that performance's "immaterial" service has always been highly material, something that became newly apparent with the contagious materiality of "essential service" during the pandemic. More on those tangles as I go.

Indeed, taken together, the essays in *Back Stages* implicitly track a tangled genealogy of theory and practice within social institutions, artistic institutions, and institutions of higher education. Two decades of my own writing coincided with what scholars and curators called "the performative turn," even if differently positioned critics had vastly different ideas of what the "performative" stood for and what it was turning from. My first book, *Lines of Activity* (2000), allied with a performative turn in the humanities and social sciences to analyze the evolution of a renowned institution of social reform, the Hull-House Settlement of Chicago. In my 2004 book, *Professing Performance*, I went in a different direction to analyze institutional patterns of connection and misrecognition around the keyword "performance," starting with early institutional debates in literary studies and moving into late twentieth-century theoretical debates in visual, social, and critical theory. My 2011 book, *Social Works*, addressed a topic that took me in yet another direction—the political assumptions and aesthetic practices of socially engaged art; this project required an investigation into how performance functioned within an expanding visual art world while also questioning the political assumptions of the "social" that such practices sought to model and to catalyze. Between and following these presumably distinct publications, however, I engaged in numerous projects that somewhat unexpectedly plotted a connective through line. From the late 1990s until now, I found myself charged with addressing a whole variety of organizational puzzles, cross-disciplinary sites, and artistic experiments, all of which revolved around the methodological challenges of analyzing and curating performance across a century when sensibilities toward social institutions changed as well. This is the line I seek to share in *Back Stages*.

The through line integrates three related methodological themes that shift and challenge each other depending on the project. A first alights on the relation between performance and social theory. This means considering how the many forms of performance (artistic, activist, ritualistic) activate our awareness of the social sphere and propel social reform. From a community parade in early twentieth-century Chicago to a public art action in twentieth-first-century Chicago, performance makes social dynamics visible and available for revision. But it also means adopting performance analysis as a scholarly method, as a multisensual, time-based form for modeling relationality and tracking the infrastructures that sustain lives worth living. Performance is thus a catalyst for social action but also a method by which social action can be interpreted and understood, aligning itself with scholarly turns in cultural anthropology, new historicism, new materialism, affect theory, and of course performance studies. A second central theme focuses on interart debates within and across various relational, participatory, and performative "turns." As I noted above and will continue to elaborate below, the consolidation of social practice in the artworld also ushered in various modes of "medium-unspecific" collaborations across art forms. At the same time, the poly-artistic curation of the performing arts inside the visual art museum brought renewed attention to the different effects, values, skills, and virtuosities of different performance forms; sometimes those interart virtuosities seemed to relate to social practice, including the political aesthetics of Occupy, and sometimes they seemed to be part of an entirely different, depoliticized conversation. Finally, both these methodological themes anticipate a third preoccupation, one largely focused on the challenges and possibilities that performance brings to practices of philosophical critique and the material revelation of context. Performance carries many connotations—it is associated with artifice, mimesis, display, excess, action, and more. While reckoning with these associations, I most often found myself focused on performance as a hyperembedded form, as a form whose boundaries with context continually blur and struggle with—and therefore must embrace— its relentless heteronomy. Performance exists in an embedded relation to the systems that surround it, a relation that exposes the surround that is simultaneously inside it. When performance becomes the object of critique, it both expands and confuses the parameters of critique, including the parameters of inside/outside, text/context, foreground/background. When taken seriously, the heteronomy of performance actually invites a different kind of formal pursuit, one linked to the goals of critique; performance offers an opportunity to explore the contextual contingency of any action, subject, or knowledge formation. That contingency is always present, if oft-disavowed; one formal effect of a global pandemic is that it makes the disavowal of material embeddedness impossible to sustain.

Not that anyone ever could.

Having introduced some central questions, let me back up to do some more scene setting, especially on the scenes that brought performance into a different kind of interart conversation. The last twenty years saw a renewal of the art and performance relationship in many experimental contexts—in museums and on stages, in studios and at civic spaces, in biennials (for the artworld) and in festivals (for the performing arts world). Following a longer century of cross-disciplinary experimentation, I found that the renewal could not be tracked fully under the rubric of "*performance* art," especially when artworld experiments began more actively to incorporate the trained skills of theater, dance, and music (i.e., the *performing* arts). I also found that the disciplinary significance of such experiments varied depending on who was watching them, and from which artistic or scholarly tradition they did their viewing. This productive structure of disciplinary misrecognition was familiar to me from *Professing Performance*, but whereas the 2004 study took that structure primarily to disciplinary questions of literature and text, these projects required an understanding of how performance (an ensemble and time-based medium) interacted with visual art (a presumably static, most often solo medium).

I used to take the year 2012 as an exemplary, pivotal moment in these transcontextual experiments. This was a year that included performance festivals like American Realness and Crossing the Line that considered the relationship between the gallery and the theater. So too, in the Performa Biennial, Roselee Goldberg focused that year's performance art biennial on the category of "theater" to grapple with the expansion of performing arts curation, even if, as she said at the time, she "hates theater."[1] The Under the Radar festival followed by hosting a conversation on the relation between the "black box" and the "white cube." In spring of 2012 Jay Sanders and Elisabeth Sussman offered a Whitney Biennial that was lauded in part for the performances curated inside it, including Wu Tsang's *Green Room*, Michael Clark's *Who's Zoo*, Richard Maxwell's installed rehearsals, and Sarah Michelson's *Devotion Study #1—The American Dancer*. The latter made history for being the first choreographic work to win the Whitney's Bucksbaum Award.[2] By fall of 2012 the Museum of Modern Art (MoMA) in New York was commissioning and acquiring all varieties of performances—from the maybe parodic, maybe activist, maybe earnest "events" of the art group Grand Openings to the siting of works conceived and commissioned by choreographers like Ralph Lemon, Steve Paxton, Faustin Linyekula, Dean Moss, Jérôme Bel, and more.[3] The year 2012 was also a pivotal transition for Tim Griffin, who left his position as editor of contemporary art publication *Artforum* to take over the contemporary performance venue The Kitchen, activating both its gallery spaces and its theater to stage a conversation across art forms. Meanwhile, non–New York-based activity had been approaching those interart stakes from different angles. The Walker Art Center in Minneapolis reconceived what it meant to "collect" when it acquired Merce Cunningham's costumes, debating along the way whether their conservation required the preservation or the eradication of the sweat marks and make-up stains of the dancers who wore them.[4] In France, Boris Charmatz and others started Musée de la Danse, putting choreography on a plinth. In the United Kingdom, the Tate Modern opened a section of the museum called The Tanks in 2012—committing "permanent" space to the presentation and exhibition of "temporary" art forms—by resiting choreographer Anne Teresa De Keersmaeker's *Fase* in its concrete space. Incidentally, the contemporaneously acquired "Crystal Quilt" of socially engaged artist Suzanne Lacy was also sited in The Tanks next door, broaching without fully reconciling a conversation about whether the museum's choreographic turn and its social turn were really part of the same performative turn.

Antagonisms remained; Marina Abramović's famous statement that "to be a performance artist, you have to hate theater" still lingered in the ears and in the atmosphere of these and many other experiments—including those inspired by Abramović's own blockbuster retrospective at MoMA two years earlier. Arguably, however, those antagonisms have been the ground for more considered critique—and a host of new experiments that now populate visual and performing arts spaces alike.[5] Though some versions of art history warned against the intrusion of temporality into visual art spaces, conversations among scholars of theater, dance, performance, and art are now increasingly hosted by art institutions; there is continual, productive debate about the stage management of live events as well as its archival and collectible potential in the projective scores and retrospective residue that performance leaves behind (e.g., texts, photographs, props, sets, sweat, promises, memories). Choreographer Anna Therese De Keersmaeker has gone on to become a signature figure in this crossdisciplinary—and cross-professional—conversation. Three years after the Tanks opening, she created a new piece of choreographic endurance; *Work/Travail/Arbeid* (2015), premiered at WIELS Center for Contemporary Art in Brussels as part of the Performatik 2015. Performatik itself was a citywide event conceived in collaboration with experimental theater spaces such as Kaaitheater and visual art spaces such as Bozar and WIELS. Its organizer, Katleen Van Langendonck, strategically decided to market Performatik as both an art "biennial" and a performing arts "festival" to invite and redefine different kinds of durational art reception.[6] Curated by Elena Filipovic, *Work/Travail/Arbeid* placed an ensemble of trained dancers within the WIELS galleries for six hours each day, inspiring them to move as sentient sculpture deliberately and responsively in and among the audience members who rotated in and out of the space each hour.[7] Audience members managed their own relationship to proximate dancers as they moved, some staying at the perimeter of the gallery, some entering the center. Some stood, some sat, some walked, and even ran along with the dancers as they rushed across the space. In a public dialogue with fellow choreographer Xavier Le Roy, De Keersmaeker spoke about the paradoxes of dance-art collaborations.[8] Both she and Le Roy remarked on how their disruptions of dance in one context actually appear to reactivate dance in another context. Le Roy noted bemusedly, "I am non-dance in the dance world, but in the art world, I am dance."[9] Even more recently, De Keersmaeker become implicated in a highly political conversation about aesthetic transcontextualization when Chris Dercon, former director of the Tate Modern, included her in his first (and last) program as incoming intendant for the Volksbuhne in Berlin.[10] More on that tangle later as well.

These interart questions of movement, stasis, embodiment, ensemble, and context speak back to the first and third themes I noted above; for one, they focused both conceptually and infrastructurally on how artists, curators, critics, and citizens delineate the parameters of the cultural object. Such infrastructural questions in the artworld had their parallel in the scholarly world. Late twentieth-century scholarly traditions—new historicism, visual culture, cultural anthropology, performance studies—increasingly emphasized the aesthetic object as contextual and situated, indeed, even unsettling conventional parameters of where the object ended and its context began. My project on Hull-House was both a symptom of and a response to such disciplinary turns, using the lens of performance to describe the embedded life of a settlement movement whose proponents sought to embed themselves across class and culture in Progressive

Era Chicago. Such disciplinary questions also informed the more metain-
stitutional work I sought to do in *Professing Performance*; in putting
performance forward as an object of analysis and debate in higher education, I suggested that it challenged epistemological conventions of
delineation and boundedness, echoing a wider scholarly context that was
challenging literary and art-historical conventions of delineation. If one
places this contextual ethos between the world of scholarship and the artworld, one can arguably understand the "performative turn" within this
hypercontextual thought structure, one that propelled artistic experiments
that embraced rather than disavowed the temporal, spatial, and embodied
contexts in which art was installed and in which social life was experienced. "Situatedness" emerges then as both a scholarly methodological
pursuit *and* as an artistic preoccupation; situatedness is a condition to
be aesthetically mined by late twentieth- and twentieth-first-century artists. Most interestingly, artworks variously called institutional critique and
social practice, or dubbed performative, relational, choreographic, and
socially engaged, were using the stuff of "context." Habits, dispositions,
spaces, money, power, institutions, and people became aesthetic material—
whether at a community organization or in a museum, theater, university,
or governmental apparatus. Throughout *Back Stages* I offer various sites
and puzzles that explore the productive dependence of art and ideas on the
social institutions that house them. In a final epilogue, I consider the "un-
housing" of such forms by the parameters of shelter-in-place, alongside
their ubiquitous rescreening and restreaming in 2020.

Of course, the "swapping of contexts" among the arts in fact exposes
artistic contexts; the experiments above and those referenced in *Back
Stages* expose the naturalized conditions and contexts that produce ordinary knowledge of what we think we know about art, theater, and the
social underpinnings of ensemble. They also expose undertheorized differences between performance art and the performing arts in the process.
Such tacit differences are part of why "performance artists" feel the need
to "hate theater" even when their own processes come so close to approxi-
mating its condition. It is no coincidence then that a focus on context
and situation simultaneously invites a reckoning with a wider genealogy
of "critique"—criticism, self-critique, and immanent critique. In various
essays throughout *Back Stages*, I find myself preoccupied with context
as artistic material, a method of analysis, and both the object and the
ground of critique. Indeed, my own perspective on the connection between
context and critique is situated in my context at UC Berkeley—a place
that holds and sometimes mixes historicist practices, cultural studies,
activist histories, and traditions of critique. Consider an exemplary essay
by UC Berkeley's Judith Butler: "What is Critique? An Essay on the Virtues of Foucault" (2001) is primarily a piece on the French expat and
Berkeley-bound Michel Foucault, but Butler starts by gathering other

contextualizing trajectories from Raymond Williams in the United Kingdom and Theodor W. Adorno in Germany. She reminds us:

> Raymond Williams worried that the notion of criticism has been
> unduly restricted to the notion of "fault-finding" and proposed
> that we find a kind of response, specifically to cultural works,
> "which [do] not assume the habit (or right or duty) of judgment."
> And what he called for was a more specific kind of response, one
> that did not generalize too quickly: "what always needs to be
> understood," he wrote, "is the specificity of the response, which is
> not a judgment, but a practice." I believe this last line also marks
> the trajectory of Foucault's thinking on this topic, since "critique"
> is precisely a practice that not only suspends judgment for him,
> but offers a new practice of values based on that very suspension.[11]

Butler goes on to note that this sense of critique as a practice also informed
Adorno's thinking:

> For critique to operate as part of a praxis, for Adorno, is for it to
> apprehend the ways in which categories are themselves instituted,
> how the field of knowledge is ordered, and how what it suppresses
> returns, as it were, as its own constitutive occlusion. Judgments
> operate for both thinkers as ways to subsume a particular under
> an already constituted category, whereas critique asks after the
> occlusive constitution of the field of categories themselves.[12]

In the case of both Williams and Adorno, critique is highly situated because
thinking is a situated activity. To practice critique is to mine not simply
what we know but *how* we think we know—the conditions that produce ourselves as knowing subjects. Williams called that situatedness, the
"specificity of the response," and it was both a clarifying act and a humble
act to avow one's own site specificity as a critic—even a critic on the floor.
For Adorno, the experience of specificity insidiously depended on a degree
of occlusion, a repression of situating factors so that one's context could
feel normal and natural rather than constructed and contingent. Every
knowledge order repressed other possibilities; it was the job of critique to
explore the productivity of a lived order as well as to ask what that habit
of living occludes. With Williams and Adorno at her side, Butler continued
to clarify the contribution of Foucault to this longer genealogy of critical
theory, one that deemphasizes evaluation per se in favor of an immanent
excavation about how terms of value are produced in the first place:

> Thus, Foucault seeks to define critique, but finds that only a series
> of approximations are possible. Critique will be dependent on its

objects, but its objects will in turn define the very meaning of critique. Further, the primary task of critique will not be to evaluate whether its objects—social conditions, practices, forms of knowledge, power, and discourse—are good or bad, valued highly or demeaned, but to bring into relief the very framework of evaluation itself.[13]

This tendency to emphasize critique's "dependence" thus exemplifies another hypercontextual thought structure; the object of critique simultaneously defines the parameters of critique's practice. If the job of critique is "to bring into relief the very framework of evaluation itself," then thinking has a kind of infrastructural quality. It is experienced in relief, suspending and suspended by frameworks, conditions, speech, health practices, and power practices. Critique's frontstage is part and parcel of its backstage.

Having started with a theme of sociality in performance, moved to contemporary performance in the art world and then on to themes of critique and context, let me highlight connections among these trajectories. Those allied with the performing arts might spy a clear link between the contextuality of critique and the contextuality embedded in theater's etymological history. Many theorists of the theater regularly invoke the etymological link between theory and theater—a place for viewing—to foreground theater as a space of critique, as a space for "viewing the very framework" of social and artistic evaluation. Such a preoccupation has a visual art genealogy as well, one demonstrated in the contextualizing practices of both art history and contemporary art, especially the artworld practice of "institutional critique." Institutional critique is the moniker given to a group of artistic practices that set their sights—and their sites—on the institutional processes of art organizations, especially the world of museums, as well as the associated financial and spatial systems of gallery, biennial, and art-market processes.[14] Institutional critique remains a catchall term for the disparate practices that extended Minimalist and conceptual art's engagement with the gallery to address the museum's wider network of economic and institutional relationships.[15] More social and political themes start to emerge here too.

Alexander Alberro, one of institutional critique's notable historians, reminds us that the Enlightenment concept of the public sphere—and art's civic function therein—was a primary motivator for "institutionally critical" practices. "The artistic practices that in the late 1960s and 1970s came to be referred to as institutional critique," Alberro writes, "revisited that radical promise of the European Enlightenment, and they did so precisely by confronting the institution of art with the claim that it was not sufficiently committed to, let alone realizing or fulfilling, the pursuit of publicness that had brought it into being in the first place."[16] Artists who identified with institutional critique staged that confrontation in a variety of ways. For Daniel Buren, such a challenge meant interrogating the decontextualizing logic of the studio-museum relation, as well as the inside-outside logic of the public museum. For Hans Haacke and Martha Rosler, the investigation of the museum's relation to public space meant understanding and critiquing its economic dependencies, including its embeddedness in the world of real-estate speculation. For Michael Asher, institutional critique meant mimicking the museum's didactic processes by turning that didacticism on the institution itself. For Mierle Laderman Ukeles, it meant exposing the gendered and classed processes of custodians and conservators that kept the museum clean. For Fred Wilson, it meant exposing the race and class processes that kept the museum secure. Dan Flavin and Lawrence Weiner unsettled the object status of the artworks on which the art apparatus depended, turning to the fragile structures of lighting or text as alternatives. For Louise Lawler, institutional critique meant "appropriating" or recontextualizing the central props of the museum within defamiliarizing didactics and conventions of display. Andrea Fraser created "counterdocent performances." Rather than offering tours of the museum's artwork, she focused on its apparatus, discoursing at length on the arrangement of the subscription desk, the sculptural proportions of the drinking fountain, or the social and economic function of the museum cafeteria.[17]

These works unfolded from the late 1960s through the 1990s and primarily measured their distance from the visual artworld; indeed, they sited themselves in the artworld as a proximate irritant within it. Alberro and others have chronicled institutional critique as an embedded practice of negation.[18] They were practices that interrupted, foregrounded, short-circuited, or otherwise redirected the apparatus of the museum and visual artworld to make its processes explicit, to make visible contingent factors that were oft-occluded. If art presented itself as autonomous and self-authorizing, institutional critique artists exposed the institution that produced that perception of autonomy. Upon considering this art-based trajectory of institutional critique, a few elements are relevant for my themes above and throughout *Back Stages*. First, institutional critique is about the revelation of context, indeed, about the incorporation of the contextual, the background, the backstage into the art itself. Institutional critique directed attention to that which was "outside" of art, precisely to expose the outside's construction of the inside. Indeed, translations of institutional critique in German and elsewhere billed it as "context art" (*Kontext Kunst*).[19] To mine that context was to mine the apparatus of knowledge production in art; it focused less on what we know about art than on the apparatus that undergirded the boundaries and schemas for what we think we know about art. More importantly for this collection of essays, the contextual expansion of institutional critique also undergirded the contextual travel of performance studies, as well as the contextual travel of the performing arts—the context swapping that I described above. The shift *to* context enabled a shift *across* context; the critique of context opened the door to new interart experiments, including those that brought new objects, bodies, actions, and theatrical gestures to expose the contextual underpinnings of the institution.

Indeed, one might further suggest that theater was/is not only an object of critique but also a vehicle for artistic self-critique. As recounted in my gloss of artistic practices above, one finds that the institutionally critical gesture consistently used theatrical techniques to expose that institutional context. As I argued in *Social Works*, art objects were placed within scenes. Visual artists made art objects into props and sometimes into scripts. Visual artists hung lights, cast actors, and engaged in ambiguous role-play themselves. Museum didactics started to sound like stage directions. The unveiling of the institutional apparatus seemed to require varied forms of theater. At the same time, those heterogeneous forms worked with different conceptions of what theater might mean. Theater became a central vehicle by which to conduct a critique, not only because of its themes, stories, and characters but also because of the contextual heteronomy of the form itself. Even as the artworld critiqued the ubiquity of theatricality in the experience economy, even if performance artists say that they hate theater, this world deployed (and deploys) theatricality to conduct its own self-critique. As such, institutional critique further contributed to the proliferation of performance described above; whether performing artists in dance or theater noticed or cared, the institutional critical gesture readied the visual art world for a wider array of bodily arrangements, spaces, objects, and actions.

Coming to terms with this heterogeneity of practice means renewing those questions about the relation between performance and social theory, including the former's interdependence with institutional and political process. Retroactively, it is now possible to see how much political ambivalence undergirds these cases, or rather, how often the sites and works reveal a growing confusion about how the political performs. Foregrounded in some places more than others, these essays track a lurking concern that the formats and sensibilities of so-called progressive "resistance" were being appropriated as conservative accommodations to neoliberal politics and economics. Around the time that I wrote *Social Works*, left activists who sought to dismantle social institutions found that conservative Tea Partiers wanted to dismantle them too. As an employee of a defunded public institution, this unwelcome left-right political alignment was particularly concerning, prompting me to ask whether a recognition of institutional dependence might be more politically radical than any simplified quest for anti-institutional autonomy. Political ambivalences continued and continue in other ways as well. As relational experiments unfolded in the artworld, many began to worry that the "experiential" ethos of participatory art was in danger, not of dismantling a late capitalist experience economy but of reinforcing its participatory compulsions. In the years following the publication of *Social Works*, political aesthetics took new form in the Occupy movement, with general assemblies, human microphones, and performative actions that yielded DIY social institutions. Looking back now at 2012, I continue to wonder if there was not, at the very least, a symptomatic relation between the interart debates of museum performance and the infrastructural aesthetics of Occupy, between the apparently depoliticized formal concerns of the former and the apparently politicized, deforming practices of the latter. Jumping ahead to the timing of this writing, liberals and progressives who once ardently upheld the values of free speech find the First Amendment being "weaponized" for corporate-funded expressions of homophobia and performances of racial hatred. Now, as this book anticipates publication, a pandemic has politicized the infrastructural proximities of performance in ways that the assemblies of 2012 could never have anticipated. Ultimately, as I reflect about such heterogenous questions, "performance" was and is hardly a medium-specific guarantee of progressive politics; nor is it a medium-specific guarantee of the opposite. Rather every site, every event, every action transpires in a knotty mix of affects, materials, and systems. The bad news is that the relationship between performance and politics has become even less clear; the good news is that lack of clarity requires more complicated thinking, curating, teaching, policy making, and art making from us all.

Indeed, if the contextual and institutional stakes of interart turns, misrecognitions, and alignments have changed, it coincides with shifts in global politics.[20] This is where the latent politics of interarts experiments become patent, even if there starts to be a routinized quality to this so-called global debate. Let me pick up one of the (prepandemic) routines. One argument with which I am routinely confronted—and which reappears throughout this collection—is the post-Fordist critique of participatory performatives. This critique places performance and the participatory turn within a wider discourse on the changing nature of work, a shift that arguably underwrites artworld experiment and experience. Bojana Cvejić and Ana Vujanović offered examples of how the thought rides in an interview with Jasbir Puar, Judith Butler, Isabell Lorry, and Lauren Berlant on the subject of precarious labor.[21] Here they cited post-operaist thinkers who theorize a turn from material production of commodities to immaterial labor of services which values "cultural-informational content—standards, norms, tastes, and (most important strategically) public opinion—by means of cooperation and communication as the basic work activities . . . Art thereby gains a new political position, and performance has a special role to play there. . . . workers are no longer obliged merely to get the job done, but also to be virtuoso performers: eloquent, open, and communicative."[22] But, and here's another tangle, while this thesis "is mostly taken as promising for the politicality of the contemporary Art World," for them and many others, such optimism is misunderstood and misplaced; they would say—and others say—that performance should be talked about less as a political practice and more "as a model of production."[23] Thus the performative turn in contemporary art and public art practice is read as a symptom of a wider turn to service in late capitalism, offering "encounter" and sociality as desirable product. From such a vantage point, social practice work, performance art, participatory art, and even the performing arts are unwittingly providing an economic service, enabling an immaterial turn that seems fully in consort with the experiential turn in late capitalism. Moreover, that turn is buttressed, or rather unbuttressed, by the increasingly intermittent conditions of artistic and performing arts labor; artists have learned to embrace the "freedom" and "creativity" of a lifestyle that strings together residencies, laboratories, shift work, and temporary working situations, the "festivalization" and "proliferation of small-scale projects, leading only to economic self-precaritization."[24]

If we take seriously this tangled scene, what are artists who are invested in these practices and dependent on their professional circuits to do? Well, first, we might notice that the interart debates I glossed above might be best framed not only for their politics but also for their underlying economics, that the classic Arendtian division between politics and labor are getting differently defined in such moments. The apparent political significance or political insignificance of a performance gesture can be thus reframed, made differently legible, when we notice that gesture's embedding in a changing context of labor and economics, the changing workplace of performance. Along the way, performance workers might have to rethink service labor, and what it means to display their skills. Or, as Cvejić and Vujanović conclude with no small degree of oratorical intensity: "The question would be how to act upon the material conditions, to no longer compose or negotiate with them, but to reclaim art as a public good in political and economic terms, which requires reconfiguring relations between the state, the public sphere and the sphere of the private capital. To do this, critical thought from within performance practice itself will not suffice, but in fact, performance practitioners will need to politically reeducate themselves as citizens in the public sphere."[25] What would such a public reeducation within the workplace of performance be? What does an enactment on material conditions look like? Throughout *Back Stages*, you will find me reasking questions about publicness and working conditions through examinations of a range of interart contexts.

Indeed, to take these questions and methods for another spin, let's turn (or return) to some case studies. Let's return first to that sentient structure in Faye Driscoll's *Thank You for Coming*, the work of a choreographer that traveled from occupied proscenium stage to occupy the galleries of museums and biennials as well. The transit across this interart context is one where modes of reading, perceiving, and servicing partake of different aesthetic legacies. When do audience members sit and performers move? When does the latter stay still while the former moves around them? In the scene of this work, the tangle of bodies eventually settle collectively onto the ground, wrapping torsos and limbs into a group amoeba-like form that shuttles across the platform: contact improv meets *Meat Joy* (1964) meets Brechtian aesthetics. Eventually, they rise in highly stylized gestures and facial expressions, communing with each other in jittery, syncopated movements while joyously calling out the names of those of us attending. Shannon . . . Patrick . . . Katya . . . Nicholas . . . Tracy . . . the names of each and every audience member who made the decision to assemble together that night are called, underscoring the parameters of attendance. Eventually, performers come down from the platform and ask us to rise. They take apart the platform and ask us to help them, rearranging us and the stage space into new infrastructures of observer and observed, now occupying the same horizontal plane. We are asked to reassemble the material conditions of the choreographic structure. They ask us to grasp ropes suspended from the ceiling and dare us to amble and swing with them into new forms and shapes together—making virtuosity in reach. Indeed, this performance certainly requires the traditionally virtuosic skills of the performing arts—the bodily core of contact improvisation, gravitational defiance of ballet, and triple threat of dancing, acting, and singing—and it also requires conceptual or cognitively virtuosic skills. The piece asks us to attend to the entwinement of artist and art in bodily service, as well as to the entwinement of audience and art in provisional copresence. For me, it is a piece that rethinks rather than rejects virtuosic spectacle, allowing its cognitive and productive dispersal among bodies who increasingly avow their need for each other. (It makes me melancholy to recall that need from inside my shelter in 2021.) Eventually, we depart, and as we make our way out, we, for the first time, receive our programs from the dancers who greet and say goodbye at the exit. Offering us our welcome in reverse, the programs remind us that the title is "thank you for coming." In a conceptually rich performance of service, the dancers' gesture enacts hospitality while making us question and rechoreograph our patterns of participation, allowing us to thank these virtuosic dancers for being so good at what they do, even as they assure us that their virtuosity is shared in the mundanity and investment of our attendance, that their virtuosity is matched by our own.

Now from the perspective of 2021, a piece like this seems to thematize and take a degree of control over the workplace of performance, its forms, material conditions, bodies, and way of being with others. That said, we have to also acknowledge that its appearance was and is contingent on the intermittent, temporary, festival structure of serial project work—Faye Driscoll's career is an assembly of some of the most distinguished venues for "project work" a performing artist can string together. If such a piece is at risk of only "enacting 'critical thought' from within" performance practice, only recomposing and renegotiating rather than, as Cvejić and Vujanović would have it, "reclaiming art as a public good," then we might turn to another example to understand the twentieth-first-century tangles of that reclaiming and its embedded global politics. Let's set this work next to a debate at a different performing arts palace, the Volksbuhne—the German palace of performing arts in former East Berlin—where the furor over the arts as a public good received an urgent exorcism. At one point in 2017, the German ministers of culture's decision to appoint the director of the Tate Modern as the new director of the Volksbuhne seemed another exemplary opportunity to advance and complicate aesthetic experimentation across the visual and performing arts. Dercon said he was ready to animate Berlin with a modernized program, one that began by transporting a range of Tate Modern performance experimenters—including Boris Charmatz of Musée de La Danse and Anne Teresa De Keersmaeker in a *Fous de dance* at Tempelhof Airport. He also commissioned relational artist Tino Sehgal to create Beckett performances, along with other artworld artists, most of whom had been part of curator Catherine Wood's program at Tate Modern years before. As interesting as this transit and transplantation might have seemed to some of us, it was roundly rejected—often before viewing—by a host of others. Indeed, the ensuing debate, protest, Occupy-like takeover, and eventual resignation of Chris Dercon as the Volksbuhne director typified—in high dramatic form—the struggles, projections, misrecognitions, and insidious politics of interart experimentation; a fleet of Berlin's citizens and its cultural laborers decried the "Tate Modernization of the Volksbuhne." Take the well-circulated 2016 open letter of Volksbuhne staff as an example. Its writers accused Dercon of representing "dance, musical theater, media art—already core elements of the Volksbuhne—as 'novelty' "—as forms erroneously discovered by the then outgoing Tate Modern director.[26] In response to Dercon's desire to move across disciplines beyond what he called the "spoken word" form of the theater, practitioners were alarmed by his desire for an alternative "polyglot stage language." His infamous assertion that Hito Steyerl and Wolfgang Tillmans were the only good performing artists in Berlin stung. In these and other exchanges, we saw a tussle around vocabulary (how strange to hear theater called "spoken word"?) and artistic literacy, as well as a confrontation of inherited artistic genealogies. It also exposed a much a wider concern about the workplace of performance in a globalizing environment. Dercon's program was critiqued by staffers as one that welcomed an empty internationalism perceived as "a historical leveling and destruction of our identity, [ushering] a global consensus culture with unified patterns of presentation and scale."[27] The outsourcing of the season to "project work" and "residencies" with

Charmatz, De Keersmaeker, Sehgal, and other international artists was seen to undermine the repertory model of resident theater. Once again, undergirding this concern about aesthetic differences or political differences is a primary concern about economics and jobs. New polyglot stage languages required a different kind of expertise from an artistic and technical staff trained in producing the "spoken word" form of theater. The open letter put it bluntly: "We fear that with these plans there will be no need for our expertise and capacities. We fear job cuts, even liquidation of entire subsections." In other words, these salaried theater artists feared (rightly) what Axel Haunschild calls the boundaryless career of the itinerant, twenty-first-century creative laborer, thereby staging what Cvejić and Vujanović might have read as a last ditch refusal to accept artistic precaritization.

This drama offers one more site in which to imagine the political reeducation for artists as citizens in the public sphere, albeit a fitful, opportunistic, incomplete, and internally contradictory one. It exemplified concerns about the performance workplace, the reskilling or deskilling of the performing arts, and the potentials and perils of an artworld embrace of performance and—in a Brexit context—of a neoliberal Londoner taking over an (East) German institution in the European Union. Never mind that he's Belgian.

At this point, it seems important to step back to situate these patterns of projection. The crisis is not fundamentally about how the visual art world is taking over the theatrical world. Indeed, over the last few decades, many of us have heard just as many accusations that theater was taking over the visual art world. Perpetuating a modernist art habit, many critics from Michael Fried to Hal Foster have lamented the invasion of performers, choreographers, and time-based artists whose work deskills and distracts attention from the contemplation of visual art. If the artworld's ambivalence toward theater is something of a modernist trope, we now find ourselves in a reversal, navigating the theater world's ambivalence toward the artworld. But look what happens when we step back from this political theater, when we take a wider view of this "place for viewing." We find that each accuses the other in similar terms; it is certainly there that we find the real symptoms of historical crisis. Each accuses the other of ushering a commercialized event culture. Each accuses the other of neoliberal takeover. Critics in both camps are concerned about the effects of globalization, whether the empty internationalism of the art biennial or the festivalization of the performance season. Rather than decide which art form is more political, or which more neoliberal, the interart debate reveals a much broader anxiety about the future of work, one in which all cultural employees have a stake. Indeed, it is striking to see how much the performing art works initially presented by Dercon anticipated the imagery of the protests against it. The virtuosic powers of the artist as political actant become, through a change in optic, a protest against the economic conditions that house it. Dercon resigned in less than a year at the urging of German cultural ministers, public-sector employees who did not want to have to sustain this kind of public reeducation. The Volksbuhne scene demonstrates the opportunities and obstacles of political reeducation, especially at a historical moment when the effort to embrace art as a public good seemed increasingly remote.

Looking Ahead: Table of Contexts

The sequence in my table of contents is largely chronological, and, not coincidentally, such a chronology allows me to divide the book into three parts devoted to (1) background disciplinary debates, (2) complex artistic projects, and to conclude with (3) "restagings" that synthesize the themes of art, performance, and the social into reimagined conversations. Several of the essays are in extended and sometimes eccentric dialogue with the three books that I glossed above. While I have published essays that offer abridged arguments of these books, I decided not to include them here; readers can find them reprinted in several places elsewhere; (and, of course, readers can read the whole books too).[28] Part 1 on "Background Stages" explores institutional puzzles across social institutions, institutions of higher education, and institutions of art, recalling legacies of artistic and scholarly practice that meet, redefine, and undo each other in different contexts and with different political implications.

1. "Performance at Hull-House: Museum, Microfiche, and Historiography." The earliest published essay in this reader coincided with the process of writing my first book on Hull-House, a process that found me analyzing social performance while simultaneously reckoning with the embodied and affective contingencies of performing history and practicing historiography.
2. "Performing Show and Tell: On the Disciplinary Problems of Mixed-Media Practice." Commissioned for a special issue of the *Journal of Visual and Cultural Studies*, this chapter compares the "turn" from theater to performance studies with the "turn" from art history to visual culture studies, asking whether their respective disciplinary stakes of tradition and revision parallel each other.
3. "Theatricality's Proper Objects: Genealogies of Performance and Gender Theory." Included in a collection focused on the keyword Theatricality, this chapter joins debates in feminism and queer theory with debates on theater and performativity, following a link between the antiessentialist turns and medium-specific politics of these subfields.

4. "When 'Everything Counts': Experimental Performance and Performance Historiography." This chapter compares the contextualist methodological stakes of new historicism and performance historiography with the contextual contingencies of Minimalist art and post-Minimalist performance, arguing for a connection between scholarly practice and artistic practice as the century turned.

5. "Resist Singularity." Responding to a special issue of *Theater Survey*, which asked, "What Is the Single Most Important Thing We Can Do to Bring Theater History into the New Millennium?" I suggest in this chapter that the field resist singularity to welcome varied aesthetic, disciplinary, and political positions to the field.

6. "Rhetoric in Ruins: Performing Literature and Performance Studies." Recalling a less-recounted genealogy of performance studies in oral interpretation, this chapter engages debates on the future of higher education while showing unexpected kinship between the narratorial experiments of rhetoric and those of experimental ethnography in cultural anthropology and performance studies.

7. "Living Takes Many Forms: Creative Time." Having assisted in the curation of *Living as Form* at Creative Time, this chapter recalls the public renewal of the arts in the 1930s under the Works Progress Administration to make a historical case for including theater, dance, and other performing art genealogies in the contemporary artworld's framing of socially engaged art practice.

Having established a network of disciplinary questions and histories in part 1, part 2 on "The Arts at Work" analyzes complex artistic projects, exhibitions, and collections that demonstrate the potentials and perils of curating performance amid the experience economies and social movements of the twentieth-first century.

8. "Life Politics/Life Aesthetics: Environmental Performance in *red, black & GREEN: a blues.*" Focusing on a performance installation that joins the work of choreographer-poet Marc Bamuthi, public artist–singer Theaster Gates, and socially engaged architect Rick Lowe, this chapter explores the link between hybrid aesthetic practice and site-specific politics.

9. "Elmgreen & Dragset's Theatrical Turn." Commissioned for a featured piece in 2011 Performa's biennial on performance art, this chapter argues for the long-term connection between theater and the practice of institutional critique by a queer male artistic duo feted in the artworld.

10. "Performativity and Its Addressee: Walker Art Collection." Responding to the signature holdings of the Walker Art Collection—along with its tradition of cutting-edge performing arts

curation—this chapter demonstrates how the term "performativity" helps us to understand the intermedia practice and spectatorial relations of experimental art.

11. "Just-in-Time: Performance and the Aesthetics of Precarity." Using the performance art theater troupe My Barbarian as a spine, this chapter links post-Fordist social theory with debates across art, theater, and performance studies, foregrounding the degree to which precarity is an occupational hazard of performance even as it simultaneously invites reflection on its own conditions of virtuosity.

12. "Seven Ways to Look at *Windows*: Harrell Fletcher." This essay uses the work of social practice artist Harrel Fletcher as a springboard for framing the disciplinary stakes of environmentally responsive, socially engaged art and performance.

13. "Countercarnival in a Performance-Friendly World: *En Mas'*." Responding to an exhibition platform devoted to integrating Caribbean carnival into visual art exhibition, this chapter mines Black Atlantic social theory to argue that carnival anticipates twentieth-first-century performance exhibition and provides a reminder of its provocative (oft-repressed) social politics.

14. "Utopian Operating Systems: Theaster Gates's Way of Working." Focusing on the expansive practice of Theaster Gates, this chapter explores the connection between the backstage materials of urban renewal and the frontstage expressions of performance and public art.

15. "Trusting Publics: Paul Ramírez Jonas." Written for a midcareer retrospective on the work of Paul Ramírez Jonas, this chapter foregrounds the role of theatrical material in public art practice, as well as the necessity of facing political ambivalence toward once-trusted public institutions.

In the final section, "Restagings," I close with more recent analyses of past and contemporary practice, reframing classic questions of aesthetics and politics to provoke new alignments across seemingly nonallied fields in drama, visual art, performance, protest, and civic reenactment.

16. "The Way We Perform Now." First shared at an Artists Space forum on the role of dance at the Whitney Biennial and published in a special issue on museums in *Dance Research Journal*, this ten-point chapter considers the aesthetic, political, and economic stakes of cross-pollination across the visual and performing arts.

17. "Drama and Other Time-Based Arts." Reaching back to classical poetics, seventeenth-century aesthetics, and literary genre theory, this chapter (not previously published) considers how dramatic conventions (along with epic and lyrical ones) offer frames for

understanding the formal and social significance for time-based art practice now. Initially developed as a Spencer Lecture in Drama at Harvard, I decided to leave much of its oral tone and mode of address.

18. "Assemblies: Public Participation, Heteronomous Worlds." Alighting on the aesthetic, democratic, technological, educational, environmental, and archaeological associations of the keyword "assembly," this chapter connects contemporary debates around civic action and climate politics with those in public art to argue to reassemble the politics and aesthetics of performance. It joins thoughts originally shared at a keynote on "Autonomy and Functionality" in Berlin with an ongoing investigation of assembly.

19. "Epilogue: Essential Labor and Proximate Performance." Serving as an epilogue to the entire book, I reflect here about the provisional and potentially permanent effects of a global pandemic on the cultural sector and on performance as a form.

As noted above, each of these essays was written for a particular venue and readership, many of whom rarely overlap with each other. With *Back Stages*, I hope to bring these varied audiences into conversation and to catalyze a cross-disciplinary conversation beyond the disciplined institutional constraints in which they continue to occur. On the one hand, some essays first appeared in publications devoted to a performing art form such as theater or dance (e.g., *Theater Survey* and *Dance Research Journal*). Some appeared in venues devoted to the interdisciplinary field of performance studies (e.g., *Exceptional Spaces, Contesting Performance* or the *Drama Review*), that is, venues whose readership occasionally coincides with the first two. On the other hand, many of the collected essays were commissioned by journals, books, and catalogues that focused on visual art in the expanded field. The readership and reach within this art expansion also varies greatly—from scholarly debates in visual culture and the humanities (e.g., *Journal of Visual Culture* and *Representations*) to those focused on formal questions in contemporary art (e.g., *Walker Art Center's Living Collections*), to publications targeted to advance the field of socially engaged art (commissioned by organizations such the Vera List Center, Creative Time, Independent Curators International, and more). Moreover, while many essays appeared in scholarly journals and edited collections, others appeared in art catalogues specifically responding to exhibitions with limited dissemination. As a critic and teacher who addresses different kinds of audiences in serial form—for example, artists at this venue, theater makers at that one, curators here, humanities scholars there—my hope with *Back Stages* is to reach a range of readers simultaneously. Whether or not I succeed, the entirety of the book is dedicated to the crew who have always been my primary interlocutors, my most provocative critics, and my most trusted supporters: my students at Northwestern, Harvard, and the University of the California, Berkeley. My work is always already for them.

Notes

1. Statement from conversations with the author. For a more detailed account of Goldberg's distinction between theater and visual art performance, see RoseLee Goldberg, ed., *Performa 11: Staging Ideas* (New York: Performa Publications, 2013).

2. Among others, see Roberta Smith, "A Survey of a Different Color: 2012 Whitney Biennial," *New York Times*, March 1, 2012, https://www.nytimes.com/2012/03/02/arts/design/2012-whitney-biennial.html; Andrew Russeth, "Whitney's 2012 Bucksbaum Prize Goes to Sarah Michelson," *Observer*, April 19, 2012, http://observer.com/2012/04/whitneys-2012-bucksbaum-award-goes-to-sarah-michelson/; and Brian Schaefer, "Sarah Michelson and the Infiltration of Dance," *Out Magazine*, January 30, 2014, https://www.out.com/entertainment/theater-dance/2014/01/30/sarah-michelson-whitney-museum.

3. Museum of Modern Art, "The Museum of Modern Art Commission Six International Choreographers to Present Dance Performances at the Museum in a Series Co-organized with Ralph Lemon," news release, October 16, 2012, https://www.moma.org/documents/moma_press-release_389341.pdf.

4. See Abigail Sebaly, "Cold Storage and New Brightness: The Cunningham Acquisition Moves in at the Walker," *Walker Art Online Magazine*, July 29, 2011, https://walkerart.org/magazine/cold-storage-and-new-brightness-the-cunningham-acquisition-moves-in-at-the-walker.

5. For elements of the original interview, see "Marina Abramović: What Is Performance Art?" Museum of Modern Art, March 21, 2010, https://www.youtube.com/watch?v=FcyYynulogY. Also see Chris Wilkinson, "Noises Off: What's the Difference between Performance Art and Theater?" *Guardian*, July 20, 2010.

6. "Performatik 2015 Presents Performances, Exhibitions, and Talks By Over 35 Artists and Curators," Biennial Foundation, January 26, 2015, http://www.biennialfoundation.org/2015/01/performatik-2015-presents-performances-exhibitions-and-talks-by-over-35-artists-and-curators/.

7. Chris Dupuis, "In the Move from Stage to Museum, a Dance Becomes Performance Art," *Hyperallergic*, April 27, 2015, https://hyperallergic.com/202056/in-the-move-from-stage-to-museum-a-dance-becomes-performance-art/.

8. "Dance and the Exhibition Form: Conversation with Anne Teresa De Keersmaeker, Xavier Le Roy and Elena Filipovic," WIELS Contemporary Art Centre, Belgium, March 22, 2015.

9. Xavier Le Roy in public conversation at WIELS Contemporary Art Centre, Belgium, March 22, 2015.

10. The political furor over the appointment and subsequent resignation of Chris Dercon as Volksbuhne director—in the year after our Frankfurt conference "Theater and Critique"—exemplify the cross-arts frictions I explored in this essay. A detailed examination of that example will require a separate essay.

For now, see, e.g., Isabelle Graw, "We Are the Revolution," *Texte zur Kunst*, December 18, 2017, https://www.textezurkunst.de/articles/die-revolution-sind -wir/; and essays in a recent Volksbuhne Special Section in *Theater Survey 59*, no. 2 (2018).

11. Raymond Williams quoted in Judith Butler, "What Is Critique? An Essay on Foucault's Virtues," in *The Judith Butler Reader*, ed. Sara Silah and Judith Butler (London: Blackwell Publishing, 2004), 304. Also see Raymond Williams, "Criticism," in *Keywords: A Vocabulary of Culture and Society* (Oxford: Oxford University Press, 1983).

12. Butler, "What Is Critique?," 305.

13. Butler, "What Is Critique?," 306.

14. See, among others, Alexander Alberro and Blake Stimson, eds., *Institutional Critique: An Anthology of Artists' Writings* (Cambridge, MA: MIT Press, 2009); and Andrea Fraser, "From the Critique of Institutions to an Institution of Critique," *Artforum* 44 (2005): 100–106.

15. For more on these disputed origins, see my "Staging Institutions: Andrea Fraser and the 'Experiential' Museum,'" in *Andrea Fraser: A Retrospective*, ed. Sabine Breitwieser and Tina Teufel (Salzburg, Austria: Museum der Moderne, 2015), 21–29.

16. Alexander Alberro, "Institutions, Critique, and Institutional Critique," in *Institutional Critique: An Anthology of Artists' Writings*, ed. Alexander Alberro and Blake Stimson (Cambridge, MA: MIT Press, 2009), 3.

17. For more on Buren; Rosler; Haacke; Asher; Ukeles; Wilson; Flavin and Weiner; Lawler; and Fraser, see their writings in Alberro and Stimson, *Institutional Critique*. See especially Buren, "The Function of the Museum" (1970), 102–9; Haacke, "Provisional Remarks" (1971), 120–29; Asher, "September 21–October 12, 1974, Claire Copley Gallery" (1974), 150–55; Ukeles, "Manifesto for Maintenance Art 1969!" (1969), 144–49; Rosler, "Lookers, Buyers, Dealers, and Makers: Thoughts on Audience" (1979), 206–45; Ivan Karp and Fred Wilson, "Constructing the Spectacle of Culture in Museums" (1992), 330–49; and Fraser, "From the Critique of Institutions to an Institution of Critique" (2005), 408–25.

18. Alberro, "Institutions, Critique, and Institutional Critique." See additional essays in Alexander Alberro and Blake Stimson, eds., *Institutional Critique: An Anthology of Artists' Writings* (Cambridge, MA: MIT Press, 2009).

19. See Peter Weibel, ed., *Kontext Kunst* (Cologne: DuMont Buchverlag, 1994). Exhibition catalogue produced on occasion of the exhibition "Kontext Kunst: The Art of the 90s" at the Steiermärkisches Landesmuseum Joanneumk, Austria, October–November 1993.

20. Although this kind of interarts investigation around that exemplary year in 2011 and 2012, the stakes of these turns, misrecognitions, and alignments have changed, sometimes subduing, sometimes coming into striking focus. To track and spark student interest and audience engagement around these episodes of disjunction, I began another "translational" or publicly engaged research initiative titled *In Terms of Performance* with the Pew Center for Art and Heritage, an organization invested in public literacies across the arts. In this coedited online site, http://intermsofperformance.site/, Paula

Marincola and I commissioned short reflections on keywords in contemporary art and performance, asking differently positioned artists, curators, and critics to mediate on terms like "composition," "live," "duration," or "character," which might have quite different resonances in different artistic domains. The site launched at Tate Modern with an array of public programming and was later exhibited at the Brooklyn Academy of Music which used the site as an audience engagement tool and educational exhibit. Many artists and curators discussed in *Back Stages* are represented n the site, and several helped us activate it.

21. Jasbir Puar, Lauren Berlant, Judith Butler, Bojana Cvejić, Isabell Lorey, and Ana Vujanović, "Precarity Talk: A Virtual Roundtable with Lauren Berlant, Judith Butler, Bojana Cvejić, Isabell Lorey, Jasbir Puar, and Ana Vujanović," *TDR: The Drama Review* 56, no. 4 (2012): 163–77.

22. Puar et al., "Precarity Talk," 175.

23. Puar et al., "Precarity Talk," 175.

24. Puar et al., "Precarity Talk," 167.

25. Puar et al., "Precarity Talk," 176.

26. "Volksbühne staff on Chris Dercon: We fear job cuts and liquidation," e-flux, June 20, 2016, https://conversations.e-flux.com/t/volksbuhne-staff-on -chris-dercon-we-fear-job-cuts-and-liquidation/3911.

27. "Volksbühne staff on Chris Dercon."

28. Shannon Jackson, "Civic Play-Housekeeping: Gender, Theater, and American Reform," *Theater Journal* 48, no. 3 (1996): 337–61; "Professing Performance: Disciplinary Genealogies," *TDR: The Drama Review* 45, no. 1 (Spring 2001): 84–95; "What Is the 'Social' in Social Practice: Comparing Experiments in Performance," in *Cambridge Handbook of Performance Studies*, ed. Tracy Davis (Cambridge: Cambridge University Press, 2008), 136–50; "Social Turns: In Theory and Across the Arts," in *Routledge Companion to Art and Politics*, ed. Randy Martin (New York: Routledge, 2014), 104–13. See also *Lines of Activity: Performance, Historiography, Hull-House Domesticity* (Ann Arbor: University of Michigan Press, 2000), *Professing Performance: Theater in the Academy from Philology to Performativity* (Cambridge: Cambridge University Press, 2004), and *Social Works: Performing Art, Supporting Publics* (New York and London: Routledge, 2011); Shannon Jackson and Marianne Weems, *The Builders Association* (Cambridge, MA: MIT Press, 2015); and Johanna Burton, Shannon Jackson, and Dominic Willsdon, eds., *Public Servants* (Cambridge, MA: MIT Press, 2016).

Part 1

✦

Background Stages

Chapter 1

Performance at Hull-House

Museum, Microfiche, and Historiography

Indeed, we shall find little in this room to declare to us the general object of the museum, which is to throw the light of history and of art upon modern industries. The historical object it has in common with all museums; the artistic object it possesses in common with all arts and crafts workshops; but the combination of the two ideals, and the concrete expression of them in the midst of a foreign population largely wrenched away from its hereditary occupations, is peculiar to Hull-House.

—Marion Foster Washburne on the Hull-House Labor Museum, 1904

Who hung this up? Does anyone know what this is doing here?

—Hull-House Museum tour guide encountering a new display, 1993

History, writes Michel de Certeau, "is the product of a place." In *The Writing of History*, de Certeau challenges historians to interrogate the institutionalized places, unquestioned practices, and constrained modes of writing that constitute what he calls "the historiographical operation." His critique incorporates contemporary understandings about the nature of representation that have dismantled the intellectual foundations on which many academic disciplines—anthropology, sociology, literary studies, etc.— formulated their objects of knowledge and assumed their legitimacy.[1] These ideas echo and extend those of metahistorians such as Michel Foucault, Michael Taussig, Hayden White, Joan Scott, and Dominick LaCapra who encourage more reflexivity in the historian's craft, questioning periodizations, narratives, categorizations, and acts of contextualization.[2] Many have also argued for a performative understanding of historical documents—how letters, autobiographies, speeches, legal documents, and essays are situated speech acts reflecting the contingencies of certain contexts and employing familiar tropes to reach specific audiences. By exploring history as an institution, however—from archival operations to collegial networks to the mundane materiality of so-called evidence—de Certeau pushes meta-historical interrogations. This essay is largely my attempt to come to terms with the "placeness" of two history-telling venues—one, the turn-of-the-century Hull-House Labor Museum and two, the set of archives, museums, and writing practices in which contemporary Hull-House researchers such as myself currently participate. The first venue (which presented the history of labor) is thus a phenomenon of the past, its extant remains located in the second venue (which presents the history of Hull-House). Each incorporates a variety of written texts, images, human beings, and objects in very different ways, demonstrating how particular media can change the meanings and rhetorical force of the histories they present. The double meaning (and double pronunciation) of the word *present* can be extended here to suggest that presentations of the past are simultaneously the exertions of a particular present, that is, of a particular place that preserves (keeps present), uses available material (what is present), and interprets (makes understandable, palatable, and useful in the present). At the same time, these remaining representations assume a referent, that is, they presume to document an absent "presence." To make explicit the partiality of these presential mechanisms, this essay continually vacillates between my interpretations of lost performances and my encounters with their extant historical signifiers. Throughout I try to understand the implications of de Certeau and other critics for theorizing past historiographical operations and for writing with an awareness of the place from which I construct them.

But First, Some "History": Originary Fieldsite Number One

The Labor Museum described by Marion Foster Washburne in my epigraph was one of hundreds of performance-based reform activities—including social clubs, pageants, citizenship classes, festivals, storytelling, theater—practiced at the Hull-House Settlement of Chicago, a symptom, reaction, haven, and self-styled antidote to what many have called one of the most volatile periods in American history. During what is now named the Progressive Era—the period from the end of the nineteenth century to the beginning of World War I—immigration, industrialization, urbanization, and the changing role of women placed the United States in a liminal zone aptly fitting Antonio Gramsci's description of transitional states: "The old is dying and the new cannot be born; in this interregnum there arises a great diversity of morbid symptoms."[3] It was during this tumultuous

Fig. 1. Courtesy of the Hull-House digital image collection, Special Collections and University Archives, University of Illinois at Chicago.

period and in what they thought were the most "morbid" locations that white, upper-middle class, predominantly Anglo-Saxon settlement workers (or "residents" as they called themselves) set up house, seeking to ameliorate the social conditions of displaced immigrants, the exploited working class, and other "unfortunates." For young, educated women (and later men) who felt stifled by the traditional activities and privileges of a bourgeois existence, the settlement also offered a socially sanctioned outlet for their energies and, as its founder and Nobel Peace Prize winner Jane Addams wrote, a way to fulfill their own urges "to learn of life from life itself."[4] For many of these reformers—and for the liberal bourgeoisie who visited—the settlement was an education in morbidity, whether it was an exposure to the disease and garbage of the "slums," an introduction to the dehumanization of the factory system, or an encounter with immigrant cultural difference—a dense and unfamiliar diversity of language, habitual behavior, hygiene, and work pattern fueling the nationalist anxieties of hereditary Americans concerned with the racial purity of the United States.[5]

The Labor Museum was a particular response to these conditions. Confounded by the older members of her immigrant neighborhood whose inability (or lack of interest) in speaking English, whose styles of dress, and whose "primitive" forms of labor "are considered uncouth and

un-American," Jane Addams wanted to find a way for them to commu-
nicate with reformers and with "the children and more ambitious young
people [who] look down upon them and are too often ashamed of their
parents." At the same time, she was also troubled by the monotonous,
repetitive labor of factory workers who "are brought in contact with
existing machinery quite as abruptly as if the present set of industrial
implements had been newly created." Her solution to both these dilemmas
was to have older immigrants of the neighborhood gather in one place
to perform and to teach the skills in craftsmanship indigenous to their
respective countries, including metallurgy, woodworking, pottery, and
textile manufacture. Using the display of these crafts, the museum would
also teach the history of labor—from its "primitive" origins to industrialized machinery—to give factory workers a sense of their advanced place
in a narrative of technological progress. Hull-House would provide tools
and supplies, schedule classes and history lectures on the weekends, and
employ older immigrants in the community as teacher-laborers. The initial
outline of the program stated three goals.

1. Industrial processes themselves will be made more picturesque and
   be given content and charm.
2. People who are forced to remain in shops and factories . . . will have
   some idea of the material which they are handling, and it is hoped
   in time a consciousness of the social value of the work which they
   are performing.
3. The older people who are now at such a disadvantage because they
   lack certain superficial qualities which are too highly prized, will
   more easily attain the position in the community to which their previous life and training entitles them.[6]

Allowing Chicago's Nineteenth Ward neighbors to see their labor in its
"historical continuity" and themselves "in connection and co-operation
with the 'whole'" would, it was hoped, both connect alienated workers
to the industrial materials they encountered daily and place the crafts of
older immigrants in a context that highlighted their significance. It would
also form cross-class and cross-cultural links between these neighbors and
the bourgeois reformers and Hull-House visitors who might too easily
dismiss the contributions of immigrant others as well as the important
function of working-class laborers.

Motivated also by the innovative educational theories of John Dewey,
Addams demonstrated an interest in adapting performance forms for
pedagogical use. She felt that the form the museum—"the word is pur-
posely used in preference to the word 'school'"—could retain some
of the "fascinations of the 'show'" and that interest could be created
around the unacknowledged practices of everyday life if they were framed

appropriately. Furthermore, Addams maintained that the structures of the traditional classroom and the dullness of book learning could not always accommodate the interests and priorities of Hull-House neighbors. "The residents of a settlement should be able to utilize many facts and forces lying quite outside the range of books, should be able to seize affections and memories which are not available in schools for children or immature youth." By giving its curriculum the "charm of human form," the Labor Museum thus employed a pedagogy of embodied performance in lieu of written text. Young apprentices "learned by doing" from actual laboring performers whose lessons contained "affections and memories" as well as a list of how-tos. Thus the Labor Museum channeled the human aspect of this exhibit, one that was capable of giving "concrete expression" to the history of labor, of "making the teaching dramatic,"[7] and of charismatically eliciting a visceral connection in participating students. Later, Addams would note how, in the textile exhibit, "the whirl of the wheels recalls many a reminiscence and story of the old country, the telling of which makes a rural interlude in the busy town of life,"[8] illustrating the emotional force of the unplanned, less tangible aspects of this pedagogical space.

Several other material factors were in place at Hull-House to motivate and make possible what would become a very well-publicized reform inspiration. Hull-House had organized a large exhibition of neighborhood handicrafts in 1897, an event that led to the founding of the Chicago Arts and Crafts Society (CACS) whose first president, George Twose, was a Hull-House resident. Twose was already teaching a class in woodworking by this time. Additionally, the Field Museum of Chicago had recently donated a collection of lithographs depicting varieties of women's textile manufacture as well as samples of these textiles. Two factories in the neighborhood had also donated pieces of "obsolete" machinery to the settlement. These donations—objects available in the present for which Hull-House found a use—would become the material basis for the story the Labor Museum presented, a montage that would be arranged to pass as historical narrative. Before elaborating, however, I want to highlight the creation of a different kind of historical montage.

Second: Originary Fieldsite Number Two

The University of Illinois at Chicago is where I go these days to "make history." One hundred years ago, the Hull-House settlement stood at the corner of Halsted and Polk, a site which now marks the University of Illinois parking lot and an entrance to the Dan Ryan expressway. On the southwest corner stand two restored buildings from the thirteen-building complex—the "original" Hull-House mansion and the Resident's Dining Hall—which contain the Jane Addams Hull-House Museum. The special collections room is one block away in the university library, the place to which the above cursory narrative is extremely indebted. In this room remnants of Hull-House's past have been helpfully preserved, indexed, and microfiched—that is, made into the documents that historians call evidence.

In history everything begins with the gesture of setting aside, putting together, and transforming certain classified objects into "documents." This new cultural distribution is the first task. In reality it consists in producing such documents by dint of copying, transcribing, or photographing these objects, simultaneously changing their locus and their status. This gesture consists in "isolating" a body—as in physics—and "denaturing" things to turn them into parts that will fill the lacunae inside an a priori totality. It forms what de Certeau calls the "collection" of documents.[9]

Two points raised by this passage are especially significant for me. First is the circumspect materiality of historical documents—the grossly "natural" existence of yellowing paper, torn laundry lists, broken combs, and ripped clothing that, if it were not for the denaturing exertions of a larger historiographical apparatus, would seem wholly unremarkable. A second point concerns the construction of the "a priori totality" that presumably redeems these preserved objects, the comprehensive collection that requires a legitimating historical narrative. It is in the temptation to create order from chaos where a circular process of preservation and interpretation instantiates historical periods and discursive categories. Whether telling the story of labor technology or the story of Hull-House, it is here that beginnings, middles, and ends are made. Deciding to observe my own process of historiography—the dubious nature of historical objects and the suspect practices by which I systematize them—has made my historiographical operations feel somewhat tenuous. I find myself a little more hesitant, more than a little nervous, as I try to come to terms with the uncanniness of my enterprise. And, as Taussig says in theorizing a larger social Nervous System (NS) and its effects on scholarly research, it can be "somewhat unsettling to be centered on something so fragile, so determinedly other, so nervous."[10]

And whenever I try to resolve this nervousness through a little ritual or a little science I realize this can make the NS even more nervous. Might not the whole point of the NS be that it's always a jump ahead, tempting us through its very nervousness toward the tranquil pleasures of its fictive harmony, the glories of its system, thereby all the more securely energizing its nervousness? Hence the sardonic wisdom of the NS's scrawling incompleteness, its constant need for a fix.

For the historian, it is the fragile nature of the so-called past that paradoxically frustrates social analysis even as it offers itself up for contemplation. The dubious status of this absent presence simultaneously invites and defers the systematic solidity of a referential statement. As I contemplate the contingencies of the historical NS, I begin to wonder whether the nervous gap between historical signifiers and their signifieds, one occasionally and cautiously filled by my researcher's desire for a "fictive harmony," will withstand a metahistorical critique.

Twinges of this nervousness arise when I use the archival index to the Jane Addams Memorial Collection. There, the Labor Museum—along with hundreds of clubs and organizations—receives its own entry. By requesting the appropriate microfiche reel, I had access to much of the quoted passages on the goals and significance of the Labor Museum, prose that I attributed to Jane Addams. In truth, the author is circumspect. The original 1900 outline of the Labor Museum was an unsigned, typed, error-ridden document, its sentences lifted and corrected to appear in a 1901 publication called "The Labor Museum: First Report," which did list "Miss Addams" as author. But the same prose appeared in quotation marks again in a 1904 article on the Labor Museum, this time printed as direct discourse attributed to "Miss Luther"—another Hull-House resident who volunteered as the museum's curator at the time. My quandary about the originator of these oft-reproduced words exemplifies a larger problematic as I try to write the Labor Museum's history and routinely catch myself searching for origins. When did the Labor Museum begin? I find myself asking. In her classic book *Twenty Years at Hull-House*, Jane Addams suggests that it began on a walk down Polk Street in an Italian neighborhood where "I saw an old woman Italian woman, her distaff against her homesick face, patiently spinning a thread by the simply stick spindle so reminiscent of all southern Europe,"[11] whereupon the idea for the Labor Museum seized her. However, investigation of the documents of the Arts and Crafts Society (a different entry) suggests that this organization must have inspired the founding of the Labor Museum, an influence that leaks through the category separation of this archival collection. Meanwhile, the Hull-House inventories (a different reel) records the philanthropic donations that were waiting to be used months before their "locus and status" were changed into the component parts of the Labor Museum's "a priori totality," the "historical continuity" and vision of "the whole" central to its pedagogy. Together, a heterogeneous account of precedents, needs, random material objects, and individual inspiration illustrate the fallaciousness of my impulse to find the beginning of the Labor Museum's story, the origin narrative that gives my historian's NS a welcome fix. Meanwhile, the ease with which I earlier turned to the figure of Jane Addams to create a satisfying narrative replicates another impulse often practiced in Hull-House historiography—one exemplified in the museum's guided tours and by the names given to the Jane Addams Hull-House Museum and the Jane Addams Memorial Collection: the tendency to attribute to a single famous individual the efforts of hundreds of Hull-House reformers. This is encouraged especially when historiographical sites present "origin-al" source material as if their modes of presentation

Fig. 2. Courtesy of the Hull-House digital image collection, Special Collections and University Archives, University of Illinois at Chicago.

did not entail human intervention. Whether filling a celebratory history of Jane Addams or incarnating the history of textile manufacture, archivists and curators preserve material to tell the stories that in turn influence how and what material will be preserved. Together they fuel a kind of interpretive inertia.

This interpretive inertia is tempting to a researcher trying to place Hull-House "in context," but the "a priori totality" embedded in the indexes and origin narratives of Hull-House historiography has already completed much of her work. Or so it would seem. But the contingencies of my presentation of the Labor Museum suggest a politics behind these acts of contextualization. Taussig has investigated the means by which social analysts surround objects of inquiry with information that encourages certain interpretations and discourages.

> [F]or a long time now the notion of contextualization has been mystified, turned into some sort of talisman such that by "contextualizing" social relationships and history, as the common appeal would have it, significant mastery over society and history is guaranteed—as if our understandings of social relations and

history, understandings which constitute the fabric of such context, were not themselves fragile intellectual constructs posing as robust realities obvious to our contextualizing gaze.[12]

Instead, he maintains "that first and foremost the procedure of contextualization should be one that very consciously admits of our presence, our scrutinizing gaze, our social relationships and our enormously confused understandings of history and what is meant by history."[13] In addition to acknowledging the unremarkable materials from which I glean historical evidence and the metaphors of causality to which I succumb to make sense of them, for me this means admitting to my own presence. My "research" also entails the carcinogenic smell of ink toxin and the waning endurance of fingertips as they grip number-two pencils, while stunned eyes remain propped open before the blue light of a projector and hunger pangs tempt me to stop research for another day. While the head archivist dismisses the "irrelevant" things I xerox, I find myself alternately bewildered, frustrated, and amused as I try to "restore behavior," using Richard Schechner's term[14]—to theorize relationships and communities, to model embodied performances—from inside a fluorescent-lit, linoleum-floored room filled with files, indexes, and microfiche reels. These remnants of the past feel more like fetish objects facilitating a scholar's ritual conversation with the dead: I use newspaper clippings instead of hair cuttings, xeroxed diaries instead of totems. My sense that the stuff from which historical data is gleaned has an absurdly mystical function rather than a solidly empirical one, which in turn provokes an uncomfortable feeling that the historiographical operation is less like fact accumulation and more like ghostbusting. Periodically, I retreat to decompress at the nearby Hull-House Museum to indulge a nostalgic romance with the settlement's past since there, as I will discuss later in this essay, the gaps between historical signifiers and their signifieds feel less wide. Other times I simply return to my Evanston apartment where hunger pains are (happily) more easily satiated. Laying bare mechanisms of contextualization means being aware of interpretive predispositions, motivated as they are by nerves and emotion as well as by contemporary intellectual constructs. It also means subjecting oneself and one's work to what Taussig calls "montage—the juxtaposition of dissimilars such that old habits of mind can be jolted into new perceptions of the obvious":

> In fact we have been surreptitiously practicing montage all along in our historical and anthropological practices, but so deeply immersed have we been in tying one link in a chain to the next, creating as with rosary beads a religion of cause and effect bound to narrative ordering of reality, that we never saw what we were doing, so spellbound were we by our narrativizing.[15]

More Categories and Contexts

Because Hull-House's reform endeavors attempted to facilitate cross-cultural awareness and communication, its museum historiography—whether in the Labor Museum or in the contemporary Hull-House Museum—is always mediated by issues of cultural diversity. Thus the histories depicted in the Labor Museum and the Hull-House Museum simultaneously construct and contextualize the ethnic heterogeneity of the Nineteenth Ward. Whether in the former's representation of past labor practices or in the latter's representation of past communities, I will argue that these curatorial acts demonstrate the collusion of ethnographic and historical frameworks. Barbara Kirshenblatt-Gimblett extends Taussig's insights about the politics of contextualization to the specifics of museum exhibition: "In-context approaches exert strong cognitive control over the objects, asserting the power of classification and arrangement to order large numbers of artifacts from diverse cultural and historical settings and to position them in relation to one another."[16] In this case, the classificatory schemas created around the turn-of-the-century at Hull-House impinge in contradictory ways on those presented at the Hull-House Museum of the late twentieth century. Both deploy acts of montage that pass as historical and ethnographic knowledge.

Several ideological factors were also in place to motivate and legitimate Addams's inspiration, an account that might create a social analysis—or a "montage"—whose juxtapositions offer new angles and revelations about the Labor Museum's cultural politics. For the "place" of the Labor Museum's history telling should also be interpreted in light of the nationalist, industrial, and evolutionist ideologies circulating in the "present" of progressive reformers, those individuals whose class privilege equipped them with the tools of historical discovery (i.e., the tools of representation). Meanwhile, although the formal apparatus of the Labor Museum distanced it from the classroom environment, it also imported a problematic legacy of exhibition and curatorial operation that offered a structural container for these ambivalent ideologies. The Labor Museum's displays gave importance and status to everyday labor practices. It sought to create an arena of more equitable and democratic social interaction, but Hull-House's bourgeois residents were still the curators who created and contextualized this arena of public communication.[17] And acts of contextualization—whether in the montage effects of museum exhibition or historical writing—are inseparably linked to questions of politics and partiality.

Specifically, the Labor Museum's idealization of primitive labor practice and respect for cultural difference found legitimation in the Arts and Crafts movement. Its espoused beliefs were channeled to respond neatly to Hull-House's more inclusive cultural mission and to fit the interpretive requirements of museum exhibition. In the United States, middle-class followers of William Morris and John Ruskin used theories of the craftsman ideal to distance themselves from the ravages of industrialization. Whether to motivate a different ideal of employment or to inspire new home decoration ideas, the image of the preindustrial artisan and his idealized relationship with nature was nostalgically invoked to unalienate the factory laborer and, more often, to reconnect the bored bourgeoisie to "life itself." Eileen Boris summarizes the movement's unique brand of "imperialist nostalgia":

> The idealistic, uplifting, optimistic yet paternalistic spirit of the movement reflects the class that turned to arts and crafts as solution to and escape from the industrial world it did so much to forge. Functional and romantic, modern and tradition, individualistic and communal, nationalist and universal—the arts and crafts movement contained contradictory tendencies.[18]

But it was precisely these contradictory tendencies that made the craftsman ideal so useful in containing and narrating Progressive ambivalence. It provided a way for many to address industrialization while ignoring a larger political economy, of mourning its ravages while still relying on its financial benefits. Linking the figure of the craftsman to the "preindustrial" parts of the world from which many American immigrants came, the museum could thus create an unthreatening evolutionary link between the lives of progressive hereditary Americans and their cultural others. Understanding difference was synonymous with understanding one's past, one's connection to the natural world, and one's origins in the human race. Thus, in an unselfconscious combination of historical and ethnographic frameworks, extant "peasant crafts" were interpreted as "early" episodes of a long human tradition. Certainly, to nuance my "montage analysis" further, Hull-House's own historical and ethnographic representations distinguished it from other definitional arenas, such as the cultural performances of the Mount Vernon Ladies Association or of Henry Ford's "melting pot," which acted as pep rallies for conservative political groups like the Immigration Restriction League. But the inclusive rhetoric of both Arts and Crafts philosophies and of Hull-House's tolerance for diversity still set extremely ambivalent terms, interpretations that maintained the supremacy of a certain class while simultaneously integrating "others" into its community. Additionally, the Progressive discourse of immigrant contributions emphasized the benefits of only some "native traditions" and celebrated certain "immigrant gifts" in a way that dictated the terms of their inclusion. Unlike foreign languages, non-Christian religions, or unhygienic domestic practices, arts and crafts were safe national contributions that spiced the American way of life without dangerously threatening the idealized dream of a clean, ordered, yet diverse America, a dream that Progressives felt they needed to fuel if immigrants were to be integrated.

Currently, a selective form of inclusion is practiced in my present. On a wall in one of the rooms of the Hull-House Museum, for instance, a picture of Ida B. Wells hanging next to those of Hull-House reformers depicts a revisionist history, insupportably suggesting an alliance between Hull-House residents and this black female activist, as if the former embraced rather than ignored her legendary statement against the near exclusion of black Americans from the Chicago World's Fair of 1893. The version of the past reproduced and narrated in 1993 at the Hull-House Museum is filtered through the lens of a contemporary United States self-consciously concerned with its own "multicultural" diversity. Unlike the turn-of-the-century past, however, my present has thought to "include" African Americans in its pluralist representation of that past. And so, functioning as Arts and Crafts ideology once did, multiculturalist contextualizations imagine the past with a liberal pluralist caution that occasionally creates blind spots and harmonious elisions more than historically grounded understanding.

If a cautiously inclusive definition of American identity undergirded (and continues to undergird) the cultural representations of the Labor Museum, Hull-House needed (and still needs) to create the vision of that pluralism, categorizing a diverse population and specifying the contribution of each culture on its own particular version of a pluralist wheel.[19] To imagine a heterogeneous American community, for instance, the curators of the Labor Museum first had to imagine the communities from which it derived.[20] In the act of preserving certain practices, therefore, they simultaneously constructed them along unproblematized divisions of ethnicity. From a confused array of donated art and equipment, from the population of a neighborhood roughly divided by cultural groups that did not always reflect distinct national identities, Hull-House gleaned its "representatives." The practices of individual agents were interpreted as metonymic embodiments of larger national cultures. Thus the spinning of a neighborhood woman named Mrs. Brosnahan came to stand for "Irish spinning." Mrs. Molinari's labor stood for "Italian spinning," despite the fact that, at this time, so-called Italians identified with their respective provinces more than with the nation of Italy. In the desire to frame these activities within a grand image of a "gallery of nations," any sense of individual creativity was erased under the larger narrative of national typicality. The inscriptions represented how, according to Sally Price, "[i]n the Western understanding of things, a work originating outside of the Great Traditions must have been produced by an unnamed figure who represents his community and whose craftsmanship respects the dictates of its age-old traditions" even if that means constructing these works as "age-old" and as part of a "tradition."[21] Furthermore, the divisions between ethnicities drew from earlier labels created by Hull-House reformers in their 1895 collection of articles, maps, and statistics titled *Hull-House Maps and Papers*. There, they distinguished "groups forming different elements in social and industrial life without confusing the mind by a separate recognition of the people of every country."[22] By this time the American industrial order had created its own discriminations, and it was this system of ethnic categorization that Hull-House replicated. In the process, originary national communities were invented. Not only did a Neapolitan woman's labor come to stand for "Italian," but the image of a spinning Polish girl named Hilda Satt Polacheck—whose family emigrated to the United States to escape Russian invasions—ironically was titled "Russian Spinning." Cultural divisions, like history, are the products of a place.

The selection and values implicit in the construction of the Labor Museum's contextualizations exerted even greater cognitive control, however, when Hull-House's unique gallery of nations also underwent a hierarchical organization. The evolutionary historical framework embedded in reform ethnography became most explicit when Hull-House resident-curators further categorized the collection by creating a progressive narrative out of the history of labor. In the textile room, the museum charted the "evolution" of spinning, one that drew, despite well-intentioned critiques of industrialism, on culturally situated interpretations of history, progress, and technology. Craft techniques from geographically disparate cultures were assembled in one space and positioned along a single timeline. Each marked a different point along a linear narrative of progress, a narrative that culminated in the machines developed and used in American industry. "Some of the old women still use the primitive form of the distaff," wrote Addams in her initial outline of the Labor Museum: "It will be possible to illustrate the history of textile manufacture, to reveal the long human effort which it represents, to put into sequence and historic order the skill which the Italian colony contains, but which is now lost or despised." Addams welcomed the fact that some women "still" used certain "primitive" methods, since it would allow the Labor Museum to give an embodied representation of an "historic order," that fictive totality created from within the Progressive Era's social Nervous System. Individual laborers were offered a holistic perspective on their labor without questioning whose perspective, whose sequential construction, the Labor Museum disseminated. Thus practitioners of extant craft techniques drawn from a geographically diverse pool found themselves unified by the temporal framework of progressive ideology, the objects of a well-intentioned chronopolitics.[23]

A description of the demonstrations and lectures that accompanied the history of spinning provide an example of how enthusiastically Hull-House residents worked to interpret labor practices using an evolutionary model. In this performance, recounted in the Labor Museum's "First

Report," a lecturer offered an historical perspective while members of different cultural groups—Navajo, Syrian, Russian, Irish, etc.—were presented as examples of different time periods.

> Even the casual visitor was able to see that there is no break in the orderly evolution from spinning of the Navajo woman with her one disc stick, trailing on the ground like a top, to the most complicated machine, and the lecturer on industrial history needed scarcely to state that history looked at from the industrial standpoint at once becomes cosmopolitan, and the differences of race and nationality inevitably fall away.[24]

Thus the craftsmanship of the Navajo woman was placed at the origin of an evolutionary model; her work in the present was emblematic of the American worker's past. Even more significant is the appeal the writer makes to performance as a means of communicating the lesson. In saying that the lecturer "need scarcely to state" the history of spinning because the embodied representation of it was so clear, the writer (Jane Addams?) indicated that performance grounded the lecture, it "realized" the history. In placing each woman and her craft in sequence, the incontestable reality of performance re-presented a curatorial idea. The moment demonstrates how the immediacy of performance can be co-opted to realize a constructed, ideologically situated historical frame. The impression of unmediated encounter reified a performance mediated by linear, ethnocentric interpretations of history and progress. Although (to add another element to my montage) this use of evolution needs to be seen in light of turn-of-the-century ideology when, as George Stocking has said, "social scientists were evolutionists almost to a man [sic]," the Labor Museum's narrative of progression still reinscribed the superiority of the practice that concluded the story.[25] While positing various labor practices as anticipating "modern" machinery gave those practices a significance they did not often enjoy, it still offered a somewhat prejudiced representation of the quotidian, an historical montage in which the Progressive American present repeatedly positioned itself as another culture's future.

In the Resident's Dining Hall of the 1993 Hull-House Museum, the reworked legacy of the Labor Museum's ethnic constructions makes an appearance. The exhibit is called *Hull-House and the Neighborhood: Settlement, Investigation, Invention, and Advocacy* and attempts to represent in a single room the social and spatial complexity of an immigrant, urban milieu. The museum's representation of the neighborhood's past existence draws, as did the Labor Museum, from the *Hull-House Maps and Papers*. An enlargement of the 1895 Hull-House neighborhood map, a color-coded document, shows the ethnicity of the occupants of each neighborhood building: green for Irish, red for Russian, blue for Italy, black for "colored," and yellow for Bohemian. As reformers ran out of colors, they resorted to striped patterns to represent smaller neighborhood national populations such as the Swiss, French-Canadians, and Dutch. Those privileged enough to be represented by the color white—a signifier used to denote the absence of ethnicity, a "cultureless" normalcy—also included all first-generation Americans and immigrant youth who spoke English and attended public school. The side walls of this contemporary museum are now themselves color coded; newspaper excerpts, photos, and didactics representing selected ethnic experiences hang on green, red, yellow, and blue walls. There is no black wall, however. Unlike the Ida B. Wells photo, no revisionist attempt is made here to show Hull-House's relationship to nonwhite migrants (i.e., those who were even "darker" than the Italians). While plenty of extant material dramatizes Hull-House's Greek festivals and German dances, as well as the Labor Museum's gallery of nations, no archival data exists to create a story about Hull-House's sensitivity to African American culture. Once again, ethnic and historical representations are simultaneously acts of invention, constrained and enabled by available ideological and material factors. In this case, documents are not available to satisfy the more inclusive multiculturalist imaginings of 1993.

What the Visitor Cannot See

It is probably somewhat misguided—perhaps reflecting my resilient desire for origins—to have used the word *legacy* above to describe the relationship between a past and present Hull-House Museum. Nevertheless, my personal reading of the latter is influenced by my investigation of the former. My so-called knowledge of the past acts as an enabling juxtaposition to my experience of the present, creating a productive montage effect that prompts me to ask different questions of an index or a contemporary exhibit, defamiliarizing historical pedagogies by foregrounding their construction. This dialogic relationship between past and present not only troubles the assumed distinction between them, but suggests that their interaction is transverse rather than unidirectional. That is, while the selective filter of the present represents the past, the (no less selective) filter of the past mediates my understanding of the present. While I sort through the heterogeneous aspects of my visits to the museum, for instance, I am reminded of another traveler-researcher-ethnographer-historian who visited this "same" corner at Halsted and Polk nearly one hundred years ago. Marion Foster Washburne, whose words appeared in my epigraph, toured the Labor Museum and published an account of his experience, an article that was "set aside" to become available to me through the microfiche machine. Often the details and affections documented in his writing seem to surface, pentimento-like, in my tours through Hull-House's contemporary

historiographical sites. Since the ghosts and legacies I have invented with
his document have proved to be enabling fictions in my research, I want to
explore this particular mediation between past and present.

Marion Foster Washburne was a journalist for *The Craftsman*, the
publication of the US Arts and Crafts movement with the widest circulation. Other articles on the Labor Museum had appeared earlier, but
Washburne's 1904 essay is particularly significant for the way he self-
consciously places his feelings, thoughts, and own predispositions directly
in the text. As a chronicle of his own experience and the experiences he
witnessed, this article is thus a fascinatingly "partial" representation of
settlement reform methods, as well as Progressive Era politics, goals, and
anxieties.[26] Additionally, his use of language and narrative techniques can
be excavated for what Hayden White called "the content in their form."[27]
For example, his extensive use of the first-person plural to dramatize how
"we came upon" the Labor Museum and how "we feel" about it recreates
the experience for an engaged reader, a gesture that is at once inclusive and
coercive. His opening paragraph describes the scene for this reader before
entering Hull-House:

> Steadfast amidst the clash of industrial warfare, true to the Eng-
> lish tongue and the English better genius in the midst of a modern
> Babel, clean and wholesome on the edge of the Ghetto, serene
> among sweat-shops and saloons, in the very center of toiling Chi-
> cago, stands Hull-House.[28]

Washburne's dramatization likens the settlement to a lone diamond in
a pile of rubble, reproducing the image of the philanthropic institution
as the single representative of civilization in a barbarous, urban world.
Tropes of the Progressive Era's ethnographic imagination recur. Washburne likens the polyglossia of the immigrant neighborhood to the most
feared mythological tale of linguistic anarchy. He will use battle, animal,
and mechanical metaphors to describe urban life throughout this text.
Smarter, cleaner, English-speaking reformers and journalists must make
bold, adventurous journeys, braving the cityscape that Upton Sinclair
made famous—a domestic version of an unknown dark continent. As he
continues "through a long tunnel-like passage . . . filled with dynamos and
the steam heating apparatus," Washburne is momentarily soothed by the
presence of "two lithographs in cheerful gilt frames"—a sign of civilization. Before entering the museum, he notes "the light windows of the labor
museum" and offers another description of an urban scene:

> [T]here a half-dozen street urchins were looking in. Swearing,
> twisting, pushing each other, using each other's backs and shoul-
> ders to obtain vantage-ground, clad in nondescript clothes, rough

> in manner, and of many nations, they looked in longingly from the cold alley where they lived upon these glorified workshops which promised pleasantness and peace. (570)

Before Washburne takes his reader into the museum, he depicts the dramatic effect this social experiment seemed to be having on the denizens of the neighborhood. He describes the behavior, dress, ethnicity, and environment of this group of boys in a way that signals their "incorrigibility" to a reading audience of bourgeois reformers. At the same time, he attributes to them a "longing" desire for "pleasantness and peace" to suggest their attraction to the signs of civilization and thus their latent potential to change—to be reformed.[29]

Of course, these boys might have been looking at something else—perhaps teasing a friend for going in rather than hoping for tranquility and solace from their depraved environment. But Washburne has placed the behavior of these boys on display within an interpretive frame that prevents alternative readings. Not surprisingly, his ideological frame determined what he would observe, note, and describe. Washburne's journalist eye contextualized and situated based on his own understanding of what was unique and unfamiliar; an ethnographic gaze made a "show" of the subject on which it landed, exemplifying Kirshenblatt-Gimblett's theory of how people and things are made into ethnographic objects: "The vitrine, as a way of looking, is brought to the site. A neighborhood, village, or region becomes for all intents and purposes a living a museum in situ. The museum effect, rendering the quotidian spectacular, becomes ubiquitous."[30] Even when he entered the museum, he continues to gaze in this way. As he describes a metal shop, "for a shop this room is in appearance, much more than a museum," he noted the "grim picturesqueness" and "general tone of brown." His description of battered, bent, and heavy machinery "spitting blue and yellow flames" anthropomorphized unfamiliar technologies, creating a picture of a sentient industrial factory in miniature. When he exclaimed once again that he "still [does] not see what it is that makes this a Museum. What is it more than a series of manual training shops?" he concluded that the spectatorial structure was all that indicated its status. "True," he wrote, "the groups of onlookers mark a characteristic difference" (572).

Washburne and my critique of his point of view remind me of my own excursions into Chicago, even to the urban campus of the University of Illinois. To leave my residence in Evanston for the Near West Side of Chicago is to substitute a suburban vista with an urban one, to exchange lawn-framed sidewalks for grass-cracked cement, to leave smooth asphalt streets arched by fifty-year-old elms to traverse pothole ridden intersections with yellowed seedlings marking the efforts of a city beautification committee. To move from Northwestern University to the University of

Illinois is to leave an enclaved private institution for a visibly public one, to encounter fingerprint-covered walls instead of spotless ones, and to ride small elevators with peeling linoleum and broken bulbs in lieu of spacious elevators with vacuumed carpet and recessed lighting. Of course, the fact that I decide to notice and attribute meaning to the characteristics of my new study environment reflects the degree to which I have internalized another aesthetic, the extent to which my view of the world is filtered by a suburban semiotic. Paralleling Washburne's ambivalent attributions, my impulse to read "dingy" into an institution that another might see as "privileged" tells you more about my point of view than it does about the thing described. Since spectatorial structures and predispositions affect what an "onlooker" is able to perceive, a student habituated to the sights, sounds, and schedules of University of Illinois—a participating insider rather than a detached outsider—would offer a different account.

Washburne, however, began to demonstrate a self-conscious awareness of the limitations of his point of view. As he walked through its rooms, he happened on a group of boys who were learning to make sleds. Washburne was at first critical of their skills and decided that the product of their labor, if it is finished, would be marginal at best. But he recognized something else:

> The direct object of such training may not be obvious to the casual observer, for it is plain that the boys have not time in these few hours of work a week to master even the beginnings of good carpentry. What does take place is what the visitor cannot see, although he may afterwards experience it himself. It is a change of mental attitude. (571)

Here Washburne acknowledged that his role as observer-visitor may not be fully capable of tracking and representing the experience of the Labor Museum for the people of the neighborhood. Since approaching the Labor Museum as an embodied laborer or apprentice characterized the experience intended for its students, perhaps it was the boys' role as "participant" that gave them full access to its pedagogy. Since the Labor Museum's effect was to be visceral, intellectual, and emotional, channeling all levels of experience to ground education, perhaps Washburne's role as the casual "observer" distanced him from that knowledge. On the other hand, while spectatorial predispositions constrained Washburne's initial encounter, they did not fully neutralize his capacity to sense that the "object" of the Labor Museum may not be "visible," that its affective power lay in "what the visitor cannot see." As the article continues, Washburne's text figures an authorial subjectivity trying to move beyond the superficial encounter of "the casual observer" so that he himself (as well as the reader) "may afterwards experience" the elusive effects of the Labor Museum.

As Washburne's outsider status prompted him to note the clothing, nationality, and manners of the boys outside the window, so this status affected his perception of the laborers inside. Concentrating on what he could observe, indeed on what he was trained to observe, he focused on degrees of cleanliness and physical deformity:

> Standing at the table is a clean old German kneading clay, his squat, bowed legs far apart, his body leaning forward, his long and powerful arms beating upon the clay like piston rods . . . one sees that he is bent and twisted by his trade, conformed to his wheel. Upon this he slaps his clay . . . (574)

To Washburne, the German potter was an emblem of the physical laborer whose work and body are one, the joints and limbs of his body likened to the machinery around him. This individual is received as a kind of living ethnographic object precisely because his audience member—one of the "group of onlookers"—seems disposed to turn him into one. However, the movements of Washburne's description are more complicated. As he continues, he seems intent on defining the human being beyond these observable characteristics, or more accurately, of sensing the invisible through the visible:

> His hands open, his thumbs work in; one almost sees him think through his skillful thumbs and forefingers. Like some mystery of organic nature, the clay rises, bends, becomes a vase . . . The old potter rises, lifts the vase in his mitten-like hands, and, bending, straddling sideways, his face unmoved, carries it tenderly to its place. (574)

To Washburne's eye, this worker seems so intent on his manual craft that his intelligence has a corporeal residence, epitomizing the bourgeois projection of the craftsman ideal and its nearly extinct unalienated laborer. At the same time, Washburne tries to "see" his thoughts, to locate an elusive sense of agency nearly imperceptible in a "face unmoved." The intense curiosity with which he notes the potter's expressionless face and "tender" comportment illustrate Washburne's only barely fulfilled hope to learn more of this German potter's subjectivity, his desires, experiences, and dispositions.

Meanwhile, as I scrutinize this text through the machine that has become the ubiquitous tool of the historian in the age of mechanical reproduction, I find myself identifying with Washburne's search. As a performance historian, I have been trained to question the logocentrism of extant evidence and to "see" beyond the surface of these representations. Attempting to negotiate the apparently nonnegotiable spectatorial structures of print and of the microfiche machine, I then feel dependent on texts like Washburne's for the invisible or ephemeral nature of the Labor Museum—its elusive agents, its structures of affect, its unplanned performances—they can make accessible to me. Mine is perhaps the frustration of a performer-ethnographer used to engaging in the experiential medium of a fieldsite or of live performance. Unfortunately, participant observation—the "intense, intersubjective encounter"[31] that many ethnographers use to ground their scholarship—is simply not an option for the historian. But mine is also the frustration of a researcher more firmly rooted in a metaphysics of presence than she would like to admit. I feel the strangeness of historical writing when reminded of the obvious and confounding fact that the Hull-House people, places, and practices about which I am writing are undeniably . . . not here. The "direct object" of my inquiry is quite simply not present. This phenomenological reminder is always at least a little unsettling. On the other hand, the conundrum of my absent fieldsite will only persist as long as I continue to imagine it in some nebulous past. For, as my earlier subtitle indicated, I do have a field, one that does not exist beyond the archives, but is the archives, its documents, museography, and employees. Of course, caught as I am in the operation of a kind of historiographical difference, these representations always seem inadequate. In fact, my longing to experience the past might well be an epiphenomenon of my encounters with these Hull-House mediators and thus another trick of an historical Nervous System. Negotiating past and present as absence and presence, historical representations posit an unmediated (now lost) presence. Thus they carry with them "the destiny of their own non-satisfaction," an always deferred promise of referentiality. Washburne's dilemma with the German potter, however, forces an extra degree of humility and an important corrective to my perceptions of lack. For even if these once-living Hull-House residents and neighbors were still here, how could I be sure that they would tell me their secrets? And even if they were somehow "present," why do I think that they would have any secrets to tell?

Washburne responds to his own conundrum by beginning a new paragraph, one that redirects its curious gaze from an external to an internal focus on the author. For the first time, Washburne uses the first-person singular and shares an internal monologue. In doing so, the text suggests that the Labor Museum's display of unfamiliar objects and humans was also a space in which visitors could begin a self-investigation:

> Looking at him, I wonder. My heart aches. My flower-pots at home made by such as he, gain a new significance. They are no longer mere receptacles for holding earth and guarding the roots of my plants. The rough, red surface of them is written all over with the records of human patience, human cooperation with nature, human hopes and fears. (574)

Washburne's reaction seems to illustrate that the goals of the Labor Museum are being fulfilled. He comes to interpret the objects occupying his own life differently for having been introduced to the people and processes that created them. Not only have workers been reconnected with their own labor processes but a member of the bourgeoisie is "unalienated" from his own material life. Other moments of consciousness raising use a romanticized anti-industrialist rhetoric as Washburne invokes Ruskin and Morris who "recognize that the commercial custom of rating a laborer at what you can buy or rent him for is as low, as inadequate a measure of a human being as could well be devised." The shift in writing style and increasing degree of self-consciousness dramatizes what Kirshenblatt-Gimblett calls "the museum effect:"

> Bleeding into the ubiquity of the common-sense world, the museum effect brings distinctions between the exotic and the familiar closer to home. Calibrations of difference become finer. The objects differentiated draw nearer. One becomes increasingly exotic to oneself, as one imagines how others might view that which we consider normal.[32]

The Labor Museum had seized Washburne's affections, evoking memories of his own life whose normalcy was defamiliarized by the museum effect. The image of the German potter juxtaposed with his own ceramic pots created a personal montage, forcing him to see the latter anew. Illustrating the transverse relationship between self and other, the text shows how the museum momentarily recontextualized Washburne's personal life even as it simultaneously contextualizes the exhibit for his reader.

Authenticity and an Historian's Nostalgia

Washburne's ceramic pots and my microfiche reels share a similarly ambivalent status, one that has a frustratingly confused effect on both of us. Each, we are disposed to believe, contains traces of a past context of production; the "surface of them is written all over with the records of human patience, human cooperation with nature, human hopes and fears" (574). As researchers, both Washburne and I hope for the ability to discern this elusive record so as to touch somehow the lost past to which these objects refer. In both cases, the recognition and subsequent decoding of the record is simultaneously exhilarating and lacking, since the connection with the past they seem to offer is always thwarted by their failure to do so. The potter is not his fingerprints; the reel is not "the real." These metonymic signifiers offer and withdraw the promise of connection, of communication. They encourage the desire to possess lost performances, the ephemeral, affective, and embodied aspects of the past that leave only partial traces of having been. This longing for what is lost periodically takes me away from the library to visit and revisit the Hull-House Museum, for there the material reality of museum exhibits suggests a closer connection to a represented past. There I can touch it, walk through it, sit down on its chair. Or so I like to imagine before I am reminded otherwise. Susan Stewart amplifies:

> Nostalgia is a sadness without an object, a sadness which creates a longing that of necessity is inauthentic because it does not partake in lived experience. Rather, it remains behind and before that experience. Nostalgia, like any form of narrative, is always ideological: the past it seeks has never existed except as narrative, and hence, always absent, that past continually threatens to reproduce itself as a felt lack.[33]

The act of preservation—whether in a museum or historical writing, whether by Washburne or myself—is intimately bound up with anxieties about authenticity and temporality. It is always about loss despite possession.

Washburne continued through the Labor Museum, each room offering a new exhibit. The text vacillates between their description and the reaction each induces in "the visitor." As a space that represents an idealized past (whether of the craftsman's labor, of American society, or of the human race), Washburne's response is mixed with more than a small dose of nostalgia. Here he describes the cooking room where Hull-House neighbors were taught nutritional science surrounded by the images, texts, and objects narrating the history of cooking:

> A low window seat to the right, and a big table before it, covered with a blue and white homespun cloth, make one wish that one could go back at once to the old colonial days, and make apple dowdy and mulled cider in this picture-booky place. (575)

Since the efficacy of nostalgia's narrative lies in what it erases from memory as much as in what it retains, the idealized and selective vision of "apple dowdy and mulled cider" substitutes for the "the colonial days," representing only that which induces longing in the visitor. Here the charm attributed to the past by means of temporal distance paradoxically makes one long to partake of it, to see the gap between past and present collapse. But the charm may be partly induced by the presential consciousness elicited by this brand of exhibit. Tangible items such as the "blue and white homespun cloth" suggest that the past is somehow accessible. This cloth is what it signifies. History is still here.

In the next moment, however, the materialized reality of this "picture-booky place" will be disrupted for Washburne as the gap between past and present, between referent and representation, reasserts itself:

> A dear little painted dresser stands next to the window seat, set out with old blue and white china; but an abrupt modern not is struck by the case of laboratory samples which hangs beside it. (575)

Washburne's rhapsodies about the charms of the "old blue and white china"—a signal of the Arts and Crafts aesthetic—are stalled by the abrupt reminder of modernity, the place from which this history is produced. His next encounter with the Arts and Crafts dishware is even more disturbing:

> Here is a fine old carved side-board with more blue and white china on it—modern blue and white, alas! and not half so pretty as the old kind. (575)

An object signifying the past but created in the present is a poor anti-dote for this peculiar form of historical anxiety. The effectiveness of these representations is proportionate with the degree that they mask the act of preservation, an activity that is, whether through "setting aside" or through reproduction, always an act of construction.

Washburne's nostalgic perception was triggered not only by the charm of objects such as the cloth and china but also by the people of the Labor Museum who doubled as historical signifiers. As earlier discussed in relation to the Labor Museum's contextualizations, his spectatorship marks the intersection of ethnographic and historical methods of interpretation, exemplified as Washburne continues into other rooms and categorizes unwitting exhibits.

> Addams hopes sometime to have the living workers in the Museum dressed in their national and historic costume as they go about their work. This Italian women, with big gold ear-rings swinging against her dark and scrawny neck, unconsciously carries out the idea. But the sweet-faced Irish woman near her, . . . her white Irish hands deftly twisting the thread, is altogether too respectable and modern to look her part. (576)

To Hull-House students, "this Italian woman" was Mrs. Molinari; to Washburne, she was an anonymous representative of Italian culture whose outward appearance read "authentic." Washburne drew on a travelers' semiotics to judge the degrees to which these human exhibitions fit the categories to which they were assigned, the degree to which they "looked their part" in an impromptu pageant. Washburne's text also signals the rupture inherent in his own semiotics and in representational practices more generally when he refers to the Irish woman's "part" as national signifier. National identity is here somewhat ironically characterized as an assembly of external props, costumes, and facial expressions. Significantly, respectable and modern, however, were adjectives used to describe the woman whose "white Irish hands" looked "less ethnic," whose outer appearance did not adequately signify an "un-American" cultural background. The presumption that one is less civilized if one evokes the past makes his description somewhat ambivalent; a "dark and scrawny neck" mingles a degree of cultural anxiety into this idealized space. His reference to modernity reflects the ideology used to contextualize these women and their labor, an act of preservation that was simultaneously a categorical and evolutionary imposition. Being labeled "modern" in this timeline meant the loss of ethnically identifiable characteristics, the "national and historic costume" that signified cultural and temporal difference to this ethnographer-historian. The Irish woman and the modern blue and white china are thus ambivalent figures—the attribution of their "modern" status simultaneously makes their authenticity questionable. Meanwhile, the Italian woman's status as authentic is secured through her primitive otherness.

Besides the pictures of Ida B. Wells and the nearby exhibition of *Hull-House and the Neighborhood*, the interior of the 1993 Hull-House mansion—a site simultaneously billed as original and restored—is filled with pictures, props, and furniture of another era. Frayed children's books and preserved immigrant newspapers are strewn on an upholstered divan and coffee table as if spontaneously left by their readers. The effect of this sepia-toned vision of lived space is disrupted, however, by "the abrupt modern note" of stark white pieces of paper whose typed black lettering contextualizes these remnants of the past: "Russian Newspaper, circa 1909" and "Children met here for Jenny Dowd's Kindergarten class, 1893–1903." Across the hall, a writing desk holds a pen poised over a pile of papers inscribed in Jane Addams's indecipherable penmanship, a hand familiar to me after hours of squinting at microfiched copies of her letters. I respond to the documents on the desk with fetishistic fascination—Did she touch these, I ask myself? The incontestable reality of this materialized exhibit lends a feeling of authenticity to the history it narrates. For a moment I imagine that I have come on a piece of the past, a piece of Jane Addams, before realizing that—alas!—the papers are themselves microfiche copies. The fickle promise of authenticity extends and retracts itself continually as I pass a fireplace, a bulletin board, a photograph. The same strange feeling occurs when I try to forget the slideshow that depicted how extensively the original mansion was torn down before it was "restored," when I try to ignore the cash register and items for sale at the foot of the staircase, or when I try to pretend that I am not standing on the linoleum floor of an addition created to accommodate the administrative and lavatory needs of museum exhibition.

In the middle of his tour, Washburne's confrontation with the paradoxes of museum representation underwent a new twist when he found an object whose relation to an historical referent was not simply questionable, but nonexistent.

> Lacking in both bones and wood is this awkward, monstrous creature, made of brown basketry . . . We are relieved to learn that it is here because a Scandinavian friend of the House made it as a masquerade costume for his son. At any rate, the figure crouches beside the window, an anomaly humped and hideous, a plain warning against things which are merely curious and ingenious. (577)

Had this been contextualized with misleading didactics and donated pictures, perhaps Washburne would have seen a significance anyway. By letting him in on the joke, the Labor Museum's workers saved him from mistaking a "curious" object for an historiographically meaningful one, from being duped into creating an outsider's interpretation of what was actually an inside joke. The moment reminds me of another one I overheard nearly one hundred years later while a museum employee was initiating a new tour guide in the practice of contextualization, an encounter that ironically reframes my anxieties about authenticity and historical narration. The two stood before an array of uncontextualized objects awaiting demystification. It was the material culture display. Objects such as a spinning wheel and sewing machine were familiar to me. And I quietly took pride in being able to recognize a cigar maker. The ensemble of wood and metal that looked like an unfinished oversized umbrella or a ("humped and hideous") deformed ostrich stumped me much as the unfamiliar machinery confounded Washburne.

"This is a drying rack," said the touring guide who helpfully extrapolated. "They would do other people's laundry at home and then hang it out to dry on these spindles."

Nearby was an enormous washtub with a mechanized apparatus of some sort in the center. "And this?" asked the initiate. "This is nice."

"Oh. They wouldn't have had it in their homes at this time, though."

"Really?"

"Yeah, that's a washtub of a later period and would have been too expensive," she laughed, "Mary Ann [the head curator] saw it and got it for a good deal or something."

The initiate nodded and pondered Mary Ann's anomalous purchase in a confused silence, perhaps wondering what she was going to be able to say about it on future tours. Whether or not future bright-eyed museum visitors receive the washtub as an accurate material signifier of the past will depend on whether the initiate ignores or incorporates this piece of unfortunate information. Whether she decides to create the satisfying (if inaccurate) narrative this dubious washtub invites, or whether she (like the Labor Museum guides before her) decides to reveal the masquerade to her visitors, "history" precariously rides on the whims and imagination of a tour guide. Her acts of contextualization may or may not redeem an object that (like an earlier monstrous creature) serves as "a warning" to museum curators against purchasing things that are "merely curious and ingenious." At the Labor Museum and the Hull-House Museum, unremarkable objects such as these tubs, racks, and brown basketry can be made remarkable. The denaturing process of historical narrative tenuously invents or erases historiographical significance.

The ensuing awkward silence in the Hull-House Museum was broken when an assistant curator joined the tour guide and the initiate. As they searched for ways to contextualize more objects, the three continued to tread along the fragile cordons of a historical NS.

They came to a pair of boots.

"So, here is a pair of boots," said the assistant curator. Slight pause. "Hmmm, Cathy, what do you usually say about this pair of boots?"

"Well," the other cautiously responded, "I usually say something about how boots from back then are really similar to boots now."

"Mmmm, yes," the other two nodded in unison.

Satisfied, they moved along on the tour while another nerve snapped.

Performative Disruptions: Accidents and Interludes

Washburne's "monstrous creature" and Mary Ann's washtub also testify to the impromptu aspects of these spaces, a performative flexibility within the museum frame that laborers, curators, students, guides, and friends can appropriate for their own use, innovation, and "masquerade." Washburne inadvertently documents more performative dislocations enacted at the Labor Museum when he recounts his conversations with two Irishwomen. While his quotations and descriptions of the two women are suspect in terms of their historical "authenticity" and suggest a great deal about his use of them to figure his own authorial subjectivity, it is useful to try to theorize the encounter through its problematic representation. In the absence of "the voices of the women themselves," such a document might be excavated for what it suggests about the agency of these "humans turned exhibit" as mediated through Washburne's own self-representation. He quotes the first woman, Mrs. Sweeney who was actually the museum's cleaning lady, replicating the phrases and lilts of an Irish speech pattern.

> Mrs. Sweeney, a neighborhood woman, employed in keeping the
> museum clean, rolls her bare arms in her little red shoulder shawl
> and examines the pictures with me.
>
> "This is an Irish lady spinnin, annyhow," she explains, pointing
> with a soaked forefinger. "Shure, I'd know her, big or little, in all
> the worrld."
>
> Perhaps she overlooks a little the Kentucky spinner, whose pic-
> ture hangs next, and disregards their blue and white quilt, which
> makes a background for the pictures; but, at least, she has seen the
> work of her own people under a new aspect: that is, with some
> historical perspective. (577)

Once again, Washburne's ambivalent tracking system determines what he
textually highlights; an eye conditioned in bourgeois propriety receives
Mrs. Sweeney's "bare," "soaked" flesh as unusual and noteworthy. On the
other hand, it shows Mrs. Sweeney deciding to conduct her own efforts
at contextualization. The Labor Museum is not a social space where she
feels silenced by her role as domestic servant and relegated to an unseen
backstage. Unlike Washburne, she probably is not examining the pictures for the first time but is taking the opportunity to highlight what
she feels is significant about the Labor Museum's pedagogy. Her selection is motivated by the cultural familiarity of the "Irish lady spinnin."
Using the image as an object of identification, Mrs. Sweeney asserts her
own place in a national community, one whose members share a cultural history and experience. Of all the other lithographs on the wall, it
seems that Mrs. Sweeney underscores only this one. Washburne notices
explicitly that she bypasses the American image of the Kentucky spinner
but recuperates Mrs. Sweeney by suggesting that she has been influenced
by the museum's efforts at contextualization—at least she has seen her
people "with some historical perspective." But did she really? It seems
instead that Mrs. Sweeney decided to ignore the historical perspective she
was offered, one that placed the labor practices of the Kentucky spinner after her own in an evolutionary narrative. By "overlooking" some
pictures, by "disregarding" certain material objects, Mrs. Sweeney conducted something like a resistant—or at least selective—reading of the
Labor Museum's textual and imagistic didactics. As a cultural receiver,
her interest in this educational performance may have had little to do
with its interpretation of "the whole." The moment suggests that, while
dominant pedagogies are prevalent, its signifiers are not necessarily
stable. An individual agent can disrupt claims of temporal inevitabil-
ity to offer a new context in which to interpret the representations of
her ethnicity.

Washburne does not name the second woman with whom he speaks.
But, having researched other inventories and memoirs, I suspect it is

probably Mrs. Brosnahan. For several years, she functioned as one of the spinner-demonstrators and thus also the display's object. By speaking, however, and participating in her own self-contextualization, she is also the subject of display. After using free-indirect discourse to report that "she herself" knows the entire process of linen making from sowing flax seed to dyeing the fabric, he quotes her directly. The decision to include such a long direct quotation suggests the impact of this encounter on him, which the text attempts to reproduce for the reader by displacing Washburne's own authorial voice.

> "But, shure, dear," she exclaims, "it is not your chemical dyeing at all, but the home-dyeing, that I know. We made the dyes ourselves from log-wood, and barks, and stuff we took out of the bogs of old Ireland. But one thing I will say for it: it never faded as your high-toned dyes do." (579)

Mrs. Brosnahan vacillates between the first- and second-person pronoun to represent her labor processes, a discursive practice that delineates her own boundaries of self and other, or between an Irish "we" and an American "you." Not unlike Mrs. Sweeney, Mrs. Brosnahan places herself within a circle of cultural affiliation to underscore the significance of past practices. In the process, the quotidian realities of daily life are held up as emblems of a delineated national culture.

Furthermore, the fact that Washburne's text began directly quoting here might suggest something of a shift in how her personal narrative was performed. After articulating the various stages in the process of linen making, did she particularly emphasize this statement? If she had been intently focused on her spinning, did she stop so that her eyes could meet Washburne's at this point in her discourse? Was it meant to be an interpretive aside that recontextualized all that had come before? Jane Addams's writings on the Labor Museum suggest that she counted on women's oral narratives in this performance space. As earlier quoted she was glad that "the whirl of the wheels" spurred "many a reminiscence and story of the old country." Here Mrs. Brosnahan deployed the mode of personal narrative—"the rural interlude in the busy town life" that charmed Jane Addams—to distinguish her history. While a Progressive hereditary American such as Washburne might nostalgically reinterpret her statement as the loss of the craftsman ideal, it also provided a space for a certain kind of self-definitional performance—one that was to become increasingly pointed and politicized.

> Presently she tells her story.
> "Yes, we all spun and wove in the old country . . ."
> "And how did you happen to come here?" I asked.

> Her serene face darkens. "Never will I forgive them that misled us to it!" she exclaims. "There in the old country we had our comforts, our own bit of land, my man making a dollar and a quarter the day, Irish money; a blissid union of ten children and never a shoe wanting to the foot of one of them. O, wirra the day that we left! I landed here with a baby in my arms—crippled—"
>
> "Crippled? how?" I cried.
>
> She passed the question. "Yes, crippled. She is a hump-back, dear, eleven by now, and none higher than my waist. The next to the baby had the spinal meningeetis soon after we landed and his reason fled . . ." (579)

Mrs. Brosnahan's story was far from the uncritical tale of a benevolent United States welcoming "the poor," "the tired," and "the hungry." In a move that was itself simultaneously nostalgic and resistant, she elegized lost national origins while defining herself against the idealizations of a progressive American ideology. As she continued, she told also of how her husband "took to the drink" in response to the sorry situation they faced. This story exceeded the conventions of the "rural interlude" Addams described picturesquely circulating around the Labor Museum. Instead, the narrative heightened the political economic realities of an immigrant American, circumstances the museum often displaced by a romanticized emphasis on cultural production. Mrs. Brosnahan thus told a different history than the one forwarded in the lithographs, glass casements, and textiles that surrounded her, using her capacity as performative signifier to push those narratives into the background. At the same time, she negotiated this new role on her own terms, evading the questions of a journalist now fascinated anew by her extra self-disclosure. Washburne would leave the museum troubled not to have known the cause of the crippled child's "mysterious" injury, another of the Labor Museum's invisible secrets. As her encounter with Washburne concludes, this Irish woman hints to the difference between her life experiences and her Labor Museum persona. It is to the latter that she eventually returns.

> "And what did you do?" I asked.
>
> "I begged on the streets, dear. Oh, I can smile and laugh with the best when I am at work here, but there's something else in my heart." She turned to a young lady pupil, whom she was teaching to spin, unreeled the broken thread, mended, and set it right with a skillful touch or two. "No I ain't discouraged," she told the young lady, in her soft, smooth voice, "for discouraging won't do for a pupil. You'll spin, dear, but it'll take a deal o'practice." A minute more and she and Mrs. Sweeney are speaking the Gaelic together, and laughing like two children. She dances a quiet shuffle under

her decent skirts. "And can I dance?" she asks. "It is a good old
Irish break-down dancer I was in my young days. You should see
me do a reel and a jig." Her hidden feet nimbly shuffle and whisper
on the wooden floor. (579)

In this passage, Mrs. Brosnahan's movements, focus, and speech change
rapidly. At the moment that she comes closest to sharing her deepest
emotions—the "something else in my heart," she quickly turns away to
her pupil instead, suggesting that her role as teacher of labor practices
(combined with the presence of a stranger) discouraged too lengthy an
indulgence in this sort of personal narrative. The next spoken words
Washburne reports have the quality of double entendre: "No I ain't discouraged." Are they said to Washburne about life in America or to her
student about her spinning prospects? "A minute more" and Mrs. Brosnahan has engaged a third interlocutor, Mrs. Sweeney, in "the Gaelic."
Washburne seems charmed as "they laugh like two children," interpreting
their conversation as another idyllically ethnic practice. Though he safely
interprets them within a harmonizing ideological frame—as unthreatening "immigrant gifts" that spiced the American way of life and delighted
the adventurer-journalist, his text also suggests the improvised creation
of an oppositional linguistic space from which he is excluded. Their code
switching masked their conversation, and so, ultimately, the secret joke
they shared. The laughter seems to have been fleeting, however. If non-
English speaking had become too extensive and stories about the trials of
immigrant life too long, the Labor Museum's idealized portrait might have
been threatened. Fortunately, Mrs. Brosnahan, however, concluded the
visit by readdressing Washburne and offering an Irish jig—another "native
tradition" that, like arts and crafts, could be celebrated as an unthreatening immigrant "contribution." Whether this dance too had a "hidden
transcript"[34] beneath its display on Hull-House's progressive public stage,
whether Mrs. Brosnahan used an open admission of self-display to parody
the ideology of cultural harmony she was supposed to signify, also remains
hidden from Washburne (and from his historian). Meanwhile, I also keep
wondering what—or who—the two women were laughing at? Perhaps
they were laughing at Washburne . . .

Sometimes—when again I catch myself searching for "elusive subjectivities" in a microfiched article—I suspect it's me.

The wanderings and wonderings of the previous paragraph are as
much an index of my authorial subjectivity—its affections, hermeneutic
gaze, perceptions of loss—as they are an analysis of the Labor Museum's
performers. More than simply a description, my narrative is partly an
attempt to come to terms with my own invented involvement in this text.
As Washburne searches to move beyond the vision of a casual observer,
I am attempting to see beyond the distanced perspective of a historian,

a move that nostalgically posits a "beyond," the lost performance of a woman whose name may not be Mrs. Brosnahan after all. She, Washburne, and I myself share a similar situation, however, in that we are all spectators in the histories we construct. Like Washburne, my position as spectator to history also makes me its producer, a double status that impinges on my narrative performance in this text. Like Mrs. Brosnahan who recounts a particular history of Ireland and immigration, both Washburne and myself construct our narrative performances in light of our own historical and cultural situation, inflected as well by the longings and identifications induced by particular tales of the past. Additionally, our historical narratives have themselves been placed on display—Mrs. Brosnahan's for Washburne, Washburne's for me, and mine for you. In all these cases, the "places" and people from which historical narratives emanate have been explicitly incorporated as part of the historical performance itself. Rather than masking or erasing this human intervention, we have acknowledged our subjectivities, points of view, and "human hopes and fears" as we interpret our own historical inventions—as we perform that which is available to us, that which moves us, and that which amuses us. In my own case, I often find myself most amused when I encounter the nervous gaps in the historiographical operation and realize that, despite tremendous efforts to disguise it, history has never been narrated any other way. I close with a final episode from the Hull-House Museum.

The initiate's tour continued throughout the museum and ended as she, the assistant curator, and the tour guide regarded a large-framed piece of paper.

"Now this is from the Tarsitano Family Reunion," said the assistant curator, holding the frame. "Mr. Tarsitano used to come to Hull-House, and now I think his family owns a grocery store. Here are the names of some of the family." The three regarded the frame for a few moments. Slyly the assistant curator looked up and met the eyes of the other tour guide who smiled slowly. Suddenly, they both started giggling.

"You know, neither of us really knows why this is here," said one.

"Yeah," said the other, "actually . . . having you here will be a good way to pin Mary Ann down on exactly what we are supposed to say about this."

She continued chuckling to herself as she turned to another wall.

"Now over here is a picture of . . . wait, it used to hang right here."

"What?"

"Well, there used to be . . . well, I guess it doesn't matter, now. It's not here," she laughed again, even louder this time. The other woman joined once more.

"You have to be careful what you say," she said. "Mary Ann always takes things away without you knowing, and you'll find yourself pointing to something that isn't there."

As they laughed at the empty space on the wall which, like a lost or misindexed archival document, will leave an empty space in future historical narratives, a fourth woman descended the stairs. The group stopped laughing as she entered. Holding her head high, the woman walked slowly through the room.

"Morning, Mary Ann," said one guide.

"Good morning," the woman replied without looking at them. She adjusted a picture frame and continued walking through to another exit. "Everything alright?"

"Yes, yeah, hmmhmm," replied the assistant curator and the guide.

Mary Ann left; the two women looked at each other for a split second. Suddenly, they burst out laughing once more.

Like two children?

Conclusion

While the story of Washburne's encounters as well as my own have been adjusted in both our recreations, the movements of these texts suggest something about their contradictory, affective impact on us. After hearing about Mrs. Brosnahan's Irish linen, her crippled child, and drunken husband, for instance, after seeing her "eyes gleam," her hands spin, and her feet dance a jig, Washburne seems profoundly moved.

> We feel that this living woman—this worker and victim and survivor—is the most precious thing that the Museum has shown us. Indeed, we suspect the founders of deliberate intention in placing her there, where she is not measured by petty, momentary standards, but by the laws which underlie human evolution. We catch a glimpse of the importance of her function in a historic industrial order; and while our minds leap to the new truth, our hearts thrill with a new sympathy. (579)

Washburne has turned his eyes inward, placing himself under examination only to grow more humble. Washburne claims to be relieved of the "petty, momentary standards" by which Hull-House immigrants are judged. His heart is able to "thrill with a new sympathy" because the Labor Museum has provided him with a way to understand her and her experience. In concluding the visit (and after attending a lecture where "these thoughts become more definite and these emotions strengthened to resolution"), Washburne feels the "museum effect" to such a degree, feels a closeness and connection to Hull-House to such an extent, that he finds a new subject position for himself as he exits Hull-House into the "riotous city."

> We, too, wistful children of a half-civilized state, look back through these windows into a warmed and light world of happy industry; and even while we shove and push for the best places, wish in our hearts that we were working within. The light and heat, even the joy of doing good work under right conditions, may be artificial and evanescent, but without, around us, all is struggle and clamor. (580)

Washburne has become one of those boys whom he earlier observed outside the Labor Museum window. He struggles for the best seat as the boys earlier pushed "to obtain the best vantage ground." He wishes he was working within, the same "longing" that he earlier attributed to the boys. However, this connection he feels—a new sympathy turned to empathy as his bourgeois superiority is redeemed by an encounter with simple primitives—is still one that retains Washburne's ideological filter. He still sees civilization in stark contrast to the city, still characterizes the urban landscape as "riotous," "struggle," and "clamor," and still presumes the "evanescence" of Hull-House. Finally, Washburne's sympathetic transformation illustrates one of the most problematic aspects of an uncritically "humanist" ideology advanced in many a museum. As Sally Price writes, such an exhibit "allows our self-recognition and personal rediscovery and permits a renewed contact with our deeper instincts; the result is that we increase our understanding of ourselves and our relationship to art."[35] Thus, "becoming exotic to oneself" can still maintain the category of the "exotic," resulting in selfish acts of personal appropriation rather than encouraging a more radical personal transformation or dismantling entrenched ideological categories. This component and its effect, however, makes such contextualizations so engaging; the affective power of the harmonious, cross-cultural links they seem to forge is precisely what masks their insidiousness.

For my part, this text is the record of a particular "effect" Hull-House and its historiographical sites have had on me. Visiting Jane Addams's Hull-House Museum is a complicated experience for someone who happens to be doing research on the settlement. While there, I do not always engage in moments of ethnographic eavesdropping or metahistorical musing on my own self-(mis)guided tours. Sometimes I cower in scholarly humility as I read a didactic that quotes a source I do not recognize or refers to a neighborhood church I did not know existed in Chicago's Nineteenth Ward. The reaction is a symptom of larger research anxieties as I adjust with intimidation and confusion to the practice of fact accumulation that seems to be so much a part of the historiographical operation. Internalizing a kind of hyperempiricism, I scribble reminders to myself—"Find poem: 'Ode to Maxwell Street' . . . Get date of photo of Greek boys' wrestling club." These are the moments when I forget Jacques Derrida's critique and succumb to the presential temptations of performance historiography. Caught in an historian's double repression, I assume the presence of the document's referent and disavow the representational nature of the document itself. While I can often maintain this functional ontology for hours at a time, inevitably the problem of absence returns. For usually these visits end with me leaving the museum to linger in bewilderment at the intersection of Halsted and Polk Streets, a place that was at one time walked by the inhabitants of an immigrant neighborhood and is now traversed by college students wearing jeans, sweatshirts, and backpacks. It is then that de Certeau's questions in *The Writing of History* resurface in my mind. "What do historians really fabricate when they 'make history'? What are they 'working on'? . . . What in God's name is this business?"[36]

Notes

"Performance at Hull-House: Museum, Microfiche, and Historiography" was originally published in *Exceptional Spaces: Essays in Performance and History*, ed. Della Pollock, 261–93 (Chapel Hill: University of North Carolina Press, 1998).

1. Michel De Certeau, *The Writing of History*, trans. Tom Conley (New York: Columbia University Press, 1988), 64.

2. See Michel Foucault, *Archaeology of Knowledge*, trans. Alan Sheridan (New York: Pantheon, 1972); Joan Scott, *Gender and the Politics of History* (New York: Columbia University Press, 1988); Hayden White, *The Content of the Form: Narrative Discourse and Historical Representation* (Baltimore: Johns Hopkins University Press, 1987), and *Tropics of Discourse* (Baltimore: Johns Hopkins University Press, 1978); Dominick La Capra, *History and Criticism* (Ithaca, NY: Cornell University Press, 1985); and Michael Taussig, *The Nervous System* (New York: Routledge, 1992).

3. Selections from Antonio Gramsci, *The Prison Notebooks of Antonio Gramsci*, ed. and trans. Quintin Hoard and Geoffrey Nowell Smith (London: Lawrence and Wishart, 1971), 276.

4. Jane Addams, *Twenty Years at Hull-House* (New York: Penguin, 1981), 72.

5. For a history of the settlement movement, see Allen Davis, *Spearheads for Reform* (New Brunswick, NJ: Rutgers University Press, 1967); for a critical analysis of Hull-House, Rivka Shpak Lissak, *Pluralism and Progressives: Hull-House and the New Immigrant* (Chicago: University of Chicago Press, 1989); and for an historical excavation of museum exhibition during the same period, Donna Haraway, "Teddy Bear Patriarchy: Taxidermy in the Garden of Eden, New York City, 1908–36," in *Primate Visions: Gender, Race, and Nature in the World of Modern Sciences* (New York: Routledge, 1989), 26–58. Words such as "unfortunates" and "slums" were frequently used in reform literature of the period.

6. All previous quotations from Jane Addams, "First Outline of Labor Museum at Hull-House," 1900, Jane Addams Memorial Collection, Reel 51.

7. Jane Addams, "First Outline of Labor Museum at Hull-House," 1900, Jane Addams Memorial Collection, Reel 51.

8. Jane Addams, *Twenty Years at Hull-House*, 260.

9. De Certeau, *Writing of History*, 73.

10. Taussig, *Nervous System*, 2–3.

11. Jane Addams, *Twenty Years at Hull-House*, 172.

12. Taussig, *Nervous System*, 44–45.

13. Taussig, *Nervous System*, 44–45.

14. See Richard Schechner's theory of performance in his *Between Theater and Anthropology* (Philadelphia: University of Pennsylvania Press, 1985).

15. Taussig, *Nervous System*.

16. Barbara Kirshenblatt-Gimblett, "Objects of Ethnography," *Exhibiting Cultures: The Poetics and Politics of Museum Display*, ed. Ivan Karp and Steven D. Lavine (Washington, DC: Smithsonian Institution Press, 1991), 390.

17. For essays on the concept of public history, see Susan Porter Benson, Stephen Brier, and Roy Rosenzweig, eds., *Presenting the Past: Essays on History and the Public* (Philadelphia: Temple University Press, 1986).

18. Renato Rosaldo, *Culture and Truth: The Remaking of Social Analysis* (Boston: Beacon, 1989), 68; Eileen Boris, *Art and Labor: Ruskin, Morris, and the Craftsman Ideal in America* (Philadelphia: Temple University Press, 1986), xiv.

19. For general discussion of pluralism in relation to American nationalism, see, e.g., Rogers M. Smith, "The 'American Creed' and American Identity: The Limits of Liberal Citizenship in the United States," *Western Political Quarterly* 41, no. 2 (1988): 225–51; Hans Kohn, *American Nationalism: An Interpretive Essay* (New York: Macmillan, 1957); Virginia Sapiro, "Women, Citizenship, and Nationality: Immigration and Naturalization Policies in the United States," *Politics and Society* 13, no. 1 (1984): 1–24. For a discussion about whether settlements (in particular Hull-House) anticipated Horace Kallen's more specific definitions of "cultural pluralism," see Lissak, *Pluralism and Progressives*. For references to conservative cultural performances, see Michael Wallace, "Visiting the Past: History Museums in the United States," in Benson, Brier, and Rosensweig, *Presenting the Past*, 137–64.

20. Benedict Anderson, *Imagined Communities* (London: Verso, 1983).

21. The term "gallery of nations" frequently titled the pageants and immigrant performances of the Progressive Era. See Sally Price, *Primitive Art in Civilized Places* (Chicago: University of Chicago Press, 1989), 56.

22. Quotation from residents of Hull-House, *Hull-House Maps and Papers* (New York: Arno, 1970), 15; for analysis of the relationship between industrialized labor and the construction of ethnicity, see Eric Wolf, *Europe and the People without History* (Berkeley: University of California Press, 1982).

23. For chronopolitics, see Johannes Fabian, *Time and the Other: How Anthropology Makes Its Object* (New York: Columbia University Press, 1983), 23.

24. Jane Addams, "First Report: The Labor Museum at Hull-House" (1902), Jane Addams Memorial Collection, reel 51:7.

25. George Stocking, *Race, Culture, and Evolution: Essays in the History of Anthropology* (Chicago: University of Chicago Press, 1982), 112.

26. My analysis is inspired by recent critiques of ethnographic writing. See, e.g., James Clifford and George Marcus, *Writing Culture: The Poetics and Politics of Ethnography* (Berkeley: University of California Press, 1985); and

James Clifford, *The Predicament of Culture: Twentieth Century Ethnography, Literature, and Art* (Cambridge, MA: Harvard University Press, 1988).

27. White, *Content of the Form*, 27.

28. All Washburne quotations are from Marion Foster Washburne, "A Labor Museum," *The Craftsman* 6, no. 6 (September 1904): 570–80. All quotations are hereafter cited in the text.

29. On youth and moral reform, see Jane Addams, *The Spirit of Youth in the City Streets* (New York: Macmillan, 1909); and Paul Boyer, *Urban Masses and Moral Order in America, 1820–1920* (Cambridge, MA: Harvard University Press, 1978).

30. Kirshenblatt-Gimblett, "Objects of Ethnography," 413.

31. James Clifford, "On Ethnographic Authority," in Clifford, *The Predicament of Culture: Twentieth Century Ethnography, Literature, Art* (Cambridge, MA: Harvard University Press, 1988), 21–54; Jacques Derrida, *Of Grammatology*, trans. Gayatri Chakravorty Spivak (Baltimore: Johns Hopkins University Press, 1976), 143.

32. Kirshenblatt-Gimblett, "Objects of Ethnography," 410.

33. Susan Stewart, *On Longing: Narratives of the Miniature, the Gigantic, the Souvenir, the Collection* (Durham, NC: Duke University Press, 1993), 23.

34. James C. Scott, *Domination and the Arts of Resistance: The Hidden Transcript* (New Haven, CT: Yale University Press, 1989).

35. Price, *Primitive Art in Civilized Places*, 34.

36. De Certeau, *The Writing of History*, 56.

Chapter 2

Performing Show and Tell

On the Disciplinary Problems
of Mixed-Media Practice

Childhood Rituals

My title is obviously an echo of both the title of this special issue of the *Journal of Visual Culture*—"Show and Tell"—as well as of W. J. T. Mitchell's essay "Showing Seeing," an assessment of visual culture studies that appeared in the *Journal of Visual Culture* and was reprinted in Routledge's *The Visual Culture Reader*.[1] It has been interesting for me to return to that essay—one whose patience, wit, and sanity I greatly admire—to review his articulations of the myths and anxieties, theses and countertheses, which circulate in discourses that surround the study of visual culture. Working as a scholar, teacher, and administrator in performance studies, I feel that I am often encountering threats and composing countertheses that have a similar shape. Those who have read Mitchell's essay know that the last section of "Showing Seeing" is where the phrase "show and tell" becomes literalized in Mitchell-the-teacher's discussion of his "return to one of the earliest pedagogical rituals in American elementary education." He describes how he asks students to become "ethnographers . . . reporting back to a society that has no concept of visual culture."[2] In a number of paragraphs, he dramatizes the range of student examples—objects, masks, costumes, and narratorial strategies—used to "show seeing." There is something about the last part of this essay that also has a familiar shape for me. When Mitchell says that these pedagogical "performances have the effect of acting out the method and lessons of the curriculum," he both announces and does not announce the fact that his students of visual culture have become students of performance.[3] Visual culture seems here to require performance for its seeing to be shown, something that perhaps seems too obvious to require analysis. But it is hard for me not to read the enthusiasm of those last paragraphs as a sign of Mitchell's performance friendliness. When he is astonished by "how much clearer the Sartrean and Lacanian 'paranoid theories of vision' " become "after you have had a few performances that highlight the aggressivity of vision,"[4] he sounds like an advertisement for what those in my field tend to call "performance pedagogy." And when that enthusiasm allows him to celebrate this "visible, embodied, communal practice" and even to take a quick dig at the conventional habits of academic practice that he calls "the solitary introspection of a disembodied intelligence," then it really becomes hard not to infer that Mitchell has been bit by the theater bug.[5]

I want to use the fact that performance slips in here in Mitchell's essay to launch an essay into the parallels, discontinuities, and enmeshments between performance studies and visual culture studies. My title "Performing Show-and-Tell" is, at some level, a kind of redundancy; the show-and-tell ritual is, to my mind, always already performance. But the fact that its redundancy is not necessarily apparent to everyone suggests the need for more clarification. My hope is that a comparison between visual culture studies and performance studies provides a way of foregrounding the stakes and the obstacles faced in their shared consolidation. Both these fields address the occupational opportunities and occupational hazards of what Mieke Bal more generally calls "interdisciplinary cultural analysis"; to me, there is something about an encounter between two interdisciplinary sites that brings their similar and quite different disciplinary legacies into higher relief.[6]

To start off, let me think formally about what it is that makes "show-and-tell" a performance and, from there, think about how that reflection illuminates the dynamics of the cross-disciplinary encounter more generally. Superficially, we could say that show-and-tell is referring to a mixture of image and word, a mixture of media and sensory modes that all theater people like to say is the particular provenance of their beloved art form. When Gotthold Ephraim Lessing is taught in a theater theory syllabus, theater is often positioned as a place where the juxtapositive element of painting and the temporal element of poetry are brought together. When we think of showing and telling as referring less to a medium than to types of signification, then that mixing becomes more complex, forcing a reminder of the number of ways that worded narrative can "show," or that text and images can be perceived as literal and as symbolic in different relations. The image-word binary becomes more unstable and inadequate when you consider all the elements that go into the show-and-tell ritual in childhood education. The image *shown* in this scene is usually something *held* and thus a particularly materialized image, an object that takes part in the tactile as much as visual register. The transmission of the verbal is also, in this case, accompanied by an embodied presenting self, one who makes use of vocal inflection, gesture, facial expression, and motion. That child also stands before a group of individuals, tries or tries not to make eye contact, pauses, paces, and races, gets down and gets back up, as she breathlessly confronts and endures the addressive relation with her audience.

Now even as I begin to elaborate what I think of as a performance-centered list of elements, differently located readers might perk up their ears. "Theater is not the only medium that is mixed," one scholar might say, perhaps quoting Mitchell's own essay where he declares all media to be mixed "with varying ratios of senses and sign-types."[7] A self-identified "digital artist" who works in the so-called multimedia of screens and networks might ask why one would mention theatrical performance at all. A literary critic might ask me to remember the specific attachment of terms like "show" and "tell" to narratology. Meanwhile, someone else would find it important to note that the tactility that I might associate with performance is part and parcel of visuality as elaborated in past and contemporary reworkings of Walter Benjamin, Georges Bataille, Roland Barthes, and more. "And we certainly don't need a theater person to talk to us about addressive relations with the spectator," might say every art historian who has had to deal with the spectator in those endless debates on the legacies of Minimalism. More and different claims of disciplinary association and differentiation could follow.

Even if I am not imagining all reactions entirely accurately, let them serve more generally as examples of the type of reactions that pervade the interdisciplinary encounter, one where the sorting out of mine, yours, also mine, and also yours happens in extended exchanges. And as such, let me use those reactions to remind you about another element of the show-and-tell ritual that you may have forgotten. The shared object in this earliest of pedagogical rituals (rituals that actually begin before "elementary school") is usually a possession. This is to say that one of its distinctive characteristics is that it is mine, and that its "mineness" becomes more urgent and anxious in the de- and recontextualizing travel that happens when a beloved object is taken from home and brought to school. Show-and-tell is threatening because of the fear that a beloved object will be passed around, abused, misused, broken, taken, and if returned, returned in different shape. Show-and-tell can be hard for child audiences too. They are required to listen patiently and to censor their own embodied desires to touch that which they see. Now, in bringing these dynamics to a discussion of the interdisciplinary encounter, it is obvious that I could abuse the "childishness" in the metaphor of what Mitchell calls a childhood ritual, and say that all the angst about recognition and "deskilling" in interdisciplinary formations such as visual cultural studies is just an example of scholars being nervous that other people are taking their toys. But partly because I happen to think that toys are very serious business, I would like not to take that tack. Instead, I want to push the metaphor one more time to foreground what I think is essential about the interaction in show-and-tell, namely, its structure as an intersubjective exchange. The sharing of the toy, the deep breath taken before a treasured object is passed around, the incorporated role of objects in the self-construction and self-extension of individual identities, and the meeting and deflection of gazes, all these elements compose show-and-tell's performance as an essential exercise in intersubjectivity. It is a place of delicate relationality and occasional reciprocity, as well as a place where we learn to deal with the inevitable asymmetry of certain exchanges. It is also valuable as a place to hear a story, a telling about what makes the shared object special, even if it is not what seems special about it to you. And so finally, the preservation of show-and-tell becomes essential as a place where—remember, this is a pedagogical ritual—you might learn something new as well.

Disciplinary Likeness

In thinking about what performance studies and visual culture studies have to do with each other, I want to preserve a sense of the weight and exchange embedded in show-and-tell exercises. You will see that, for me, learning something new is often about learning something "old," about deciding that the memories, traditions, experiences, and skills attached to the shared object are worth incorporating into any new game that you happen to want to play with it.

So, how much is performance studies like visual culture? The focus of my comparison will be based on two points framed in Mitchell's essay. The first concerns his positioning of visual culture studies in a supplemental relation to the tradition of art history and aesthetics. The second concerns his implicit adoption of that supplemental insight to argue for the inherent mixedness of all media in "varying media-ratios and sign-types."[8] To take up the first talking point, if visual culture studies is conceived as some kind of newer formation that "supplements" the traditions of aesthetics and art history, then we can see a similar relation of supplementarity between performance studies and the traditions of "theater studies." Paralleling Mitchell's staging of visual culture's substitutions, there is a way that performance studies enacts its supplementarity in that now classically deconstructionist sense as both an addition to and replacement of theater studies. Performance studies refers to domains outside the proscenium-staged theater event to modes of behavior and cultural forms—carnivals, protests, storytelling, everyday life rituals, the *homo ludens*—that can be added to the array of objects that traditionally encompassed drama and theater history. But that incorporation can never be benignly additive but always anxiously substitutive. Like the art history–to-visual culture movement described by Mitchell, the theater-to–performance studies movement similarly (1) "indicates an incompleteness in the internal coherence" of the tradition of theater as if it "somehow failed to pay attention to what was most central" to itself, and (2) opens the field "to 'outside' issues that threaten" its boundaries.[9]

Both performance studies and visual culture have celebrators and detractors of this expansion of relevant objects of inquiry. While someone like Nicholas Mirzoeff might welcome the field's expansion to studies of CNN, milk ads, and Japanese anime, someone like Thomas Crow might remain more suspicious of what he called "the vast vertical integration of study, extending from the esoteric products of fine-art traditions to handbills and horror videos."[10] Similarly, performance studies professor Richard Schechner vehemently embraced a world where students of performance studied "rock concerts, discos, electioneering, [and] wrestling," while theater scholar Richard Hornby vehemently lambasted that same world where "figure skating" and wrestling matches were placed on the same analytic plane as Shakespeare.[11] The invocation of a list of expanded objects is, of course, not unique to visual and performance studies, but is part of the rhetoric of interdisciplinary humanities practice more generally. And while I do not think that the politics of expansion always play out in the same way, it certainly has been attached to various attempts to rectify the gendered, raced, intercultural, and classed exclusions of the arts and humanities curriculum. While US pundits like William Bennett worried about whether the expansion of the Western canon would mean the replacement of Shakespeare by Alice Walker, counterparts in theater worried whether the expansion of the performance canon would mean the replacement of Shakespeare by Tonya Harding. But, of course, there are concerns voiced from even more temperate scholars about the possibility of these lists getting out of hand, and about whether individuals will have the capacity to reckon with so expanded an "expanded field." While visual scholars worry about the appropriateness of studying baseball cards or wonder if their colleagues really know enough about bioimaging to think anything worth saying, parallel scholars in theater and performance worry about the prospects of someone who studies the "performance of picnics" and wonder if their colleagues really know enough about "the performance of surgical practice" to say anything worth hearing.

A list of expanded objects is only one way of characterizing interdisciplinarity. There are the professional indexes, the conferences, the "studies" appendages in the naming of subfields, and the visual culture readers that have their parallel in the performance studies readers as well. We also endure similar confusions of alignment between subfields and circulating conceptual terms. The term "visuality" has a kind of parallel (though I do not think equivalence) in the term "performativity." Both are theoretical concepts that percolate throughout the humanities and that are derived often from philosophical explorations into subjectivity. They both sound like they belong to particular sides of the cutting-edge disciplinary equation (visuality to visual culture studies and performativity to performance studies) but are, in fact, terms with which some but not all visual culture scholars identify and with which some but not all performance studies scholars identify. Finally, in thinking about shared disciplinary questions and methods that seem to propel both performance and visual culture studies, it is hard not to notice the number of times that something like "anthropology" or "ethnography" have been held up or criticized as the route to new interpretations in both fields. I think that Hal Foster's impressively neat summary of the reasons behind anthropology's prominence in visual studies bears out in performance studies as well.[12] Anthropology seems a useful discourse not only because it "studies culture" but also because it does so by "addressing alterity"; it has an approach whose mixture of humanistic and social science methods can help to "arbitrate the interdisciplinary." It also, at least since the 1980s, incorporated "self-critique"—or what I learned to call "self-reflexivity"—into scholarly presentation.[13]

I see more significance in this list of reasons why, as Foster puts it, anthropology becomes the "compromise discourse of choice," particularly because of how he characterizes the relation between anthropology's "contextual" approach and that of contemporary artists who, Foster writes, "aspire to fieldwork in the everyday."[14] This seems a reminder of something else that the turn to visual culture and the turn to performance studies might share: namely, a history of art practice that incorporated the contextuality of art into the art itself. This is to remember the familiar series of art-historical movements—Dada, surrealism, Bauhaus, Happenings, conceptualism, Minimalism—not simply as art that, like everything else, needs to be contextualized. The artworks affiliated with such movements were themselves explorations of the category of the contextual, unsettling the boundaries of art and its surround, sussing out the latent symbology of the contextual (à la New Historicism), reckoning with the permeation of object and world, asking receivers to decide if and why such divisions need to be reinstantiated. Martin Jay asked for a similar remembering when he said in that notorious *October* questionnaire of 1996 that "the crisis of the institution of art . . . has been as much internal as external, arising from changes within 'art' itself and not merely resulting from the importation of cultural models from other disciplines."[15] In other words, the sensibility of visual culture is an artist's thing, not just a scholar's thing. The visual culture interest in the imagery of advertising, for instance, was presaged in some ways by the iconic representation of popular culture imagery in visual art (remember Andy Warhol's Brillo Pad Boxes and Campbell Soup Cans). Upon considering the institutional formation of performance studies, it is noteworthy how often the sensibility of performance studies was an artist's thing as well. The turn to anthropology and sociology—to reading Victor Turner on Ndembu ritual or Erving Goffman on the front stages and back stages of daily life—followed after certain experiments in the arts, after say the large-scale Happenings of people like Allan Kaprow or small-scale "events" of people like George Brecht, attempted to explore the nature of collectivity and to take a rhetorical stance on the everyday. In fact, two of these performing artists, Michael Kirby and Richard Schechner, founded what would become the scholarly department of performance studies at New York University. This is an interesting moment when the lessons learned by the humanities from "anthropology" were, at some level, also being taught by artists. Clifford Geertz wasn't the only person noticing that "art" and "common sense" were "cultural systems" or that "local knowledges" were rhetorical.

To summarize thus far, as fields that consolidated at a similar historical moment, performance studies and visual culture studies bear a structural resemblance and can be seen as both cause and symptom of a similarly fraught, similarly opportunistic, intellectual and artistic milieu. As such, we are also heralded and scolded in language that sounds the same. In addition to that anxious list of objects or those pesky references to anthropology, selected elements of performance studies can, like selected elements of visual culture, endure affirmation and ridicule depending on the interests of the argument. Performance studies' theoretical bent gets accused (both internally and externally) of being "too theoretical"; performance studies' relationship to poststructuralist theories of representation can get accused of advancing a "textualized" paradigm; and performance studies' politics can get accused of being "politically correct." Meanwhile, what feels like interdisciplinary innovation to some feels like "deskilling" to others. All these terms and conundrums should sound familiar to anyone who has read the vast number of essays, position pieces, questionnaires, or symposium notes devoted to the "state" of our respective fields in the last ten years. Finally, there does seem to be a high tolerance for mixture—formal, theoretical, disciplinary, and medium based—in both performance studies and visual culture studies. To invoke the title of Mitchell's own contribution to this special issue—"There Are No Visual Media: That's Why We Need Visual Culture Studies"—Mitchell's notion that all media are mixed—"with varying ratios and sign-types"—sounds quite familiar to performance studies affiliates. The only difference is that we usually hear the conclusion differently phrased: Yes, all media are mixed, "that's why we need performance studies."

Disciplinary Difference

At this point, it sounds like performance studies is to theater what visual culture is to art history, both paralleling perhaps what cultural studies is to literary studies—or perhaps to the humanities more generally. It might seem time for the members on one side of each pair to lock arms in shared struggle against the opponents on the other side of each pair. If all agree that media are mixed, perhaps what we "need" in fact is a unified front. But there is actually one other tendency that these presumably newer formations share, one that for me ends up producing episodes of unwitting or often unwelcome differentiation. Articulations both for and against these so-called newer fields tend to disavow their relation to particular disciplinary histories. That disavowal ends up doing at least two things: (1) it tends to homogenize the "traditions" from which they are presumably breaking free, and (2) it obscures the specific history of particular types of analysis and method from the critics who employ them or, if you will, are employed by the skills that they use. Both these symptoms of disciplinary disavowal end up producing a number of obstacles in our contemporary moment. Let me offer a brief example of the first tendency—the homogenization of tradition. In both art history and theater studies, in fact, "traditional" scholarly forebears can be found cavorting with anthropologists. In the late nineteenth and early twentieth centuries, long before Clifford Geertz, James Clifford, and the ethnographic watershed of the 1980s, Hal Foster and others have noted that Alois Riegl and Aby Warburg were two foundational figures who redefined art history in anthropological terms.[16] Similarly, early figures in the formation of theater studies such as Arthur Pickard-Cambridge and later Francis Fergusson made extensive use of Cambridge anthropology to develop a notion of theater as the transmission of ritual behaviors.[17] This kind of impure disciplinary tradition can get conveniently sidestepped by contemporary arguments that seek to surpass the traditional by turning to anthropology. This kind of impure disciplinary tradition also can get conveniently sidestepped by arguments that seek to *defend* the traditional by turning *away* from anthropology.

Recently, I have spent a great deal of time examining the effects of varied, and variously repressed, disciplinary pasts on how intellectual debates in theater and performance studies are currently framed. While I do not feel that I am in a position to do the same for art history and visual culture studies per se, I am interested in comparing my understanding of the heterogeneous precedents of visual culture studies to the heterogeneous precedents of performance studies to show that they are not exactly the same heterogeneity. Indeed, the examination of this nonmatch is a reminder that the study of performance and the study of visual material have been antagonistic to each other on occasion. More importantly, the legacies of these cross-purposes are destined to erupt (indeed, in many a graduate seminar, do erupt) lest we too easily assume their shared purpose in the present.

Having considered how the theater/performance studies pair and the art history/visual culture pair are useful analogies, let's now consider why they aren't. Once we stop assuming that all old things are the same (and similar in their difference from the new), what happens when we investigate visual and performance genealogies for what Michel Foucault would call their "non-identity through time"?[18] One place to begin comes with the realization that the predecessors of performance—whether cast as drama or theater—do not have the same purchase on the received indexes of tradition. Some of you might have noticed a slip in my comparison between theater's disciplinary history and Mitchell's account of "art history and aesthetics," since theater studies has not had the same kind of partnership with aesthetic theory that the visual arts—and, it probably goes without saying, the literary arts—have enjoyed. While proponents crafted theater theory syllabi that characteristically moved "from Aristotle to Artaud," those movements did not usually help to define or redefine the terms with which aesthetic theory understood itself. (The generic exploration of tragedy is, to my mind, the exception that proves the rule here.) In fact, a look at the institutional history of theater in the academy suggests that it has been something of a question mark in the humanities—shakily defined as a liberal art, dangerously defined as a technical field, not clearly high or low, not clearly avant-garde or mass culture—which makes its relation to the biggest questions of aesthetic or humanistic inquiry somewhat insecure. The first departments of theater were divided about its proper institutional location. At many Ivy League schools, it was a spin-off of the English department, a literary form adjacent to but different from poems and novels. At Carnegie Tech and Cornell, it was placed in schools for painting, sculpture, and the industrial arts.[19] Cornell's first theater department was actually located in a revamped machine shop. The difference in the literary or visual arts location betrays confusion about what kind of form it actually it is; in fact, theater is a genre at some universities and a medium at others.

While I think that theater's partial fit in a literary curriculum and partial fit in a visual arts curriculum makes it intriguingly liminal to us now, the fact of the matter is that such partial fittings made it uncomfortably liminal, indeed, institutionally insecure, in the early twentieth century. Theater's insecurity derived not only from its mixedness but also from what modernists and postmodernists might retroactively call its nonautonomy, its enmeshment in the cultural and the contextual. Indeed, it has always been hard to decide where the autonomous theatrical art piece ended and its context began—in the play text, in the acting of the play text, in the acting and design of the play text, in the theater space, in the seating arrangement of the audience? The necessity of all these elements to be coordinated again and again, every night, for weeks in a row, in order for the theater to be itself bespeaks a hypercontextuality that has been hard to disavow, even when—under Crocian aesthetics, early twentieth-century formalisms, or New Critical paradigms—it was trendy to disavow contextuality. This kind of history makes it hard to draw equivalences between the effects of a late twentieth-century "turn to culture" in literature and art history and those it had in theater studies. If a cultural turn is characterized as an incorporation of the social and extra-aesthetic surround of the art object—a surround that includes more than conventional histories of artistic precedence and influence—then that surround has actually been a fundamental part of how the traditional discipline of theater studies has been conceived and not something that theater studies waited for performance studies to do for it. In no way would I argue that the earlier disciplinary histories of theater already produced the terms of our interdisciplinary future. The theoretical and political language of poststructuralism and newer culturalisms rarely appears in the defensive empiricisms or proproduction appeals of earlier theater scholars. But I do want to say that such heterogeneous pasts mean that our innovations in the present might also need some differentiation. The "dominant" disciplines of the past are not equivalent in their domination. Indeed, older paradigms in each field did not only *share* power but also *exerted* power over each other, an historical fact that gives each of us a more complicated relationship to the different traditions that we are supposedly rejecting.

The inexactness of pairing and eliding theater/performance studies and art history/visual culture also becomes clear when one considers not only methodological pasts but also recent history and varied historiographies of experimental artistic production. One way of characterizing the major shifts of twentieth-century art is, of course, to chronicle the development of modernism and its eventual giving way to postmodernism. One way of characterizing the artistic history of *that* shift is to focus on modernism as a quest for medium purity and postmodernism as a violation of medium purity. So when Mitchell says that all media are mixed media, it is a statement that seems to be made possible by a postmodern turn. What becomes interesting, I think, is how various art forms—however mixed they appear to be—get positioned inside this account of modernism and postmodernism. Indeed, to whom they appear mixed and to whom they don't is one of the questions. The debate over the theatrical in visual arts is a much labored example, so much so that the complexity of its residual effects in the present can be simplified. But for scholars and artists identified with visual culture and performance studies, I think that it is worth remembering, even before Michael Fried, the reaction of people like Clement Greenberg and Hilton Kramer to Harold Rosenberg's theatrical characterization of the action in action painting. Rosenberg argued that such canvases were "an arena in which to act—rather than a space in which to reproduce, re-design, analyze or 'express' an object, actual or imagined. What was to go on the canvas was not a picture but an *event*."[20] Greenberg in turn chastised him for moving Abstract Expressionist painting to the same domain as "breathing and thumbprints";[21] Hilton Kramer was baffled: "painting being painting, and not the theater, what does he mean by the canvas 'as an arena in which to act?' "[22] For modernist critics who needed painting to stay "specific"—and, moreover, needed that medium specificity to be "flat"—the idea that painting could be mixed, that it could have or, after Mitchell, always already does have embodied, durational, tactile, and environmental elements was not conceivable. The references to a threatening "theatrical" would, of course, multiply as the twentieth century wore on, reaching their much touted apex in Fried's deployment of the term to refer to, well, a number of things—literalism over pictoriality, entry of the durational into what should be a juxtapositive realm, addressive relation (the need for an audience) "that a modernist sensibility finds intolerable," as well as a more general antiart stance.[23] More to the point for a discussion of medium specificity, theatricality was an index of mixture and liminality that was profoundly antimodernist. Fried used "theatrical" to characterize an "in-between" state in which forms belonged to no essential artistic medium; to work across media, that is, to violate medium specificity, was to inhabit the "in-between" that "is theater."[24]

When we take this recent history of the visual arts debate back to our analogies between the "from" foundations of theater and art history and the "turn-to" moves of visual culture and performance studies, it becomes even harder to connect the dots among shared terms, labels, and movements. Such histories remind us how often the turn away from modernism (and thus the turn toward postmodernism) in the visual arts has been characterized as theatrical. The t-word, "theater," comes in not to characterize an old stodgy form as it might in performance studies, but to refer to the subversive invasion of the latest fad. Nor is there room for either the term theater or performance to inhabit modernism's medium specificity. If the practices that come under those terms, in traditional or avant-garde form, incorporate more than one artistic register and "exist for an audience," then it is hard for any of them to be modernist. This is another place where the legacies of performance have a qualified relationship to the traditional indexes of (here "modernist") tradition. Performance from this history looks less like its own specific medium than like the means by which visual media undo their specificity. From this view, performance is not so much a parallel field to visual culture, but a mechanism by which art history starts to cultivate the sensibilities of visual culture.

That is, of course, a certain way of showing and telling a particularly located history. To pursue the addressive relation between art and receiver, as so much experimental theater did and continues to do, is not a violation of medium specificity if your starting medium happens to be theater. In fact, what might be a violation of medium specificity from one angle of vision is hypermedium specificity from another. Even more confusing is how often the experiments in performance art, Happenings, and Fluxus experiments of the sixties and seventies used an antitheatrical language themselves. Their referent for antitheatricality was, I would submit, very nearly the opposite of the antitheatricality referent of concern to the

visual arts.[25] Performance experimenters were interested in foregrounding the durational, environmental, and addressive nature of performance
in ways that they did not feel were being exploited by the conventions of
theater itself. It was precisely what they called their "antitheater" extensions into duration, environment, and address that visual art critics called
"theatrical." Again, this is only one more relevant disciplinary history that
precedes any articulation of a relationship between performance studies
and visual culture studies. But I think that it is useful as an index of how
the heterogeneity of different pasts can have the odd effect of both confusing and overdetermining the position of performance in visual culture
studies. If performance is the vehicle by which the boundaries of the visual
arts unsettle themselves, then its subversive status becomes strangely normalized and its relationship to longer histories of cultural forms somewhat
skewed.

Disciplinary Self-Difference

For the sake of enlarging our sense of the occupational hazards of interdisciplinary exchange, it is worth remembering how often similar processes
are at risk when we work from a different direction or on different encounters. If a self-identified "visual culture" person came to a theater history
seminar, then I think that there are interesting ways that her "subversive
status" would also become "strangely normalized" and her relationship
to longer histories of cultural forms would become "somewhat skewed,"
demonstrating that what Jon McKenzie has called "the liminal norm" in
performance studies operates in a variety of interdisciplinary encounters.[26]
When visual culture and literary studies meet, the projections, substitutions, and skewed referentiality proceed differently; one possible starting
point would consider how very different the referent for Clement Greenberg's critiques of "the literary" were from most contemporary literary
critics' understanding of their cherished term. And when visual culture
and anthropology meet, the disciplinary foregroundings and forgettings
are different too; from the perspective of anthropology, we might do well
to remember, visual culture is something being done to anthropology, not
only something that anthropology is doing to art history. Meanwhile, the
digital and technological component of visual culture studies is one that
has produced a variety of analyses whose relationship to "art history"
often receives, I think, an oddly retroactive articulation.

At this point I want to suggest a qualification, not only to an analogy
between the theater-is-to–performance studies what art history–is-to-visual
culture constructions, but to what it means to consolidate "theater" and
"art history" as the relevant "traditional" pasts at all. The fact of the matter, and the difficulty of the matter, it seems to me, is that the membership

of visual culture studies is not only individuals whose background is art history or aesthetics. Some are from film, some from English, and some from website design. The same goes for performance studies, where the variety of scholars from film, folklore, anthropology, area studies, gender studies, and English means that each scholar is weighted with a different notion of what is traditional and is implicitly employing (and being employed by their relation to) inherited frames and different skill sets. As a result, the barometers and boundaries that individuals use for registering the mixedness of media vary as well. This means that "the ratios" and "sign-types" mixed in mixed media are not simply *there*—in the cultural form, awaiting elaboration—but also something produced by the perceptual habits of particularly located receivers. I think that scholars tend to stack our ratios and apply different "differentials" to gauge media mixing and sign-type labeling. If the place from which I approach, say, a Fluxus event, is painting, then the way I gauge its media ratio is different from the gauge I might apply if I measured its distance from theater, both of which would differ from how one might gauge Fluxus's difference from poetry or from music. I might also have different notions of whether an element is part of a media ratio or part of the surrounding context or of whether a sign type is iconic or indexical depending on my discipline's habits for locating indexicality. I might wonder whether a sign is really a sign or part of the apparatus. Even in an artistic and scholarly context that is working to blur the lines between art and context, sign and apparatus, I will not register the crossing of the line if I do not work with the same notion of where the line is.

Mitchell's argument about the ratios and sign-types of inherently mixed media is a response, I believe, to Carol Armstrong's concern that the difference between a painting and a novel will be a "nonproblem," the capacity to differentiate between verbal representations, temporal significations, and "marks made on a thickened material surface" drowned in a sea of interdisciplinary indifference.[27] What I am suggesting here is that, while I support Mitchell's ideal vision of visual culture studies, the fact that not everyone makes the same differentiations can make *not* differentiating them (or not differentiating how we differentiate) seem appealing. At the least, a less detailed formal understanding in interdisciplinary media analysis can sometimes make for an apparently more harmonious—if always short-lived—interdisciplinary encounter. Meanwhile, variously positioned scholars' relationship to the heterogeneous past can go unremembered as well. Earlier, I referred to the sensibilities of both visual culture and performance studies both being "artist's things," sensibilities that have a kinship to those cultivated by interdisciplinary artists in advance of interdisciplinary scholarship. What is perplexingly productive now, I think, is that students can declare an interest in one of the list of expanded cultural forms—milk ads and rock concerts, CNN and wrestling—without understanding a connection (or even knowing about) that artistic history. Students who did not begin with art history come to visual culture to study "home product advertising" without knowing about Warhol's *Brillo Boxes*, much less Èdouard Manet's *Le déjeuner sur l'herbe*. Students who did not begin in theater come to performance studies to study rave culture without knowing about Happenings, much less "The Cherry Orchard." Once we factor in the heterogeneity of the fields from which students of visual culture and performance studies now derive, we also need to notice that the artistic sensibility that propelled scholarship across the humanities and social sciences will not always result in a scholarly paradigm that remembers the artists who cultivated that sensibility. And then, we need to take a deep breath and decide how everyone feels about that.

I hope that it is apparent that I do not think that we need to recentralize a unified history. But I do think that we could do a better job of differentiating how we differentiate—both in the perceptual analyses that we employ and in the relevant object histories that we deploy. What we show-and-tell, how we do the showing and telling, and how patiently or impatiently we listen to the performance will vary with inherited skills and inherited notions of what makes an object special. Any way of arguing for innovation, break, or change in cultural practice always assumes certain traditions and likenesses across cultural practices too. If Alice Walker threatens Shakespeare, then Shakespeare is textual and literary, and a genre. If Tonya Harding threatens Shakespeare, then Shakespeare is visual, durational, and embodied, and a medium. Different differences need different samenesses. Meanwhile, a shared interest in mixedness does not in itself dispel the fact that we have different ways of registering it. If an antagonism to opticality did, on some level, drive the innovations toward exposing mixture in the Conceptualist movement, then that turn is similar to but different from the mixed arts analysis that Svetlana Alpers finds in cultural models. Both these revelations of mixture are similar to and different from how a philosophy of visuality exposes visibility's dependence on sensorial mixture or, to quote Kaja Silverman, "upon a confluence of the phenomenal, the psychic, the specular, and the social."[28] At some level, all this work places the visual in relation to "breathing and thumbprints," but it will still produce different positionings depending on whether you think of thumbprints phenomenologically, materially, or indexically. It will also produce different positionings depending on whether you are used to thinking about breathing as part of a depiction, as part of the medium used to create the depiction, or as part of the apparatus used to support the medium. And it will make a bigger difference if you aren't used to thinking about breathing at all.

Since barometers for gauging mixedness and sign-types vary, the possible disciplinary connections between them will be most interesting when they have been argued rather than assumed. I think that I am finally asking for scholarship that shows its tracks and writes with an awareness of its contingency. By differentiating how we differentiate, I think that we will find more utility in the project that so many readers of this journal actually share. The game of show-and-tell acquires a certain pleasure when it adopts a self-reflexive pedagogy, when everyone takes that breath before a treasured object, method, or discipline gets touched, turned, and passed around—and then takes another breath before that object is returned, inevitably . . . in a different shape.

Notes

"Performing Show and Tell: On the Disciplinary Problems of Mixed-Media Practice" was originally published in "Show and Tell: The State of Visual Culture Studies," edited by Martin Jay, special issue, *Journal of Visual Culture* 4, no. 2 (2005): 163–77.

1. W. J. T. Mitchell, "Showing Seeing: A Critique of Visual Culture," in *The Visual Culture Reader*, ed. Nicholas Mirzoeff, 2nd ed. (London: Routledge, 2002), 86–101.

2. Mitchell, "Showing and Seeing," 97.

3. Mitchell, "Showing and Seeing," 99.

4. Mitchell, "Showing and Seeing," 99.

5. Mitchell, "Showing and Seeing," 99.

6. Mieke Bal and Bryan Gonzales, eds., *The Practice of Cultural Analysis: Exposing Interdisciplinary Interpretation* (Stanford, CA: Stanford University Press, 1999).

7. Mitchell, "Showing and Seeing," 91.

8. Mitchell, "Showing and Seeing," 91.

9. Mitchell, "Showing and Seeing," 88.

10. Nicholas Mirzoeff, "The Subject of Visual Culture," in *The Visual Culture Reader*, ed. Nicholas Mirzoeff, 2nd ed. (London: Routledge, 2002), 11; Thomas Crow, "Visual Culture Questionnaire," *October* 77 (Summer 1996): 35.

11. Richard Schechner, "A New Paradigm for Theater in the Academy," *TDR: The Drama Review* 36, no. 4 (1992): 10; Richard Hornby, "The Death of Literature and History," *Theater Topics*, 5, no. 2 (September 1995): 145.

12. Hal Foster, "The Archive without Museums," *October* 77 (Summer 1996): 104–6.

13. Foster, "Archive without Museums," 105.

14. Foster, "Archive without Museums," 105.

15. Martin Jay, "Visual Culture Questionnaire," *October* 77 (Summer 1996): 44.

16. Hal Foster, "Antinomies of Art History," in Hal Foster, *Design and Crime: and Other Diatribes* (London: Verso, 2002), 91.

17. See Shannon Jackson, *Professing Performance: Theater in the Academy from Philology to Performativity* (Cambridge: Cambridge University Press, 2004), 94–108.

18. Michel Foucault, *The Archaeology of Knowledge; and, The Discourse on Language*, trans. A. M. Sheridan (New York: Pantheon Books, 1972), 33.

19. See Jackson, *Professing Performance*, 40–78.

20. Harold Rosenberg, "The American Action Painters," *ARTnews* 51 (December 1952): 22. Emphasis added.

21. Clement Greenberg, "How Art Writing Earns Its Bad Name," *Second Coming Magazine* 1, no. 3 (March 1962): 59.

22. Hilton Kramer, "The New American Painting," *Partisan Review* 20, no. 4 (July–August 1953): 423.

23. Michael Fried, "Art and Objecthood," in *Art and Objecthood: Essays and Reviews* (Chicago: University of Chicago Press, 1998), 163.

24. Fried, "Art and Objecthood," 164.

25. Jackson, *Professing Performance*, 109–45; Philip Auslander, *From Acting to Performance: Essays in Modernism and Post-Modernism* (London: Routledge, 1997), 56; Jon Erickson, *The Fate of the Object: From Modern Object to Postmodern Sign in Performance, Art, and Poetry* (Ann Arbor: University of Michigan Press, 1995).

26. Jon McKenzie, *Perform or Else: From Discipline to Performance* (London: Routledge, 2001).

27. Carol Armstrong, "Visual Culture Questionnaire," *October* 77 (Summer 1996): 28.

28. Kaja Silverman, *World Spectators* (Stanford, CA: Stanford University Press, 2000), 3.

Chapter 3

Theatricality's Proper Objects
Genealogies of Performance and Gender Theory

> The institution of the "proper object" takes place, as usual, through a mundane sort of violence. Indeed, we might read moments of methodological founding as pervasively anti-historical acts, beginnings which fabricate their legitimating histories through a retroactive narrative, burying complicity and division in and through the funereal figure of the "ground."
>
> —Judith Butler, "Against Proper Objects"

> I've tried acting, but I just can't do it.
>
> —Judith Butler

As a theory of performativity reemerged in the United States during the last decade of the twentieth century, the question of its relationship to theatricality often followed close behind. Is the performative related or opposed to the field of "acting?" Is acting related or opposed to the concept of theatricality? What, ultimately, does performativity have to do with theater? The different intellectual assumptions and institutional allegiances behind such questions structured numerous conversations and determined patterns of disciplinary inclusion and exclusion. For American scholars and graduate students in theater and performance studies, the circulation of the term "performative" exerted contradictory force, paradoxically elevating and eclipsing our favorite objects of study. On the one hand, its theoretical prominence in the antifoundationalist work of critical theorists such as Jacques Derrida and Judith Butler seemed to pull theater and theatricality into the critical spotlight. On the other hand, performativity's location inside a tradition of speech-act theory that was indifferent and, in some cases, hostile to all things theatrical dimmed that light considerably. This complex theoretical context was further confounded by the specific investments—political, philosophical, aesthetic, disciplinary—in which such terms appeared. In rhetoric, literary studies, critical race theory, art history, postcolonial theory, and other critical circles, terms such as theatricality and performativity were easily and differently aligned with the traditions, vocabularies, conflicts, and goals of each field.

In this essay I investigate the theoretical complications of theatricality and performativity by using "gender studies" as both an allied theoretical field and a case study. Because issues of gender are intimately linked to both theories of the theatrical and of the performative, gender serves as a useful counterpoint. In the United States, in fact, some of the most productive work on the theatricality/performativity debate occurred in the field of gender studies. Prominent sex/gender theorists took up the idea of performativity while feminist theater theorists came to terms with its theoretical fallout. Furthermore, the discourse of gender and the discourse of theatricality are both similarly divided, varied, and dispersed. As such, their simultaneous investigation gives an illustration of the kind of confounded theoretical investments described above. For many of us, there is not an equivalence between the study of performativity and the field of performance studies. Nor is either of these inquiries equivalent to the study of theatricality. Similarly, for many of us, there is not an equivalence between queer theory and lesbian and gay studies. Nor is either of these inquiries equivalent to feminist studies. Nevertheless, all these fields and terms can be elided with each other—and often are—in even the most careful discussions. Coming to terms with the gendered fate of theatricality in the late twentieth century thus means disaggregating a series of hurried equivalences and dismantling a series of defensive oppositions. Such instances will testify to the curious status of gender and theatricality as both fields and critical concepts—the conflicted way in which they and their researchers could be elevated and eclipsed, critically central and abjectly peripheral, at the same moment in the very late history of twentieth-century theory.

My two epigraphs offer abstract and symptomatic ways of framing this critical context. Judith Butler, a scholar widely associated with the most provocative research in gender theory and performativity, placed her cautionary note about disciplinary histories in an interrogation of the vexed relationship between feminist and queer theory. While her reflections might be applied to any kind of disciplinary relationship, I argue that the conflicted status of gender theory has had a great deal to do with the internally discontinuous status of theatricality as a critical term. This partnership has produced several debates, discussions that draw lines around the "proper objects" of different fields and produce their own "retroactive narratives" of disciplinary formation. In debates about theatricality—in theater studies, in performance studies, in speech act theory, as metaphor, as act, and as object—questions of equivalence, redundancy, tradition, distinction, and supercession constantly inhere. Is theater a subset of performance? Is performance a foundation for or a symptom of performativity? Is performativity's act the same as "acting"? What is the difference between performance studies and performativity studies? Meanwhile, those questions are inflected by the equally complicated field of gender. Can feminism accommodate a theory of sexuality? Is sexual difference a foundation or a symptom? Is gender's act the same as "acting"? What is the difference between gay/lesbian studies and queer studies? It is often the provisional and erratic answers to these and other questions that reproduce disciplinary wars.

While I seek to clarify various "antihistorical" acts of "buried complicity" in disciplinary debates around gender and performance, I am aware that the impulse to do so can produce its own kinds of friction. The effort to disentangle disciplinary equivalences can transform into the territorial quest to erect impermeable boundaries. And given that this kind of line drawing happens within a field of institutional power, an engaged conversation can have the character of confrontation. As Butler said of her own investigation into the "proper objects" of feminism and queer theory, "it seemed that an exploration of the 'encounter' . . . was timely and potentially productive, but I forgot at that moment how quickly a critical encounter becomes misconstrued as a war."[1] My desire to pursue this project comes from a frustration with the occasionally defensive, proprietary, and antihistorical conversations that can occur within and outside theater and performance studies. Rather than offering definitional coherence or hierarchical evaluation of different concepts, I hope to offer tools for discursive navigation.

To assist in the navigating, I make a central claim for the discursive operations of "theatricality" as we move from the twentieth to the twenty-first century. I suggest that theatricality functions ubiquitously and contradictorily because of the term's flexible essentialism. Depending on context, convenience, and polemics, theatricality can as easily find itself on the essentialist as antiessentialist side of a conceptual binary. Theatricality is used as a metaphor for representation and, in other contexts, as an antirepresentational ground for the authentic. While a history of Western thought associates theatricality with the figural, allegorical, and surrogated nature of representation, a host of critical theorists in the late twentieth century used theatrical examples to characterize the literal, stable, or naively metaphysical "real." Thus different invocations of the theatrical can often be diametrically opposed to each other, assuming its antiessentialist associations with mimesis and construction on the one hand and its essentialist associations with the given and concrete on the other. Moreover, this constant repositioning is not always self-conscious and hence not necessarily "strategic." Instead, the flexibility has made for a great deal of theoretical confusion, sometimes producing the defensiveness described above. Sometimes, however, that confusion can be experienced as enabling. When gender studies (feminist, queer, and otherwise) became involved with theatricality's flexible essentialism, the combination proved both useful and confounding. The flexible associations of both the concrete and the mimetic made an all-too appropriate match for a feminist theoretical struggle that wanted to maintain a political project and to de-essentialize it, too.

I.

To create a place from which to theorize an intellectual history, I will discuss the work of three theorists in the United States: Elin Diamond, Sue-Ellen Case, and Judith Butler. As feminist theater theorists and sex/gender theorists, each of these scholars has contributed significantly to our understanding of both theatricality and gender in their various guises. They have each worked on and from within the discursive current of the last decade of the twentieth century, and their texts serve as indices of those debates. In 1988 Elin Diamond published the much-circulated essay entitled, "Brechtian Theory/Feminist Theory," propelling an epistemological shift in the study of feminist theater. In 1989 Sue-Ellen Case published "Toward a Butch-Femme Aesthetic," a piece that would become central to an emerging canon of feminist theater as well as to that of lesbian and gay studies. In 1990 Judith Butler published *Gender Trouble*, disseminating her groundbreaking arguments on the nature of gender performativity. As the twentieth century came to a close, each would review the central concepts of her own writing, sometimes by coming to terms with work of one of the other. In Diamond's *Unmaking Mimesis* (1997), Case's *Domain Matrix* (1996), and Butler's *Bodies That Matter* (1993), "Against Proper Objects," and revised introduction to *Gender Trouble* (2000), they reckoned with the political productivity and political fallout of a decade of critical theory.[2] I hope that an investigation of the stakes, terms, shifts, revisions, and retrenchments of this intellectual genealogy will help to focus a discussion of theatricality and its gendered alliances in the very late twentieth century. Superficially, these three theorists can be construed as illustrations of three strains of gender studies—Diamond's association with "feminist theory," Case's with "lesbian feminist theory," and Butler's with "queer theory." I hope to show that, while this retroactive positioning is conceptually convenient, it also obscures important histories and significant connections for theories of both gender and theatricality.

A number of issues in feminist and critical theory came to the fore in the late 1980s, and Diamond, Case, and Butler tried to reconcile them in related ways. For the purposes of this essay, I will focus on two political and epistemological crises. Feminists needed to grapple with the issue of sexuality and the philosophical effects of something conveniently called "poststructuralist" (sometimes "postmodernist") thought. These crises turned out to be related. The concerns of sexuality constellated around two related movements within feminism, namely the homophobia of the feminist movement and the antipornography efforts of a certain strain of feminism. As feminists worked on the former issue, they came face to face with the myopias of the latter. The argument against the "oppressions" of pornography—most notably found in the work of Catherine MacKinnon and Andrea Dworkin—argued that sexual objectification within pornographic fantasy structured and supported male domination of women.[3] This position extended to other realms of sexuality—including lesbian sex—resulting in a feminist intolerance for sex practices and experimentation between women that did not embody a literalized ideal of "sexual equality." As a consequence, the effort to dismantle sexual discrimination continually faced condemnations of sex practice. A feminist commitment to sexual equality could actually rationalize feminist homophobia. As varieties of feminists debated the issue of sexuality, they also came to terms with the impact of poststructuralist thought. In a critical foment that included revisionist takes on the complexity of the psyche, analyses of the constitutive role of discourse, and a deconstructionist stance on the instability and self-differentiality of apparently singular identities, feminists wondered how to maintain a viable political project. While the issue of sexual inclusion and the issue of poststructuralist destabilization were not always connected, at times they appeared intimately related. With the work of Michel Foucault and with revisions in psychoanalysis and deconstruction, sexuality emerged as a conceptually rich frame from which to theorize the heterogeneity of the subject and the effects of discourse more generally.[4]

To understand the impact of these two concerns on theories of theatricality and gender, it is important to remember the relationship between sexuality and poststructuralist thought—and equally important not to assume an equivalence. For many feminist theorists, the political ambivalences of poststructuralism were too confounding; hence, they considered postructuralism's proponents and paradigms "patriarchal" and, ultimately, racist and heterosexist in effect. For others, however, the poststructural critique was central to the undoing of patriarchy; from this angle, those who maintained a belief in the singularity and authenticity of sex/gender identity risked succumbing to a patriarchal ideology. For some, a focus on "women's experience" and female "agency" was necessary for feminism; for others, such emphases were naive and assumed a reductive conception of the female subject. Thus, in this complicated political and epistemological scenario, it was not uniformly clear what it meant to work in gender studies, what it was to be a feminist, or what it meant to theorize sexuality. None of these efforts were equivalent to each other or even to themselves but varied with a critical and political context. As I noted above, "gender

studies" was and is an internally discontinuous field and, like the fields of
theater and performance studies, positions within it were and are retroactively and relationally construed.

Diamond's "Brechtian Theory/Feminist Theory" was a prescient articulation of a feminist theatrical practice that addressed this complex critical
context. The central effort of her essay was to integrate feminist goals
and Brechtian theatrical technique. She began the essay admitting that this
was an "unlikely" grouping and that "feminists in drama studies might
greet this coupling with some bemusement."[5] That this combination now
sounds so very "likely" testifies both to Diamond's foresight and to her
historical timeliness. The use of Brecht enabled Diamond to make an
argument for theater as a feminist political practice. A creative revision of
Brecht's concepts of alienation also matched the destabilizations of poststructuralist thought with a suitably ironic theatrical practice. At the same
time, Diamond's argument for theater invoked the "embodied" nature of
the medium, "grounding" this articulated practice in a materiality that
warded off antipoststructuralist suspicions. A feminist Brechtian theater's
status as both overtly representational and overtly material, as ironic and
embodied, made for a flexibly essentialist practice that suited the internal
discontinuities of feminist theory.

Diamond relocated concepts of *Verfremdungseffekt*, the "not, but," and
"historicization" to theorize a Gestic feminist criticism. At this historical
moment, a feminist focus on "women's experience" appeared problematic. Feminist theater that positioned itself within this expressive paradigm
risked exclusion (which women?) and risked presuming experiential
authority and authenticity. The defamiliarizing appeals of *Verfremdungseffekt* provided a different paradigm. The quest to defamiliarize the
normal—to make "something ordinary and immediately accessible into
something peculiar, striking, and unexpected"[6]—could be directed at an
effort to denormalize masculinity and femininity. Rather than speaking
unproblematically of women's experience, a feminist Gestic theater would
make strange the category of woman itself. The defamiliarizing effort
continued through a process of Brechtian "historicization," a mode of performance that placed the historical contextuality of gender production on
display for analysis and critique. Diamond made, to my mind, her most
innovative theoretical move when she used the Brechtian "not, but" as the
basis for staging the differential character of sexuality. Her presentation
is worth quoting at length as an illustration of a shifting epistemology in
feminist theory.

> Gender critique in artistic and discursive practices is often and
> wrongly confused with another topos in feminist theory: sexual
> difference. I would propose that "sexual difference" be under-
> stood not as a synonym for gender oppositions but as a possible

reference to differences within sexuality. I take my cue here partly from the poststructuralist privileging of "difference" across all representational systems, particularly language. Derridean deconstruction posits the disturbance of the signifier within the linguistic sign or word; the seemingly stable word is inhabited by a signifier that bears the trace of the word it is not.[7]

Diamond thus found, in a contemporary discussion of deconstruction, language that resonated with the destabilizing articulation of Brechtian theater. "When an actor appears onstage," Brecht wrote and Diamond quoted, "besides what he actually is doing he will at all essential points discover, specify, imply what he is not doing . . . Whatever he doesn't do must be contained and conserved in what he does."[8] By making a link to Brecht's discussion of the "not, but," she proposed a theater that could perform this kind of sexual self-differentiality.

Using Derrida as her theorist, Diamond's theory thus explicitly engaged the connection between poststructuralism and sexuality, using the sensibility of the former to foreground the heterogeneity of the latter. "Deconstruction thus wreaks havoc on identity, with its connotations of wholeness and coherence: if an identity is always different from itself it can no longer *be* an identity. Sexual *difference*, then, might be seen to destabilize the bipolar oppositions that constitute gender identity."[9] Furthermore, Diamond labeled this theory a "gender critique," explicitly delineating her feminist theory from its "confused" associations with sexual difference as "gender opposition." For her, the differential nature of sexuality was a question imaginatively conceived and resolutely explored within something that called itself feminism—and that knew itself to be something other than the study of "men" versus "women." The work of Gayle Rubin served as a significant intertext. Rubin's discussion of how a "sex/gender system" exacerbates male and female difference at the expense of other kinds of commonalities supported a deconstructionist stance. According to Diamond, "to paraphrase Gayle Rubin, women and men are certainly different, but gendering coercively translates the nuanced differences within sexuality into a structure of opposition: male vs. female, masculine vs. feminine, etc. In my reading of Rubin, the 'sex-gender system,' the trace of the difference of sexuality is kept alive within the sterile opposition of gender."[10] A feminist Gestic theater would thus perform with an awareness of this sexual trace, using it to unravel and denormalize sterile oppositions.

Diamond's essay also addressed the field of film studies. Because some of the most exciting work on gender representation came from within this field, the medium of film became a favored object of analysis in feminist theory. "Brechtian Theory/Feminist Theory" made an explicit intervention in this critical milieu: "Now feminists in film studies have been quick to appropriate elements of Brecht's critique of the theater apparatus . . .

[They] have given us a lot to think about, but we [feminists in drama and theater studies], through Brechtian theory, have something to give them: a female body in representation that resists fetishization and a viable position for the female spectator."[11] For Diamond, the active and embodied nature of the theatrical medium distinguished it from film, creating a unique relation between actor and spectator: "Brechtian theory formulates (and reformulates) a spectatorial state that breaks the suturing of imaginary identifications and keeps the spectator independent . . . Film semiotics posits a spectator who is given the illusion that he creates the film; theater semiotics posits a spectator whose active reception constantly revises the spectacle's meanings."[12] Diamond qualified a Brechtian sense of embodiment by integrating it with a feminist awareness of gender and desire. Even as she argued for embodiment as a unique condition of the theatrical medium, her discussion exemplified a deconstructionist critique of presence: "I want to be clear about this important point: The body, particularly the female body, by virtue of entering the stage space, enters representation—it is not just *there*, a live, unmediated presence."[13] Thus, while arguing for theater's embodied particularity, Diamond also insisted on the mediated nature of that embodiment. For her, the representational was part and parcel of what it meant to be theatrical.

Finally, Diamond's essay used theatrical practice to make an argument about the political viability of feminist theatricality. Many a political and social theorist could use a theatrical language to discuss political action. Not as many, however, would use that language to argue for "theater" itself in feminist politics. For those of us for whom the term "theatricality" is tied to an object and an institutional allegiance as much as a social paradigm, the difference was crucial. Diamond's effort meant arguing against the prejudice of theater's irrelevancy or a sense of theater as "just" play: "Recalling such performances should remind us of the rigorous self-consciousness that goes into even the most playful gender-bending . . . When gender is alienated or foregrounded, the spectator is enabled to see a sign system *as* a sign system . . . the gender lexicon becomes so many illusionistic trappings to be put on or shed at will."[14] Diamond thus emphasized theatrical practice as an arena of thoughtful rigor and hence female agency.

Case's 1989 article also marked a critical moment in theater criticism's relationship to feminist politics. As the latter changed, so did the imaginative capacities of the former. This article was also written in advance of a decade in which "queer" theories of "performativity" would enhance and confuse the status of something that called itself "feminist theater." Like Diamond's "Brechtian Theory/Feminist Theory," Case's article contended with a range of related issues and goals. It addressed the impact of poststructuralism—or "postmodernism"—on feminism. It contended with the heterosexism of the feminist movement. And it made an argument for theater as a favored site for feminist possibility and a favored object for feminist analysis. It also foregrounded the imaginative work of Split Britches, the troupe whose performances at New York's WOW Café activated an emerging feminist theater theory. Case's first paragraph described a "recent conference on postmodernism" that addressed the impact of Foucault. Here she articulated a concern that would become the repeated refrain in critical theory—that the theoretical trajectory associated with postmodernism "denies both agency and gender to the subject." Because they "suggest no subject position outside of the ideology, nor do they constitute a subject who has agency to change ideology," such theories disabled political activism.[15] Case's initial suggestion that poststructuralism was sexist and heterosexist, however, emphasized only part of the story. In fact, a sense of poststructural possibility also galvanized her theorizing of the butch-femme aesthetic. A poststructural critique of binary discourses conceived sexuality as a field of differences, a heterogeneity unrecognizable within the constraining polarities of "sexual difference." Hence, and as I suggested above, a poststructural critique could cut both ways. While it theoretically short-circuited politicized identity claims, it also helped a project of sexual expansion. Consequently, Case's theorizing of Split Britches also cut both ways; an oft-quoted passage, for instance, invoked both of these "bad" and "good" possibilities: "These are not split subjects, suffering the torments of dominant ideology. They are coupled ones that do not impale themselves on the poles of sexual difference or metaphysical values, but constantly seduce the sign system, through flirtation and inconstancy into the light fondle of artifice, replacing the Lacanian slash with a lesbian bar."[16] In this model, being "split" could mean many things. One could be tormented by ideological self-division, or one could be enabled by its inconstancy and artifice. Case would use the terms of theatricality—as concept and as practice, as norm and as act, as essentialist and as antiessentialist—to settle into a flexible paradigm that intersected with all these roving associations. In the process, theatricality's referent would change dramatically.

Psychoanalytic theory and the revisionist work of Jacques Lacan functioned as significant, if not explicitly quoted, intertexts. Case looked to Joan Rivière's work on Lacan, particularly to a discussion of how a choice between "having" and "being" the phallus constituted male and female sexual difference. Since women—for Lacan, Rivière, and a host of psychoanalytic theorists—are not able to possess the phallus and, with it, the capacity to render themselves intelligible and signifiable, women are compelled instead to occupy a compensatory role as a vehicle for and partner in male-identity formation. Helpfully for theater theorists, both Rivière and Lacan used a theatrical metaphor to theorize the female side of this normalizing operation—the term "masquerade." In this formulation, a theatrical mode was associated with processes of convention, constraint, reaction-formation, and gender constitution.[17] It was a "mask" worn unconsciously by a female "both to hide the possession of masculinity and to avert the reprisals expected if she was found to possess it."[18] Masquerade was thus not playful or liberatory but rather the defensive mechanism by which "womanliness" became internalized and consolidated. In "Toward a Butch-Femme Aesthetic," Case rehearsed the idea of masquerade as normalization. Yet, as the essay proceeded, the term underwent redefinition.

> Rivière notes a difference here between heterosexual women, and lesbian ones—the heterosexual women don't claim possession openly, but through reaction-formations; whereas the homosexual women openly display their possession of the penis and count on the male's recognition of defeat . . . I suggest that this kind of masquerade is consciously played out in butch-femme roles . . . If one reads them from within Rivière's theory, the butch is the lesbian woman who proudly displays the possession of the penis, while the femme takes on the compensatory masquerade of womanliness. The femme, however, foregrounds her masquerade by playing to the butch, another woman in a role; likewise, the butch exhibits her penis to a woman who is playing the role of compensatory castration. This raises the question of "penis, penis, who's got the penis," because there is no referent in sight; rather, the fictions of penis and castration become ironized and "camped up."[19]

In the butch-femme scenario, Case argued, the processes of sexual differentiation were replayed but also played with; masquerade returned, but its theatricality was of a different order. Rather than the site of female normalization, masquerade became the site of feminist resistance.

The essay made use of two associations of theatricality—as habituated convention and liberatory action—and linked them both to masquerade, allowing the theorist to effect a theoretical move while using the same term. Interestingly, the pivot between these two associations rested on the presence or absence of consciousness. Unlike the *feminine* masquerader, the *feminist* masquerader "foregrounds," "openly displays," and "consciously plays."[20] A kind of will or choice determined which kind of theatricality was at work and at play. For a feminist movement preoccupied with the location of agency, the second sense of theatricality dovetailed nicely. Case's language echoed the revolutionary formulations of the feminist movement: "From a theatrical point of view, the butch-femme roles take on the quality of something more like character construction and have a more active quality . . . these roles qua roles lend agency and self-determination to the historically passive subject, providing her with at least two options for gender identification and with the aid of camp, an irony that allows her perception to be constructed from outside ideology, with a gender role that makes her appear as if she is inside it."[21] By developing the inside-outside positionings, this form of lesbian feminist theatricality addressed the political conundra of poststructuralist and feminist theory. It posited a subject with an outsider's "perception" and the capacity for "agency" and "self-determination" while also acknowledging her embodiment within social convention, gendered "roles," and sexual "appearances."

Like Diamond, Case also used film and feminist film theory as a specific counterpoint to her own theorizing. Case noted a connection to Mary Ann Doane's theorizing of female masquerade. In Doane's use of Rivière, a female spectator would "flaunt her femininity . . . and reveal 'femininity itself as a mask.'"[22] Case suggested that the "masquerade that Doane describes is exactly that practiced by the femme—she foregrounds cultural femininity. The difference is that Doane places this role in the spectator position, probably as an outgrowth of the passive object position required of women in the heterosexist social structures."[23] Despite the connection, Case thus made an explicit argument about the difference between film and theater. By emphasizing the role of the actor in the theater, she claimed an activist position for feminism. Because film theory focused on the figure of the spectator, the discipline of film, in Case's reading, could not claim the "more active" stance of "a theatrical point of view." By "reinscribing [flaunting] within a passive, spectatorial role, [Doane] gags and binds the traditional homosexual role players, whose gender play has nothing essential beneath it, replacing them with the passive spectatorial position that is, essentially, female."[24] Thus Case's theory claimed an antiessentialism for lesbian feminist theater (one that "has nothing essential beneath it") while at the same time invoking the "tradition" of homosexual role-playing as well as the "essentially" "passive" and "female" nature of spectatorship. The film-versus-theater duality framed Case's claims for the exceptional bodiedness of performance. As opposed to "theorized spectators in darkened movie houses . . . [where] the erotics are gone, [her] theoretical maneuvers [would] maintain what is generally referred to as 'presence.'"[25] Case's theorizing thus exemplifies the tendency to grant theatricality a theoretically useful flexible essentialism. At times, she used the antiessentialist language of theatrical mobility, instability, and dynamism. The butch-femme performance was a duo that together inhabited a subject position; the actor-character was thus a doubled and therefore unstable figure. But Case also used the more stabilizing language of the theater at other times. She would oppose theater and film by virtue of the former's corporeality, thus allowing—if not necessarily arguing—for a link between the theater and the feminist privileging of "experience." She would also differentiate butch-femme masquerade from the reaction- ormation of antifeminist masquerade by giving the actor "self-consciousness" and—like Diamond—the capacity to inhabit and uninhabit various roles "at will." As the reference to bodies echoed the language of the feminist experiential, so this reference to actor intention reinforced a political commitment to "self-determination" and a "more active" "agency." In a feminist struggle that wanted to maintain a political project *and* to de-essentialize it, theater's flexible essentialism allowed feminism to have it both ways.

Judith Butler's *Gender Trouble*, the text that many credit with the inauguration of queer theory, appeared in 1990 to address a similar set of conundra. Butler sought to reckon with the homophobia of the feminist movement and was particularly "enraged" by the assumptions of sexual difference and sexual morality mobilized by the antipornography crusade.[26] She also used poststructuralist paradigms to place even more pressure on the foundational assumptions and foundational texts of feminist studies. Indeed, if there was a recurrent theme in *Gender Trouble*, it lay in its repeated critique of the concept of foundation itself. The first paragraph offered an efficient précis of essentialist feminist thought: "For the most part, feminist theory has assumed that there is some existing identity, understood through the category women, who not only initiates feminist interests and goals within discourse, but constitutes the subject for whom political representation is pursued."[27] Butler's text inserted Foucault and Derrida in its first two footnotes and, by page two, countered the "for the most part" assumptions of feminist theory with the paradigmatic arguments of poststructuralist theory and its radically antiessentialist implications.

> Foucault points out that juridical systems of power *produce* the subject they subsequently come to represent. . . . If this analysis is right, then the juridical formation of language and politics that represents women as "the subject" of feminism is itself a discursive formation and effect of a given version of representational politics.[28]

Butler thus argued against the notion of a "prior" identity, psyche, or feminine language that could somehow exist before or beyond the productive operations of discursive regulation. She followed the Foucauldian articulation with a Derridean critique of the subject: "In effect, the law produces and then conceals the notion of a 'subject before the law' in order to invoke that discursive formation as a naturalized foundational premise that subsequently legitimates that law's own regulatory hegemony."[29] The rest of *Gender Trouble* came to terms with the impact of these opening statements. Butler reviewed and resituated key arguments in critical, social, and feminist theory by thoroughly testing and incorporating poststructuralist positions on identity and representation.

Butler's philosophical intertexts were wide-ranging. She invoked Descartes, Leibniz, Engels, Marx, Nietzsche, and Levi-Strauss. While the speech-act theory of J. L. Austin was not explicitly cited in *Gender Trouble*, Austin's sense of the performative appeared in various parts of the text. The notion that language could be constitutive rather than simply expressive dovetailed nicely with her argument on the power of discourse to produce that which it sought to describe. Working with the notion of woman as a discursive "effect" and against the idea of a female consciousness "before the Law," Butler also reconsidered a variety of familiar feminist texts and intertexts, including the work of Lacan, Rivière, and Rubin. Arguing that Lacan was imprecise in his theorizing of "masquerade," she suggested various possible interpretations: "Does it serve primarily to conceal or repress a pregiven femininity, a feminine desire which would establish an insubordinate alterity to the masculine subject and expose the necessary failure of masculinity?"[30] The belief in an "insubordinate alterity" and in masculinity's "failure" would have been embraced relatively easily by a feminist movement that wanted female resistance and self-determination. Indeed, Case isolated and redefined masquerade by foregrounding the insubordinate alterities of butch-femme performance and by counting on "the males' recognition of defeat."[31] Butler, however, emphasized a some-what different reading: "Or is masquerade the means by which femininity itself is *first* established, the exclusionary practice of identity formation in which the masculine is effectively excluded and installed as outside the boundaries of a feminine gendered position?"[32] Working with the assump-tion of regulation as simultaneously constraining and productive—and with an antiessentialist critique of the subject—Butler's text argued that female identity came into being through a process that simultaneously negated it. A similarly structured argument informed her reading of Rubin. Rubin's discussion of the overpolarizing operations of the sex-gender sys-tem "sets the stage," argued Butler, "of a Foucaultian critique."[33] Focusing on Rubin's reading of the incest taboo as simultaneously prohibitive and constitutive, Butler asked whether it could be "reconceived as a produc-tive power that inadvertently generates several cultural configurations of gender?" including the assumption of sexual difference in the first place.[34] Paralleling Diamond's move in her redefinition of sexual difference within feminist theater, Butler questioned the notion of biological sex as existent prior to gendering, radicalizing Rubin's insights into the sex-gender system to undo the sex-gender distinction itself.

The final chapters of *Gender Trouble* tried to come to terms with the significance of these arguments for activism. These pages would be the most often read, remembered, misread, and debated. These pages would also propel and confuse the status of theatricality as a term and a prac-tice during the course of the next decade. Given the gendered subject's perpetual enmeshment in and constant citation of gender norms, conven-tional notions of liberatory action or subversive alterity were not possible in Butler's frame. She thus advocated the performance of "gender parody" as a way of differently citing gender normalization. It was here that she proposed drag performance as a mode that "fully subverts the distinction between inner and outer psychic space and effectively mocks both the expressive model of gender and the notion of a true gender identity . . . *In imitating gender, drag implicitly reveals the imitative structure of gender itself—as well as its contingency*."[35] Redeploying terms such as imitation, "cross-dressing," drag, and parody, Butler made alternative use of a theatrical language. In a model that could not subscribe to conventional notions of a self-determining feminist resistance, parodic repetition became a form of theatrical politics: "The task is not whether to repeat, but how to repeat, or indeed, to repeat and, through a radical proliferation of gender, to *displace* the very gender norms that enable the repetition itself."[36] While the language may have sounded familiarly theatrical, a particular distinction lay in the "complex temporality" that Butler theorized, one in which neither the actor nor gender norms preexisted each other. Parody was Butler's way of imagining a political practice within what was still a recursive process, that is, the performative means by which representation installs a gender that it seems to describe. Finally, queer theories of performativity emerged in tandem with this radically antiessentialist critique of gender; the recursion of identity formation was key to both theoretical developments. The "queer" theoretical move is thus related but not wholly equivalent to either feminist or gay and lesbian studies. As such, it also had an attenuated relationship to the field of feminist theater and performance. Fields and concepts would become elided and equated, of course, ultimately creating confusing assumptions about epistemological boundaries, "burying complicities" and intellectual kinships whose resilience still confuse us now.

II.

In many ways, all three theorists came close to theorizing parallel modes of theatricality. For Diamond, a Brechtian feminist theater would defamiliarize the ideological operations of the sex-gender system. For Case, a dynamic and self-conscious butch-femme masquerade displayed and "camped up" the reaction-formations of feminine masquerade. For Butler, a drag performance of gender parody would repeat but displace the norms of gender performativity. All these theorists attempted to address a poststructuralist awareness of gender normalization. They were all critical of a homogenized notion of "women's experience," and all were critical of feminist homophobia. Many of their intertexts—Lacan, Rivière, Rubin, Foucault, and Derrida—were the same, even if they were put to different use. Most significantly, Diamond, Case, and Butler all found ways of using a theatrical mode to face the mixed metaphors and epistemological conundra of late twentieth-century feminist and critical theory. This meant conceiving of theatricality as something that worked within as well as against the conventions it sought to critique. It meant finding a way to "resist" domination while remaining aware of its pervasiveness. In other words, it meant deploying both the conservative and progressive dimensions of theatricality within the same theory; sometimes theatricality was invoked as a norm (feminine masquerade) and sometimes as an action (feminist masquerade); sometimes these two axes were given different labels, and sometimes the same term was retheorized. Whether it was Gestus, camp, or drag, however, a countergender theatricality could no longer install itself unproblematically outside patriarchal ideology or inside an uncontaminated feminist subject. Instead, these savvy theatricalities would use the techniques of defamiliarization, irony, and parody. They would have the "both/and" character, the "yes/but" quality that characterized so many critical theories of resistance in the 1990s.

Diamond, Case, and Butler, however, would not find themselves entirely allied with each other over the course of the next decade. To track the ways in which their differences would be emphasized (and the ways in which complicity would be buried) tells us something about the conceptual ambivalences of feminism and queer theory, as well as about theatricality and performativity. As a presumably "experimental" or "active" medium, theater could be undone as much as enabled by queer theories of performativity. One central factor to consider—and one that has been shadowing this argument—revolved around the critique of presence. Like other insights associated with poststructuralism, the critique of presence unsettled conventional assumptions of Western metaphysics and, with them, some of the assumptions of theatrical discourse. Derrida's critique of orality and embodiment stalled some of the central features by which proponents of theater and performance art argued for performance's exceptionalism. When Derrida asserted that the desire for presence—an unmediated state of being outside of writing, textuality, and inscription—was an epiphenomenon of writing itself, his move kept scholars of theater and speech from appealing to embodiment and orality in purely celebratory terms. References to the body and to the spoken, to immediacy, spontaneity, and presence now sounded naive, literal, unsophisticated, and reductive. In actuality, there was nothing about Derrida's argument about writing that made it impossible to study bodies and speech. In fact, theatricality's flexible essentialism means that it does not necessarily occupy one position in a critique of presence. Theater's longstanding associations with artifice, figuration, and representation suggest that it could function as the ultimate figure of deconstructionist self-difference. At the same time, its assumed status as a "copresent" medium in "real time" makes theater ripe for caricature within deconstruction. Theatrical discourse constantly vacillates between these sensibilities. "This is about copies," some might assert; "this is about real bodies," another group will respond, all of them waving hands in the air or bringing fists to the table depending on context, convenience, and polemics. In the late twentieth century, a number of contexts emphasized the latter set of associations, however, and often with a negative spin. Not only did Derrida use performance-based examples—of speech, of Antonin Artaud—in his critiques of metaphysical naivete, influential figures such as art historian Michael Fried used the word *theatrical* as a synonym for literality.[37] Hence, at a moment in intellectual history when it became fashionable to be associated with the figural, critical theorists linked theater to the literal real.

The impact of the critique of presence on the theorizing of theatricality paralleled its impact on feminism. Since feminism also laid claims to the "body" and to "experience," such references could also sound reductive—especially when viewed in hindsight. When proponents of "feminist theater" such as Diamond and Case reviewed their earlier work, they were both placed in the position of defending themselves against accusations of metaphysical naivete. For Diamond, this meant returning to her earlier discussion of the "female body"—reasserting that in no way had she suggested that such a body was "just there, live, unmediated." So important was it by the mid-1990s "to be clear about this point" that Diamond elected to reprint the entire passage in italics.[38] Case created a different "amulet to ward off haunting spirits," however, remaining skeptical of the political and disciplinary effects of the deconstructionist critique.[39] As she had earlier located the butch-femme aesthetic in "what is generally referred to as 'presence,' "[40] so she remained unwilling to accept the argument of writing's pervasiveness and supercession. Joined to a theory of performativity, the deconstructionist move was for her ultimately "a privileging of print culture."[41] Arguing that this critical context was "burying the live body," Case thus found it necessary for theater, feminism, and women to "bring home the meat" of live performance and, in a partnered move, to "recharge essentialism."[42] Some might argue that, when Derrida and others referred to writing, they did not intend to refer to "print" per se. And when theorists of performativity referred to citational processes, they did not assume that citations only occurred in print texts. What Case indirectly identified, however, is how an unequal institutional context can exert unintended pressures and exacerbate disciplinary inertias. The principle that writing is everywhere—that there is "nothing outside the text"—does not necessarily encourage disciplinary expansion. And in this context, any reference to bodies or to speech can prompt the accusation of essentialism and intellectual naivete—whether in feminism, or theater, or feminist theater.

A second theoretical conundrum affected the theatricality/performativity debate, specifically the issue of "choice" inside the operations of performance. Butler's extrapolation of Derrida for feminism and for speech-act theory emphasized the absence of a prejuridical consciousness that could formulate intention and will before and outside the law. The absence of such a preexistent consciousness or identity was fundamental to both her critique of feminism and her theorizing of performativity. In the delight and furor that followed *Gender Trouble*'s publication, however, the most common misreading assumed the presence of a self-consciously performing agent behind the performance of gender. Butler took great pains in numerous discussions to correct this notion. In "Critically Queer"—republished later in *Bodies That Matter*—her statement explicitly critiqued the concept of will and choice—and did so by distinguishing performativity from performance.

> In no sense can it be concluded that the part of gender that is performed is therefore the "truth" of gender; performance as bounded "act" is distinguished from performativity insofar as the latter consists in a reiteration of norms which precede, constrain, and exceed the performance and in that sense cannot be taken as a fabrication of the performer's "will" or "choice"; further, what is "performed" works to conceal, if not to disavow, what remains opaque, unconscious, unperformable. The reduction of performativity to performance would be a mistake.[43]

When taken back to the context of feminist politics, this kind of statement was hard to swallow and would ultimately drive a retroactive wedge between concepts of performativity and theatrical performance. The assumption of a conscious feminist performance was critical to the theorizing of several types of feminist and sexual activism in the early 1990s. As Butler said, "The publication of *Gender Trouble* coincided with a number of publications that did assert that 'clothes make the woman,' but I never did think that gender was like clothes, or that clothes make the woman."[44] For Case, the presence of an intentional domain distinguished the feminine masquerader from the feminist masquerader. Case had also used her focus on the female actor—in artistic and social terms—to argue for the theatrical as a "more active" basis from which to theorize feminist practice. In *Domain Matrix* Case remained suspicious of Butler's theorizing, ultimately accusing her models of functioning as a reversed metaphysics in which "regulatory norms" occupied the grammatical position of a primary, self-generating principle in lieu of a conscious agent.[45] For Diamond, too, a feminist Gestus had entailed a "rigorous self-consciousness" that would expose the illusion of gender as something to "be put on or shed at will."[46] When her revised essay reappeared in *Unmaking Mimesis*, Diamond addressed the tension. She was more willing to accept Butler's theorizing of a "complex temporality" in which neither norms nor performer consciousness preceded the other. She also adjusted particular phrases to address a new discursive context, one in which clothes definitely did not make the woman. In lieu of "gender is exposed as a sexual costume,"[47] she argued that "gender is relentlessly exposed as 'performativity,' as a system of regulatory norms which the subject cites to appear in culture."[48] Diamond also deleted the reference to a performer's ability to shed the illusion of gender "at will," substituting instead a lengthier discussion of the impact of queer performativity on feminist theatricality. Her revised argument made a disciplinary claim. While acknowledging that Butler's charge that theatrical performance "implies one who ontologically precedes and then fabricates gender effects . . . is irrefutable," she also suggested that it promoted a theoretical insularity.

> Though "performativity" is not an "act" but a "reiteration" or "citation," why should we restrict its iterative sites to theory and to the theorist's acts of seeing? . . . Performance, as I have written elsewhere, is the site in which performativity materializes in concentrated form, where the "concealed or dissimulated conventions" of which acts are mere repetitions might be investigated and reimagined.[49]

As Case charged that a critique of performativity circumscribed the range of favored analytic objects to "print" forms, so Diamond argued that the term required analytic expansion. Indeed, in an institutional context where scholars of theatrical performance still fought for legitimacy, Butler's use of the term "reduction" in reference to performance had a painfully exclusionary ring. Case's and Diamond's arguments for theater's "rigorous self-consciousness" were thus specifically directed at an institutional establishment (in higher education and elsewhere) that was quite used to assuming that theater people actually did not know what they were doing. Less than a decade later, however, the critical context had changed. Feminist attempts to correct the assumption of theater's irrelevant instability in the 1980s ended up justifying a critique of theater's overly stable assumptions of relevancy in the 1990s. Just when it became theoretically interesting *not* to be an intentional agent, a theory of performativity "reduced" theatricality to a state of a simplistic intentionality.

III.

Whether it was through a critique of presence, embodiment, and experience or a critique of action, will, and intention, proponents of theatrical performance could find their terms and their objects both critically central and abjectly peripheral in late twentieth-century theory. If we can be vigilant—rather than defensive or territorial—about how this paradox happened, perhaps we can learn to navigate it better. Theoretical explorations of both queerness and performativity prompted emulation, revision, and critique from feminist theater theorists. Diamond would see the need to delete references to the "sex-gender system" in *Unmaking Mimesis*, substituting "heterotopia of difference" in its place.[50] Case's antiessentialist theory of feminist theatricality looked more essentialist in hindsight. But it is exactly this kind of retroactive attribution that is most dangerous for disciplinary discussion. Recall Butler's statement in my opening epigraph, where she—the unintended architect of "queer theory"—called for more awareness of the mundane violence at work in the impulse to divide feminism and queer theory. In her analysis of the introduction to *The Lesbian and Gay Studies Reader* and its quest to delimit the "proper object" of *sex* to gay and lesbian studies, Butler describes a complicated process of disavowal and terminological relocation, where "commonality must be denied, through elision or through the semantic splitting and redistribution of its constitutive parts."[51] In Butler's example, feminists constructed a sex/gender paradigm that announced a distinction between sex as "sexual difference" (the opposition between men and women) and gender as social construction. In queer theory's retroactive construal, however, the feminist interest in "gender" was redefined as the opposition between men and women (sexual difference), thereby equating the second term with a much less interesting association to which it had previously been opposed. Recall that it was precisely this "confused" equation that Diamond, along with many other feminists, sought to redress in the late 1980s. A similar process of elision could be said to occur in many a theatricality/performativity debate, one where the quest to be more interesting also prompted a semantic splitting and redistribution. To engage theatricality is to engage both a longstanding association with the figural and a longstanding debate about the intentionality of the actor. That history, however, was sidestepped by the frame of performativity, one that equated theater with the real and the intentional to celebrate (or condemn) theories of performativity for their engagement with the play of representation.

To elide and align completely the processes of these two debates would be extreme. However, the articulations of gender theory and of performance theory do share in a similar "antihistorical" act of disavowal in the shaky quest for intellectual transcendence. The antiessentialist dimensions of the "first" term (feminism, theater) are backgrounded by the discourse surrounding the "next" term (queer, performativity) to prop up the latter's claims to radical antiessentialism. In this relational process, feminism and theater are caricatured retroactively as bastions of political and formal essentialism. Proponents of both feminism and theater, it should be noted, can participate in the same process of partial recall. Resistances to both queer theory and theories of performativity often have an essentialist inertia, making claims to "experience," "embodiment," "ground," and the "real" to stall the presumably groundless and "textualist" spin of post-structuralist theorizing. In the process, all these moves participate in the "burial" of both feminism and theatricality as arenas of representational complexity.

Delineating the "proper object" of theatricality is a difficult endeavor because of the term's essentialist flexibility and the shifting relational contexts in which it is theorized. In this complicated scenario, it is perhaps most important to be vigilant about the shaky hierarchies, chronologies, oppositions, equations, and synecdochic fallacies that we bring to bear on this process. For those of us who have a professional commitment to theater as a discrete event and a valued practice, the invocation of a *t*-word has certain stakes. For many of us, the metaphors of social theory are attached to specific objects, disciplines, and institutional locations. Just as a term such as "juridical" may have specific resonances for legal scholars, so a term such as theatrical rings more intensely and acutely in the ears of theater and performance scholars who seek legitimacy for their favorite objects of study. Moreover, there are gendered reasons why debates about theatricality have become particularly difficult as we move from the twentieth to the twenty-first century. The issue of sexuality—and particularly a sexuality that exposed the self-difference of identity—was an intrinsic part of feminist discussion. The self-difference of identity was, furthermore, part of feminist theatrical discussion as well. Diamond theorized the "not, but" of deconstructive sexuality within feminist discourse. That such a thought structure would become associated with queer theory and performativity—sometimes to the exclusion of feminism and theatricality—testifies to our habits of disciplinary forgetting, as well as to an unequal field of institutional power. When it comes to disciplinary allegiances and oppositions, it might also be important to proceed with caution. We might be careful of equating a field with a concept, assuming that one scholar can stand in for an entire field, homogenizing distinct inquiries into entire fields, or assuming that one field necessarily "preceded" the other. For instance, to study performativity is not equivalent to being a "performance studies" scholar; indeed, there is a disciplinary strain within the latter so committed to a discourse of presence, practice, and intention that its assumptions would seem very nearly the opposite of those who work on performativity—and more aligned with those who work on theater (at least some theaters). Similarly, queer theory is not equivalent to "gay and lesbian studies"; indeed, there is a disciplinary strain within the latter so committed to a discourse of presence, practice, and intention that its assumptions would seem nearly the opposite of those who work on queer theory—and more aligned with those who work on feminism (at least some feminisms).

Finally, when coming to terms with theatricality's flexible essentialism, we might also recognize that essentialism is itself relationally produced and sometimes an unintended effect. Feminism and theater are construed as essentialist only through a process of selective association and relational remembering. Furthermore, for all its critiques of normalization, queer theory can have normalizing effects. In 1989, Case foreshadowed the dangers of "contemporary theory seem[ing] to open the closet door to invite the queer to come out, transformed as a new, postmodern subject."[52] By 1997, Butler acknowledged the misogyny perpetuated by a queer "coming out" that excluded gender from sexual critique.[53] Meanwhile, no person, argument, term, or field can be said to be purely essentialist or antiessentialist. When Case elected to "recharge essentialism," she appealed to an earlier time when feminist theory was "describing a life—a full time commitment that is more inclusive than a vocation, or a delimited goal." She contrasted this effort to make a life with "the work in the late 1980s [that] celebrates slippage, setting oscillation against full-time political struggle."[54] By the year 2000, Routledge published the tenth-anniversary issue of *Gender Trouble*. In a new preface, Butler—the critic who would be repeatedly slammed for neutralizing the conditions under which "life" could be described—reminded us that the legibility of life, in all its variety, had always been her hope. She invoked a personal history in which she came to "understand something of the violence of gender norms"—an uncle, gay cousins, lost jobs, lovers, and homes.[55] She wrote, therefore, "from a desire to live, to make life possible, and to rethink the possible as such . . . This book is written then as part of the cultural life of a collective struggle that has had, and will continue to have, some success in increasing the possibilities for a livable life for those who live, or try to live, on the sexual margins."[56] By offering her readers "a sense of solace that there is someone here," Butler herself could be said to engage in an essentializing act.[57] Of course, the fact that she lodged the reminder within a discussion of language and subjectification unsettled any secure reference to that person or to that here. In their entirety, her statements seem to describe vulnerability while at the same time to acknowledge that such descriptions are part of a citational process. Emotions are generated, and they are no less volatile and no less felt for being constituted. Proponents of theatricality should be the first to acknowledge the possibility, viability, and necessity of such a speech act. And, *pace* past repudiations, perhaps none of us should be surprised to find out that Butler "can act" after all.

Notes

"Theatricality's Proper Objects: Genealogies of Performance and Gender Theory" was originally published in *Theatricality*, ed. Tracy Davis and Thomas Postlewait, 186–213 (Cambridge: Cambridge University Press, 2003).
EPIGRAPHS: Judith Butler, "Against Proper Objects," *Feminism Meets Queer Theory*, ed. Elizabeth Weed and Naomi Schor (Bloomington: Indiana University Press, 1997), 1; Butler, private communication with the author on theatrical performance.

1. Butler, "Against Proper Objects," 1.

2. Sue-Ellen Case, *The Domain Matrix* (Bloomington: Indiana University Press, 1996), and "Toward a Butch-Femme Aesthetic," in *Making a Spectacle*, ed. Lynda Hart (Ann Arbor: University of Michigan Press, 1989), 282–99; Elin Diamond, *Unmaking Mimesis: Essays on Feminism and Theater* (New York: Routledge, 1997); and Judith Butler, *Bodies That Matter: On the Discursive Limits of "Sex"* (New York: Routledge, 1993), "Against Proper Objects," *Feminism Meets Queer Theory*, ed. Elizabeth Weed and Naomi Schor (Bloomington: Indiana University Press, 1997), 1–30, and *Gender Trouble: Feminism and the Subversion of Identity* (New York: Routledge, 2000).

3. Andrea Dworkin, "Prostitution and Male Supremacy," *Michigan Journal of Gender and Law* 1 (1993): 1–12; and Catherine A. MacKinnon, "Sexuality, Pornography, and Method: 'Pleasure under Patriarchy'" *Ethics* 99, no. 2 (January 1989): 314–46.

4. Michel Foucault, *The History of Sexuality, Volume 1*, trans. Robert Hurley (New York: Random House, 1990).

5. Elin Diamond, "Brechtian Theory/Feminist Theory," *TDR: The Drama Review* 32, no. 1 (1988): 82, 83.

6. Bertolt Brecht, *Brecht on Theater*, ed. John Willet (New York: Hill and Wang, 1964), 143; quoted in Diamond, *Unmaking Mimesis*, 84.

7. Diamond, *Unmaking Mimesis*, 85.

8. Brecht, *Brecht on Theater*, 137; quoted in Diamond, *Unmaking Mimesis*, 86.

9. Diamond, *Unmaking Mimesis*, 85.

10. Gayle Rubin, "The Traffic in Women: Notes on the Political Economy of Sex," in *Toward an Anthropology of Women*, ed. Rayna Rapp (New York: Monthly Review Press, 1976), 157–210; quoted in Diamond, "Brechtian Theory/Feminist Theory," 86.

11. Diamond, "Brechtian Theory/Feminist Theory," 83.

12. Diamond, "Brechtian Theory/Feminist Theory," 88.

13. Diamond, "Brechtian Theory/Feminist Theory," 89.

14. Diamond, "Brechtian Theory/Feminist Theory," 85.

15. Case, "Toward a Butch-Femme Aesthetic," 282.

16. Case, "Toward a Butch-Femme Aesthetic," 283.

17. Jacques Lacan, "The Meaning of the Phallus," in *Feminine Sexuality*, ed. Juliet Mitchell and Jacqueline Rose (New York: W. W. Norton, 1986), 74–85; Joan Rivière, "Womanliness as Masquerade," in *Formations of Fantasy*, ed. Victor Burgin, James Donald, and Cora Kaplan (New York: Routledge, Chapman, and Hall, 1986), 35–43.

18. Rivière, "Womanliness as Masquerade," 38.

19. Case, "Toward a Butch-Femme Aesthetic," 291.

20. Case, "Toward a Butch-Femme Aesthetic," 291.

21. Case, "Toward a Butch-Femme Aesthetic," 292.

22. Mary Ann Doane, "Film and Masquerade: Theorizing the Female Spectator," *Screen* 23, no. 3–4 (1982): 81; quoted in Case, "Toward a Butch-Femme Aesthetic," 292.

23. Case, "Toward a Butch-Femme Aesthetic," 292.

24. Case, "Toward a Butch-Femme Aesthetic," 293.

25. Case, "Toward a Butch-Femme Aesthetic," 289–90.

26. Butler, "Against Proper Objects," 1.

27. Butler, *Gender Trouble*, 1.

28. Butler, *Gender Trouble*, 2.

29. Butler, *Gender Trouble*, 2.

30. Butler, *Gender Trouble*, 48.

31. Case, "Toward a Butch-Femme Aesthetic," 291.

32. Butler, *Gender Trouble*, 48.

33. Butler, *Gender Trouble*, 72.

34. Butler, *Gender Trouble*, 72.

35. Butler, *Gender Trouble*, 137, italic in the original.

36. Butler, *Gender Trouble*, 148.

37. Jacques Derrida, *Of Grammatology*, trans. Gayatri Spivak (Baltimore: Johns Hopkins University Press, 1974, 1967), and *Writing and Difference*, trans. Alan Bass (Chicago: University of Chicago Press, 1978); Michael Fried, "Art and Objecthood," *Artforum* (June 1967): 12–23.

38. Diamond, *Unmaking Mimesis*, 52.

39. Sue Ellen Case, *The Domain Matrix* (Bloomington: Indiana University Press, 1996), 6.

40. Case, "Toward a Butch-Femme Aesthetic," 290.

41. Case, *Domain Matrix*, 17.

42. Case, *Domain Matrix*, 17, 186, 11.

43. Judith Butler, *Bodies That Matter: On the Discursive Limits of "Sex"* (New York: Routledge, 1993), 234.

44. Butler, *Bodies That Matter*, 231.

45. Case, *Domain Matrix*, 16.

46. Diamond, "Brechtian Theory/Feminist Theory," 85.

47. Diamond, "Brechtian Theory/Feminist Theory," 85.

48. Diamond, *Unmaking Mimesis*, 46.

49. Diamond, *Unmaking Mimesis*, 46–47.

50. Diamond, *Unmaking Mimesis*, 48.

51. Butler, "Against Proper Objects," 4–5.

52. Case, "Toward a Butch-Femme Aesthetic," 288.

53. Butler, "Against Proper Objects," 23.

54. Case, *Domain Matrix*, 153, 155.

55. Butler, *Gender Trouble*, xx.

56. Butler, *Gender Trouble*, xx, xxvi.

57. Butler, *Gender Trouble*, xvii.

Chapter 4

When "Everything Counts"

Experimental Performance and
Performance Historiography

In 1973 an artist named Mierle Laderman Ukeles presented a series of fifteen performances in conjunction with exhibits of her work at a range of US museums and galleries. In one such iteration, "Hartford Wash: Washing Tracks, Maintenance Inside" at the Wadsworth Atheneum in Hartford, Connecticut, Ukeles descended to her hands and knees to wash the inside floors and exterior steps of the museum. Ukeles engaged continuously and for hours in the repetitive motions of crouching, squeezing, scrubbing, standing, dumping, crouching, squeezing, scrubbing, standing, and dumping that constituted her avant-garde experimental practice of "maintenance art."

In 1998 the Wooster Group first opened their production of *House/Lights* at The Performing Garage in New York City, presenting a show that would tour in Germany, Belgium, Canada, France, Scotland, and Norway before being revived again at St. Ann's Warehouse in Brooklyn in 2005. Joining the routinized plots and gestures of the brothel depicted in Joseph P. Mawra's 1964 film *Olga's House of Shame* with the looping phrases and scenarios of Gertude Stein's 1938 text *Doctor Faustus Lights the Lights*, the production coordinated a system of words, actors, and mediating machines to create a house and playhouse that were decidedly off-kilter.

I am interested in these performance practices in part for what they say to each other. Both have female performers at their center. Both engage in a dynamic construction of space, whether we understand their movements to extend within or beyond an aesthetic frame; neither performance seems to have fixed ending points. Both invoke the metaphor of the "household," of playing house and a house at play, even if together they straddle the two opposing poles of female stereotype embodied in the cleaned house tended by a wife and the unclean whorehouse tended by its mistress. Both make productive use of repetition, whether to comment socially on female labor or to unhinge linguistic referentiality via the tropes of female modernism. Whatever these performances share thematically and formally, they are also each imbricated in art histories and theatrical histories that differ from each other. And it is that difference and the relationships across their differences that most concern me in this essay. In brief, I will consider how and whether a spatial turn in experimental art of the late twentieth century is allied with a spatial turn in late twentieth-century theater history scholarship. Located in a collection on the "historiography of performance," one that follows from and supplements the earlier important collection, *Interpreting the Theatrical Past*, the above examples also represent two different domains (though by no means all domains) in which the vocabulary of "space" and "experimental performance" might apply.[1] I want to think through some of the conceptual parallels and conceptual puzzles that different disciplinary methods bring to bear on the site of performance, exploring methods of theatrical history, art history, and cultural history in which varied groups of scholars have reckoned with the politics of location. My use of words such as "site" and "location" is not coincidental, since I am most interested in exploring what I have elsewhere called the "hypercontextual" nature of theater and performance, an enmeshment in site and location that always seems to make the notion of "situated performance" something of a tautology.[2]

In what follows, I will present and compare different kinds of scholarly approaches to "sitedness" in performance, using two contemporaneous publications as touchstones for my presentation: theater scholar Ric Knowles's 2004 *Reading the Material Theater* and art historian Miwon Kwon's *One Place after Another: Site-Specific Art and Locational Identity*, published in hardback in 2002 and in paperback in 2004.[3] I then use the fact of their shared language to tease out some of the conceptual convergences within theatrical and visual art-historical methods at our present moment. At the same time, I also explore their conceptual differences to foreground the methodological tensions in an interdisciplinary performance historiography more generally. If, following Louis Mink, "space" is a key term in the production of historical understanding, spatial understanding for performance historiography is particularly intriguing, moving as it does across Mink's distinctions between concepts we think *about*, concepts we *use*, and a priori concepts we think *with*.[4] If for Mink space is one of those a priori concepts with which we encounter the world, it is also one that performance consistently redefines as posteriori, as arising from experience rather than preceding it. Performance makes the process of *thinking with* space into a process of thinking about space and a process of using it. In so doing, performance brings the contingency of spatial knowledge into higher relief, asking us to notice our own situating habits and the changeable ways we locate ourselves. As it happens, different artistic practices and scholarly methods can vary in their sense of spatial contingency. Hence, before we can devise a spatially nimble performance historiography, we first have to situate how we situate.

Materialist Categories

In the same decade that saw the publication of *Interpreting the Theatrical Past*, progressive scholarship in the humanities, social sciences, and history and philosophy of natural science took seriously, vociferously, if also variously, the politics of situated identity. In what would retroactively be homogenized under the phrase of "identity politics," scholars and activists called attention to the gendered, classed, raced, and homophobic discourses that structured our habits of interpretation and tacit exclusion. The vocabulary and conceptual frames of identity-based scholarship varied enormously; indeed, many questioned the stability of anything like a volitional, self-intending entity like "identity," prompting an internal rift between varieties of feminist, antiracist, and queer scholarship. Often repolarized as a debate between essentialist and antiessentialist concepts of identity, proponents of the latter argued that the former reproduced hegemonic identity categories by claiming to speak as woman or as black. Meanwhile, the former accused the latter of evacuating the political efficacy of identity by questioning the stability of its material existence. Within this mix of positions, it is no coincidence that the language of "site" and "situation" emerged to sustain progressive critique. Probably one of the most well-circulated essays on feminist location came from Donna Haraway who used her unusual position as a feminist critic of science to forward the concept of "situated knowledges."[5] In these and related scholarly movements, the concept of "site" helped scholars and activists navigate some of the perils and contradictions of identity-based critique. By pointing to the sited construction of identity, one could theoretically embrace a sense of identity's instability and constructedness while simultaneously analyzing the concrete material location in which that construction occurred.

While the progressive debates of the 1980s and 1990s gave a particular urgency to the methodological tasks of contextualization in theatrical analysis, it would be imprudent to assume that the identity turn invented the situating methods of theater scholarship. Indeed, the hypercontextual form of the theater has meant that theater scholarship has long been preoccupied with the situatedness of its events, even if the techniques and politics of how that situating happens have changed over time. In early twentieth-century iterations of the discipline of theater studies, emerging scholars mimicked and adapted the epistemological conventions of their time to contextualize the theatrical event. In most cases, a reference to the limitations of the hermetically sealed dramatic script became the foil on which an expanded theatrical field rested. As scholars and artists argued for the necessity of considering performers, design, buildings, and audiences in addition to the dramatic text, the language used to analyze these other situated registers varied. Some employed philological conventions of fact-based contextualization and Darwinian preoccupations with genus and species to chart theater's evolutionary expansion.[6] Proponents of Cambridge anthropology adapted models of ritual to interpret drama within a network of event-based processes.[7] Scholars of medieval and Renaissance theater knew full well that the deepest resonances of the form only came forward with knowledge of its embodied gestures, guilds, wagons, churches, and street layouts—what a later generation of scholars would call its material conditions.[8] Earlier American institutional figures, meanwhile, formulated their own kind of situated discipline by promoting the artistic act of performance production as essential to the understanding of a play-text.[9] All these quite different approaches can be understood as different attempts to "situate" theater, albeit with quite different vocabularies and visions of scholarly discipline. Additionally, at different moments in the scholarly pendulum, all these gestures contended with other scholarly movements that argued for the importance of autonomy in art and art criticism, whether in the New Formalism of the mid-twentieth century or further back, when Joel Elias Spingarn, defending his critical compatriot Benedetto Croce, grumpily declared that to analyze the *production* of drama was akin to incorporating "a history of the publisher's trade" into one's analysis of poetry.[10]

As Richard Knowles shows in *Reading the Material Theater*, scholarship in theater studies has drawn from other approaches over the twentieth century to reckon with the extended nature of the form. Working toward what he calls a "materialist semiotics" for theater studies, he cites two more trajectories for situated analysis. One lies in the "cultural materialism" of Antonio Gramsci's theories of cultural production who, Knowles reminds us, referred to the "theatrical industry" as early as 1917.[11] The other lies in the midcentury adaptations of Prague-school semiotics to theater studies methodology, a preoccupation with signifying systems of production and reception that propelled highly influential European and Euro-American theater scholarship such as that of Keir Elam, Patrice Pavis, Marco de Marinis, Michael Quinn, André Helbo, and Marvin Carlson.[12] While Knowles refers to a certain methodological exhaustion with the taxonomic tendencies of semiotics, he adapts its categories to Gramscian-inspired movements in cultural studies and New Historicism through the late twentieth century. He cites scholars who, in the words of one collection, sought to "redraw the boundaries of literary study."[13] He cites another collection, inserting his own parenthetical, to position "texts (including, here, performances) as inseparable from the conditions of their production and reception in history; as involved, necessarily, in the making of cultural meanings which are always, finally political meanings."[14] Indeed, Spingarn's earlier admonitions became prognostications, for it was in the context of New Historicist and cultural materialist literary criticism that many a scholar did in fact begin to consider the role of printing presses, "the publisher's trade," and other forms of material

writing in the analysis of poetry.[15] Knowles goes on also to expand beyond
the Renaissance-based scholarship of new historicism to cultural studies
scholarship on twentieth-century forms of popular production and reception to notice the relationship between Stuart Hall's models of "encoding/
decoding" and the inherited models of theatrical semiotics.[16] Knowles
adapts the graphic habits of theater semiotics to offer a chart that "fleshes
out a triangular model" for reading the material theater: (1) conditions
of production (i.e., encoding), (2) performance text, and (3) conditions
of reception (i.e., decoding). Each work is "in concert or in tension both
within their own 'corner,' and along the axes that hold the poles together
in tension with one another. 'Meaning' in a given performance situation—
the social and cultural work done by the performance, its performativity,
and its force—is the effect of all of these systems and each pole of the
interpretive triangle working dynamically and relationally together."[17]

Thus, in creating triangular frameworks for a "materialist semiotics,"
Knowles gathers and modifies a vocabulary for the situation of performance, one that places the myriad dimensions of a site into divided if
relationally defined categories for making a text and receiving a text, and
for the text itself. So productive and entrenched is this theatrical triangle
that we might find it difficult to notice the hermeneutic act that such a spa-
tializing of space entails. First of all, in adapting Dollimore and Sinfield's
disquisition on the necessity of considering texts' production and reception, Knowles inserts his own parenthetical to be sure that we know that
"texts" are "(including, here, performances)." Despite the apparent ease
of that substitution, it is worth noting that, for a differently positioned
scholar, the elements of "performance" might well qualify as elements of
its extratextual situation. While some theater scholars might locate the
designed set of a play within the diegesis of the "performance text," the
scholarly habits of another might position that same component as an exe-
getic element of a dramatic text, better located as part of its "conditions of
production." Both scholars may claim to be equally committed to "situating" theatrical texts, but they may possess different disciplinary habits for
gauging what elements of theater belong to the "text" corner of a material
semiotic triangle and what to the "production/encoding" corner.

It is certainly not the case that either Knowles or the scholars he cites are
unaware of this hermeneutic contingency. Indeed, when Knowles quotes
one of Tony Bennet's essays to say that "neither text nor context are conceivable as entities separable from one another," he invokes one of the
most significant contributions of new historicist methodology, that is, the
conceptual sense, not only that texts need contextualization but also that
the text/context division is itself a contingent construct.[18] But even that
recognition does not in itself bypass the fact that differently positioned
scholars locate the space of the text/context implosion in different places,
since the barometer for "redrawing the boundaries of literary study"

between text and context, between performance and situation, depend on inherited generic assumptions of where those boundaries were in the first place. By looking more closely at some of the ways that Knowles defines the elements of these different corners, we can get an even better sense of how fragile and contingent methodological dispositions can be. Under "Performance Text," Knowles places "script, *mise en scene*, design, actors' bodies, movement, and gestures, etc. as reconstituted in discourse." Consider the relation between these elements and those that are placed under conditions of production such as "actor," "director," "training," "working conditions," "stage and backstage architecture," or "historical/cultural moment of production." The categories require a curious separation between "actor" and "actors' bodies"; meanwhile, they must uphold a firm boundary between mise-en-scène and "working conditions." The conceptual difficulties continue with the extended definitions of other points on the triangle, such as when "conditions of production" also include "backstage architecture and amenities" that are presumably distinguished from other elements that appear under "Conditions of Reception" such as "publicity" or "front-of-house, auditorium, and audience amenities."[19] The spatial elements of a theatrical building are thus placed in different semiotic registers; the auditorium is naturalized as part of a frontstage reception and distinguished from backstage architectural features. Meanwhile, publicity is something received rather than something produced. And a scholar would have to make a determination about which "amenities" qualify as production and which as reception.

Site Specificity

Around the same time that Knowles composed his manuscript for *Reading the Material Theater*, another scholar in the field of art history was simultaneously composing hers. While Knowles developed his "materialist semiotic" frames whose "theoretical rigour and located reading" could "provide a model for site-specific performance analysis that takes into account the specifics and politics of location,"[20] Miwon Kwon's *One Place after Another* adopted a subtitle in quite similar terms—"*Site-Specific Art and Locational Identity*." Filtered through an alternate disciplinary lens, the same words "site specific" and "location" were differently loaded and differently expansive for Kwon, whose project was in fact to scrutinize and compare the range of sensibilities and goals that had collected under the notion of site specificity. Concerned that the term had been "uncritically adopted as another genre category by mainstream art institutions and discourses," she wondered with other critics whether the "unspecific (mis) uses of the term 'site-specific' are yet another instance of how vanguardist, socially conscious, and politically committed art practices always become domesticated by their assimilation into the dominant culture."[21] At the same time, she also wanted to track the resistance of some site-specific artists to institutional absorption, noting that others had formulated yet new terms—"context-specific, debate-specific, audience-specific, community-specific, project-based"—to "forge more complex and fluid possibilities for the art-site relationship."[22]

Like that of many other scholars grounded in the field of visual art history—Hal Foster, Rosalind Krauss, T. J. Clark, or Benjamin Buchloh along with other art historians expressly concerned with performance/ live art such as Amelia Jones, Jane Blocker, Rebecca Schneider, Adrian Heathfield—Kwon's terminology and her concerns overlap with those of theater and performance studies scholars.[23] With terms like "context-specific" and especially "audience-specific," it seems that visual art experiments are reproducing and perhaps reinventing theatrical art traditions. At the same time, the intellectual and artistic trajectories supporting Kwon's project and positioning her implied interlocutors are part of a different set of artistic coordinates and movements. In titling her book *One Place after Another*, Kwon echoes and plays with a phrase from Minimalist sculptor Donald Judd whose 1965 essay "Specific Objects" tried to give a vocabulary to the redefinition of visual art at work in the period. Distinguishing what he called "three-dimensional work" from previous painting and sculpture, Judd argued that he and allied artists wished to challenge the inherited material and spatial constraints of traditional visual art forms, especially painting. For Judd, "The main thing wrong with painting is that it is a rectangular plane placed flat against the wall. A rectangle is a shape itself; it is obviously the whole shape; it determines and limits the arrangement of whatever is on or inside of it."[24] Integral to the Minimalist gesture, then, was a resistance to the framed flatness of the painting frame, and by extension the bounded limits placed on the conventional props, plinths, and pedestals of sculpture. Key to this resistance was an engagement with an extended spatiality: "Three dimensions are real space . . . Obviously, anything in three dimensions can be any shape, regular or irregular, and can have any relation to the wall, floor, ceiling, room, rooms or exterior."[25] Frank Stella was one of the many artists invoked by Judd to help him articulate the effects of "specific objects": "Stella's shaped paintings involve several important characteristics of three-dimensional work. The periphery of a piece and the lines inside correspond. The stripes are nowhere near being discrete parts. The surface is farther from the wall than usual . . . The order is not rationalistic and underlying but is simply order, like that of continuity, one thing after another."[26] The serial proposition of "one thing after another" was thus Judd's phrase for articulating a certain kind of boundary reorganization in the visual arts, one whose parameters neither reproduced traditional visual distinctions nor used traditional material infrastructures for the support of the aesthetic object, thereby reworking distinctions between background and foreground, canvas and wall, core and periphery, under and above, inside and outside.

For Judd and others to disparage "the main thing wrong with painting" was at this time for him to challenge, not only a long durée of European Masters but also a more contemporaneous context of modernist art practice and criticism. In developing a critical vocabulary for the nonrepresentational explorations of Abstract Expressionism and modernist painting, powerful visual art critics such as Clement Greenberg and his former student Michael Fried famously called for a mode of formal criticism that took seriously these painters' engagement with the intrinsic qualities of their medium. For Greenberg, this medium of pure engagement respected the classical definition of the spatial, juxtapositive, nondurational nature of the plastic arts, a respect for the all-at-once encounter that from Gotthold Ephraim Lessing to Joshua Reynolds had distinguished painting and other static arts from the durational arts of poetry and drama.[27] Crucially (especially for a spatially complex performance historiography), painting's spatiality was nondurational and highly circumscribed by the essentially flat medium of the canvas.

> It quickly emerged that the unique and proper area of competence of each art coincided with all that was unique to the nature of its medium. . . . It was the stressing . . . of the ineluctable flatness of the support that remained most fundamental in the processes by which pictorial art criticized and defined itself under Modernism. Flatness, two-dimensionality, was the only condition painting shared with no other art, and so Modernist painting oriented itself to flatness as it did to nothing else.[28]

The focus on flatness as a condition of modernist legitimacy prompted such critics to value paintings that replicated the wholly present encounter of classical painting via a meditation on the flatness of the canvas. By extension, for both Greenberg and Fried, modernist painting required a criticism that did not engage with either the corruptions of other media or the historical contingencies of its social conditions. Significantly, such an intrinsic criticism did not consider itself to be uninterested in criticality, but understood the modernist engagement with its medium to constitute its own form of "self-criticism." The younger Fried spent a good deal of time grappling with and defending his mentor's scholarly method: "[I]n general, criticism concerned with aspects of the situation in which it was made other than its formal context can add significantly to our understanding of the artists' achivement. But criticism of this kind has shown itself largely unable to make convincing discriminations of value among the works of a particular artist."[29] For modernist critics like Fried and Greenberg who were well aware of situating and contextualizing methodologies in art historiography, modernist art had the label it did because of its wholly present, formal resistance to social contingency; it hence required a criticism that understood that gesture.

As complicated and powerful as intrinsic modernist art criticism was in the period, it became in many ways a convenient foil for artists and art critics who would go on to celebrate an expanded and "situated" field for art practice. For pro-Minimalist (or "three-dimensional") artists and their supportive critics, modernism's medium purity functioned much as "dramatic literature" did for the field of materialist theater, as the internally focused foil on which externally minded appeals to spatial situatedness could rest. Fried would go on to write a polemic against the theatricality of Minimalist art in "Art and Objecthood," an infamous essay that only propelled the aesthetic expansion it sought to forestall. Fried's decision to align Minimalism's "literalism" with "theatricality" came from his sense of its concern with "actual circumstances" in "*a situation*" that "*includes the beholder*," even "the *beholder's body*."[30] As with Spingarn's "publisher's trade," this was another moment when admonition became prognostication. Fried's italicized disdain only emboldened situated art practice, even as it implicitly supported (albeit negatively) the sense of theatricality as a figure for hypercontextuality, situatedness, and dependence on a spectatorial "receiver," that is, exactly the registers that have been so central to the materialist and semiotic study of the theater. Moreover, as Kwon's substitution of "place" for "thing" suggests, artists and critics began to offer new kinds of answers to the question of how far an artistic work could engage its situation. Could "place" be made as specific as an object, that is, its fundamental registers exposed and its inherited barometers, boundaries, and supporting infrastructures reorganized? Those varied answers are at the heart of what it means to produce and to analyze "site-specific art" and "locational identity" from within the field of visual art history.

In giving a history and a vocabulary to the site-specific turn in contemporary art, Kwon recounts some of the familiar Minimalist gestures and public art controversies around works such as Robert Smithson's *Spiral Jetty* (1970) and Richard Serra's *Tilted Arc* (1981).[31] At the same time, site-specific art encountered a paradox as artists and curators faced new questions about what exactly "the material context" contained and whether there had been implicit conceptual boundaries within those early boundary-breaking calls. Moving beyond Judd and Serra to consider artists such as Michael Asher, Marcel Broodthaers, Daniel Buren, Hans Haacke, and Andrea Fraser, Kwon analyzes a mode of practice that began to engage not only the phenomenological registers of the art object and the gallery walls but also the social and institutional forces that shaped the space of presentation. Repeating what is now a familiar art historiographical move "from Minimalism to institutional critique," she considers how Mel Bochner's *Measurement Room*, Hans Haacke's *Unfinished Business* or Andrea Fraser's *Museum Highlights* pushed the Minimalist envelope, extending its engagement with situation beyond the *materials* of the artistic environment to the *materialist* processes of the artistic institution. While Judd had celebrated the many possible "relations" of "three-dimensional work" to "the wall, floor, ceiling, room, rooms or exterior," institutional critique began to push the concept of site to ever new "exteriors," considering not just the walls and the ceilings but the institutions, funding structures, real-estate deals, and construction contracts that built the walls in the first place.[32] As a result, Minimalism's phenomenological reaction to medium purity began retroactively to look "pure" itself.

Convergences

In each of the theatrical and art-historical trajectories tracked thus far, there is a persistent interest in the material sitedness of the artwork. At the same time, the parameters for dividing or imploding divisions between art and site shift historically amid debates and confusions about what elements constitute a "site" and where divisions between intrinsic texts and extrinsic engagement lie. Much as theatrical historians have made assumptions about whether the production of drama was intrinsic or extrinsic to the dramatic text, so art historians have made assumptions about the diegetic or extradiegetic status of a painting's canvas, and its paint and its wall. Moreover, spatial boundaries have changed with different sensibilities and different innovations. The wall is the beginning of "context' from one vantage point but incorporated into the artwork from another. The "performance" is part of "conditions of production" from one vantage point but incorporated into the concept of "text" from another. Additionally, every situating gesture has met different critical resistances from those who object to deautonomizing methods in both art and criticism, whether in Croce and Spingarn's critical avoidance of stage architecture, audiences, and printing presses or in Greenberg and Fried's scandalized reaction to finding themselves "in a situation," that is, amid artworks "where *everything counts.*"[33]

As much as variations in contents and boundaries of site change within discrete art histories, it is my sense that those variations become more ubiquitous and differently defamiliarizing when we begin to join the formal and analytic habits of more than one field into the interdisciplinary pursuit of performance historiography. For one, there is an implicit question around how much a given work understands itself to be site specific versus how much site specificity is something a critic finds in it. In other words, for whom is "space" a form of a priori knowledge and for whom is it something to use? Moreover, how do the parameters of space extend and retract for differently positioned artists and scholars? For Knowles, the language of materiality and site specificity emerges most often to describe the work of the scholar who assembles information around various registers of textuality, production, and reception to understand the total theatrical event, often deploying such registers to offer interpretations that theater-makers had not always anticipated themselves. In Kwon's world, the language of materiality and site specificity most often describes the goals of artists who consciously try to reorient their work away from the framed painting or pedestaled sculpture and into the extended environment of production and reception. Along the way, artists encounter elements of the situation that they might not have anticipated—and Kwon goes on to analyze institutional and community experiments where such surprises occurred—but the artistic impulse toward situated engagement is one that the artwork seeks to create, construing heretofore contextual elements of a site into the art itself. Indeed, it is in this kind of site-specific work that we see a contemporaneous artistic version of the New Historicist trope, an ever expanding attempt to recast context as text and to unsettle any desire to reinstitute the boundary between them.

It would be completely misguided if we did not notice that certain theatrical artists also actively seek situated engagement, understanding situatedness to be the material of their work and not only the materialism that a theater scholar finds in it. Brechtian techniques of alienation clearly extended the boundaries of the theatrical situation, as have, in different ways, movements in environmental, feminist, protest, and community theater. What becomes interesting to me, then, is how we bring the formal vocabulary for understanding site specificity in visual art history into conversation with theatrical history and a performance historiography. What can we learn from each others' preoccupations with site? And how might each others' analytic habits and medium-specific knowledges embolden each other as well as foreground the medium specificity of the spatial concepts we deploy? Does the "street" in street theater have a different valence if we think about it through the lens of a site-specific artist? Does the body in theater resonate differently when we think about it as a material akin to clay, wire, or oil paint? Conversely, does the post-Minimalist preoccupation with the receiver get a more sustained kind of attention if joined to theatrical scholarship on the role of audiences? Does the current curatorial habit of letting artists create not only displayed artworks but also engagements in the lobbies, shops, cafés, and promotional material of the museum look different to a theater historian who specializes in the analysis of "amenities?"

In many ways, a number of scholars and historians have been posing different versions of similar questions, whether a cross-disciplinary conversation between theater and the visual arts was explicitly thematized. Nick Kaye's work on site-specific art tracks a Minimalist genealogy from the visual arts to contextualize different kinds of environmental theater, building on the work of Henry Sayre and Jon Erickson.[34] A host of live-art scholars ranging from Adrian Heathfield to Amelia Jones to Rebecca Schneider to Jane Blocker have approached the body of the performer as a material, an approach that differs significantly from a theater historian's approach to "actor training." At the same time, we might wonder about forms of rapprochement that have yet to occur explicitly, say a conversation around place between New York art historian Rosalind Deutsche's *Evictions* and New York theater scholar Marvin Carlson's *Places of Performance* or another conversation that might join Patrice Pavis's mise-en-scène to fellow Frenchman Nicolas Bourriaud's *esthétique relationnelle.*[35] To focus this wider, defamiliarizing cross-disciplinary conversation, I would like to return to the opening of this essay. What does it mean to place Mierle Laderman Ukeles and her maintenance art next to a troupe like the Wooster Group and their *House/Lights*? As it happens, Kwon includes Ukeles in her disquisition on institutional critique, and in fact her decision to do so shows how earlier feminist reactions to Minimalism give the history of institutional critique an earlier and differently politicized genesis. Ukeles's maintenance performances actually accompanied photographic exhibitions of her maintenance art as a wife and mother at home, framing documentation of her dressing children, washing diapers, and cleaning the house as a brand of devalued everyday art. The *Washing Track* series showed the reliance of not only the household but also the institution of the museum on daily forms of gendered, classed, and raced labor. Ukeles thus acted as institutional critic of the museum, exposing the labor required to keep the walls of the gallery white and the phenomenological encounter with its stone steps clean. As Kwon argues, "she forced the menial domestic tasks usually associated with women—cleaning, washing, dusting, and tidying—to the level of aesthetic contemplation."[36] In the language of theater historiography, Ukeles moved "working conditions" into the territory of the mise-en-scène.

What is interesting then is how Kwon goes on to analyze the significance of work such as Ukeles within her larger attempt to give a vocabulary and specific history to the changing orientation of site-specific art, an argument that is worth quoting at length.

> [T]he site of art begins to diverge from the literal space of art, and the physical condition of a specific location recedes as the primary element in the conception of a site . . . it is rather the *techniques* and *effects* of the art institution as they circumscribe and delimit the definition, production, presentation, and dissemination of art that becomes the sites of critical intervention. Concurrent with this move toward the dematerialization of the site is the simultaneous deaestheticization (that is, withdrawal of visual pleasure) and dematerialization of the art work. Going against the grain of institutional habits and desires, and

continuing to resist the commodification of art in/for the marketplace, site-specific art adopts strategies that are either aggressively
antivisual—informational, textual, expositional, didactic—or
immaterial altogether—gestures, events or performances brack-
eted by temporal boundaries. . . . In this context, the guarantee
of a specific relationship between an art work and its site is not
based on a physical permanence of that relationship (as demanded
by Serra, for example) but rather on the recognition of its unfixed
impermanence, to be experienced as an unrepeatable and fleeting
situation.[37]

First, as we move here from a discrete notion of an art*work* to a process-
based notion of the *work* it takes to make art, I find it interesting to think
about Ukeles and this analysis in relation to the triangulated frameworks
of theater historiography. In many ways, Ukeles seems to be exposing the
"conditions of production" for visual art. She trains the attention of the
receiver away from the framed canvas or the Minimalist block in the center toward the institutional processes and material conditions required to
maintain the walls and floors that support them. As much as the attempt
to expose production resonates with what we might call Brechtian techniques of theater making, this performance also confounds theatrical
conventions for delineating its object. First, such site-specific performance
does not usually uphold the divisions of labor we find in the theater; principles that would divide actor from director from designer in the face of
work where spatial design, conception, and performed execution are credited to a single artistic intelligence. Furthermore, Ukeles's performance is
in some ways less easily located on the "performance text" portion of
theater historiography's analytic triangle. As someone trained as a sculptor
and craftsperson, Ukeles's turn to performance was an extradiegetic move
away from sculpture's diegetic form; the movements and motions of performance were very explicitly the vehicle for enabling Ukeles's "contextual
turn." In other words, what might look like a "performance text" to a performance critic was in fact an attempt to unhinge the "text" corner of the
analytic triangle, perhaps to unhinge the semiotic logic of any triangle that
would imagine even a fragile boundary between performance text, production, and reception. It seems to me quite significant that performance
is understood here, less as its own medium or text, and more as a vehicle
for exposing visual art's conditions of production and reception.

This kind of framing also informs Kwon's language of "dematerialization," a term that became ubiquitous in visual art history in conjunction
with post-Minimalist art movements. Used early on by art critic Lucy
Lippard and John Chandler, the language of dematerialization has been
used subsequently to mark the artistic preoccupation away from discrete
objects and toward situations and processes.[38] Kwon's disquisition on the

dematerialization of site in turn invokes the language of ephemerality and impermanence, reminding us of the art-historical genealogies that support Peggy Phelan's theorizing of performance's ontological ephemerality.[39] At the same time, I think it is important to ask, to whom does Ukeles's crouching, squeezing, and scrubbing appear dematerialized? By what logic is this "gesture" and its institutional critique im-material? This seems to me an important place to notice the medium-specific knowledge that supports an analysis, since it is by measuring this performance's distance from painting and sculpture that its processes come to appear antivisual and receive the dematerialized label. To another kind of theatrical eye accustomed to the durational and gestural language of stylized theater, the everyday tasks of washing might look hypermaterial; it might be read as an explicitly concrete enactment when measured within and against a theatrical medium that happens to think of durationality and embodied gesture as essential materials. The theatrical eye might also offer a different take on performance's role in enabling a contextual engagement. While breaking with the medium purity and formal integrity of painting and sculpture, I cannot help but wonder whether Ukeles found herself reckoning with the conventions and skills required of another medium, that is, a theatrical one. She may not ever have had "actor training," but did she find herself cultivating some attributes of the actor's body nonetheless? Did she develop a performing persona (or try not to)? Did she participate in bodily training, stretching, and breathing to sustain her endurance performance? Did she cultivate reflexive skills for managing her own reactions to audience involvement? In other words, by resisting the modernist definitions of the medium she inherited, Ukeles might well have found herself adopting the medium-specific definitions of a new one. The extrinsic engagement of visual art needed the intrinsic elements of theatrical performance.

Having reengaged Ukeles and Kwon through a theatrical lens, what happens when we try to reverse the lens to consider how visual art history might engage materialist theater historiography? As the book continues with case studies showing materialist semiotics in action, one of the most intriguing examples occurs in Knowles's analysis of the text, production, and reception of the Wooster Group's *House/Lights*. Starting off with "an unlocated, formalist reading," we learn that *House/Lights* places a 1964 cult lesbian bondage flick, *Olga's House of Shame*, into "productive contact" with Gertrude Stein's *Doctor Faustus Lights the Lights*, mixed together with filtered voices, bodily prosthetics, and sound and video bites drawn from *I Love Lucy, Young Frankenstein*, Esther Williams, Yiddish theater, classical ballet, and Cantonese opera.[40] Such a mix of disparate references is characteristic of the Wooster Group's oeuvre and one of the central reasons they were dubbed, by both scholars and journalists, "a postmodern theater company." That attribution, however, becomes somewhat troubled through the course of Knowles's analysis, beginning with his interest in the importance of "landscape" both to Gertrude Stein and to the Wooster Group's compositional aesthetic. He quotes Elinor Fuchs's sense of the Wooster Group's landscape-based creations of "the multi-focal scene," as well as Fuchs's argument that "landscape to Stein was wholly present to itself, simple and un-anxiety-provoking to the spectator."[41] Significantly, this inherited sense of landscape offers its own kind of hermetic encounter, creating in Peter Sellars's words, "a classical repose . . . beneath the busy surface level."[42] Whether appearing in pastoral depictions of the natural or later in Steinian and Wooster Group creations of a busier but wholly present encounter, the impulses toward landscape are in fact not to be confused with the impulses toward site specificity. Indeed, the refusal of the referential and material contingencies of the world outside the depiction is part of its signature. When Kate Valk acknowledges that the Stein "landscape is as abstract as the landscapes we make," it provides Knowles with a vehicle for attributing the modernist label to the Wooster Group instead: "it is the very abstraction of Stein's landscapes—their lack of social referent—that made her work recruitable for high-modernist formalism."[43] What might appear then to be postmodern multireferentiality turns out to be modernist a-referentiality instead. Here is a place where different concepts of space collide, paradoxically where the classically, antidurational, all-at-once encounter of visual art appears in a theater space that seeks not to engage the "situatedness" of theater's extended hypercontextuality. Despite the shared use of a spatial metaphor, to create a landscape is not to engage a social situation. Within this frame, the Wooster Group's *House/Lights* has far less kinship with the site-specific performances of Mierle Laderman Ukeles and far more kinship with the wholly present encounters and internally critical ambitions of modernist painting.

Once we begin to think of the Wooster Group's work within the formalist, asocial, wholly "present" discourse of modernist painting, the intervention of Knowles's materialist analysis of the group is brought into higher relief. In interviews, Elizabeth Le Compte and Kate Valk resist the idea that there is anything iconically "American" about their work, even as it is marketed as the quintessential example of an American avant-garde in the publicity of all their tours. In reacting to the referential readings some give to their work, Le Compte firmly recircumscribes its parameters, saying that it is a theater made only from "who we were in the room."[44] "They replied that they didn't think of themselves has having . . . even a New York orientation, but thought of themselves as quite specifically located in Manhattan, and more particularly lower Manhattan."[45] That lower Manhattan is, of course, specifically SoHo (South of Houston), a "location" that is most notable for transforming from an artists' community to a high-end district of expensive lofts and boutiques. Analyzing SoHo tourist guides, Knowles finds that such "amenities" also claim the Wooster Group as part of the SoHo location, advertising the group's experimental cult status as part and parcel of its tourist appeal.[46] Here is a materialist framing of the Wooster Group unanticipated by the Wooster Group themselves, orienting from the people "in the room" to new "exteriors" that suggest their enmeshment within an expanded site of economic and real estate development. The noncontingent, a priori understanding of the Wooster Group space becomes highly contingent, fettered by an extension of its spatial parameters. The cheekiness of Knowles's analysis then lies in his decision to locate a theater company that seeks not to be locatable.

Locating Location

Throughout this essay I have tried to highlight the disciplinarity and medium specificity of what space can mean for performance historiography. As performance historiographers draw from methods in a variety of disciplines, our cross-disciplinary engagements and medium-impure experiments might be more medium specific than we realize. The forms that we find ourselves historicizing are embedded in medium-specific genealogies that do not only differ in "content" but also in form. Such differences in form affect how we understand the parameters of words such as "space," "site," and "location," fretted as such terms are with implicit assumptions about what is interior and exterior to an art object. In the end, a located historiography in performance means coming to terms with different ways of locating location. It means contending with the degree to which an analysis of materials might differ from a materialist analysis and to which the situated art event may or may not seek to engage its context. It means thinking about the degree to which certain projects refuse a boundary between art and situation and the degree to which others adamantly seek to uphold it. It also means deciding on one's role as a scholar of such practices and what conceptual boundaries and frames we bring with us when we analyze. It means deciding whether we understand the materialist critic's job to lie in the locating of another context unanticipated by the contextualist gesture, another exterior to even the most externally engaged art or performance practice. It means tracking the vacillation of spatial concepts between different registers of historiographical understanding—as object or as tool, as a priori knowledge that precedes experience or as posteriori knowledge that derives from it. Meanwhile, the way we conceive background and foreground, art and apparatus, text and context, inside and outside, vary with medium-specific histories and disciplinary locations. If, as Fried said, contending with theatricality means contending with forms where "everything counts," a locational historiography of performance requires vigilance about how we interpret, categorize, and sometimes implicitly circumscribe that "everything."

Notes

"When 'Everything Counts': Experimental Performance and Performance Historiography" was originally published in *Representing the Past: Essays in Performance and Historiography*, ed. Charlotte Canning and Thomas Postlewait, 240–60 (Des Moines: Iowa University Press, 2010).

1. Thomas Postlewait and Bruce A. McConachie, eds., *Interpreting the Theatrical Past: Essays in the Historiography of Performance* (Iowa City: University of Iowa Press, 1989).

2. Shannon Jackson, *Professing Performance: Theater in the Academy from Philology to Performativity* (Cambridge: Cambridge University Press, 2004).

3. Ric Knowles, *Reading the Material Theater* (Cambridge: Cambridge University Press, 2004); Miwon Kwon, *One Place after Another: Site-Specific Art and Locational Identity* (Cambridge, MA: MIT Press, 2002).

4. Louis O. Mink, Brian Fay, Eugene O. Golob, and Richard T. Vann, *Historical Understanding* (Ithaca, NY: Cornell University Press, 1987), 205.

5. Donna Haraway, "Situated Knowledges: The Science Question in Feminism and the Privilege of Partial Perspective," in *Simians, Cyborgs and Women: The Reinvention of Nature* (New York: Routledge, 1991), 183–202.

6. See, e.g., Brander Matthews, *The Development of the Drama* (New York: C. Scribner's Sons, 1903).

7. See Shelley Arlen, ed., *The Cambridge Ritualists: An Annotated Bibliography of the Works by and about Jane Ellen Harrison, Gilbert Murray, Francis M. Cornford, and Arthur Bernard Cook* (Metuchen, NJ: Scarecrow Press, 1990).

8. See, e.g., E. K. Chambers, *The Medieval Stage* (London: Oxford University Press, 1903); Richard Southern, *The Medieval Theater in the Round: A Study of the Staging of the Castle of Perseverance and Related Matters*, 2nd ed. (London: Faber, 1975); Richard Beadle, ed., *The Cambridge Companion to Medieval English Theater* (Cambridge: Cambridge University Press, 1994); A. M. Nagler, *Theater Festivals of the Medici, 1539–1637*, trans. George Hickenlooper (New Haven, CT: Yale University Press, 1964); and Ronald W. Vince, *Renaissance Theater: A Historiographical Handbook* (Westport, CT: Greenwood Press, 1984).

9. See Wisner Payne Kinne, *George Pierce Baker and the American Theater* (Cambridge, MA: Harvard University Press, 1954); Susan Harris Smith, *American Drama: The Bastard Art* (Cambridge: Cambridge University Press, 1997); and Jackson, *Professing Performance*, 40–78.

10. Benedetto Croce, *Guide to Aesthetics/Breviario di estetica* (South Bend, IN: Regnery/Gateway, [1965] 1979); Benedetto Croce, Remo Bodei, and Hiroko Fudemoto, *Breviary of Aesthetics: Four Lectures* (Toronto: University of Toronto Press, 2007); Joel Elias Spingarn, *Creative Criticism and Other Essays* (New York: Harcourt, Brace, 1931), 31; noted also in Marvin A. Carlson, *Theories of the Theater: A Historical and Critical Survey from the Greeks to the Present*, expanded ed. (Ithaca, NY: Cornell University Press, 1993), 312.

11. Knowles, *Reading the Material Theater*, 11.

12. Knowles, *Reading the Material Theater*, 12. See also Keir Elam, *The Semiotics of Theater and Drama* (London: Methuen, 1980); Patrice Pavis, *Languages of the Stage: Essays in the Semiology of the Theater* (New York:

Performing Arts Journal Publications, 1982); Marco De Marinis, *The Semiotics of Performance* (Bloomington: Indiana University Press, 1993); Michael Quinn, *The Semiotic Stage: Prague School Theater Theory* (New York: Peter Lang, 1995); André Helbo, *Les mots et les gestes* (Lille, France: Presses universitaires de Lille, 1983); Marvin A. Carlson, *Places of Performance: The Semiotics of Theater Architecture* (Ithaca, NY: Cornell University Press, 1989); and Erika Fischer-Lichte, *Semiotics of Theater* (Bloomington: Indiana University Press, 1992).

13. Stephen Greenblatt and Giles B. Gunn, *Redrawing the Boundaries: The Transformation of English and American Literary Studies* (New York: Modern Language Association of America, 1992).

14. Jonathan Dollimore and Alan Sinfield, *Political Shakespeare: New Essays in Cultural Materialism* (Manchester: Manchester University Press, 1985) ix; quoted in Knowles, *Reading the Material Theater*, 12–14. Parentheses added by Knowles.

15. Jeffrey Masten, Peter Stallybrass, and Nancy Vickers, *Language Machines: Technologies of Literary and Cultural Production: Essays from the English Institute* (New York: Routledge, 1997); Jeffrey Masten, *Textual Intercourse: Collaboration, Authorship, and Sexualities in Renaissance Drama* (Cambridge: Cambridge University Press, 1997); Meredith L. McGill, *American Literature and the Culture of Reprinting, 1834–1853* (Philadelphia: University of Pennsylvania Press, 2003).

16. Stuart Hall, "Encoding, Decoding," in *The Cultural Studies Reader*, ed. Simon During (New York: Routledge, 1999), 507–17.

17. Knowles, *Reading the Material Theater*, 19.

18. Quoted in Knowles, *Reading the Material Theater*, 19.

19. Knowles, *Reading the Material Theater*, 19.

20. Knowles, *Reading the Material Theater*, 12.

21. Kwon, *One Place after Another*, 1.

22. Kwon, *One Place after Another*, 2.

23. See, e.g., Hal Foster, *The Return of the Real: The Avant-Garde at the End of the Century* (Cambridge, MA: MIT Press, 1996); T. J. Clark, *Farewell to an Idea: Episodes from a History of Modernism* (New Haven, CT: Yale University Press, 1999); Rosalind E. Krauss and Marcel Broodthaers, *A Voyage on the North Sea: Art in the Age of the Post-Medium Condition* (New York: Thames and Hudson, 2000); B. H. D. Buchloh, *Neo-Avantgarde and Culture Industry: Essays on European and American Art from 1955 to 1975* (Cambridge, MA: MIT Press, 2000); Amelia Jones, *Body Art/Performing the Subject* (Minneapolis: University of Minnesota Press, 1998); Jane Blocker, *What the Body Cost: Desire, History, and Performance* (Minneapolis: University of Minnesota Press, 2004); Rebecca Schneider, *The Explicit Body in Performance* (London: Routledge, 1997); and Adrian Heathfield, ed., *Live: Art and Performance* (New York: Tate Publishing, 2004).

24. Donald Judd, "Specific Objects," in *Donald Judd: Complete Writings 1959–1975* (Halifax: Press of the Nova Scotia College of Art and Design, in association with New York University Press, 1975), 181–82.

25. Judd, "Specific Objects," 184.

26. Judd, "Specific Objects," 183–84.

27. Gotthold Ephraim Lessing and Irving Stone, *Laocoön: An Essay upon the Limits of Painting and Poetry* (New York: Noonday Press, 1957); Joshua Reynolds, *Discourses on Art* (New Haven, CT: Published for the Paul Mellon Centre for Studies in British Art [London] by Yale University Press, 1975).

28. Clement Greenberg, "Modernist Painting," in *The New Art: A Critical Anthology*, ed. Gregory Battcock (New York: E. P. Dutton, 1973), 68–69.

29. Michael Fried, "Three American Painters, Kenneth Noland, Jules Olitski, Frank Stella: Fogg Art Museum, 21 April–30 May 1965," in *Art and Objecthood: Essays and Reviews* (Chicago: University of Chicago Press, 1998), 215.

30. Michael Fried, "Art and Objecthood," *Artforum* 5 (1967): 56.

31. Kwon, *One Place after Another*, 12.

32. Donald Judd, "Specific Objects," in *Donald Judd: Complete Writings, 1959–1975* (Halifax: Press of the Nova Scotia College of Art and Design, in association with New York University Press, 1975), 183.

33. Michael Fried, "Art and Objecthood," *Artforum* 5 (1967): 56.

34. Nick Kaye, *Site-Specific Art: Performance, Place, and Documentation* (London: Routledge, 2000); Henry M. Sayre, *The Object of Performance: The American Avant-Garde since 1970* (Chicago: University of Chicago Press, 1989); Jon Erickson, *The Fate of the Object: From Modern Object to Postmodern Sign in Performance, Art, and Poetry* (Ann Arbor: University of Michigan Press, 1995).

35. Rosalyn Deutsche, *Evictions: Art and Spatial Politics* (Cambridge, MA: MIT Press, 1996); Patrice Pavis, *La mise en scène contemporaine: Origines, tendances, perspectives* (Paris: A. Colin, 2007); Nicolas Bourriaud, *Relational Aesthetics*, trans. Simon Pleasance and Fronza Woods (Dijon, France: Les Presses du réel, 2002).

36. Kwon, *One Place after Another*, 23.

37. Kwon, *One Place after Another*, 19–24. Emphasis in original.

38. John Chandler and Lucy Lippard, "The Dematerialization of Art," *Art International*, February 20, 1968, 31–36.

39. Peggy Phelan, *Unmarked: The Politics of Performance* (London: Routledge, 1996).

40. Knowles, *Reading the Material Theater*, 148, 149.

41. Knowles, *Reading the Material Theater*, 152, 153; quoting Elinor Fuchs, "Another Version of Pastoral," in *The Death of Character: Perspectives on Theater after Modernism* (Bloomington: Indiana University Press, 1996), 92, 95.

42. Knowles, *Reading the Material Theater*, 149.

43. Knowles, *Reading the Material Theater*, 152.

44. Robert Coe, "Making Two Lives and a Trilogy," *Village Voice*, December 11, 1978; quoted in Knowles, *Reading the Material Theater*, 155.

45. Knowles, *Reading the Material Theater*, 159.

46. Knowles, *Reading the Material Theater*, 155.

Chapter 5

Resist Singularity

That may sound like an evasion. If the question under discussion is asking for a single direction and a plan of action, a stand and a silver bullet, it partly is. To "resist singularity" has the ring of poststructuralist relativism, the now clichéd way that many seem to have evaded action and avoided taking any kind of a stand.

I will admit that my interest in developing a formula for resisting singularity is indebted to poststructuralist thought. But the version I want to offer is one that itself resists the shibboleths and pat relativisms that have reduced poststructuralism to easy one-liners. And certainly, I am not the first to notice that poststructuralism's call for radical openness occasionally has manifested itself in a closedness to several kinds of scholarly practice. To "resist singularity" in one's scholarship, conception of theater, and conception of history means learning to value varieties of thinking that you do not share and (even more to the point) varieties of practice in which you do not excel. By valuing, I mean more than tolerating but allowing that difference to be both a source of intellectual defamiliarization and a means of crafting multiple lines of cross-disciplinary affiliation on behalf of a provisional, critical collectivity. While resisting singularity does not have the shape of a silver bullet, while it proceeds in more than one direction, it is to my mind a plan of action and also a way of taking a stand.

The idea that theater history has to be brought into the twentieth-first century obviously betrays anxiety about its continued relevance, though the assumption that the contributors will have plans to offer suggests that there is hope. Of course there is something about this kind of reflection that has been pervasive lately as variously located scholars speculate on the interdisciplinary, theoretical, and occupational future of humanities teaching. In a recent issue of the art history journal *October*, for instance, similar kinds of questions were asked about that discipline. Several scholars and artists in the field of visual art—Rosalind Krauss, Hal Foster, Benjamin Buchloh, David Joselit, Andrea Fraser, Martha Rosler, Richard Serra, and more—were invited to speculate on the relevance of "our original project."[1] The editor of that special issue, George (no Pierce) Baker, gave it a less than cheery title—"Obsolescence," but the bleakness of the idea of an obsolescent field received a partial Benjaminian recovery. Isn't there, Baker asked, something potentially resistant in the "outmoded?" As theater reconciles itself to new presentational media—whether "film" in the twentieth century or "new media" in the twentieth-first—Walter Benjamin's decision to see a liberating potential in the obsolescent machinery of the past has and continues to be important for theater and its cumbersomely industrial technologies. The same might be said not only for theater as a form but also for theater history as a scholarly practice. Indeed, my own reservations about *auras* notwithstanding, I think that there is something useful for us in the challenge of Benjamin's angel of history to models of progress, including models of scholarly progress.[2] Benjamin's articulation of the dynamic copresence of past, present, and future forces us to consider the historical residue that clings to calls for the future, as well as the capacity of history luminously to erupt and relocate our definitions of the contemporary. My recent sense of what it means currently to "profess performance" has been informed by an excavation of our multifarious disciplinary histories.[3] Inspired by the notion that our perceptions of what constitutes the past— and what the future—are shakily dependent on which way the angel turns, I have been interested in concretizing different ways of thinking about temporal enmeshment and temporal movement. That is, I am interested in how disciplinary pasts and disciplinary futures can be saturated with each other at one moment and trade places in the next.

In what follows, I offer a few ways of conceiving the resistance to singularity. Whether articulated in methodological, disciplinary, institutional, or professional terms, I consider what it means both to value multiplicity and to imagine the past and future of the field in intimate coimbrication. Throughout I will also be working with the idea that theater history is in fact already in the twentieth-first century. Since we can all produce lists of provocative scholars who currently publish under the banner of theater history, we could say that theater history is here as long as such people keep writing. But I also agree that it is important to come to grips with what their research means, what their similarities and differences signify, and what histories and hopes are instantiated with each sentence that they write today.

Certainly one way of orienting disciplinary friction over the practice of theater history has to do with contentions over methodology. What counts as an argument? What kind of work must be done to support it? What is rigor? What is research? What is the difference between a theory and a proof, between a close reconstruction and a close reading? Are these various practices compatible with each other? If some of us make use of archives, others fieldwork, others textual explication, and others theoretical excavation, can we constitute even a provisional collectivity from our varied membership?

Debates over appropriate methodology are neither new nor exclusive to the field of theater history. Indeed, it is the not-newness of the argument and its relation to other fields that help to defamiliarize the terms of the debate. Within the American Society for Theatre Research constituency— along with other historical fields—recent methodological controversy often revolves around a presumed opposition between theory and history. Depending on training or disposition, various constituencies will criticize the former as jargon-infused hot air and the latter as flat-footed fact collecting. Others, including me, will attempt to argue against the opposition, though how to take that argument farther than a generalized distaste for binary thinking often remains unclear. This is where a consideration of the history of theater history—as well as the history of other humanities fields—provides at least one way of recasting the discussion. As I and others previously have argued, the consolidation of theater as a scholarly field occurred in the early twentieth century when the empirically rigorous, contextualizing practices of philology offered humanities professors a means of defining and evaluating their own professional expertise.[4] The reaction to this intellectual trend was mixed as disgruntled students, belles lettres faculty, and concerned citizens decried the ruination of the arts and humanities by the historical formulas, vocabularies, and irrelevant musings of self-important professional intellectuals. In other words, this was a moment when the abstract beginnings of our field's fact collecting sounded to many like jargon-infused hot air. A century of theater history's routinization and normalization now obscures the radical intellectual shift that its practices once signaled, as well as its earlier perception as a fashionable, self-indulgent threat to traditional intellectualism. History sounds a whole lot like theory from the perspective of this disciplinary genealogy.

To use the term "genealogy" to characterize this puzzle is obviously indebted to Michel Foucault. His Nietzschean inspired counter to historical models of "unbroken continuity" is compatible with, if not equal to, Benjamin's counter to historical progress.[5] That Foucault had earlier critiqued the formation of knowledge by arguing that "the non-unity of discourse" had to be a principal operating assumption in the study of disciplinarity further supports his relevance to our own questions about the field.[6] To consider genealogies of the field is to "maintain passing events in their proper dispersion"; it "is to identify the accidents, the minute derivations—or conversely the complete reversals—the errors, the false appraisals, and the faulty calculations that gave birth to those things that continue to exist and have value for us."[7] By extension, an excavation of theater history's practices is an examination of its many references and its shaky self-oppositions, requiring an awareness of their "non-identity through time, the break produced in them, the internal discontinuity that suspends their permanence"[8] The nonidentity through time of the "theory-history" opposition exposes one of those discontinuous puzzles, a terminological polarization whose permanence is worth suspending. In such discontinuity we see how a feared or feted "future" (e.g., theory) and a discredited or feted past (e.g., history) can be both enmeshed with each other and to trade places. To "resist singularity" in the history of theater, as well as the history of theater history, is thus also about recognizing a methodological heterogeneity that has always been there.

If Foucault's critique of knowledge involved a critique of the places where knowledges are constructed, then the valuing of disciplinary difference also means incorporating a recognition of institutional variety, the very different configurations of departments, schools, journals, societies, and responsibilities that produce and are produced by our knowledge categories. Over the last two decades, the knowledge formation "performance studies" has been offered as a way of resisting singularity in our conceptions of theater history. As someone who both has a doctorate in performance studies and helps to run a doctoral program under that banner, I have been in the business of taking up and extending such an offer. I think that it is erroneous, however, to prescribe one kind of institutional practice for every university. When, in the early 1990s, an offer of intellectual expansion turned into an institutional prescription—"theater departments should become performance studies department"—that kind of prescription occurred. Meanwhile, recent discussions over which programs are and are *not* allowed to count as performance studies show how very singular a vision of intellectual multiplicity can actually be.

I think that living as a scholar of theater and performance in the twentieth-first century will involve a loosening of anxieties, prescriptions, and oppositions around the t-word and the p-word. Oppositions between theater and performance, between "theater history" and "performance studies," between theatricality and performativity, also have a discontinuous history and are by no means equivalent to each other. There might be no better way to untie those terminological knots than to recognize and value the institutional heterogeneity that supports scholars working under these and related labels. Rather than neat oppositions, rather than fights over which term plays umbrella to whom, our interdiscipline is better characterized as a collection of practices that bear more and less relationship to each other, depending on person, context, topic, and approach. The contributors to *Theater Survey* may work from several different kinds of departments—as do the contributors to the *Drama Review*. *Text and Performance Quarterly* may be just as likely to publish a study of Surrealist performance as *Theater Journal*. The unit on "puppetry" might be just as likely to appear on the "Introduction to Theater" syllabus as on the "Introduction to Performance Studies" syllabus. And when categorical divisions between method or topic do seem relevant, those categories do not seem to confine the output of particular individuals who themselves take up and set aside intellectual affiliations with each project, performance, and publication.

   The theme of affiliation anticipates the last register that I would like to consider, the professional—and preprofessional—heterogeneity of our field's membership. Quite often, the much-invoked opposition between theory and practice confuses our understanding of the professional entanglements we all share and perpetuate. Whether historians, performers, directors, activists, educators, theorists, designers, or administrators, the circumstances of our employment call for an investment in certain standards of professional practice. Often, however, our discipline's habit is to use the terms "professional" and "practitioner" to characterize the work of artmakers. To enter "the life of the mind," however, is not to exit from the professional world. Nor does it mean that professors are allowed to ignore our enmeshment in the postgraduate occupational anxieties of all our students. When Barbara and John Ehrenreich located "college professors" in their critique of the professional managerial class, they isolated the enmeshment of "salaried mental workers" in the indirect reproduction of capitalist relations.[9] They argued that it saturated the occupational lives of academics of both the left and the right who might otherwise imagine themselves as outside careerist domains. Whether everyone accepts all aspects of the Marxist critique behind this insight, it is nevertheless a vehicle for loosening the strict polarizations and neat equivalences we often draw among different sets of skills. Graduate students in MFA programs and graduate students in PhD programs are both entering professional domains. Theater undergraduates who become actors enter a professional world, and so do those who become management consultants or Green Party campaign managers or liberal arts professors. Performers who try to work on Broadway may have different professional lives from those who try to get Stove-Top stuffing commercials. Performers who try to work at LaMama or P.S. 122 may have different professional lives from both. Some may try for all three; others may ultimately end up trying for the PhD. Meanwhile, theater directors who work on campuses and theater directors who work at equity houses may both be "practitioners," but their professional risks and obligations differ. Throughout, the critical and curricular object of "theater history" might play different imaginative and pragmatic roles for students and teachers who try to adapt its artistic content, research practices, and writing requirements into skills for a personal future. This is a kind of professional heterogeneity that can be neither strictly polarized nor strictly equated. But it is the shared ground on which a provisional critical community can be constructed. It is also the unsettling source of a professional defamiliarization that will be both personal and perpetual. I think that the trick is to allow that defamiliarization to propel self-reflexivity rather than a self-interested call for the silver bullet that you happen to own.
   Disciplinary friction often derives from basic differences in what each of us is good at doing. Some struggle with the idea of using Foucault; some struggle with the idea of using a finding aid. Some are more comfortable

dealing with cubic feet at the library, others with linear feet at the scene shop. Some can accept the idea of "oral history" but cannot stand the idea of conducting multiple interviews with informants who aren't always nice. Some can accept the idea of "theory" but cannot stand the idea of conducting multiple readings of texts that aren't always clear.

Disciplinary variety is something that seems particularly heightened in the academic history of theater and its related disciplines. As such, it is both a burden and an opportunity, an edginess that might both renew and confound the analysis of the obsolescent. To resist singularity seems to be both the challenge and necessity of a field that cannot possibly disavow its methodological, institutional, and professional heterogeneity. As such, this critical element of our discontinuous past will be an integral part of any future that we hope to invent.

Notes

"Resist Singularity" was originally published in "What is the Single Most Important Thing We Can Do to Bring Theatre History into the New Millennium?" edited by Jody Enders, special issue, *Theatre Survey* 45, no. 2 (2004): 241–46.

1. The editors, introduction to "Obsolescence," special issue, *October* 100 (Spring 2002): 3.

2. Walter Benjamin, *Illuminations: Essays and Reflections*, ed. Hannah Arendt, trans. Harry Zohn (New York: Schocken, 1968).

3. Shannon Jackson, *Professing Performance: Theater in the Academy from Philology to Performativity* (Cambridge: Cambridge University Press, 2004).

4. See, e.g., Jackson, "Institutions and Performance," in *Professing Performance*, 40–78; and Joseph Roach, "Reconstructing Theater/History," *Theater Topics* 9, no. 1 (March 1999): 3–10. See studies such as Gerald Graff, *Professing Literature: An Institutional History* (Chicago: University of Chicago Press, 1987), for the effects of philology on literary study.

5. Michel Foucault, *Language, Counter-Memory, Practice*, ed. Donald Bouchard, trans. Donald Bouchard and Sherry Simon (Ithaca, NY: Cornell University Press, 1977), 146.

6. Michel Foucault, *The Archaeology of Knowledge*, trans. A. M. Sheridan Smith (New York: Pantheon Books, 1972), 32.

7. Foucault, *Language, Counter-Memory, Practice*, 146.

8. Foucault, *Archaeology of Knowledge*, 33.

9. Barbara Ehrenreich and John Ehrenreich, "The Professional-Managerial Class," in *Between Labor and Capital*, ed. Pat Walker (Montreal: Black Rose Press, 1979), 5–45.

Chapter 6

Rhetoric in Ruins

Performing Literature and Performance Studies

> The problem that students and teachers face is thus not
> so much the problem of what to believe as the problem of
> what kind of analysis of institutions will allow any belief to
> count for anything at all.
>
> —Bill Readings, *The University in Ruins*

The posthumously published *The University in Ruins* was Bill Readings's
attempt to reflect on the university's position as a social institution and an
occupant of an unstable zone in the increasingly globalized world of higher
education. To reflect on the university in this way meant focusing one's
attention less on the content and micromoves within "the culture wars" of
the 1990s and more on analyzing the social, cultural, and institutional status
of those debates themselves. Readings's book and other works have been
helpful in my own attempts to come to terms with the institutional place
of performance studies in higher education now.[1] My charge in this essay
is a little more precise for the purposes of this collection; it is to give both
local and abstract accounts of some different kinds of performance studies pedagogy that developed in the United States throughout the twentieth
century, practices signified by the gently mocked term "oral interpretation"
whose history differs from the histories of performance studies that are most
often told. In coming to terms with oral interpretation—what some call the
"Northwestern tradition" of American performance studies education, or
with what I and others have called the "NCA tradition"—I will be tracking
a rhetorical genealogy that simultaneously requires a rhetorical stance on
itself. Indeed, it might well be this rhetorical stance—one that emphasizes
not only *what* is valued in a field but *how* we do our valuing—that is the
most vital element of the NCA tradition. Moreover, this emphasis on rhetorical performance might well be one particularly vitalizing element offered by
performance studies to what Readings called "a posthistorical university"
more generally, vitalizing precisely because it feels itself to be dying.

Before recounting a history of oral interpretation as it changed and expanded in the twentieth century, a few notes about Bill Readings's argument might be necessary to suggest how the notion of "ruins" could signify the erosion of belief in performance studies even as it simultaneously renews a commitment to the field. Readings's analysis offered its own take on an oft-recounted but rarely internalized history of the academic profession—tracking its transforming processes of self-legitimation from a "Kantian University of Reason" to a "Humboldtian University of Culture," and now to the technobureaucratic "University of Excellence" with which universities across the globe are becoming increasingly familiar. To academics used to thinking of themselves as perpetual "resisters" of institutional structures, his arguments were soberingly inconvenient. Some of his most inconvenient claims were directed at a late twentieth-century intellectual climate in the humanities that celebrated "interdisciplinarity," fought the "culture wars," propelled the "rise of theory," and gathered around journals, centers, and occasionally societies that were affiliated, with varying degrees of commitment, with something called "cultural studies." While Readings's book was in sympathy with these and other movements that sought to diversify university curricula, he simultaneously noticed other unannounced premises and unintended consequences of their arguments. Most generally and reductively, Readings noticed the ways that such debates and transformations were, not so much resistant to the technobureaucratic evolution of the overly managed university, but actually a symptom and, occasionally, a propeller of such administrative consolidation. As he and people like John Guillory noticed, the so-called culture wars of the 1990s became as heated as they did precisely because a notion of culture had begun to matter less and less in United States society. Furthermore, if the Humboldtian notion of culture—in both its conservative and progressive orientations—was being eroded by technobureaucracy, then cultural studies' critique of culture only helped that process along. Indeed, Readings's argument was that a new University of Excellence was supported in large part by a process of "dereferentialization," one where there ceased to be any galvanizing principle or value beyond the leveling reductions of administrative accounting. While the exact implications of Readings's argument have been debated in several quarters, it has provided a set of questions that remain provocative and vexing for anyone trying to understand an interdisciplinary discipline. At the very least, they ask us to think about how performance studies' own critiques of culture—however revolutionary or well intended they might have felt—might well be disconcertingly compatible with performance's techno-bureaucratization as a discipline. Perhaps all those claims about performance studies as an "antidiscipline"—claims that certainly enticed my graduate student self in the 1990s—were actually symptoms of the dereferentializing impulses of a bureaucratic imaginary? Indeed, the erosion of intellectual standards for assessing a discipline unintentionally could allow accounting standards of assessment to enter in their place.

Readings's argument should obviously be important to a collection such as *Contesting Performance* that seeks to combat the exclusively "Americanized" story of the rise of performance studies. While, to my mind, the term "techno-bureaucracy" was undertheorized in Readings's book, not always making distinctions between antigovernmental capitalist or progovernment socialist versions of "bureaucracy," it does give us a way of viewing some of the more insidious elements of academic employment right now—whether the ideology of the "bottom line" that animates more universities in the United States or the "Research Assessment Exercises" endured by academics in the United Kingdom, Australia, New Zealand, and Singapore. I would also submit that there is a particular generational consciousness exemplified in Readings's book, one that is symptomatic of many of us who were trained in the academy after its so-called revolutions. There is something about being trained in the space of erosion that seems to require an unusual amount of metadisciplinary reflection, something that academics used to do most often just before retirement. The difference now is not only that metareflectors are getting younger (not just me, but also the editors of this collection) but also that a kind of critical suspicion overrides any articulation of such histories. Ours is a generation who, in Marquard Smith's terms, is

> too young for punk and should have been too old for raves, their formative years lived with the threat of nuclear war at the forefronts of their nihilistic minds, with sexualities fashioned in a climate gripped by the fear of AIDS, and a political consciousness created wholly within and in opposition to the Thatcher-Reagan nexus, and thus attuned to both the consequences and pointlessness of organized politics.[2]

The impulse to reflect about the profession does not come then from the place it usually does, the place of nostalgia for what the university was and the lament over what it has become. It is hard to be nostalgic if you cannot even pretend to claim access to a better Boomer past, whether "better" is a university of the highest and noblest aspiration, or "better" is the activist university of a 1968 protest culture. Unable to narrate with the exquisite pain and pleasure of someone who was *there before now*, the task for many of us is to explain performance studies without ever having known anything else and to come to terms with what interdisciplinarity must be without really having known what a discipline was.

The narration of a rhetorical tradition of performance studies in the United States thus necessarily takes place within this awkward space of partial recall. But there is also something uncanny about the fact that this tradition was so often "unstoried," to quote Paul Edwards, even in the self-conscious debates about performance studies in the 1990s in the United States.[3] It is thus strange to be writing this story of a US gene-alogy in a book that simultaneously seeks to combat the Americanized story of the rise of performance studies. Yet if we understand globaliza-tion to be wrapped up simultaneously with something that we loosely call Americanization and if, furthermore, we understand the current state of universities across the globe to exist in a determining relationship with processes of Americanization, of which Readings's "techno-bureaucatic University of Excellence" is an example, then I think that we need also to think about how US American disciplines and universities have also been Americanized. Indeed, paradoxical as it may seem, the internal regional and disciplinary debates about the "two" strains of performance studies themselves exemplify the process of Americanization. The rhe-torical genealogy of performance studies, including and especially its obfuscation, is itself a demonstration of Americanization in action in the United States.

What Is Oral Interpretation? A Brief History

Answering the question "What is oral interpretation" might be just as hard as answering "What is performance studies?" In this section I want to offer a brief representation of the histories and experiences that collect around this rhetorical genealogy.[4] At the grandest, most Humboldtian level—one where the myopias of Western intellectual histories are perpetuated, even when they are never remembered very deeply—we can position rhetorical performance studies in the longest of classical genealogies, one that con-nects the act of orally performing a narrative to Western ancient traditions that are both rhetorical and poetic. This is to remember the Platonic and Aristotelian debates about the *rhetor's* social function, techniques, and effects. This is to remember that the field of rhetoric has been historically linked to the goals of persuasion, as well as to an analytic sensibility that understands how intimately the audience participates in the constitution of the *rhetor's* expression. The more contemporary habit of understand-ing knowledge as socially constructed and as discursively produced is of course indebted to a longer strain of rhetorical thinking that has gone in and out of favor with changing intellectual trends. Meanwhile, another genealogy of rhetorical performance studies begins later but is still long, and it is the one that coincides with concept of "literature" as a category. As Paul Edwards rightly points out, the oral interpretation of literature as it became known in the nineteenth and twentieth centuries needed a con-cept of literature to become itself.[5] As Margaret Robb has told the story, the oral interpretation of literature descended from a certain disciplinary

Fig. 3. The Wooster Group's *Point Judith (an epilogue)*, 1979, directed by Elizabeth LeCompte. *Left to right*, Matthew Hansell, Libby Howes, and Spalding Gray. Photograph copyright Nancy Campbell.

moment at the turn of the twentieth century when the humanities fields that we now know as philosophy, literature, classics, or art history began to take distinct form.[6] Coincident with what historians of the university call the transition from a classical to a vernacular curriculum, the study of literature became a distinct field that sought professional legitimation. Moving from the study of Shakespeare and classical texts to the inclusion of novels and then contemporary poetry, the field of literary studies formed. At the time of this syllabification, however, other elements of the nineteenth-century curriculum were gradually discarded or syphoned off to fields other than the literary. One of those elements was oral argumentation and performance, as both a form of "public speaking" and as a hermeneutic form of oral poetics.

As I have argued elsewhere, the performing professor was gradually defined as the opposite of what a growing literary professoriate felt itself to be or felt that it needed to be to secure professional legitimacy for literary inquiry.[7] As various groups formed and broke with each other in the history of the professionalization of literary studies—forming and reforming organizations like the Modern Language Association and National Council of the Teachers of English (NCTE)—teachers of oral performance and public speaking attached and detached themselves at various moments. As Paul Edwards describes it, one crucial moment occurred in 1914 when a small group of public-speaking teachers, marginalized under "Oral

English" within the NCTE, "decided to remain in a Chicago hotel until they could come up with a better idea. They emerged as charter members of the National Association of Academic Teachers of Public Speaking."[8] This is the organization that relaunched the academic fields of rhetoric and speech communication as they are variously known in the United States today, eventually changing its name to the Speech Communication Association and most recently to the National Communication Association. And it is within this organization that the oral interpretation of literature would find its new home, casting off its delegitimized and feminized associations with elocution and maintaining departmental wings and professional focus groups in the performance of literature, renamed the Interpretation Division in 1970 and renamed again as the Performance Studies Division in 1991. Departments around the United States maintained this strain of the rhetoric and speech, hiring and reproducing curricula in the land-grant and state colleges that supported the field of communication studies most actively. Along the way, these professors of the oral interpretation of literature had to explain themselves continually to an increasingly "scientizing" field of communication studies, arguing for the importance of literature to communication studies colleagues who were simultaneously developing the subfields in "corporate communication" and "organizational behavior." When NCA changed the name of its Interpretation Division to Performance Studies, those communication studies departments—from North Carolina to Louisiana to Texas to Arizona to California to Minnesota to Illinois to Maine—followed suit. A performance studies curriculum existed and exists within schools of speech or departments of speech communication in these and other states around the country. Northwestern University was one of the only places where an entire department—rather than a departmental wing—had been devoted to interpretation, and hence its change to Performance Studies received the most attention, prompting some erroneously to assume that rhetorical performance studies was only a "Northwestern" thing rather than a part of a national scholarly apparatus that had been in existence since 1914.

The rhetorical performance studies genealogy plots a slightly different story within the larger and uneven transitions from Humboldtian Universities of Culture to a techno-bureaucratic Universities of Excellence. If the American story of performance studies more often centers on the East Coast, then theater was the "high cultural" site from which it claimed to be breaking. One way of telling this story institutionally is to see performance studies practitioners questioning the genre conventions and models of culture inherited from traditional disciplines of drama and theater. To recount the genealogy of rhetorical performance studies, on the other hand, is to see similar and different connections to these intellectual trends and disciplinary dismantlings of the late twentieth century. Oral interpretation had a delegitimated relation to literature departments, but not exactly the same delegitimated one that "drama" professors had to the literary field. At the same time, this is also to tell a story about forms and practices that tried fervently to maintain a connection to a Humboldtian practice of culture, potentially doing so precisely because they had to survive within departments of communication studies whose increasingly social scientific fixations in "organizational communication" already were allied with technobureaucratic definitions of knowledge. As oral interpretation professors tried to maintain their literary performance classrooms next to colleagues who were graphing the effectiveness of new corporate communication strategies, oral interpretation functioned as the last bastion of a University of Culture in departments that had already sold their souls to the University of Excellence.

What Is Oral Interpretation: A Brief Practicum

The practice of oral interpretation is based on the exploration and presentation of literature through techniques of performance. It is based on the belief that there is value in this process, a value that might be cast in critical, pedagogical, and artistic terms. In midcentury literary studies, it both resisted and reproduced New Critical values, positioning performance as a more public, potentially more unseemly form of literary exploration while simultaneously casting it as the ultimate form of textual close reading. Such a value translated to the pedagogical realm where professors of oral interpretation found their students more energized by, more engaged with, and more discerning of the formal attributes of literary texts when such students took up the task of performing those texts in the classroom. Not only did the presumptuous act of performance force a minute attention on the innovations of an author's literary technique, the public presentation of those texts to a roomful of fellow students required a care and commitment that one could not fake. One might start with any piece of prose—say, Grace Paley's short story, "Wants."

> I saw my ex-husband in the street. I was sitting on the steps of the new library.
> Hello, my life, I said. We had once been married for twenty-seven years, so I felt justified.
> He said, What? What life? No life of mine.
> I said, O.K. I don't argue when there's real disagreement. I got up and went into the library to see how much I owed them.
> The librarian said $32 even and you've owed it for eighteen years. I didn't deny anything. Because I don't understand how time passes. I have had those books. I have often thought of them. The library is only two blocks away.[9]

This text goes on to exemplify much of what Grace Paley is known for—the incorporation of the mundanely domestic within the political, the simultaneous incarnation of a minute-to-minute temporality within larger chronological sweeps of time, the creation of a narrative voice that seems to be both inside and outside her life with an equal mix of awkwardness and erudition, a portrait of the poignant and painful operations of relationality that bring each of us, provisionally, into being. The premise of oral interpretation, its perpetually challenged hypothesis, and hence animating principle, is that performing this text will make a reader more aware of these effects and the techniques that produce them. Such an act would have to consider acutely, for instance, when and where the speaker is at any moment, vacillating between what might be the scene of the story (at the library) and the scene of its telling (here in performance). Does the speaker say, "I saw my ex-husband in the street," to the audience? If so, at what point does she sit on the library steps to enter the past scene of the story? Before she tells us where she is? As she tells us? Or perhaps she enters the scene of the story only at the moment that she says, "Hello, my life." A workshop of this text would probably try out all these ideas and more. Along the way, participants might end up reckoning with the way that the text confounds neat temporal distinctions between such diegetic and extradiegetic realms. Indeed, such a strategic conflation is arguably central to this text's effects, central to creating the sense of time as something to be endured and something to be recalled in strange and unanticipated shifts.

A slightly different but related set of questions would come into play when we hear the response of the ex-husband: "He said, What? What life? No life of mine." The distinctiveness of this and so many other instances of reported speech in Paley's texts lies in the fact that she does not resort to quotation marks, or to what narratologists call "direct discourse," to represent it. The words of speakers and their interlocutors are given only modest separations of punctuation and indentation, making the decision about whether to turn this prose into a "dialogue" an open one. A performer might change all registers of performance—focus, bodily comportment, and vocal tone—to create an entirely separate and continuous representation of a second character. "What? What life? No life of mine," this fully formed ex-husband might say back. But, taking a cue from Paley's own roundabout representation of speech, the performance of the line might try not simply to represent a completely different character but also to convey the effect of that character's speech on the ex-wife who narrates him: "He said, What? What life?" she reports, performing the sounds of the exclaimed interrogative but also, possibly, the sting it attempts to instill. "No life of mine," his voice and hers continue together, one couched in the narrative of the other. The performance of these short phrases might thus attempt to use the simultaneity of their voices to perform the attachment of a detached relationality, conveying both the illocutionary intent of his dismissal and her attempt to refuse to be hurt by it. No life of mine, indeed.

Are you following me? Probably not unless you try it yourself.

The passage continues, and the choices and experiments of oral interpretation would too. I invite you to sound them out and try out different ones. The narratological experimentation (and the problem of presenting it again) only becomes more complicated when oral interpretation moves into ensemble performance. Along the way, it is important to notice the narrotological complexity of any choice. Whether playing with tense, pronoun, or physical and verbal discontinuity, the performer is often in several places at once. It is this kind of subtly unsettled position that Wallace Bacon called the "tensiveness" of oral interpretation, a "matching" between performance and text that never has the feel of perfectly sealed lamination.[10] Not coincidentally, it was this kind of performance style that made Bertolt Brecht's concept of the "not, but" (along with all his other tense and pronoun exercises in "A New Technique of Acting") much more comprehensible to me as a performer, in some ways restoring an actual narrotological sense of what "epic" acting should be.[11] I am aware, however, that an illustration of oral interpretation might be challenging to read for a number of reasons. As a practice that exists in the embodied, social, and temporally fleeting realm of a performance, it is a brand of performance studies research that appears awkwardly within the archival conventions of print representation. It shares what all fieldsites share and thus replicates what all fieldworkers experience when they become ethnographers—how exactly to represent the simultaneous experience of several registers adequately in the serial sentences of print? How to select words to represent the affect created or the gesture shared? The pedagogical and experimental aspect of the process, furthermore, is one whose significance lies as much in what is tried and tossed out as in what is tried and kept for a final performance. Indeed, a student performer's clarity about the manipulation of textual and performance techniques is something that emerges through repetitions, failures, alterations, and more repetitions. Thus the elements that make a performance workshop seem so exciting are often exactly the elements that make a printed account of a performance workshop seem so boring. They also, not coincidentally, stubbornly refuse comprehensive "accounting" in the spreadsheets and tallies that might legitimate the field in a University of Excellence. As a repertoire of vocal and gestural techniques that are perpetually revised and resituated, oral interpretation offers yet another illustration of the complex, asymmetrical relationship that Diana Taylor finds between the "archives" and the "repertoires" of performance research.[12]

The other concern of course is that a one-minute example cannot give a sense of the vast diversity of performance texts encountered in rhetoric performance classes, especially as the late twentieth-century scholars and activists expanded canons along gendered and cosmopolitan lines and as these and other scholars challenged the literariness of the text to include a whole variety of so-called nonfictional texts. Before moving to analyses of one such expansion, it is worth noting at the same time how significant the oral interpretation brand of performance pedagogy and practice was for many artists in Chicago and beyond. Indeed, just as the "East Coast" genealogy has its artistic stars whose experiments are lauded and whose occasional brushes with mainstream success are discussed with mixtures of pride, suspicion, and jealousy, rhetoric performance studies has its stars too. Mary Zimmerman or Frank Galati arguably function as its Spalding Gray or Elizabeth LeCompte. David Schwimmer is its Willem Dafoe. The Lookingglass Theatre Company functions as rhetorical performance studies' Wooster Group. Indeed, the range of influence extends to many artists and theater groups, from directors such as Jessica Thebus, Eric Rosen, Martha Lavey, and Jim Lasko to theatrical institutions such as About Face, Red Moon Puppet Theater, and Steppenwolf. But the lineup also produces other kinds of exclusions, training attention on artists who have been influenced by rhetorical performance studies rather than other experimental companies; until recently, Goat Island paradoxically received it most lavish attention from performance studies scholars outside Chicago. Nevertheless, a basic awareness of the art practices developed and revised in this milieu might help a reader and audience member rehear some of the Tony, Academy, Emmy, and Macarthur genius award–winning work that emerged from it. The adaptation-derived performance mode is behind Frank Galati's Broadway staging of *Grapes of Wrath* and the reason for his collaboration with Terrence McNally's adaptation of *Ragtime*. It is behind his hiring and, we like to think, his merciful firing from the *Seussical* musical. And it is the reason that Tony Kushner's *Homebody/Kabul* had its best staging at the Brooklyn Academy of Music under Galati's direction; it took a narratologist to figure out how to handle the abrupt change in tense, pronoun, and address between those two acts. More recently, it also took a narratologist (and rhetorical performance studies artist), Mary Zimmerman, to figure out how to stage the stories of transformation, hubris, and loss in Ovid's *Metamorphoses* in New York in the year following September 11, 2001. Rhetorical performance studies continues as one long experiment in the art and ethics of the addressive relation.

Expanding Oral Interpretation in Performance Studies

Not every example of every performance influenced by rhetorical performance studies suits everyone's taste or politics. And with that, it shares much with every other performance style one can possibly think of. Indeed, just as theatrical and other art movements altered contents and forms with changing political climates, so these techniques were revised and redeployed in a variety of academic and artistic contexts as the twentieth century wore on. If international performance studies scholars are familiar with any figure from the NCA tradition, that figure is most often Dwight Conquergood. Conquergood was an assistant professor of Interpretation at Northwestern University in the 1980s and helped to guide the name change to Performance Studies both in his department and in the subfield's division of the NCA. In 1995 he was a keynote speaker at the first annual meeting of what would become Performance Studies International (PSi). As the performance studies department chair in 1996, he hosted the second annual meeting of PSi at Northwestern and was the central master of ceremonies. As I and others have argued, he is the person most consistently "credited or blamed" with the move from oral interpretation to performance studies.[13] Conquergood is most known primarily for his ethnographic work in cross-cultural performance and particularly for the advocacy position he adopted on behalf of the people he studied and with whom he worked: Hmong refugees in Chicago and Laos, Latin King gang members in Chicago and elsewhere in the United States, death row inmates, and other disenfranchised groups in US society. To those more familiar with this work, it might be interesting to know that Conquergood's scholarly formation was quite solidly in oral interpretation. Indeed, just to reinforce a sense of alternate disciplinary histories, his dissertation used the figure of "the Boast" in Anglo-Saxon England to investigate longer political histories around the division between literacy and orality.[14]

How exactly a scholar trained in an exceedingly "early" form of "oral English" became a performance studies scholar in contemporary ethnography is a question too large to receive adequate answer in this essay.[15] But this kind of expansion certainly began to happen through a pedagogical route as much as any other when Assistant Professor Conquergood took over Northwestern University's course in "Performance of Nonfiction." There, propelled by a significant amount of postdoctoral reskilling in courses with anthropologist Mary Douglas, Conquergood began to encourage students to conduct cross-cultural interviews as the basis for their performance work. The process of interviewing and reperforming an Other was thus positioned as a pedagogical means of confronting difference and defamiliarizing one's sense of self. Conquergood had himself participated in this brand of performance research in his own emergent work as an ethnographer of Hmong refugees in Chicago, re-presenting the voices of interview subjects who had fled invasion and encountered prejudice upon arrival in the United States. Most often, such performances were presented in community centers, courtrooms, or other civic sites where cross-cultural communication was necessary.

As graduate students at Northwestern, we all read an essay that was Conquergood's earliest attempt to come to terms in print with this change in his focus as a teacher and researcher, "Performing as a Moral Act: Ethical Dimensions of the Ethnography of Performance."[16] Published in 1985 in *Literature in Performance*, the journal that would have changed its name to *Text and Performance Quarterly* by the time Conquergood published in it again, the essay was a self-conscious echo of Clifford Geertz's "Thinking as a Moral Act: Ethical Dimensions of Anthropological Fieldwork in the New States."[17] We taught it in every syllabus of our introductory courses in performance studies. But its appearance in syllabi in the 1990s did not go without a fight in the 1980s; we also all knew the story behind Northwestern's former Interpretation department chair, Lilla Heston. After reading the essay, she reportedly stomped down the hall to Conquergood's office and stood in his doorway as he watched her systematically rip it to shreds. Resistances notwithstanding, the essay was both symptom and propeller of the shift that brought the rhetorical practice of oral interpretation into the disciplinary formation of performance studies in the United States. The touchstone for these courses and subfields in ethnographic performance derived in part from the fact that the social sciences were undergoing a period of self-reflection. In the 1970s and 1980s, a number of essays, collections, and books appeared that investigated the status of the social science researcher, especially the ethnographic researcher in the midst of a fieldsite where the imperative to "write up" the site coexisted uneasily with the fact that that site was often opaque to the researcher thus charged. For Conquergood, and many other rhetorical performance studies scholars and students, the dilemmas of ethnography intimately paralleled the dilemmas of performance.

It is important to emphasize how much this expansion beyond the field of oral interpretation was simultaneously indebted to it. A match between ethnographic ethics and performance ethics could be imagined because "performance" had been debated and practiced by these scholars as an act of translation and adaptation across worlds and across textual and embodied media for seventy-five years. While the world expanded and the politics of media were revealed in their complexity, Geertz's isolation of the ethnographic dilemma as a relation between "being there" and "being here" echoed the language of adaptation and its own preoccupations between the "scene of the story" and the "scene of the telling." When James Clifford or Johannes Fabian critiqued the "ethnographic present," the mode of writing that sought to create cultural immediacy but that risked cultural typification, rhetorical performance studies practitioners who worried constantly about the effects of tense felt that they knew what was meant by "chronopolitics."[18] And when Clifford, George Marcus, Geertz, and Renato Rosaldo all experimented with the use of the first-person, that is, their own first person, in an attempt to situate themselves as unstable researchers in a fieldsite, rhetorical performance studies scholars were as attuned to the open vulnerability invited by a first-person narrator as they were to the fact that that same narratological choice could over-determine the ethnographic story.[19] The sense of performance not only as a narratological experiment but also as a cross-media experiment similarly supported the connection between rhetorical performance studies and ethnographic practice. The effort to represent the embodied, intimate, affective, ephemeral, perpetually revisable encounters of performance had been a source of institutional insecurity for performance, but it now had the possibility of generating an intellectually legitimizing opportunity for field practitioners. Indeed, a performer's mode of attention seemed exactly the mode of attention necessary to grapple with ethnographic dilemmas. When Edward Said critiqued the assumption that "knowledge means rising above immediacy," performance studies rhetors clapped.[20] When anthropologist Michael Jackson said that "textualism tends to ignore the flux of human interrelationships," we cheered.[21] And when anthropologist Talal Asad said, "Indeed, it could be argued that translating an alien form of life, another culture, is not always done best through the representational discourse of ethnography, that under certain conditions a dramatic performance, the execution of a dance, or the playing of a piece of music might be more apt," we thought that we had won the lottery.[22] The representational "problems" of performance appeared for a while to be the representation "solutions" to ethnography.

Concluding

Whether all elements of the opportunity of performance studies have been actualized, this was a particular kind of conversation between ethnography and performance—one about narratological politics and about cross-media translation—that rhetorical performance studies offered and still offers to performance studies. It is important to notice that this particular conversation between performance and ethnography was as much or more about *how* to research than about *what* to research. While, for other types of performance scholars, the anthropological expansion of performance was about widening the objects of the canon to include performance forms from around the world, for many in the NCA tradition, performance ethnography was just as significantly an invitation to reflect about the politics and practices of exactly how to perform that expansion. It was and continues to be part of an ongoing investigation in the art and ethics of addressive relations.

I have come to realize, however, that the difficulty of writing this essay is partly about the difficulty of "accounting" for an investigation and a genealogy that is so linked to pedagogy, where pedagogy's intimacies, fleeting illuminations, mindful interventions, daily diligence, and moment-to-moment encounters are both intensely transformative and intensely undocumentable. Performance pedagogy is a *repertoire* if ever there was one, a space of human accountability that resists professionalized modes of accounting. In a move that might seem its own act of wishful thinking, however, I find myself wondering if it is exactly this obstacle to accounting in which we might find the potential for rhetorical performance in the ruined university. To think about rhetorical performance studies in ruins then is not only a naming of the fall of rhetoric but also actually a naming of the function of rhetoric in navigating higher education. My suggestion is made explicit in the figure to whom Readings turns at the end of his book. There, after one hundred fifty pages that read like conspiracy to many, Readings turned to pedagogy amid the ruins, using language that managed to be committed and unbelieving at once. To value pedagogy was, for Readings, to value a site of social interdependence.

> In place of the lure of autonomy, of independence from all obli-
> gation, I want to insist that pedagogy is a relation, a network of
> obligation. In this sense, we might want to talk of the teacher as
> *rhetor* rather than as *magister*, one who speaks in a rhetorical
> context rather than one whose discourse is self-authorizing. The
> advantage here would be to recognize that the legitimation of the
> teacher's discourse is not immanent to that discourse but is always
> dependent, at least in part, on the rhetorical context of its reception.
> The *rhetor* is a speaker who takes account of the audience, while
> the *magister* is indifferent to the specificity of her addressees.[23]

What I find intriguing about Readings's elaborations of this rhetorical pedagogy is how much it mirrors the exchanges of the rhetorical performance studies classroom.

> If pedagogy is to pose a challenge to the ever-increasing bureau-
> cratization of the University as a whole, it will need to de-center
> our vision of the education process, not merely adopt an opposi-
> tional stance in teaching. Only in this way can we hope to open
> up pedagogy, to lend it a temporality that resists commodification,
> by arguing that listening to Thought is not the spending of time
> in the production of an autonomous subject (even an oppositional
> one) or of an autonomous body of knowledge. Rather, to listen
> to Thought, to think beside each other and beside ourselves, is to
> explore an open network of obligations that keeps the question of
> meaning open as a locus of debate.[24]

Whatever its limits, this is what the rhetorical performance classroom looks like. Performance practitioners of all varieties know the "think-ing together" that is rehearsal. Rhetorical performance studies adds to that interpersonal performance sphere a legacy of committed reflection on rhetorical contingency, about the politics of who is speaking, where and when, and about how those decisions betray subtle shifts of power that make different kinds of exchanges more or less possible. It is also medium-specific thinking together, one that does not fetishize the particularity of one real-time, copresent medium but that uses cross-medium acts of translation to foreground the dependence of thought on the medium of its enactment. The thing about performance pedagogy, too, is that it is also terribly inefficient, requiring enrollment limits that do not make financial sense, requiring extended hours that challenge the classroom schedulers. This brand of performance is based on a perpetually renewed space of obligation that simultaneously does not "perform, or else."[25] Indeed, it is a brand of performance that refuses to be measured by the system of inputs and outputs that structure the "performance evaluations" of academic departments with increasing frequency.

The trick for us now is to argue for the perpetuation of such a space while simultaneously knowing that it cannot be posited as a solution. "Creating and addressing such an audience will not revitalize the University or solve all our problems," says Readings of a next generation of teachers, "It will, however, allow the exploration of differences in ways that are liberating to the extent that they assume nothing in advance."[26] The generational task—and I do read the impulse to "assume nothing in advance" as a symptom of a certain perspective learned and adopted by a generation of scholars raised in the context that I was—is to take our inheritances and figure out what to do with their oddities. It probably will not be to affirm the greatness of the literary writers as they were or to perfect one's ability to "know the other" as might once have seemed possible. Oddly enough, it might be to notice the less legitimated aspects of our inheritance, since we come from senior scholars who never had the stature or institutional recognition that the "fathers" of other disciplines once had. Our literature professors were too theatrical for literary studies; our communication professors were too cultural for communication science; and our anthropology professors were accused of "going native" in their political interventions and in their performing. The perpetuation of a relentlessly illegitimate, if undernoticed, discipline for now over a century suggests that there are various ways of moving in and under the radar of whatever University (of Reason, Culture, or Excellence) one happens to be in. It can happen even in Americanized universities in the United States. Working through this essay—and, not coincidentally, cutting half of it to be "accountable" to my word limit—has helped me to remember that largely unarchived network of practices and "thinkings together" that remain central to my formation in the pedagogy of rhetorical performance studies, a network that has always been struggling to find itself and that, upon entering the performance classroom, provisionally always does.

Notes

"Rhetoric in Ruins: Performing Literature and Performance Studies" was originally published in *Performance Research* 14, no. 1 (2009): 6–16.

1. See, e.g., Gerald Graff, *Beyond the Culture Wars: How Teaching the Conflicts Can Revitalize American Education* (New York: Norton, 1992); John Guillory, *Cultural Capital: The Problem of Literary Canon Formation* (Chicago: University of Chicago Press, 1993); Jean-François Lyotard, *The Postmodern Condition: A Report on Knowledge*, trans. Geoff Bennington and Brian Massumi (Minneapolis: University of Minneapolis Press, 1994); and Pierre Bourdieu, *Homo Academicus* (Paris: Éditions de Minuit, 1984), to name a few.

2. Marquard Smith, "Visual Studies, or the Ossification of Thought," *Journal of Visual Culture* 4, no. 2 (August 2005): 245.

3. Paul Edwards, "Unstoried: Teaching Literature in the Age of Performance Studies," *Theater Annual: A Journal of Performance Studies* 52 (1999): 1–147.

4. Edwards, "Unstoried."

5. Edwards, "Unstoried."

6. Mary Margaret Robb, "The Elocutionary Movement and Its Chief Figures," in *The History of Speech Education in America*, ed. K. R. Wallace (New York: Appleton-Century-Crofts, 1954): 178–201; and, by the same author, *Oral Interpretation of Literature in American Colleges and Universities: A Historical Study of Teaching Method* (New York: H. W. Wilson, 1941).

7. Shannon Jackson, *Professing Performance: Theater in the Academy from Philology to Performativity* (Cambridge: Cambridge University Press, 2004).

8. Edwards, "Unstoried," 76. Even more recently, Soyini Madison and Judith Hamera's new edited collection, *The SAGE Handbook of Performance Studies* (Thousand Oaks, CA: SAGE, 2006), represents a wider, longer, and more varied history of performance studies in the United States, including a section on performance and literature and on performance and pedagogy, umbrellas that allow the rhetorical performance studies genealogy a more secure footing in the histories of the field.

9. Grace Paley, "Wants," in *You've Got to Read This: Contemporary American Writers Introduce Stories That Held Them in Awe*, ed. R. Hansen and J. Shepard, 1st ed. (New York: Harper Perennial, 1994), 469.

10. Wallace A. Bacon, *The Art of Interpretation*, 3rd ed. (New York: Holt, Rinehart and Winston, 1979).

11. Bertolt Brecht, "Short Description of a New Technique of Acting Which Produces an Alienation Effect," in *Brecht on Theater: The Development of an Aesthetic*, trans. J. Willett (New York: Hill and Wang, 1992), 136–47.

12. Diana Taylor, *The Archive and the Repertoire: Performing Cultural Memory in the Americas* (Durham, NC: Duke University Press, 2003).

13. Shannon Jackson, "Caravans Continued: In Memory of Dwight Conquergood," *TDR: The Drama Review* 50, no. 1 (Spring 2006): 28–32.

14. See a publication from that dissertation in D. Conquergood, "Literacy and Oral Performance in Anglo-Saxon England: Conflict and Confluence of Traditions," in *Performance of Literature in Historical Perspective*, ed. David W. Thompson (Lanham, MD: University Press of America, 1983), 107–45.

15. E. Patrick Johnson is working on a collection of Dwight Conquergood's many essay publications that will contribute significantly to the documentation of this important intellectual history.

16. Dwight Conquergood, "Performing as a Moral Act: Ethical Dimensions of the Ethnography of Performance," *Literature in Performance* 5 (April 1985): 1–13.

17. Clifford Geertz, "Thinking as a Moral Act: Ethical Dimensions of Anthropological Fieldwork in the New States," in *Available Light: Anthropological Reflections on Philosophical Topics* (Princeton, NJ: Princeton University Press, 2001), 21–41. Originally published under the same title in *Antioch Review* 28 (1968): 139–58.

18. James Clifford, "On Ethnographic Authority," *Representations* 1, no. 22 (Spring 1983): 118–46; Johannes Fabian, *Time and the Other: How Anthropology Makes Its Object* (New York: Columbia University Press, 1983).

19. James Clifford, *The Predicament of Culture: Twentieth-Century Ethnography, Literature, and Art* (Cambridge, MA: Harvard University Press, 1988); James Clifford and George Marcus, eds., *Writing Culture: The Poetics and Politics of Ethnography* (Berkeley: University of California Press, 1986); Clifford Geertz, "Thick Description: Towards an Interpretive Theory of Culture," in *Interpretation of Cultures: Selected Essays* (New York: Basic Books, [1973] 2000), 3–32; and Renato Rosaldo, *Culture and Truth: The Remaking of Social Analysis* (Boston: Beacon Press, 1989).

20. Edward Said, *Orientalism* (New York: Vintage Books, 1979), 36.

21. Michael Jackson, *Paths Toward a Clearing: Radical Empiricism and Ethnographic Inquiry* (Bloomington: Indiana University Press, 1989), 184.

22. Talal Asad, "The Concept of Cultural Translation in British Social Anthropology," in *Writing Culture: The Poetics and Politics of Ethnography*, ed. James Clifford and George Marcus (Berkeley: University of California Press, 1986), 159.

23. Readings, *University in Ruins*, 158.

24. Readings, *University in Ruins*, 164.

25. See Jon McKenzie, *Perform or Else: From Discipline to Performance* (London: Routledge, 2001).

26. Readings, *University in Ruins*, 164–65.

Chapter 7

Living Takes Many Forms

Creative Time

> The power of these theaters springing up throughout the
> country lies in the fact that they know what they want . . .
> They intend to remake a social structure without the help of
> money—and this ambition alone invests their undertaking
> with a certain Marlowesque madness.
>
> —Hallie Flanagan

So that was Hallie Flanagan, director of the Federal Theater Project
(FTP) inside the Works Progress Administration (WPA) that was so
central to implementing Franklin Delano Roosevelt's New Deal. She
was recalling her work as the leader of a federally supported theatrical movement charged with responding to the reality of the Great
Depression. The FTP addressed timely themes—with new plays that
dramatized issues of housing, privatization of utilities, agricultural
labor, unemployment, racial and religious intolerance, and more. And
the FTP devised innovative theatrical forms—staging newspapers,
developing montage stagecraft, and opening the same play simultaneously in several cities at once. The goal was to extend the theatrical
event to foreground the systemic connectedness of the issues endured.
Social and economic hardships were not singular problems but collective ones; as such, they needed a collective aesthetic. Like other WPA
culture workers—its writers, mural painters, and photographers—
FTP artists used interdependent art forms as vehicles for reimagining
the interdependency of social beings. They gave public form to
public life.

Support Systems

As we think about the twenty years of work represented in *Living as Form*, it seems important to remember prior histories of socially engaged art, both in North America and in the many regions of the world represented in the archive.[1] To do so is to remember that now is not the first time that an international financial crisis threatened to imperil the vitality of civic cultures; it is also to acknowledge that the effects of economic crises and economic prosperity vary depending on what demographic position on the globe one happens to occupy. From Saint Petersburg, Russia, to Harare, Zimbabwe, from Los Angeles, California, to Glover, Vermont, the booms and busts recounted from 1991 to 2011 were socially produced and differentially felt. Accordingly, artists dispersed among different global sites—Chto Delat, Uhuru Collective, Los Angeles Poverty Department, Bread and Puppet Theater, and more—faced unique and complex economies as they developed cultural responses to social questions around education, public welfare, urban life, immigration, environmentalism, gender and racial equity, human rights, and democratic governance. Those economies are now distinctively "mixed" in an era that is ostensibly "post-1989," less often fueled by the capitalism-communism opposition of the long Cold War than by Third Way experimentation whose allegiances to public culture are as opaque and variable as its allegiances to public services.[2] As artists reflect on these and other social transformations, they also reckon with the mixed socioeconomic models that support the art itself. Artists based in Europe can still seek national arts funding, but groups such as the Mobile Academy or Free Class Frankfurt might worry and wonder about the encroachment of neoliberal models that chip away at the principles behind it. Public sector funding interfaces with other financial models. Some artists seek commission, and others depend on royalties. Others sell documentation of socially engaged work in galleries, joining the likes of Phil Collins, Thomas Hirschhorn, Paul Chan, or Francis Alÿs whose political practices enjoy artworld cachet. Still other artists such as Mierle Laderman Ukeles or Rick Lowe mobilize social-sector initiatives in service of the arts, transforming after-school programs, public sanitation, or urban recovery projects into aesthetic acts. Finally, people like Josh Green stay to the side of larger systemic processes, choosing to develop micro-DIY networks of shared artistic support instead. But whether you are organizing potlucks to combat the effects of Turkey's Deep State, responding to a coalition government's equivocal faith in the culture industries of the United Kingdom, or celebrating the release from social realism by speculating in China's booming art market, there is no pure position for socially engaged artmaking. As an archive produced by nonprofit public arts organization, the projects of *Living as Form* are necessarily impure as well, even as they provide countless examples of how to make form from the stuff of this life.

Fig. 4. Mierle Laderman Ukeles, *Touch Sanitation* Performance, 1979–80. Citywide performance with 8,500 sanitation workers across all 59 New York City sanitation districts. Date unknown. Sweep 3, Manhattan 3. Photograph by Robin Holland. © Mierle Laderman Ukeles. Courtesy of the artist and Ronald Feldman Gallery, New York.

Which Art Forms?

To recall the FTP inside the WPA is not only to prompt consideration on changing socioeconomic contexts but also to reflect on the varied art forms from which social engagement springs. The WPA expanded the practice of photographers, architects, easel painters, actors, designers, dancers, and writers, and the *Living as Form* archive includes practices that measure their expansion from different art forms as well. The installations of Phil Collins sit next to the community theater of Cornerstone. The choreography of Urban Bush Women moves near the expanded photography of Ala Plastica. As a *Living as Form* curator asked to secure examples from theater and dance history, I found myself reflecting on the unwieldiness of the charge. How to choose among the very many examples of artists and groups from around the world whose work varies in technique, goal, situation, and style? I attend many symposia and festivals devoted to socially engaged performance, and I can imagine how laughable it would be if one of their organizers asked a curator to produce a complementary list of socially engaged visual arts. Where would one start? Or stop?

But even if the WPA moment is a reminder that socially engaged work develops from different art traditions, the willingness to capture the heterogeneity of contemporary work is striking and unfortunately rare.

Across the world, we have artists and institutions celebrating "hybrid" work that is socially engaged. But such hybrid artists still measure their distance from traditional art disciplines, and their conversations and support networks often remain circumscribed by them. Expanded theater artists talk to other expanded theater artists and are presented by an international festival circuit. Postvisual artists talk to other postvisual artists and are represented in the biennial circuit and by the gallery-collector system. The habits of criticism reinforce this inertia, routinely structuring who is cast as post-Brechtian and who is cast as post-Minimalist. It is hard to find contexts that enable conversation across these networks and critical vocabularies. Certainly, the difficulty is due in part to the wide range of skills different art forms require. Not everyone knows how to design a house or produce a film. Not everyone can fabricate a three-story puppet to be graceful or inscribe African diasporic history in a rotation of the hip, so it makes sense when architects, videographers, puppeteers, and choreographers seek conversations with fellow specialists. But the necessity of creating platforms that stitch together the heterogeneous project of socially engaged art remains—and continues to become increasingly urgent. Meanwhile, genuinely cross-disciplinary artists should not have to cultivate some talents and repress others to conform to particular legitimating contexts. It sure would be nice, for instance, if Theaster Gates did not to have to choose between standing in a gospel choir or sitting at his potter's wheel.

Which Social Forms?

The challenge of *Living as Form* thus lies in its invitation to reflect on what living means in our contemporary moment and to reckon with the many kinds of forms that help us to do that reflection. That challenge is itself embedded in different barometers for gauging aesthetic integrity and social efficacy. The question of art's social role has been a hallmark of Western twentieth-century aesthetic debate, whether sociality is marked by eruptions at Café Voltaire or by the activisms of 1968, whether it is called Constructivist or Situationist, realist or relational, functional or (after Adorno) "committed."[3] Russia's Chto Delat's renewal of Lenin's historic question "What is to be done?" is both an earnest call and a gesture that makes the question into an artifact, asking what "doing" could possibly mean in a twentieth-first-century global context. Their pursuit resonates with that of choreographer Bill T. Jones who finds himself recalibrating his sense of the role of politics in art: "I now choose to fire back that 'political' is an exhausted term and most certainly more and more irrelevant in regard to my work. To make a work that says, 'War is bad!' is absurd. I find myself saying with growing confidence that the works that I make now are concerned with moral choice as in, 'What is the right thing to do, particularly when we seem to have many choices and no real choice at all?' "[4]

Even if ethical and pragmatic questions of "doing" activate contemporary art, modernist legacies of thought and practice carry forward habits of enthusiasm and suspicion. Habits structure what work is defined as subversive and what as instrumentalized, what looks efficacious and what looks like "the end of art." Artist groups such as Alternate Roots are quite clear in their desire to craft aesthetic solutions to social problems. Meanwhile, Hannah Hurtzig's Mobile Academy worries more about the ossification of goal-driven "knowledge," ironically hoping to create "a tool to find problems for already existing solutions."[5] To some, Cornerstone Theater's mission statement provides necessary inspiration: "We value art that is contemporary, community-specific, responsive, multilingual, innovative, challenging, and joyful. We value theater that directly reflects the audience. We value the artist in everyone."[6] To others, such a "mission" risks social prescription. These critical tussles depend on how each receiver understands the place of art—should art mobilize the world or continually question the reality principles behind its formation? Should art unsettle the bonds of social life or seek actively to bind social beings to each other? Acts of aesthetic *affirmation* coincide with equally necessary acts of aesthetic *refusal*. I have offered a longer disquisition on this topic in a recent book, so I do not want to reproduce those arguments here.[7] But as we come to terms with the growing of hybrid socially engaged art, no doubt every citizen will find herself jostled between competing and often contradictory associations that celebrate and reject varied visions of the "social." Often this is a matter of what we used to call "taste," a regime of sensibility that we like to pretend that we have overcome. Nevertheless, our impulses to describe a work as ironic or earnest, as elitist or as literal, as critical or as sentimental show that many of us have emotional and conceptual investments in certain barometers for gauging aesthetic intervention and aesthetic corruption. Such differences will also affect how each of us assesses the role of functionality, utility, and intelligibility in a socially engaged work. Jeremy Deller's reenactments in "The Battle of Orgreave" may look radically functional to some of us and will look curiously useless to others. Francis Alÿs's works may seem strangely unintelligible to one group but will look overly didactic to another.

What Social Art Forms?

Reactions to socially engaged art thus renew historic questions around the perceived autonomy and heteronomy of art, whether it should be "self-governing" or commit to governance by "external rules." As many have argued, that opposition always cracks under pressure. Arguments in favor of aesthetic autonomy disavow their enmeshment in privatized art markets. Arguments in favor of aesthetic heteronomy backtrack when "the artist's freedom of speech" seems threatened. But as specious as the opposition is, questions of perceived aesthetic autonomy and heteronomy affect our relative tolerance for the goals, skills, and styles of different art forms. The legacy of antitheatrical discourses in modernist art criticism offers a case in point. Many signature Minimalist gestures purportedly laid the groundwork for social engagement now—the turn to time-based work, the entry of the body of the artist, the explicit relation to the beholder, the avowal of the spatial and institutional conditions of production.[8] Such gestures were criticized in their time for being "theatrical," and arguably the pejorative connotations of that term now linger in the many criticisms and defenses of the formal properties of social practice. But such a discourse was less potent for artists who actually worked in theater and other performing arts, people for whom time, bodies, space, and audience were already incorporated into the traditions of the medium. Thus, for socially engaged theatermakers and choreographers, the effort was not to introduce such properties—they were already there—but to alter the conventions by which such properties were managed. It meant that time might not be narrative, that bodies might not be characters, and that space could exceed the boundaries of the proscenium. It meant that people like Augusto Boal would seek to dynamize the audience relation into a new kind of "spect-actor."[9]

Now if we bring work that derives from theatrical, visual, architectural, textual, and filmic art forms under the umbrella of socially engaged art, it seems important to register their different barometers for gauging skill, goal, style, and innovation. We might call this the medium specificity of social engagement. The performing bodies of political theater may not be traditional characters, but to a sculptor, they still appear to be acting. The installation art piece may exceed the constraints of the picture frame, but to an environmental theatermaker, it still appears relatively hermetic. Postdramatic theater may be nonnarrative, but to a postvisual artist, it looks exceedingly referential. In other words, our enmeshment in certain art forms will affect how we perceive tradition and innovation in a work. It will also affect how we understand its social reach, functionality, and relative intelligibility. What reads as earnest to a conceptual artist will look snobby to a community organizer. Heteronomous engagement in one art form looks highly autonomous to another. But the harder work comes in a willingness to think past these initial judgment calls. Whose to say that the feminist content of Suzanne Lacy's projects on rape prevent them from getting formal credit for being a Happening? Whose to say that there isn't a radical refusal of social convention in Cornerstone's notion that there is "an artist in everyone?" Finally, the cultural location of specific artists will influence their definitions of what qualifies as social. I am reminded of Urban Bush Women founder Jawole Willa Jo Zollar's reflections on the subject: "I don't know that I could make a work that is not about healing. What would that be about? Being? Well, you know, it's interesting, a European director said to me, he says, you know, your work is old-fashioned because you have this obsession with hope . . . and I said, you know the values in my community that I have also internalized are that. So no, it's not about nihilism for me or this train-spotting angst. No, that's not my culture. So it can be corny to you. That's fine."[10]

Once we develop a tolerance for different ways of mixing artistic forms, however, we can get to the inspiring work of seeing how they each address the problems and possibilities of living. The WPA—like other instances of public, nonprofit, and privately funded efforts at civic culture throughout the world—knew something about the active making of life. At a time of fiscal danger, the arts were not positioned as ornamental and expendable but as central vehicles for reimagining the social order. Existing economic and social structures did not remain intact, contracting and expanding with the decrease or increase in financial flows. Instead, it was a time when different social sectors underwent redefinition and engaged in a significant amount of cross-training. Sectors in the arts, health care, housing, commerce, urban planning, sanitation, education, science, child development, and more received joint provisions that required joint collaboration. It meant health policy advanced educational policy and cultural policy in the same moment. It meant that citizens were not asked to choose between supporting employment programs or supporting arts programs as both sectors were reimagined together. In theater, journalists became playwrights, WPA laborers became actors, and public utility companies hung the lights. But this interdependent social imagining was not without its own dangers, especially when such forms of imagining were retroactively cast as politically corrupt. The statement from Hallie Flanagan that opened this essay was quoted when she was brought before the Dies Committee who argued that her directorship of an arts-based American relief program had been in fact un-American. "You are quoting from this Marlowe," noted Dies Committee member Joe Starnes: "Is he a communist?"[11]

The history lesson shows the potential and peril of coordinating public forms of aesthetic inquiry. Funny how acts of citizenship suddenly become unpatriotic. In our contemporary moment, we tend to use the word *neoliberal* to describe moral regimes based on highly individuated and market-driven measures for determining value. And the ease with which the privatized financial crisis of 2008 transmogrified into a national and global distrust of public systems shows how robust the psychic as well as financial investment in neoliberalism actually is. I thus find myself emboldened by artists who continue to renew our understanding of what cross-sector collaboration can be, even if they also remind us that it is hard to do. Mierle Laderman Ukeles has worked across the domains of the arts and public sanitation for decades, but her artist-in-residence position remains unpaid. Moreover, as Rick Lowe reminds us, cross-sector collaboration means reskilling: "I have to keep trying to allow myself the courage to do it, you know, because as we open ourselves up and look around, there are many opportunities to invest that creativity. But it's challenging. Oftentimes, as an artist, you're trespassing into different zones. . . . Oftentimes . . . I know nothing. I have to force myself and find courage to trespass . . . Artists can license ourselves to explore in any way imaginable. The challenge is having the courage to carry it through."[12] It is of course in that trespassing that art makes different zones of the social available for critical reflection. Cross-sector engagement exposes and complicates our awareness of the systems and processes that coordinate and sustain social life. For my own part, this is where social art becomes rigorous, conceptual, and formal. The nonmonumental gestures of such public art works address, mimic, subvert, and redefine public processes, provoking us to reflect on what kinds of forms—be they aesthetic, social, economic, or governmental—we want to sustain a life worth living. Whether occupying an abandoned building, casting new figures as public sector workers, or rearranging the gestural gait of the street, such aesthetic projects embed and rework the infrastructures of the social. This is where the notion that living has a form has a degree of traction. Living here is not the emptied convivial party of the relational. Nor is it the romantically unmediated notion of "life" whose generalized spontaneity Boomers still elegize. By reminding us that living is form, these works remind us of the responsibility for creating and recreating the conditions of life. Form here is both socially urgent and a task for an aesthetic imaginary. Living does not just "happen" but is in fact actively made.

In the end, the stakes of maintaining a robust and bracing public culture are too dear for us not to cultivate awareness and respect for the many ways that fellow artists contribute to the effort. Our conceptions of expanded art need to stay expansive. In *Living as Form* we find a tool to help us widen awareness. It is a tool that invites discussion of what form might mean. It is a tool that invites discussion of what living could mean for future occupants of a world full of potential and in need of repair.

Notes

"Living Takes Many Forms: Creative Time" was originally published in *Living as Form: Socially Engaged Art from 1992–2011*, ed. Nato Thompson, 86–93 (Cambridge, MA: MIT Press, 2012).

EPIGRAPH: Flanagan, quoted in Roy Rosenzweig and Barbara Melosh, "Government and the Arts: Voices from the New Deal Era," *Journal of American History* (September 1990): 596.

1. *Living as Form* was a 2011 exhibition presented by Creative Time, with the goal to "provide a broad look at a vast array of socially engaged practices that appear with increasing regularity in fields ranging from theater to activism,

and urban planning to visual art." *Living as Form*, Creative Time, 2011, https://creativetime.org/programs/archive/2011/livingasform/about.htm.

2. Anthony Giddens, *The Third Way: The Renewal of Social Democracy* (Cambridge: Polity Press, 1999).

3. The secondary literature here is vast, but see, e.g., Roselee Goldberg, *Performance Art: From Futurism to the Present* (London: Thames and Hudson, 2001); Maria Gough, *The Artist as Producer: Russian Constructivism in Revolution* (Farmington Hills, MI: Thomson Gale, 2006); and Tom McDonough, ed., *The Situationists and the City* (London: Verso, 2010). And, of course, Theodor W. Adorno, *Aesthetic Theory*, trans. Robert Hullor-Kentor (Minneapolis: University of Minnesota Press, 1998).

4. Bill T. Jones, "'Political' Work?," October 4, 2006, https://web.archive.org/web/20071209124832/http://www.billtjones.org/billsblog/2006/10/political_work.html, accessed November 23, 2021.

5. Quoted in Bojana Cvejić, "Trickstering, Hallucinating, and Exhausting Production: The Blackmarket for Useful Knowledge and Non-Knowledge," in *Knowledge in Motion: Perspectives of Artistic and Scientific Research in Dance*, ed. Sabine Gehm, Pirrko Husemann, and Katharina von Wilcke (Bielefeld, Germany: Transcript Verlag, 2007), 54.

6. Cornerstone Theater, "Mission and Values," July 2011, http://www.cornerstonetheater.org/.

7. Shannon Jackson, *Social Works: Performing Art, Supporting Publics* (New York and London: Routledge, 2011), and see many other works cited in these debates. See, e.g., Grant Kester, *Conversation Pieces* (Berkeley: University of California Press, 2004); Jan Cohen-Cruz, *Local Acts: Community-Based Performance in the United States* (New Brunswick, NJ: Rutgers University Press, 2005); Claire Bishop, "The Social Turn: Collaboration and Its Discontents," *Artforum* (February 2006), https://www.artforum.com/print/200602/the-social-turn-collaboration-and-its-discontents-10274; and "Antagonism and Relational Aesthetics," *October* 110 (Fall 2004): 51–79; Liam Gillick, "Contingent Factors: A Response to Claire Bishop's 'Antagonism and Relational Aesthetics,'" *October* 115 (Winter 2006): 95–106; and Nicolas Bourriaud, *Relational Aesthetics*, trans. Simon Pleasance and Fronza Woods (Dijon, France: Les Presses du réel, 2002).

8. Once again, the conversation around Minimalism and theatricality is a long one, but see, e.g., Michael Fried, "Art and Objecthood," *Artforum* (1967): 12–23; James Meyer, *Minimalism: Art and Polemics in the Sixties* (New Haven, CT: Yale University Press, 2001); and Hal Foster, "The Crux of Minimalism," in *The Return of the Real: The Avant-Garde at the End of the Century* (Cambridge, MA: MIT Press, 1996).

9. Augusto Boal, *Theater of the Oppressed*, trans. Charles McBride and Maria-Odilia Leal McBride (London: Pluto Press, 2019).

10. Jawole Willa Jo Zollar quoted in Nadine George-Graves, *Urban Bush Women: Twenty Years of African American Dance Theater, Community Engagement, and Working It Out* (Madison: University of Wisconsin Press, 2010), 204.

11. This story is oft-recounted. See, e.g., Roy Rosenzweig and Barbara Melosh, "Government and the Arts: Voices from the New Deal Era," *Journal*

of American History (September 1990), 596; and Ted Morgan, *Reds: McCarthyism in Twentieth-Century America* (New York: Random House, 2003), 198.

12. Greg Sholette, "Activism as Art: Shotgun Shacks Saved through Art-Based Revitalization: Interview with Rick Lowe," *Huffington Post*, November 22, 2010.

Part 2

✦

The Arts at Work

Chapter 8

Life Politics/Life Aesthetics

Environmental Performance
in *red, black & GREEN: a blues*

Life includes drawing and dominoes and rolling down hills,
and it also involves alternate energy and conservation and
food activism and poetry and art. The idea is to place all
these things on the same continuum so that there's less isolation and a greater emphasis on interdependence—socially,
intellectually, and practically.

—Marc Bamuthi Joseph

Yeah, I'm a space doctor.

—Theaster Gates

In April 2011, a dozen artists and designers gathered in the large warehouse of the Z Space Studio in San Francisco. These busy people traveled
from Chicago and various parts of California, leaving other art projects
on hold and finding someone else to take care of their children. That
the packed schedules of such busy people had reconciled to develop and
rehearse *red, black & GREEN: a blues* was itself an achievement, but
everyone knew it was going to be worth the effort. "I don't know what
this is yet," said Marc Bamuthi Joseph, clearing a safe space for himself
and the other members of the group who gathered in a circle to hear his
text in process. He began to read, starting with a preamble that described
the cast: "Four characters. One speaks through text and body, one speaks
through character and movement, one speaks through song and sculpture,
one lives in sound and fury." The lyrical phrasing outlined the contours of
the collaboration that was about to begin.

Marc Bamuthi Joseph's *red, black & GREEN: a blues* is a multidis-
ciplinary performance experiment. It mixes visual art, spoken word,

choreography, theater, and film in ways that expose the boundaries that still exist among these art forms; its composition is an aesthetic act that integrates ritual, critique, and community engagement at once. Along with this experiment across form, *red, black & GREEN: a blues* is also an experiment in content, specifically the content of the environmental movement. As I describe in this chapter, Bamuthi and his collaborators join a large group of activists, community organizers, and policy specialists who are thinking about issues of race and justice in the US environmental movement. In what follows, I would like to use forms and themes of *red, black & GREEN: a blues* to address the "politics of space" on both social and aesthetic fronts. The parameters and objectives of the US environmental movement are themselves embedded in a politics of space. On the one hand, environmental movements seek to expose the systems and fragilities of the spaces we occupy every day, encouraging new acts of care and maintenance to preserve life on the planet. On the other hand, the assumptions and reach of environmental pedagogies have their own complexities and blindspots, especially when we try to expand "environment" beyond the confines of reusable coffee cups and organic produce and into the more conflicted territory of toxic dumping, food security, public housing, and economic justice. Meanwhile, the performance space also has an aesthetic politics, or what Jacques Rancière calls its "space-time sensorium."[1] It structures inherited divisions between so-called static and so-called temporal art forms; it structures inherited hierarchies between those forms as well, reinforcing the highness and lowness of particular kinds of practice. I argue that the projects and propositions of *red, black & GREEN: a blues* create arenas to address these social and aesthetic spatial conundrums together, developing vexed but interdependent artistic forms to expose the vexed but interdependent content of environmental justice.

Let me first offer some background. We can start with the journey of Marc Bamuthi Joseph himself—he who "speaks through text and body"—and recall his roots as a champion spoken word artist who has launched a successful career in both solo and ensemble performance. Bamuthi has created signature intermedia pieces such as *the break/s: a mixtape for stage* and *Word Becomes Flesh*, testing conventions for speaking about race, masculinity, class, and cultural difference and earning awards such as the United States Artists Rockefeller Fellowship and the Alpert Award, as well as recognition from *Smithsonian Magazine* as one of "America's Top Young Innovators in the Arts." Bamuthi simultaneously cofounded Youth Speaks with James Kass, expanding from the spoken word form to create school and community programs that developed the expressive skills of young people. "At heart, I am a 10th-grade English teacher," says Bamuthi during a recent interview with *The Root*.[2] We can also recount his shock upon hearing in 2007 that the Environmental Protection Agency under President George Bush had decided to loosen rather than strengthen environmental restrictions, a moment that prompted him to focus his own performance practice on environmental issues while also bringing a more complicated racial perspective to Green politics. That pursuit was buoyed by the likes of Van Jones, whose 2008 vision of a "green collar economy" hoped to solve the problem of job creation and the problem of planetary salvation at once.[3]

Bamuthi began working in his own way, organizing gatherings in the parks of underresourced communities that asked citizens to reflect on environmental issues, from toxic dumping to toxic eating, that affected their communities. The effort prompted one of many recalibrations: "I was using a vocabulary and a world view that I had inherited from scientists, and that wasn't appropriate because we had a different project. . . . Our message was about creating a safe space for learning, which has been a problem for the Green movement."[4] The experience provoked a name change and a philosophical one: "we moved toward Life."[5] Deemphasizing a Green rhetoric that seemed not to address the basic needs of daily survival in underresourced communities, Bamuthi decided to focus on the language of Living. Mixing song, dance, games, public art, and food, each event asked neighbors to discuss "what sustains Life" in their communities. The invitation prompted a wider imagining of what qualifies as sustenance and what counts as Life. That imagining would ultimately find its way back into the text of *red, black & GREEN: a blues*, a performance piece precommissioned to open at Yerba Buena Center for the Arts in San Francisco and to tour to many other experimental performance spaces in the United States.

Ultimately then, Life is Living, a multicity festival started in 2008 for which Bamuthi serves as artistic director, and *red, black & GREEN: a blues* are part of a shared project that seeks to create different kinds of performance spaces for the exploration of environmental questions, using the living media of performance to focus attention on the spatial politics of life itself. Bamuthi's environmental art practice coincides with a wider movement in environmental justice and with a longer history of Black environmental thought. The Bush decision to loosen environmental regulations on corporate polluters is not an abstraction to a large segment of underresourced Black communities. Environmental activists of the 1970s and 1980s became more aware of the unequal demographic effects of environmental pollution.[6] Many locate the emergence of the environmental justice movement when consciousness of civil rights met the "energy crisis" of the 1970s.[7] The phrase "environmental racism," which was coined soon after, was, according to Benjamin Chavis,

> racial discrimination in the deliberate targeting of ethnic and minority communities for exposure to toxic and hazardous waste sites and facilities, coupled with the systematic exclusion of minorities in environmental policy making, enforcement, and remediation.[8]

Legal scholars in the United States, such as Sheila Foster, warn that employing the term "racism" may have little legal traction in a context that needs to locate "deliberate intent," but they argue that the legal grounds of environmental law should provide resources for addressing such inequalities.[9] By the mid-1990s—before Van Jones was hired as an environmental advisor to the Obama administration—scholars such as Jim Schwab and Robert D. Bullard published analyses of labor and environmental laws that exposed the racist effects of inadequate public policy.[10]

The recounting of this kind of story follows a particular pattern, one in which the concept of race is "added" to an ongoing environmental movement. Often the directive is to bring race to the Green movement and to bring the Green movement to communities of color. But what such a frame misrecognizes is that so-called Green values are already deeply enmeshed in the history of African American communities in the United States. In a special Green issue of *The Crisis Magazine*, a historic journal for the dissemination of Black thought and activism founded by W. E. B. Du Bois, Dorecta Taylor recently proffered such an argument: "Blacks who were still enslaved were forced to transform the environment with their labor. In so doing, many developed environmental expertise that they used to escape bondage and forge new lives for themselves in freedom."[11] Whether recalling Harriet Tubman's ecological awareness of the river currents and moss growth that guided her escape plans for slaves or whether positioning W. E. B. Du Bois's *The Philadelphia Negro* as a precursor to the ethnographies of environmental justice, Dorceta Taylor's opening essay argued that what we might now call a "Green" consciousness has been fundamental to Black survival in the United States. Similarly, as contributors to a recent collection on Black environmental thought remind us:

> Most slaves' waking hours were spent in labor on the land, but that labor gave them knowledge of the land that was intimate and precise. . . . For African American slaves, the wilderness was a place of potential deliverance—a site of healing, a meeting spot, a place where a decisive edge of resources could be added to meager plantation rations, and a place where salvation could be gained.[12]

Thus Bamuthi's decision to turn "Life" into a galvanizing term came from an awareness that environmental training was not new for African Americans. "I don't need to tell black folk how to sustain themselves. . . . Black folk have been behaving in environmental ways for centuries."[13] Indeed, from a certain angle of vision, the history of Black intellectual life is intimately tied to a history of agrarian politics, whether in the rural democratic vision of Booker T. Washington, the soil studies and peanut farming of model citizen and scientist George Washington Carver, or the vision of a natural connection to African land embodied in Marcus

Garvey's Pan-African ideals. Both integrationist and separatist models of Black thought have used agrarian metaphors to galvanize themselves, whether as a vehicle for the virtuous integration of Black agrarian laborers or as a vehicle for establishing the autonomy of pan-African identities. Even if the underresourced neighborhoods with whom Bamuthi worked in Life is Living are "urban" or "semiurban," his goal is to foreground the contemporary behaviors that sustain and care for the health, feeding, and shelter of each community. This brand of environmentalism coincides with progressive urban planning movements as well. It recalls the worldview of AbdouMaliq Simone, who argues that "people" function more deeply as a self-sustaining "infrastructure" in urban neighborhoods where traditional material infrastructures have broken down.[14] Life is Living thus seeks to redefine Green history and Green practice to recall the expanded environmentalism that is already a part of African American life.

Having offered a basic background on the politics of these social spaces, I now return to the behaviors and networks of the aesthetic practices of red, black & GREEN: a blues. The 2011 rehearsal space that opened this chapter brought artists of different media—choreography, theater, song, spoken word, ceramics, architecture, and video—to sustain a collaboration. Bamuthi asked Michael John Garcés, the artistic director of Cornerstone Theater (one of the most important community theaters in the United States) to direct; he asked Stacey Printz to contribute choreography and Eli Jacobs-Fantauzzi to allow his documentary footage of Life is Living to appear in red, black & GREEN: a blues. Tracy Tolmaire would dance and play a variety of roles, while Tommy Shepherd acted and served as percussionist simultaneously. Perhaps most unusually, Bamuthi asked ceramicist, urban planner, gospel singer, and visual artist, Theaster Gates, to design the set and perform in the show, an invitation that Gates accepted just before his notoriety in the art world went, in Bamuthi's words, "through the roof."[15] The red, black & GREEN: a blues ensemble thus parallels those of other spaces that seek to develop a cross-disciplinary aesthetic. In this early twenty-first century, those of us who try to keep tabs on the creativity of contemporary artists find them blurring boundaries of all kinds. Choreographers are siting their work in museums as often as theaters; sculptors are organizing interactions instead of creating objects; and videographers are creating installations in spaces other than the cinema. Meanwhile, much of this cross-media work aspires to social engagement, searching for new ways to activate viewers and mobilize communities.[16] Such collaborations turn up a different politics of theatrical space. If, as Marvin Carlson reminds us, the turn to "theater" was a specifically spatial turn from the text-based study of dramatic literature, it looks slightly different from the perspective of visual art forms that already understand themselves to be "spatial."[17] Recall Gotthold Ephraim Lessing's famous delineations of the proper "departments" of the arts and his argument that "space" is the proper domain of the painter, whereas "time" is the proper domain of the poet. The objects and structures of Theaster Gates's oeuvre thus already typically appear "in space"—in, for instance, the Whitney Biennial, Milwaukee Art Museum, Miami Basel, or Seattle Contemporary Art, to name a few recent appearances. From this vantage point then, the turn to theater is an opportunity to ask what happens when spatialized objects are given a life "in time?"

In fact, Gates—he who "speaks in song and sculpture"—had been asking himself such questions long before *red, black & GREEN: a blues*. For over a dozen years, he has cultivated a profile as a ceramicist, learning the techniques of Japanese pottery, as well as those of the largely white, male craftsmen of the California school. Gates began to think more deeply about what it meant to be an African American craftsman, creating contexts for pursuing that question that simultaneously exposed the repressed racial politics of the object world. African American material practices appear only fleetingly in conventional art histories. As John Michael Vlach argues, while the history of African American performance forms (in dance, gospel, jazz, orature, and more) are often studied, it takes a bit more effort to turn up the equally rich traditions of African American craft in basketry, metallurgy, quilting, wood carving, and pottery, in part because such traditions bore no "artistic signature."[18] One celebrated exception is African American potter Dave Drake, a slave who signed his works "Dave" and adorned some of them with snippets of poetry and song. After emancipation, he used the last name "Drake" and has since become an iconic figure in the fragile history of African American craft. In reckoning with this precarious legacy, Gates created his own personal and material excavations of Dave the Potter, including a series of performances where he seeks to embody the figure of Dave in song and laboring gesture, urgently creating a tradition of historical transmission while simultaneously positioning himself inside it. From within the internal politics of the visual arts, however, such laboring performances speak—not only to a history of African American artmaking but also to the embodied practices attached to the practice of "craft" as such. Indeed, as craft historians such as Glenn Adamson and Valerie Cassel Oliver argue, the presumably static craft object has been both enlivened and devalued by its attachment to the laboring body who makes it, as well as to the laboring body who uses it.[19] Whether remembering the "live demonstration" that typically accompanies the display of craft or the utilitarian ethos that places the craft object "below" the art object, craft is already associated with bodily enactment.[20] While I cannot do justice to such histories and debates in this short chapter, I flag these issues for what they say back to the inter- and intra-aesthetic politics of space. The *red, black & GREEN: a blues* collaboration is an opportunity to think about the time-space divisions and time-space hierarchies between performance and the visual arts, but it also has the chance to advance a conversation about the divisions and hierarchies within the visual artworld itself. While the visual artworld has increasingly incorporated embodied and time-based work inside its galleries, the embodied and temporal contingencies of craft can occupy a curious blind spot. Gates's work helps to correct the oversight, serving as a reminder that the craft object has never been comfortable as static display. To place craft within the space of performance is thus to foreground its latent performance history, to reembody the labor of craft performance that is already there.

With these histories and issues in mind, I want to go inside the forms and content of *red, black & GREEN: a blues*, allowing that entry to turn up yet more social and aesthetic puzzles. After staging three city festivals and anticipating a fourth in Oakland, the process of writing and developing *red, black & GREEN: a blues* returned Bamuthi to an artworld of studios and theaters. That return meant distilling and reembodying the practice of Life is Living, since the form and content of the festivals activated the form and content of *red, black & GREEN: a blues*. Bamuthi channeled the spoken words of neighbors and activists from different cities to draft a spoken word text that made poetic their hopes, pain, and everyday rituals. In the opening passages of the text, for instance, Bamuthi's poem play "Chicago/ Sudan" received an airing. In rehearsal and later performance, Bamuthi sliced watermelon while speaking with conversational lyricism to share a poem written after he met a Chicago mother and African immigrant who had lost her son to urban violence: "Me and the woman whose son just died are sitting on a bench."[21] The conversation was pivotal for Bamuthi in the redefinition of his own relationship to the Green movement. "I ask a mother about environment / She tells me of guns / Of emotionally disabled boys," says Bamuthi's character, chronicling a new self-reflexive awareness of what it meant for him to "throw an eco-party in the hood." Stunned into a political sense that "if you brown you can't go green until you hold a respect for black life," Bamuthi quietly beseeches those who have assembled to hear:

> So think of this brother brown
> Now see this mother black
> See how dark the day becomes when you bury the sun
> How you set the future back.

Such words would find their way inside a modular set built by Theaster Gates with the help of his studio collaborators in Chicago. The structure was composed almost entirely of found materials, creating nooks and crannies where video could be projected, handwritten notes could be pinned, and performers could circulate. As stories unfolded and bodies danced, the set expanded to represent the four cities of Life is Living's urban engagement—Chicago (red), Houston (black), New York (green), and Oakland (blue); each of them was occupied by distinctive characters who fielded the complex politics of poverty, violence, and gentrification.

If today's urban neighborhoods rely on a living infrastructure of exchange and support, *red, black & GREEN: a blues* thus sought a form to represent that relational reality in material movement and embodied gesture. When asked about the difference between the creation of community festivals and the creation of scripted and choreographic works like *red, black & GREEN: a blues*, Bamuthi says,

> I don't see them as two different types of creativity. In general, we seek to be collaboratively generative. We seek many ways to create safe space, whether it is in a classroom, in a community, or in the frame of performance art. The frame for development of these things is all pedagogical, all environmental, the impulse is to enable an active participation, an immersion, an ownership, among as many platforms as possible in order to advocate for that safety.[22]

Both platforms were in fact active in the same month; the final Life is Living festival in Oakland took place the week before *red, black & GREEN: a blues* opened at Yerba Buena Center for the Arts. The coincidence prompted further reflection from Bamuthi:

> However many people see *red, black & GREEN: a blues*, there never will be as many as those who come to Life is Living. Life is Living is not monetized; it does not take place in an institutionally traded environment. We want people to think about where art takes place, and the relationship between the two spaces complicates that question. . . . We want to shift the codified performance piece away from the center of the experience. We want to re-center community exchange. Five or six thousand people came to Life is Living; together with *red, black & GREEN: a blues*, that means eight thousand people were a part of this work during that one month. And no part of the piece was higher or lower than the other.[23]

For Michael John Garcés, directing such a collaborative process meant remaining "rigorous about the inquiry and attentive to how themes change in response to a process."[24] Bamuthi's method of working between Life is Living and *red, black & GREEN: a blues* parallels Garcés's own work at Cornerstone Theater, where projects similarly vacillate between large-scale civic dialogues and theatrical rehearsals where artists work to "distill" and "create a form around what we have learned."[25] Such processes thus seek to link and question the "relationship between" different types of performance spaces, positioning neither as "higher or lower," positioning neither as more or less "authentic," but conceiving their interdependence as the foundation of a total work.

The performance is divided into three stages, each with its own form of relational encounter. First comes *The Colored Museum*, a performance installation that redefines the concept of the "preshow," followed by *Colors and Muses*, a hybrid performance offered to audiences from a theatrical stage; in most venues, the performance ends with an extended discussion with all artists and audience members gathered in the installation, a step that seeks to redefine "postshow" discussion. To encounter a "museum" in the first stage of the performance is already a challenge to a theater-going audience accustomed to taking their seats quietly in the dark. Upon entry, spectators stroll in and around the playing space, moving between walls and peering into the windows of a living installation. Meanwhile, four performers occupy different zones of the installation, dancing, singing, drumming, speaking, and pausing; their movements and voices expand and contract to sustain an energy that is shared and passed on. Bamuthi's script says it "is like a game of Simon . . . with a garden in the middle, and odd projection surfaces in unexpected places."[26] Recalling but redefining the form and content of George C. Wolfe's canonical play *The Colored Museum*, four quadrants of the space are activated to anticipate the stories and movements that will grow in the four urban regions.[27] In early rehearsals, performers tried performing Bamuthi's spoken word text during *The Colored Museum* but found that the spectacular and auditory overload of the environmental installation drowned out the script. They soon realized, however, that this dynamic museum had the chance to create a different kind of "immersive" experience that paralleled the process of social engagement. "When you first go into a new place," says Garcés,

> it can be intensely emotional and experiential. You're there for a purpose, but it's not your world, and you're in that space of emotional intensity. . . . I thought of the installations as representing that emotion, of what it was like to live through the festivals in the different cities. Installation is immersive and experiential; you're not grasping a story yet; you are just in the midst of this creative world.[28]

The "space-time sensorium" of living installation thus matched the rhythms and experience of a city's living infrastructure.

The Colored Museum lasts for over thirty minutes, and while the "story" may not be fully graspable by the receivers, it is in fact structured in four rotations. The four players rotate between stations, at times overlapping, but for the most part staying in a quadrant; while there, they improvise around stories and images that will be developed later, introducing "Theaster in New York building an alter of spray paint . . . Tommy in Houston in the posture of Mr. Aaron . . . MBJ in Oakland, washing gravel."[29] As receivers begin to wonder about this mix of visual and auditory associations, they find themselves in the midst of a space that is both anticipatory and documentary. Bamuthi calls it "an echo of the as yet . . . a precognitive *déjà vu* . . . a memory masquerading as present tense."[30] This is also a space of interarts politics and interarts exchange. Within an immersive environment that is not yet fully legible, audiences must modulate literally and metaphorically their own relationships to an assembly of images, structures, sounds, and texts. As a mode of reception, the "museum" form makes that modulation particularly acute through an encounter that is proximate, intimate, and mobile. Receivers can get close to the structure; they can touch it if they want. Decisions to stand, walk, or walk faster belong to them. Receivers can move in close to hear a refrain better; they can also find themselves backing away. Each decision has an ethics. While the mobility of museum reception takes the theater audience out of its seats, aesthetic conventions are also challenged in reverse. Indeed, the safety and control of museum reception is challenged when the exhibition is embodied and unfolds in time. While *The Colored Museum* is a more resonant title than *The Colored Performance Installation*, an installation is in fact what receivers have before them. In this place of time-space recalibration, the traditionally static becomes temporal and the traditionally temporal finds itself stalled. Both Bamuthi and Garcés note that such an interarts revision is also central to what they would call a "hip-hop aesthetic." "I'm a champion of hybridity . . . , an aesthetic manifestation of hip-hop culture, the blending of styles," says Bamuthi, "hip-hop culture permeates everything I do, the advanced attack on urban oral literacy and that permeates my parenting, my cooking, my everything."[31] In this hybrid interarts space, a traditionally mobile museum spectator has to figure out what to do when the displayed object talks back, as well as when she meets her gaze.

If *The Colored Museum* section of *red, black & GREEN: a blues* is a space of aesthetic recalibration, a place where the conventions of performing art and visual art fields are redefining each other, then it is also a place to reflect further on Theaster Gates's infrastructural contribution to this encounter. Even as Gates's ceramic practice developed in one performative direction, it also expanded in others, specifically within the field of urban planning where he received a master's degree in design. Saying that "urban planning taught me to make big projects,"[32] he began to cast space and the built environment as materials for his artwork; reinhabiting abandoned houses in his native Chicago, he has since remade structures into libraries, bookstores, and "soul food" kitchens, undoing the interiority of a private home for local public use.[33] Gates says of his practice:

> I want to enunciate PLACES that already exist and occupy those Places with happenings. . . . While I may not be able to change the housing market or the surety of gentrification, I can offer questions within the landscape. . . . Beautiful objects belong in blighted spaces and creative people can play a pivotal role in how this happens.[34]

As Gates's visual art practice "expanded" along architectural lines, his work coincided with that of other socially engaged architects such as Houston-based Rick Lowe.[35] Known most widely for his Project Row Houses, Lowe argues for the use of art in urban recovery and was a key collaborator in the Life is Living festival in Houston; he appears as a character in the *red, black & GREEN: a blues* text. Most interestingly, the vernacular spatial form with which Rick Lowe works—the "shotgun house"—provided the key structural form for Gates's set. While shotgun houses appear in neighborhoods throughout the United States, they are particularly associated with the landscape of southern working-class neighborhoods. With Project Row Houses, Lowe repaired and replaced a shotgun house neighborhood in Houston, inviting artists to reimagine the spatial possibilities of these homes while simultaneously creating a system of social and housing support for single mothers, senior citizens, children, and neighborhood caregivers. John Vlach historicizes the rooms and front porches of these modest homes as objects of and settings for African American folklife, speculating that the term "shotgun" may have been an adaptation of the Afro-Haitian term "to-gun," which means "place of assembly."[36] Inspired by the "assemblies" of Lowe's social work and social design, Gates's "set" creates its own assemblies. It collects resonant recycled materials from four neighborhoods into what Bamuthi calls "brick and mortar ethnographies of neighborhoods"; at the same time, the structures were created to be rolled, detached, and reattached, creating a mobile modularity that makes different kinds of "happenings" possible. Thus, as rotations occur textually, they also occur architecturally. Performers rotate scenery in different permutations, opening and closing the spaces as different parts of the narrative require. The same structure that signifies an exterior porch in one scene will become part of an interior parlor with a single turn; elements in the background suddenly rush to the foreground. Meanwhile, performers occupying this set will find themselves differently exposed and protected with each shift. As in Gates's own reinhabited houses—as in most experiences of urban dwelling—performers in this space have to become comfortable with constant shifts in their experience of privacy and publicity

After *The Colored Museum* ends, audiences return to their seats to bear witness to the *Colors and Muses* portion of the evening. For Garcés, this second part ideally transports the audience out of the space of immersion and into a space of speculation: "How do you take that experience and share it aesthetically, what are you going to do with that experience?"[37] If *red, black & GREEN: a blues* is a place where Gates's ceramic objects become "props" and his sculptures become "sets," this is also a place where his own performance skills find a hearing. Gates comes to this work as a trained gospel singer, a talent that is in danger of being repressed in visual arts contexts but that is newly integrated here with the performance idioms of hip-hop (Bamuthi), theater (Garcés), and choreography (Stacey Printz), as well as the composition and performance training of Tommy Shepherd and Traci Tolmaire. In *Colors and Muses*, this interarts integration happens with renewed intensity. The theatrical performance takes us on rotations from city to city, extending beyond the conversation with the Sudanese mother in Chicago to introduce us to central figures in Houston, New York, and Oakland. Along the way, Bamuthi's questions around environment and racial justice refract and change. After asking "a mother" about environment, he will "ask a sculptor about environment" too, receiving answers such as those of Rick Lowe who (played by Tracy Tolmaire) describes his community practice.

> For me as an artist, I was looking for something where I could make work that was more . . . both . . . symbolic and poetic but at the same time had practical application. And found these houses that were in a great state of disrepair in one of the worst places in the neighborhood . . . but there's a certain kind of beauty within the . . . you know . . . simple design. Once we started to clean this place up, people could see that beauty. And so that became one of our mantras . . . how to honor the architecture of this community without replacing it with something different.[38]

Throughout, citizens demonstrate that neighborhood rituals of trust and bonding are central to "sustaining life" in communities. "The 3rd ward I am coming to know is social sculpture fashioned in melanin and clay," says Bamuthi's character, "hung by shotgun on birch wood frames / dim blue porchlights / boxing rings / young mothers / workshop space / flower men." The phrase "social sculpture" belongs to Joseph Beuys, a German conceptual and activist artist who coined the term to incorporate the actions of the social world into his art practice.[39] In applying the famous concept to the imperiled sociality of underresourced neighborhoods, Bamuthi calls the bluff of artworld avant-gardism by recounting the practice of neighbors highly skilled in the durational work of social belonging:

> I ask a sculptor about environment
> He speaks to me of misters
> Old men gathered to pastime
> Play young

men games
Share news
Insult
Seed comfort
Cultivate friendship.

Meanwhile, the text calls the bluff of the Green movement's clinical do-gooderism as well, especially one that would fixate on the benefits of organic food without noticing the inequities of an urban infrastructure that make it inaccessible to the urban poor. Issues of food security and Black agrarian politics are most resonantly consolidated in the character of Marcela, a Houston activist and neighbor who launched her own community garden cooperative to address the implicit injustice. "You have the right to education, clean water, you should have the right to fresh food," she says in a monologue also performed by Tolmaire.

> You shouldn't have to get on a bike or bus and ride for 20 minutes to get fresh healthy food. . . . Grocery stores around here are 20 minutes away in one direction and there's one across the freeway. And you know everybody doesn't have a car so they can't just hop in the car. You can't go to the corner store and go pick up a salad. We hope that by growing things people like and enjoy they'll come out here and pick food locally.[40]

Marcela is a descendant in a long history of African American female ecological creativity, one that proceeds from the skills learned under the violent circumstances of enforced slavery to the hard-won agency-exerted postslavery in a Progressive Era context. As Dianne Glave argues,

> African American women were the creative sources of gardening in their communities from slavery to the early twentieth century. By using yards in different ways, women took possession of them. They manipulated and interpreted the spaces for sustenance, comfort, joy, and sometimes profit. In the early twentieth century, they effectively blended gardening techniques that had come down from slavery and freedom with those taught by Home Demonstration agents at African American schools.[41]

As played by Tracy Tolmaire—who recites her stories while crouched on the ground, gently miming the actions of digging and planting—Marcela is clearly continuing to "use gardens in different ways." Once again recalling the life-sustaining behaviors of Black environmentalism, she blends long-transmitted skills of gardening to the specific limits and opportunities of a contemporary urban landscape.

As the piece moves from city to city, we encounter similar stories of environmental justice but also reflections that demonstrate the distinctive landscape of different cities. In New York, the overwhelm of a large, concentrated city brings a unique rhythm to the performance; here, Life is Living activists find that they have "more people to accommodate in the same amount of minutes / in new york, you literally cannot go green fast enough." Appropriately, it is in Harlem that we also encounter a poetics that reflects more on the title of the piece as well as its relationship to a history of Black literature and culture:

> In winter the harlem bells can't ring loud enough . . . /
> Red blood black people green land and such/
> Red black and green like a mossiah messianic dream/
> Like an afternoon wedding shot dead at dawn in queens/
> Silent. Bell.

With the underpunctuated stream of words, Bamuthi's torrent sees today's Harlem residents as descendants of those who first launched the historic red, black, and green of the Pan-African flag. Designed in 1920 by Marcus Garvey and his followers, the flag was created strategically to define African peoples as citizens and unite them as comrades. Red referred to the blood that they shared and shed, black to their distinguished race, and green to the verdant natural resources of the African continent. The pedigree of the play's title thus also makes another aspiration of the play clear. Evan as Bamuthi seeks to introduce a racial consciousness in an environment movement, he is also asking us to shake free a new understanding of "GREEN" in the long history of African American and civil rights movements. If agrarian expertise has been central to the history of African peoples in United States and if the color green has mobilized civil rights, it is also time to complicate its referents, to question any association that would position "Africa" romantically or exploitatively as a natural resource capable of infinite bounty.

Audiences can watch and listen as different elements of a social puzzle emerge and recede, adding layers of emotion and complication with each story. The "people" who form the infrastructure of these American cities are embedded in tangled networks of affect and responsibility. Moreover, representing these people requires its own artistic network—collaborators whose relations of affect, responsibility, and technical skill produce their own living infrastructure. All *red, black & GREEN: a blues* artists had a sense of themselves as seeders and growers of the piece. Having contributed choreography for other Bamuthi pieces (*Word Becomes Flesh, Scourge,* and *the break/s*), Stacey Printz already had a keen sense of how movement figures in Bamuthi's cross-disciplinary aesthetic: "Oftentimes when you do theater pieces or spoken word, you don't get people who are able to think about movement as deeply. . . . But Marc is such a big and passionate mover."[42] Printz's charge was to develop what Bamuthi calls the "Kasé" sequences of the piece, specifically the moments "when the best way to speak is to move." Printz's movement phrases function as supplements to some of the most volatile moments of the piece, taking over when the Sudanese mother's despair needs visceral expression, channeling the rage that rises from stories of environmental injustice into a "recommitment to working." These phrases underscore the text, advance and "punctuate it," and also transition between different sequences. Printz also used the set pieces as vehicles for launching bodies and propelling new gestures. For his part, Gates was only too happy to imagine performers jumping off his modular sculptures: "My objects can be objects that need people to touch them and respond them and react to them."[43] Gates's lack of preciousness toward his contributed art coincides with Bamuthi's aspirations. "It's not a 'don't touch the art' kind of party," says Bamuthi: "Leave your DNA on the floor. Here's the set, play it."[44]

With all these artistic intelligences in the room—performers, sculptors, choreographers, along with video, mural, and lighting designers, creating the conditions for effective collaboration was still a process. Bamuthi's hope was that "everyone involved grows by the exponent of collective investment," and Garcés's focus as a director was to make sure that happened.[45] For Garcés, "collaboration is two or more people coming together to reach a goal that is as yet unclear, and that means they share a willingness to try things, and being willing to change them, trusting that we'll get there."[46] Perhaps more than we recognize, such sentiments expose the latent politics of the cross-arts space. It should be said that many artists—trained in their respective fields of playwriting, choreography, or visual art—would find it impossible, aesthetically as well as temperamentally, to commit to such a process. As Garcés noted, "there was always an interesting set of strong authorial intentions in the room."[47] Collaboration across the arts meant not only "working with others" but also dismantling the boundaries (and yes, hierarchies) between art forms; it meant that the script would change when the actors performed it, a sculpture would be overturned and moved in unexpected ways, and a documentary film could suddenly serve as "background" for a "happening."

For Gates, who has often had to choose between performing and visual artworlds, the cross-arts exchange was particularly welcome.

> People are always like, "are you a visual artist with performance interests, or are you a performance artist with visual tendencies?" . . . This time I felt like I was wholly a collaborator, not just an actor, not only a potter. . . . I felt I was being asked to collaborate in the structure of the piece itself.[48]

Moreover, the move between the worlds of performance and visual art also meant reckoning with different artistic conventions around authorship. Gates is an object-maker whose work has been acquired by prominent collectors and museums, and thus his art often circulates in a space where the unique artistic signature is paramount. Calling this fixation on the "single maker" "unnatural," Gates already deviates from the conventions of other high-end visual artists by including the names of the fabricators and builders, such as John Preus, who assist in making his objects and site-works: "The artist with more force, with more generosity, with more single-mindedness, with more connective and collaborative ability, might be able to generate more impact per square block."[49] The interesting thing is that Gates seeks to maintain this philosophy in a world where his own authorial signature is gaining such traction. Indeed, as I write, he is coordinating his appearances on the *red, black & GREEN: a blues* tour with simultaneous commissions and retrospectives at biennials and museums around the world. Even as *red, black & GREEN: a blues* tours as a collaborative work, the "set" he has created also circulates as a sculpture, one that would no doubt generate a bidding war at an art fair. Such economies thus further heighten the politics of the interarts space.

If the hope for *red, black & GREEN: a blues* is to encourage growth "by the exponent of collective investment," then that sense of collectivity continues—intermittently—in the third and final portion of the piece. At the end of the show in most venues, audience members are asked to enter the playing space for conversation. *Colors and Muses* ends with the shotgun house set "closed" in a final tableau. The invitation to enter the space coincides with a reopening of the house structures, welcoming audience members into the installation for continued dialogue. A community of partial strangers thus explores the central topics and techniques of the work, sharing their own thoughts about "what sustains life in our communities" and thereby transforming the gathering into an extension of the Life is Living movement. Of all stages in the work, this one arguably involves the most risk and willingness to confront the unknown. Who will talk? And what will they say? Who will disagree, and how will this highly provisional community deal with that disagreement? For Bamuthi, it is essential that the conversation exceeds the conventions of a typical postshow discussion, but it is also hard to achieve. When performing in Houston's Mitchell Center for the Arts, they found that the height and distance of the proscenium space inhibited spatial access on the part of the audience. As they anticipate new appearances in Minneapolis, Chicago, New York, and other cities, the *red, black & GREEN: a blues* ensemble will continue to work on developing this third stage of the piece. As working on issues that depend on a responsiveness to dialogue, this element of the work is essential to the form. Says Garcés,

Bamuthi challenges notions without making assumptions of those notions. . . . He came in with an inquiry that was about the Green movement and people of color, and his sense of the goal changed because of how people answered him when he asked them questions. And I think that's fairly rare. . . . The process really defined what the show became.[50]

The hope then is to allow subsequent calls and responses from audiences to redefine it further. While the rigor of the process has involved researching the arguments of environmentalists and racial justice advocates, this dialogue also means stepping away from the professional "glossary" of sustainability when necessary. For Bamuthi,

There has to be a certain protection of terms to maintain a standard and efficiency, but in this case, we are talking about our environment. So while there has to be a certain standard, it's also in all of our best interests to be as inclusive as possible. . . . I am a language guy, so I get it. . . . I could say that this is about obesity, diabetes, and food justice, but the purpose of using broad language is to acknowledge that all of these things are like an eco-system.[51]

Postshow conversation is thus about broadening this already broad language, devising new glossaries together and reminding each other of who and what resides in the ecosystem that we share.

More than likely, that reminding and that devising will not unfold without tension or fear. If disclosure and deliberation are difficult, some audience members might feel enabled by Bamuthi's own self-reflexive relationship to the material presented. Throughout the text, rather than assuming the righteous tone of the environmental know-it-all, Bamuthi cracks jokes at his own expense, positioning himself as a "Starbucks activist" in need of education himself. Moreover, he refuses to allow his racially marginal position to keep him from reckoning with his own privileges of gender and class. Calling himself "a gentrifier arriving in the dark," Bamuthi knows that no one occupies a position of purity in the decidedly complicated puzzle of urban reimagining. But a conversation about life is always going to be a dodgy one. As noncontroversial as the word *life* may sound, it comes loaded with conceptual history from different quarters. The word *life* was a signature term for avant-garde artists of the 1960s who touted "Art-into-Life" as a mantra for dismantling the institution of art and for staging radical experiments with groups of (largely white) kindred spirits. If "life" was a generalized term for many of these artists, "life is living" brings forward other urgent connotations, implicitly asking whether and how the issues of survival and justice can animate the life experiments of the artistic avant-garde.

It is also important to note that the *red, black & GREEN: a blues* "call and response" will have to grapple with situations where the term "life" simply seems too thin, too naively hopeful, to address an historic system of racial inequality. For those who consider the degree to which "social death" has been a structural activator of African American experience, life does not do justice to a deep history of injustice. For social historian Orlando Patterson and subsequent generations of African American thinkers who gave up on Garveyism long ago, no vision of African American subjectivity is complete without a clear-eyed understanding of the systemic obstacles to racial survival.[52] Bamuthi says he gets this too: "Green isn't necessarily a shared value; life isn't necessarily a shared value for Black males under the age of twenty-four. The leading cause of death for Black males ages sixteen to twenty-four is violence perpetrated on each other. So injecting that word 'Life' is to shift the perception of what it means to be environmentally literate and what it means to sustain our communities."[53] The awareness that life is not necessarily a shared value is perhaps most wrenchingly conveyed in the text when Bamuthi's character decides to "ask a junky about environment" and hears this response.

> I'm a hail storm
> Chilled hate frozen in the shape of a needle mark tryin to heal my
>   broken heart
> a junkie walking through the twilight
> Waving high to the noon in delirium
> All my salutations sound like eulogies to the future in memoriam
> Temperature climbing
> This is the high life
> And I'm fallin
> I poem my addictions I rhyme these tracks I god my wishes I scrawl I
>   black I barren I crawl I'm calling . . .
> Collect
> From tomorrow
> I'm broke thanks, wondering if you'll buy back this backpack of
>   sorrow . . .
> Can I trade from some smack?
> I got a needle filled with black boy promise you can borrow if you can
>   stomach the fucked up ways it make you act
> All the fucked up things it makes you say
> All of the healers have been killed or betrayed . . . and ain't nobody
>   fighting because nobody knows what to save . . .

Life then is not a given, nor is it a given that life is good. But in a dire context, loaded with irony and justified pessimism, Bamuthi argues for what he calls a "rite to heal." As it turns out, that process means navigating "multiple authorial intentions" that are political and aesthetic, practical and social. Recalling Rancière's "space-time sensoriums," the environments of *red, black & GREEN: a blues* become political by virtue of a commitment to formal experimentation. The artistic coordination and artistic disruption of time, space, body, and text activate a living environment that seeks a new kind of environmentalism. To claim such a right and to craft such a rite become—together—a charged, potent, and interdependent political act.

Notes

"Life Politics/Life Aesthetics: Environmental Performance in *red, black & GREEN: a blues*," was originally published in *Performance and the Politics of Space: Theatre and Topology*, ed. Erika Fischer-Lichte and Benjamin Wihstutz, 276–96 (New York: Routledge, 2013).

EPIGRAPHS: Margret Aldrich, "Marc Bamuthi Joseph: Less about Green and More about Life," UTNE Reader, August 19, 2011; Abraham Ritchie, "The Slant on Theaster Gates," *ArtSlant* (May 2010), accessed June 2011.

1. Jacques Rancière, *Die Aufteilung des Sinnlichen: Die Politik der Kunst und ihre Paradoxien*, trans. Maria Muhle, Susanne Leeb, and Jürgen Link (Berlin: b_books, 2006), 77.

2. Simone Jacobson, "Marc Bamuthi Joseph: Sustaining Life Is Going Green," *The Root*, https://www.theroot.com/marc-bamuthi-joseph-sustaining-life-is-going-green-1790862665.

3. Van Jones, *The Green Collar Economy: How One Solution Can Fix Our Two Biggest Problems* (New York: Harper One, 2008).

4. Marc Bamuthi Joseph, interview by the author, June 2011.

5. Bamuthi Joseph, interview by the author, June 2011.

6. In the United States such concerns received mainstream coverage in publications like Richard A. Taylor, "Do Environmentalists Care about Poor People," *US News and World Report*, April 2, 1983, 51–52, as well as in prescient pieces such as Nathan Hare, "Black Ecology," *Black Scholar* 1, no. 6 (April 1979): 2–8.

7. See Kwasi Densu, "Theoretical and Historical Perspectives on Agroecology and African American Farmers," in Jeffrey Jordan, Jerry Pennick, Walter Hill, and Robert Zabawa, eds., *Land & Power: Sustainable Agriculture and African Americans* (College Park, MD: SARE, 2007), 94.

8. Benjamin Chavis, foreword to *Confronting Environmental Racism: Voices from the Grassroots*, ed. Robert D. Bullard (Boston: South End Press, 1993), 31.

9. Sheila Foster, "Race(ial) Matters: The Quest for Environmental Justice," *Ecology Law Quarterly* 20 (1993): 721–53.

10. Jim Schwab, *Deeper Shades of Green: The Rise of the Blue-Collar and Minority Environmentalism in American* (San Francisco: Sierra Club, 1994); Robert D. Bullard, ed., *Unequal Protection: Environmental Justice and Communities of Color* (San Francisco: Sierra Club, 1994).

11. Dorceta Taylor, "Green Power," *Crisis Magazine* 118, no. 2 (April 2011): 16–18, 18.

12. Jeffrey L. Jordan, Jerry Pennick, Walter Hill, and Robert Zabawa, "Introduction to Sustainable Agriculture and African American Land and Power," in Jordan et al., *Land & Power*, 5.

13. Marc Bamuthi Joseph, interview by Michael Krasny, *National Public Radio* (October 18, 2011).

14. AbdouMaliq Simone, "People as Infrastructure: Intersecting Fragments in Johannesburg," *Public Culture* 16, no. 3 (Fall 2004): 407–29.

15. Bamuthi Joseph, interview by the author, June 2011.

16. For my own take on how cross-arts engagement intersects with social goals, see Shannon Jackson, *Social Works: Performing Art, Supporting Publics* (New York and London: Routledge, 2011).

17. Marvin Carlson, "The Theatre *ici*," in Erika Fischer-Lichte and Benjamin Wihstutz, eds., *Performance and the Politics of Space: Theatre and Topology* (New York: Routledge, 2013), 15–30.

18. John Michael Vlach, *By the Work of Their Hands: Studies in Afro-American Folklife* (Ann Arbor, MI: UMI Research Press, 1991).

19. Valerie Cassel Oliver, "Craft out of Action," in Valerie Cassel Oliver, ed., *Hand + Made: The Performative Impulse in Art and Craft* (Houston: Contemporary Art Museum Houston, 2010), 5.

20. See Glen Adamson, "Craft and the Romance of the Studio," *American Art* 21, no. 1 (Spring 2007): 14–18.

21. Script for *red, black & GREEN: a blues* (September 2011 version) shared with the author. All passages quoted are from this version.

22. Bamuthi Joseph, interview by the author, June 2011.

23. Marc Bamuthi Joseph, interview by the author, December 2011

24. Michael John Garcés, interview by the author, June 2011.

25. Michael John Garcés, interview by the author, December 2011.

26. Script for *red, black & GREEN: a blues*.

27. George C. Wolfe, *The Colored Museum* (New York: Grove Press, 1988).

28. Garcés, interview by the author, December 2011.

29. Script for *red, black & GREEN: a blues*.

30. Script for *red, black & GREEN: a blues*.

31. Bamuthi Joseph, interview by Michael Krasny.

32. See Betty Nobue Kano, "Cultural Collisions for a New Public Space," *International Review of African American Art* 23, no. 2 (2010): 15–17.

33. See, e.g., "The City as Studio: Theaster Gates," Pulitzer Arts Foundation, 2009, http://vimeo.com/9055177; and projects posted on his website at http://theastergates.com/projects.

34. Theaster Gates, "The Candy Store and Other Dorchester Thoughts," https://web.archive.org/web/20100418125726/http://theastergates.com/section/31729_The_Candy_Store_and_Other_Dorchester.html.

35. Of the many writings on Lowe's work, see Aimee Chang, "The Artist and the City: New Models for Creative Public Practice," in *Transforma: 2005–10* (New Orleans: Transforma 2010), 11–24; and Michael Kimmelman, "Art Is Where the Home Is," *New York Times*, December 17, 2006, https://www.nytimes.com/2006/12/17/arts/design/in-houston-art-is-where-the-home-is.html.

36. John M. Vlach, "Shotgun Houses," *Natural History* 86, no. 2 (1977): 51–57.

37. Garcés, interview by the author, December 2011.

38. Script for *red, black & GREEN: a blues*.

39. See, e.g., Mark Rosenthal, *Joseph Beuys: Actions, Vitrines, Environments* (New Haven, CT: Yale University Press, 2005); and Thierry de Duve, *Kant after Duchamp* (Cambridge, MA: MIT Press, 1996).

40. Script for *red, black & GREEN: a blues*.

41. Dianne Glave, "A Garden So Brilliant with Colors, So Original in Its Design: Rural African-American Women, Gardening, Progressive Reform, and the Foundation of an African American Environmental Perspective," *Environmental History* 8, no. 3 (2003): 10.

42. Stacey Printz, interview by the author, June 2011.

43. Theaster Gates, interview by the author, June 2011.

44. Bamuthi Joseph, interview by the author, June 2011.

45. Bamuthi Joseph, interview by the author, June 2011.

46. Garcés, interview by the author, June 2011.

47. Garcés, interview by the author, December 2011.

48. Gates, interview by the author, June 2011.

49. Abraham Ritchie, "The Slant on Theaster Gates,"*ArtSlant* (May 2010), accessed June 2011.

50. Garcés, interview by the author, June 2011.

51. Bamuthi Joseph, interview by the author, June 2011.

52. See Orlando Patterson, *Slavery and Social Death* (Cambridge, MA: Harvard University Press, 1985); and, more recently, Jared Sexton, *Amalgamation Schemes: Antiblackness and the Critique of Multiculturalism* (Minneapolis: University of Minnesota Press, 2008); and Frank Wilderson, *Incognegro: A Memoir of Exile and Apartheid* (Durham, NC: Duke University Press, 2015); and *Red, White, and Black: Cinema and the Structure of U.S. Antagonisms* (Durham, NC: Duke University Press, 2010).

53. Bamuthi Joseph, interview by the author, June 2011.

Chapter 9

Elmgreen & Dragset's Theatrical Turn

In my dream we were *successful* artists, we had something
big coming . . .
— Elmgreen & Dragset, *Happy Days in the Art World*

On a blustery late morning in Rotterdam in 2011, a group of people assembled on a stone sidewalk in front of a defunct city post office. In front of this "deaccessioned" civic space, an exquisite plinth and glass vitrine had been installed. Members of the group began to circle it. Some meandered; some laughed with each other; some photographed; some took video footage of people taking photographs. Inside the vitrine, a perfectly smooth metal cone shone in the available light, reflecting and refracting the images of viewers who peered at it. Near the top of the cone, a metal handle was attached, evoking the shape of a designer tool or household fixture fabricated for the Alessi consumer. More cameras and a larger crowd of Rotterdam's civic figures came forward to welcome assembled guests. As the clock approached noon, they formed an expectant circle around the plinth. A bespectacled wiry gentleman in khaki and gray adjusted his flat cap and stepped forward to unlock the vitrine; he pulled out the cone by the handle, transforming the sculpture into a megaphone by raising it to his mouth. As the noon bell began to toll, the gentleman called out in international English, "It's never too late to say sorry." He spaced his words evenly and enunciated clearly, as if he wanted to make sure that all Dutch citizens within earshot were appropriately reassured. He then carefully replaced the megaphone, relocked the vitrine, and walked out of the crowd and down the block. His gait and costume blended into the moving landscape of the city street as the bell tolled behind him.

To reckon with performance in the work of Michael Elmgreen and Ingar Dragset (Elmgreen & Dragset) means reckoning with performance itself. Having collaborated together for over fifteen years, their projects have been contextualized within a variety of vocabularies, including terms such as theatrical, spectacular, exhibitionist, active, live, camp, durational, performative, and performance art. The use of this eclectic performance-based vocabulary has also coincided with other artistic vocabularies drawn from Minimalism, institutional critique, public art, relational aesthetics, and queer theory. What does it mean to extract performance-based work from the long arc of this duo's career? To what extent is this "*p*-word" referring to a discrete genre of practice? And to what degree does it coincide with other structures deployed in their many sculptural, institutional, and public projects?

Such questions are particularly opportune at a moment when a "performative" terminology circulates in so many artworld contexts, one with a vexed and sometimes opaque relationship to words like theater, acting, or theatricality. Performativity—with its distinctive suffix—is used to describe all varieties of contemporary art practices that seek, in Dorothea von Hantelmann's rephrasing of J. L. Austin, "to do things with art."[1] The term derives from a philosophical school of speech-act theory that focused on the world-making power of language. Its application in contemporary art expands on the classical etymology of the word *perform*, stemming from a root meaning "to furnish forth" or "to carry out." While all art practice arguably has the capacity "to furnish" the world it simultaneously describes, some contemporary art is more self-consciously aware of its world-making actions. In J. L. Austin's *How to Do Things with Words*, such actions depended on what he called the "happy uptake," that is, enabling conditions for "felicitous" reception that allowed the performative act to affect the thing it sought to do. A piece such as *It's never too late to say sorry* fits nicely into this capacious frame, employing as this piece does a durational and spatial structure that simultaneously seeks to reach, and potentially absolve, an unspecified addressee. We might then ask a follow-up question: How would the performative aspects of such a work interface with its theatrical aspects? A theatrical frame would focus not only on the audience's "uptake" of a particular speech act but also on the *casting*, *costuming*, and *blocking* of the performer who raises a *prop* to express a *script*. Such a focus would align with the etymology of "theater" as a term, one that derives from a root meaning "a place for viewing." The theatrical focus would emphasize not only what is viewed but also how the act of viewing itself becomes a subject for reflection. Odd as it may seem, the fact is that the vocabulary of performativity and that of theatricality are only occasionally brought into the same space. Precisely because Elmgreen & Dragset have experimented so widely, however, the interpretation of their work requires an open and inclusive vocabulary. Indeed, the span of their work across genres of performance art, live installation, public sculpture, theater, and even opera provides occasion not simply to document their hybrid practices but also, more interestingly, to reflect on the conventions we use to understand them. In what follows, I invoke different projects to track varied types of intervention, noting that structures of the performative and the theatrical appear in projects labeled performance art and in projects labeled institutional critique or public art. I then turn to what might be an especially radical cluster of performative projects precisely because their focus is so traditional: the theater. I conclude with a return to *It's never too late to say sorry* and with an anticipation of *Happy Days in the Artworld*, positioning them as integrations and expansions of Elmgreen & Dragset's performative performances.

Expanded Performance Art

> Such instant complicity . . . we were cross-peeing in a
> cruising park. Two steaming golden diagonals . . .
> —Michael Elmgreen, *Happy Days in the Art World*

In many ways, performance was the form that brought Elmgreen and Dragset together in the first place—well, perhaps the second place. Born in Denmark and Norway, respectively, the two had varied backgrounds when they met in the mid-1990s. Elmgreen had some art training, wrote poetry, and had odd jobs as an interior decorator. Dragset studied the Lecoq tradition in theater school and also worked as a theater instructor for children. After spending the first year "doing nothing together but being boyfriends," they decided to begin collaborating. Dragset recounts:

> Since we had so many other things in common, and were getting along so well on most matters, we thought that we would try to combine my theater experience and Michael's visual art experience . . . I started helping Michael preparing a show in Stockholm. That was because I could knit, and he wanted to do these knitted pieces. Some abstract pets, that the art audience could hug and nurse and feel confident with.

To which Elmgreen counters:

> . . . but in Stockholm nobody feels relaxed at openings, so we had to show the audience how to feel confident and how to use these knitted pets, and then everybody thought it was a performance—so it became our first performance . . . by coincidence.[2]

The coincidental turn to performance thus came about through an act of demonstration, a primary action aimed to provoke more actions in others. Whether viewers were moved to "hug and nurse," Dragset's recounting shows objects being transformed into performance. The involvement of the artists' gestures before a group was enough to transform beholders into theatrical spectators. Because these beholders decided to receive the demonstration not only as a performative invitation to act themselves but also as an extroverted display, a lesson about the object world became "a place for viewing"; the attempt to "furnish forth" became a time-based piece of theatrical art. If the action "was a performance," a shift in perceptual convention made it so.

Elements of this origin tale reappear in other early performance art by Elmgreen & Dragset. Dragset's knitting skills came in handy in a piece at the Institute of Contemporary Art London in 1996, a kind of craft-based endurance performance where the artists unraveled and reknit a hundred-meter piece of white cloth for hours on end. (Appropriately, the piece was remounted in Paris in 1998 during *Nuit Blanche*.) Incorporating the subtext of "being boyfriends," the unraveled knitting was given an erotic transcontextualization in another piece where the pair donned knitted skirts while performing in public toilets and soccer clubs; the unraveling of the skirt thus coincided with a camped-up act of seduction (*Untitled*, 1996). Other pieces made use of different theatrical elements. *Human Rights/Funky Hair* (1996) parodied the normalization of gay parenting by dyeing a child's hair orange, positing the boy's hair as the nonbiological inheritance of the yellow and red lacquered into the hair of his temporary "parents," Michael and Ingar. This kind of self-transformation and self-costuming also appeared in *Into Me/Out of Me* (1995), which documented the two artists cross-peeing in a stream. Wearing identical clothing and sporting bleached hair, the geometry of the "golden diagonals" anticipated the doubled geometry that would undergird later sculptural projects such as *Powerless Structures, Fig. 255* (2008; a transparent glass pavilion with two urinals installed back-to-back) and *Boy Scout* (2008; metal bunk bed with the top bunk upside down). Most importantly, the captivating twinness of the duo isolated one of queer theory's central theoretical challenges to psychoanalysis. Responding to the heterosexism of a Freudian model that separates those whom we desire from those with whom we identify, the boy-boy structure aligned an object of identification with an object of desire in a single figure.[3] In this piece, the person one wants *to be* is simultaneously the person one wants *to have*; liking and being like coincide in instant complicity. Finally, the camera documented the event for us to recall decades later, a visual capture that reciprocally heightens the fleeting quality of the action. If the event was a performance, the camera retroactively made it so.

Early pieces such as *Try* (1996) and *The End of Natural Behavior* (1996) reused but also extended this nascent theatrical vocabulary. Arranging beer and walkmen invitingly on comfy rugs, *Try* asked three men to bring in favorite books and to relax in the setting. Titling the piece with a verb made the invitation clear, obviating the need for demonstration. It is worth recalling that this piece took place around the same time that Nicolas Bourriaud curated his famous exhibition *Traffic* in Bordeaux, an event that coincided with the French publication of *Esthétique relationnelle* and the attempt to gather a variety of performative, interactive work within a relational art movement. *Try* echoed Bourriaud's characterization of relational aesthetics, since here "intersubjectivity" is the "material substrate" of the art event.[4] But in this case that substrate had a queer erotics, one that gave the abstract "relational" a heightened specificity, anticipating later works such as *Cruising Pavilion/Powerless Structures, Fig. 55* (1998) and *Home Is the Place You Left* (2008) in which relational encounters have a distinct sexual politics. At the same time, the fact that those who "try" will also be "watched" joined participation and theatrical display. As a place for viewing that is also a space for connecting, *Try* exposed the fine line that separated the extroversion of the theatrical from the relative introversion of the relational. Finally, *The End of Natural Behavior* brightened the line between the theatrical and the relational more intensely, returning to identical costumes and to semichoreographed activities placed squarely on display. As the boy-boy duo performed their sailor routine, art and life playfully revised each other. Interestingly, the placement of this performance inside "The Ark"—the name given to the Arken Museum of Modern Art's evocatively designed museum building—gave the piece a degree of site specificity. By surfacing a queer sailor subtext within the museum's seafaring metaphor, *The End of Natural Behavior* exposed and questioned the naturalized structures of the art institution. In other words, it was a performance that took a step toward institutional critique.

Installations, Institutions, Theatricality

> We used to discuss Foucault and his "Powerless Structures," the "smooth spaces" of Deleuze and Guattari . . . We used to talk about important stuff.
> —Michael Elmgreen, *Happy Days in the Art World*

By the late nineties, Elmgreen & Dragset's interest in "performance art" diminished. With the launch of a new series of works under the title *Powerless Structures*, they began to develop a reputation as practitioners of institutional critique, albeit a mode that expanded publicly and often entered the territory of queer politics. Inspired by Felix Gonzalez-Torres's practice, their connection to institutional critique came primarily from a fairly self-conscious decision to turn to the post-Minimalist geometries and formal interventions of an object-based practice.

"We were always curated to be the funny guys in the corner. If some curator wanted to have a more light activity in a very stiff exhibition . . . very much like becoming a stereotype of yourself . . . So it was fun suddenly to do installation works, 'cause that was a big surprise for everybody: 'oh

they *can* do art objects.' "[5] Indeed, they worried that the gestic world of
performance interacted with their sexual identity to fix them inside queer
stereotypes. "I mean the performances we did were very important on a
personal level and also on the level of artistic development for us; but
you felt you were becoming too much of a gay icon, and that's where our
Powerless Structures series started. That was also an emancipation from
this stereotypical image of gay people or being a gay couple. So we opened
up our own artistic expression to include all kinds of material, historical
and cultural."[6]

The "all kinds of material" meant developing a stronger relationship
with the traditional materials of visual art but using them to explore the
material structuration of powerful public spaces. It was at this point that
they also decided to move to Berlin to reorient their careers. In 1997 *Powerless Structures* launched a series of related spatial interventions where
the autobiographical bodies and identities of the artists were placed at a
remove. Acknowledging that the title "is derived form our misreading Foucault,"[7] Elmgreen & Dragset began to explore the reciprocal structuration
of selves and institutions, creating formal interventions within institutional
structures to propose new alternatives for inhabiting the world.

Even as we acknowledge the turn *from* "performance art" *to* "art
objects" in *Powerless Structures*, it is worth noticing that performance-
based techniques—both the constitutively "performative" and the
explicitly "theatrical"—still animated many of these projects. *12 Hours of
White Paint/Powerless Structures, Fig. 15* (1997) oriented itself toward the
white cube of the gallery; like many institutional critique projects in the
late twentieth century, it questioned the presumed neutrality of the visual
art space by exposing its construction. In this case, Elmgreen & Dragset
painted, rinsed, and repainted the white walls of the gallery, positing "neutrality" as a construction that could be layered and removed. Interestingly,
that construction and layering required the action of a laborer. Whether
performing as artists who mimicked the housepainter in 1997 or, with
Zwischen anderen Ereignissen (2000), hiring professional housepainters
instead, a critical stance on the museum gallery came about by exposing
the labor required to produce it. Most importantly for the purposes of this
essay, the attempt to expose the contingency and structure of the museum
required performance. In fact, performance-based turns would animate
several spatial interventions, including their well-publicized decision to
place an aesthetic umbrella over the construction and rehab process of
the Kunsthalle in Zurich with *Taking Place* (2001–2). Consider Daniel
Birnbaum's extended account:

> When the crowd walked through the doors, they encountered a
> construction site in which two men were busy demolishing a con-
> crete wall with sledgehammers while another pair of workers were

erecting a new one. Still another duo was removing the rubble and emptying the director's office of its furniture. The wreckage was everywhere and the noise was deafening. What was going on? Had there been an accident? Was it all a misunderstanding concerning address or date? In fact, everything was proceeding according to plan. What the crowd was experiencing and participating in was a performance piece, *Taking Place*, 2001–2002, involving six men restructuring an art center in the largest city in Switzerland. Why not put the office at the entrance to the building instead of hiding it in the back? the artists asked. Why not open up the reading room and make it more welcoming? . . . The construction work, carefully choreographed by the artists, took place only when the museum was open to the public. After the first few days' din of sledgehammers and concrete smashing, things quieted down. The show grew calm, approaching the solemn state we associate with the experience of art: The last weeks were about white paint, primarily; the very last days exclusively about degrees of whiteness and the fine-tuning of light.[8]

This project—like others by artists ranging from Hans Haacke to Mel Bochner to Andrea Fraser to Daniel Buren to Santiago Sierra and more— sought to expose the apparatus of the artworld, sometimes through explicit revelation or spatial reorganizing, and sometimes by withdrawing, destroying, or rebuilding elements of a gallery structure. Interestingly, *Taking Place*'s act of infrastructural avowal created a temporal experience. The exposure and reordering of the material space became a "performance piece," one that was not simply fabricated but "choreographed." The dismantling of the supporting apparatus of object-based art simultaneously opened the door to a new kind of time-based art. A certain kind of cross-medium encounter thus enabled an anti-medium-specific gesture. For Elmgreen & Dragset, this was another way to combine "his visual art experience" with "my theater experience."

Other projects exemplify a latent theatricality within practices of institutional critique and expanded public art. Several projects focused not only on representing the laborers behind the construction of a public space but also on the people responsible for maintaining it. The museum security guard is a constant if functionally invisible figure in most venues of artistic display. In *Reg(u)arding the Guards* (2005), Elmgreen & Dragset decided to call attention to this figure by defining a group of guards as an art installation. In a move that provoked reflection on employment practices within post–welfare state nations, they hired unemployed citizens to be cast as uniformed "guards," seating them in chairs within a single room of the museum gallery.[9] These performers both watched over the artwork and occupied the place of the artwork itself. Meanwhile, receivers faced

Fig. 5. Elmgreen & Dragset, *Re-g(u)arding the Guards*, 2005. Chairs, uniformed museum guards in an empty gallery. Space and number of performers variable. Courtesy of Galleri Nicolai Wallner. Photograph by Thor Brødreskift (Bergen) and Stephen White (London).

sentient sculptures who looked back at them in return. *Reg(u)arding the Guards* thus conducted an institutional critique via a theatrical enactment, one that itself troubled who was beholding whom in this place for viewing.

The exposure and deployment of an institution's latent theatricality appeared in several other projects that involved the creation of new character-laborers. *Tate Modern Walks–A Power Station Revisited* (2004) redefined the performance of the docent tour by giving spectators an alternate tour of the Tate's backstage and repressed history as a power station. The *Butler Guard* of *The One & The Many* (2010; ZKM Karlsruhe, Germany), the *Sauna Boys* of *Amigos* (2011; Galería Helga de Alvear, Madrid), and the *Real Estate Agents* of *The Collectors* (2009; fifty-third Venice Biennale) all adapted an existing labor performance to the needs of an artistic experience, choreographing gestures and rehearsing monologues that commented on the classed experience of work and art in the same breath. Finally, other works heightened the theatricality of the viewing relationship to reflect on the menace and pleasure of seeing and being seen. The infrastructural intervention of *Taking Place* took a more intimate turn in *How Are You Today?* (2002) when the artists constructed an enlarged peephole between Galleria Massimo de Carlo in Milan and the personal apartment of a neighbor above it. The female neighbor's everyday actions thus "became a performance" by virtue of being watched. At the same time, the viewer's head appeared inside a large bubble visible to the neighbor, providing the opportunity for her to watch the viewer watch. Once again, an institutional critical gesture partook of a theatrical structure:

> You popped into her domestic setting like an alien . . . And you looked into this stranger's private life from a floor level perspective as if you were a bug or a frog . . . After having talked so much about "the missing link" between the exhibition space and the everyday life taking place right outside its wall, it was such a great satisfaction suddenly being able to drill this hole into the ceiling—and by this simple gesture making a very concrete connection between the art space and its immediate surrounding.[10]

While some projects created surveillance schemes in which viewers remained relatively anonymous, several projects installed this kind of reciprocal surveillance into their structure. In *Paris Diaries* (2003), for instance, young men were each seated at desks in a gallery and asked to write in their diaries for hours on end. When visitors entered, they could peer over the shoulders of the writers to read the journal, deciding at the same time how far to tread into private territory. Eventually, however, the diary writers began to record the behaviors and experience of the gallery itself; hence, when visitors peered over the writers' shoulders, they suddenly realized that they themselves were being surveilled.

Theatrical Returns

> As far as I can see, there is only a big black void like an endless darkened auditorium filled with a bored, exhausted, and invisible audience.
> —Michael Elmgreen, *Happy Days in the Art World*

After several years of proving that they could "make art objects" within the *Powerless Structures* series, Elmgreen & Dragset began to recall and expand some of their earlier performance art and theatrical interests. Of course, as the above section argues, such interests never entirely receded. Even as they were critically undoing and reassembling museum structures, they also took such infrastructurally critical practices to the space of the theater. At the Odense Performance Festival in 1998, they created a piece that involved the deinstallation of the theater's stage and lighting equipment before an expectant audience. In *Erste Reihe (Front Row)* (2001), they removed seats from the Schauespielhaus in Hamburg, replacing them with a large velvet replica that put the act of theatrical viewing on display. Meanwhile, *Safety Curtain* (2002–3) positioned a huge vinyl eye on the safety curtain of the Komische Oper Berlin, questioning concepts of security and surveillance with its countergaze. In fact, in an artworld context, this kind of engagement with the theater building was unusual. Most institutional critiques positioned the museum as the institution in need of critique, a habit that paradoxically legitimated the museum as the custodian of "art," even if the espoused desire was to question it. But if there remains some ambivalence toward the theater as an institution—even if we are amid a self-consciously performative moment in contemporary art—some curators and commissioning bodies began to offer new opportunities to stage a theatrical return. Elmgreen & Dragset jumped at the chance to do a set design for the Opéra de Lyon for *Faustus, The Last Night* (2006) and also tried out filmmaking in *L'amour de Loin* (2008).

A far more explicit foray into theatermaking came about in their creation of *Drama Queens* (2007), a play that used a theatrical stage to comment on the conventions and quirks of visual artworld behavior. Conceived by Elmgreen & Dragset with text by Tim Etchells of the British theatre troupe Forced Entertainment, the play premiered at Skulptur Projekte Münster in Germany and then moved to the Old Vic in London with a celebrity cast performing the voice-overs. The play embodied as characters seven iconic art works: Alberto Giacometti's *Walking Man* (1960), Hans Arp's *Cloud Shepherd* (1953), Barbara Hepworth's *Elegy III* (1966), Sol Lewitt's *Four Cubes* (1971), Ulrich Rukreim's *Untitled (Granite)* (1987), Jeff Koons's unstoppable *Rabbit* (1986), and a cameo appearance from Andy Warhol's *Brillo Box* (1964). The text alternates between group dialogue and caricatured soliloquies that repeat art-critical statements as the internalized monologue of a sculpture. Says Koons's Rabbit, "They said I was nothing, an empty gesture, a superficial if kind of clever decoration. Others said that I embodied a devastating critique of the economy of the superficial."[11] The play thus puts a first person "I" behind each sculpture who narrates his or her fraught history, loves, losses, and merits as an art object with excessively egoistic subjectivity. In the text, Walking Man speaks with old-world weariness. Elegy and Four Cubes flirt; Rabbit runs about the stage, recounting critiques of himself and occasionally getting the other figures to disco with him. The play ends with a silent cameo from the Brillo Box that brings an end to art-celebrity jockeying.

If "performance" was something that Elmgreen & Dragset felt that they had to give up in order to be taken seriously as gay male artists, then the creation of *Drama Queens* marked a different kind of return to the form. This performance piece was wholly different from their knitting pieces because it not only took place in a storied theater rather than a "gallery corner" but also conformed to the conventions of a "play" rather than "performance art." As a play, it used techniques similar to those recognized by theatermakers: script, proscenium stage, actors, movement, and lighting. At the same time, it also recalled modernist art definitions of theatricality, sending up Michael Fried's anxious response to the theatricality of Minimalist sculpture. If Fried had famously articulated his anxiety with Minimalist sculpture as the scandalized encounter with "the silent presence of another person," then *Drama Queens* heightened the threat by imagining that figure loudly talking to him.[12] Meanwhile, other modifications made these sculptural interventions durable within the time-space contingencies of the theater. The sizes of the sculptures were adjusted slightly to give them proportional stage presence as an ensemble. To provide a mechanism for motorization, every one of the sculptures appeared on a plinth, with the exception of *Untitled (Granite)* who incorporated his own. With such plinths, the production both conformed to some quite traditional sculptural rules and broke those rules by making those plinths move. At the same time, the moving plinths neutralized whatever gravitational statement each had made in its time by equalizing each artwork's relation to the raised ground plane of the Old Vic stage. While Cloud Shepherd had appeared onstage in the Münster production, it was cut by the time it reached London due to "sightline and space issues."[13] Apparently, its bulbous bulk could not be tracked mechanically by the remote or tracked visually by the hyperfrontality of a proscenium stage. What Tim Etchells called a "a preposterous object-drama," another critic called "The 'Robot Wars Meets Samuel Beckett,'" expressing relief that it was "not serious or snobbish, not political or peripheral, but clever and entertaining."[14]

The extroversion of *Drama Queens* came into higher relief for some critics who contrasted it with quieter "living installations." During the premiere of *Drama Queens*, Elmgreen & Dragset installed another piece nearby titled *Have You Come Here for Forgiveness* (2007). The piece consisted of a young man, perched on a short and squat plinth inside the Sprengel Museum Hannover, reverently and compassionately handing out business cards with the title of the piece imprinted on them. While in another context, such a piece might have been perceived to be excessively "live" or "theatrical," the comparison with *Drama Queens* prompted critics to perceive it as "placid and dry," a response that shows that the assessment of introversion and extroversion is highly relative.[15] In fact, the relative calm of *Have You Come Here for Forgiveness* was an intended component of the piece. Elmgreen & Dragset hoped that this living sculpture would provoke questions about the values and affective affirmation that many seek when visiting an art institution, especially in situations where organized religion no longer provides a potent spiritual service.

The theme of forgiveness brings us back to where this essay began, standing before an unassuming Dutch citizen who boldly offered the possibility of forgiveness to anyone who decided to listen. Compared to the larger and more stylized *The One and the Many*, which opened the same day in Rotterdam, *It's never too late to say sorry* might also have seemed relatively "placid" or even "dry."[16] However, the piece's site-specific and temporal parameters created (and as I write, are still creating) a performative structure with an intriguing durability and transformational capacity. After extensive auditions, Elmgreen & Dragset selected Wim Konings to play this role, an individual with a dual career as an artist and a postal carrier. As a piece installed before a deaccessioned post office, the casting could not be more apt: "The city had to close down the building," said an assistant in Rotterdam's sculpture project, "because all of the mail systems are becoming privatized. Some think it might be made into a mall for high end shops."[17] As Konings finished his announcement and walked down the block, heading firmly in the direction of city hall, the piece begged the question: who needs to say sorry? And for what? Do civic leaders need absolution? Prospective retail owners? Dutch anti-immigration activists? Or the citizens of Rotterdam who are reckoning with their own relationship to imperiled public and civic systems? Interestingly, there will be ample time to consider different answers to such questions. The city of Rotterdam has committed to constant public reminding, authorizing Elmgreen & Dragset's piece to be repeated each day at noon for 365 days. What might come of this ongoing act of public penitence? We can imagine that its content and its addressee will transform throughout the year, subject to more and less felicitous forms of uptake by the people who choose to listen and those who choose to ignore. The city and its citizens will contend with the happiness and unhappiness of "saying sorry" as the conditions of performance change each day.

> ID: We'll wait.
> ME: Nothing more to add.

The premiere of *Happy Days in the Art World* at the 2011 Performa Biennial provides the occasion for this essay and an occasion to survey a range of performative and theatrical work. The play itself is its own survey, told from the biographical position of two middle-aged queer male artists who wonder what if any sense their lives have made. The title of course cites Sarah Thornton's widely read *Seven Days in the Art World* while also corralling the central metaphors and figures of Samuel Beckett, a reliable go-to resource for existential reflection.[18] The play does not so much recall *Happy Days* and its buried female monologist as it does plays like *Waiting for Godot* and *Endgame*. Elmgreen & Dragset expose a queer male subtext in Beckett's familiar male pairings, transforming Vladimir and Estragon into ID and ME who occupy *Boy Scout's* bunk bed and anxiously "wait" for a new round of curatorial interest. Meanwhile, Beckett's classically context-less visitor is contextualized as a BI "SpedEx" mail carrier; BI is perpetually in need of a "signature" and erupts into a jargon-ridden theoretical monologue that recalls the run-on monologue of *Endgame*'s Lucky.

Fig. 6. Performance of Elmgreen & Dragset's *Happy Days in the Art World* at the Tramway, Glasgow, in 2011. Courtesy of Performa 11.

Beckett became famous as a playwright who broke theatrical tradition. But, relative to the performative offerings usually commissioned by Performa, this piece is quite strikingly "a play." More than any knitting-based performance art, more than the talking sculptures of *Drama Queens*, Elmgreen & Dragset's contribution is not simply theatrical but also quite shockingly "theater." It is a script written by the artists, edited by playwright Tim Etchells, and directed by Toby Frow. It has a set with props. It casts actors who play characters, wear costumes, memorize lines, exchange witty dialogue, and move about a stage space with rehearsed blocking night after night. Elmgreen & Dragset have, of course, been creating sets, employing actors, devising costumes, exchanging witty dialogue, and reblocking the art world for their entire careers. With *Happy Days in the Art World*, they seem to be asking us whether "a play" can be "performance art." In pondering the question, we might find ourselves realizing that Elmgreen & Dragset have been making theater all along.

Notes

"Elmgreen & Dragset's Theatrical Turn" was originally published in *Elmgreen and Dragset: Performances, 1995–2011*, ed. Performa 11, 11–28 (Cologne: Walter Koenig, 2011). Reprinted in *BIOGRAPHY* (Oslo: Astrup Fearnley Museet, 2014).

1. Dorothea von Hantelmann, *How to Do Things with Art: The Meaning of Art's Performativity* (Zurich: JRP Ringier, 2010). See also J. L. Austin's classic, *How to Do Things with Words*, 2nd ed. (Cambridge, MA: Harvard University Press, 1975).

2. Hans Ulrich Obrist, "Performative Constructions: Interview by Hans Ulrich Obrist," in *Powerless Structures:Works by Michael Elmgreen and Ingar Dragset*, exhibition catalog (Reykjavik: Dug Down Gallery, 1998), 27.

3. For a queer critique of this psychoanalytic frame, see Diana Fuss, *Identification Papers: Readings on Psychoanalysis, Sexuality, and Culture* (New York: Routledge, 1995).

4. Nicolas Bourriaud, *Relational Aesthetics*, trans. Simon Pleasance and Fronza Woods (Dijon, France: Les Presses du réel, 2002).

5. Obrist, "Performative Constructions, 30, italic in the original.

6. Ingar Dragset, in Obrist, "Performative Constructions," 31–33.

7. Brian Sholis, "Interview: Michael Elmgreen and Ingar Dragset," *Ten Verses* (June 1, 2003), https://web.archive.org/web/20150906063101/http://www.briansholis.com/interview-michael-elmgreen-and-ingar-dragset/.

8. Daniel Birnbaum, "White on White," *Artforum* (April 2002): 99.

9. For a fuller analysis of visual art and performance issues as well as this work in the context of Elmgreen & Dragset's "The Welfare Show," see Shannon Jackson, *Social Works: Performing Art, Supporting Publics* (New York and London: Routledge, 2011), chap. 6.

10. See Ivanmaria Vele, "Elmgreen & Dragset: Boiler's Choice," *Boiler* 1 (2003): 117 (includes interview with Elmgreen & Dragset).

11. *Drama Queens*, a play by Elmgreen & Dragset with text by Tim Etchells, 2007.

12. Michael Fried, "Art and Objecthood," *Artforum* 5 (1967): 12–23.

13. Tim Etchells, "More Drama," August 12, 2008, https://timetchells.com/more-drama/.

14. Ossian Ward, "Art Shows in Kassell and Munster," *TimeOut London*, June 27, 2007, www.timeout.com/london/art/features/3089/Art_shows_in_Kassell_and_Munster.html, accessed January 2012.

15. "Michael Elmgreen and Ingar Dragset have hired an attractive young man to stand composed on a pedestal at the same venue, handing out cards to viewers that read (in English): 'Have you come here for forgiveness.' The duo's living sculpture is placid and dry when compared with *Drama Queens*, their profoundly funny, parodic theater work staged for Skulptur Projekte Münster." Michelle Grabner, "Made in Germany," *Artforum* (August 15, 2007), https://www.artforum.com/picks/made-in-germany-15678.

16. Michelle Grabner, "Made in Germany," *Artforum* (August 15, 2007), https://www.artforum.com/picks/made-in-germany-15678.

17. Elmgreen & Dragset, interview by the author, June 2011.

18. Sarah Thornton, *Seven Days in the Art World* (New York: W. W. Norton, 2008); Samuel Beckett, *Happy Days*, 1961.

Chapter 10

Performativity and Its Addressee

Walker Art Collection

> The difficult time is when there is nobody . . . when we are
> waiting to be seen but no one is there.
>
> —Eiko

In November 2010, visitors to the Walker Art Center perambulated as usual through its gallery spaces. They lingered before paintings and circled around sculptures, eventually happening upon a gallery that housed an enclosed room. Upon entering, visitors found leaves, rocks, water, and minerals. They might have discerned a tremor in a small pile of leaves, looked twice at the pallor of what appeared to be a stone before realizing that the structure also contained live bodies, two of them. With barely perceptible movements, Eiko and Koma lay prone in what might have been defined as an ecological art piece, never fully still but not exactly moving either, poised precisely to prompt awareness of the precarious nature of aliveness itself. When asked to discuss what it was like to perform this signature work, *Naked*, they said that the hardest part was not the length of time or the discomfort of being gazed on by strangers but the peculiar hollowness of moments when they were alone. As Eiko notes in the epigraph to this essay, the absence of a spectator brought not relief but a strange tenuousness: it was as if the work, "waiting to be seen," did not quite exist without anyone there to witness it.

Eiko and Koma are artists whose work—along with that of thousands of others—has been characterized as performative in some way. Now we might ask what that characterization means. Are their works performative because they are performance artists? Can art be performative without being performance? Can performance not be performative? Are some types of art performative and some not? While I do not want to ignore this tangle of questions, I do want to take another philosophical tack to chart our way through them. Most generally, I would like to consider the philosophical history of the term "performative," focusing especially on what

Fig. 7. Eiko & Koma, *Naked*, Walker Art Center, 2010. Photograph by Cameron Wittig for Walker Art Center, Minneapolis.

the concept implies about the position of the receiver. As it turns out, the receiver's role—the role of the figure we might variously call the audience, beholder, visitor, interlocutor, participant, or spectator—is fundamental to understanding the uses of the term "performativity." Indeed, the reception by the audience is key to constituting any artwork, action, speech, or event as performative in its power. This factor creates new philosophical tangles when we consider what it means to "collect" an artwork; an institution or collector does not simply acquire a performative object but also a structure for renewing its relations of reception.

Let us first consider performativity in contemporary art discourse—along with its varied, fuzzy, and sometimes contradictory uses. The hazy understanding of the term arguably contributes to its ubiquity, as performative becomes a catchall in an art and performance scene that has undergone incredible expansion. First of all, performativity is often used to describe work that seems to partake of performance but does not quite conform to the conventions of the performing arts. Cross-media pieces might incorporate a body, exist in time, or perhaps ask their visitors to do something. But what is their medium? Their genre? They might be choreographed but are not quite "dance." They are theater-like but not theater. Some might call such works performance art, and yet others would be unsure about the use of such a term, especially if the piece lacks the chocolate (of Karen Finley), the scissors (of Yoko Ono), the loaded gun (of

Marina Abramović), or the oozing blood (of Ron Athey) that would confirm its place in the increasingly canonical history of that genre. In the face of critical confusion, the term "performative" comes in to save the day. It seems to provide an umbrella to cluster recent cross-disciplinary work in time, in space, with bodies, and in relational encounters—even if the term does this work without saying anything particularly precise. Let me call this phenomenon the *intermedial* use of the performative vocabulary. As we will see, the audience—the receiver—in fact plays a central role in navigating this intermedial interplay. Depending on what art form they understand the work to be challenging, their reception will take different forms and make different judgments. Their responses gauge a work's closeness and distance to sculpture, to dance, to theater, to film, to painting, or to other mediums. Indeed, such calibrations will in turn affect whether the receiver calls herself a beholder, an audience member, a spectator, a viewer, a visitor, or a participant. The imprecision of "performative work" in terms of medium thus gets tested most urgently in the encounter with someone who is deciding what kind of receiver she wants to be.

There is a second cluster of hazy and contradictory uses, however, although they are uses that acknowledge the more philosophical understanding of the term as linguistic action in the world. In this cluster, performative art seeks most specifically to do something, to bring a world into being with its action. The term "performative" comes from a longer tradition of speech-act theory that explores the worldmaking power of language. In this school, language is understood not simply to describe the world but to constitute it. Speech shapes our perception and also alters the conditions in which we live, structuring how we think about ourselves, our relationships, and our environment. As a term that arose within a strain of Western philosophy, it coincided with a Western history of post–World War II art practice, one that was itself preoccupied with philosophical and political questions of subjectivity, action, and autonomy. This is where Dorothea von Hantelmann, in her essay "The Experiential Turn," steps in to argue that, by such a definition, all artwork is performative. "It makes little sense to speak of a performative artwork," she says, "because every artwork has a reality-producing dimension."[1] Indeed, in the long history of aesthetics, scholars have debated the question but have largely concluded that representational acts of art are always reality-producing actions, contingent on their conditions of production. Interestingly, it is precisely at this point that the position of the receiver comes in once again to advance and consolidate this process. As we will learn from examining the work of one of the most formative speech-act theorists, J. L. Austin, the reality-making capacity of the performative happens in the moment of a receiver's "uptake." A world is made in that exchange. This is something that Eiko and Koma seem to understand with some degree of urgency. The reality made by their artwork is all too fragile, dependent on someone to be there.

In what follows, I explore the frames and stakes of both the *interme-dial* and *reality-making* contexts of performative practice, clustering my reflections around selected artworks and selected philosophers that span the mid-twentieth century to the present day. By reflecting on these uses, I find it important to understand and value the impulses behind them. Given the wide range of expanded, cross-media practices that we find ourselves encountering in museums, on stages, and in the streets, it seems impor-tant to develop a more precise and varied vocabulary for what they might be doing. While this essay focuses on correspondences across twentieth-century Western philosophy and Euro-American art practice, we will also see that those correspondences are revised and critiqued by practices that engage a wider global history. After introducing some key concepts and conundrums, I focus on three different historical moments that are framed by different performative vocabularies. For the purposes of this essay, I will somewhat reductively call them the "action" turn, the "Minimalist" turn, and the "relational" turn, although we will soon see that such nam-ings are themselves performative speech acts with their own blind spots. Together, I hope that a general consideration of these three turns can help us get back inside what are indeed true artistic puzzles about how we encounter and evaluate contemporary art and contemporary performance, and their many antecedents. Following the position of the receiver in these varied contexts provides a way to navigate their forms and their effects.

Acting with Words, Acting with Painting

In 1955 Austin delivered the prestigious William James Lectures at Har-vard University. In advance of his appearance, he had been offering earlier versions of these thoughts in a course at Oxford that he called "Words and Deeds." It was the Harvard version, however, that would be remembered, transcribed, and ultimately distributed. The propositions, explorations, and qualifications that appeared in those lectures ultimately became a book, *How to Do Things with Words*, which received a good deal of attention in its own time and would become required reading for many students of critical theory as the twentieth century wore on.[2] I will explore later why interest in speech-act theory resurged in our contem-porary moment, but first perhaps it is worth remembering a network of related developments at midcentury. This was also a moment in the art-world when Abstract Expressionism had established itself as a distinctively American post–World War II art movement that invoked but reworked the nonfigurative abstractions of the European and Russian schools. As many critics tried to come to terms with the large allover canvases of Abstract Expressionist painters, some found themselves just as preoccupied with the movements and processes by which painters made such energetic works. Harold Rosenberg would give a name to this approach, defining "action painting" in the United States in 1952 at the same time that Austin was rethinking the nature of words and deeds across the Atlantic.[3] For Rosenberg, the distinctiveness of "American" Abstract Expressionist canvases came from a change in attitude toward painting itself. The conventions of two-dimensional representation were undone by painters who no longer viewed painting as a domain to "reproduce, re-design, analyze, or 'express,'" instead regarding it as an "arena in which to act." As Rosenberg described it, "What was to go on the canvas was not a picture but an event."[4] He attempted to call such actions "American," somewhat speciously mixing metaphors of politics, spontaneity, and individual liberation; meanwhile, a variety of (usually male) artists were placed under this umbrella, including Willem de Kooning, Franz Kline, Robert Motherwell, and Cy Twombly. Jackson Pollock would of course become the most emblematic "American" action painter of his time. That notoriety was solidified when Hans Namuth documented his painting in action, following the cigarette-smoking, hypermasculine American artist as he moved deftly and determinedly with his drip brush across a canvas that was propped horizontally in the great outdoors.

I cannot do justice here to the histories and debates that surround both speech-act theory and action painting. But for the confined purposes of this essay, it is worth noting that their pursuits share a number of implications and consequences. Without overdrawing equivalences, we can spot a parallel between Austin's attempt to overcome a purely descriptive understanding of language's function and Rosenberg's attempt to describe the stakes of action painting's refusal to represent. Said Rosenberg, "The painter no longer approached his easel with an image in his mind; he went up to it with material in his hand to do something to that other piece of material in front of him. The image would be the result of this encounter."[5] The canvas was thus a documentary trace of an action, an encounter that was a "doing" to the canvas rather than a brushstroke aimed to represent a prior "image in his mind."

A similar if not equivalent desire to dissolve the referential relation—that is, the "prior"-ness of the referent, the image, or the signified *before* a signifier—preoccupied Austin. "It was for too long the assumption of philosophers that the business of a 'statement' can only be to 'describe' some state of affairs, or to 'state some fact,'" he wrote. Rather than statements whose integrity was determined by the veracity of their description—that is, their representational or descriptive accuracy—he focused on statements that approached the world with the intent "to do" something to it. Considering linguistic phrases like, "I bet" or "I promise" or, most famously, "I do," he found them most interesting for their implosion of the referential relation. Indeed, it was by virtue of that implosion that such phrases transformed reality. He called such phrases "performative utterances," choosing the root *perform*, he said, because "it indicates that the issuing of the utterance is a performing of an action."[6] Both these 1950s Western intellectuals were thus interested in reorienting our understanding of their respective mediums, a reorientation that foregrounded the capacity of language and that of painting not simply to represent an already given world but to install transformative encounters that brought the world into being.

This decade followed and preceded a number of transformative and self-consciously "active" art experiments in Europe, Latin America, Asia, the Soviet Union, and the United States: Dada, surrealism, Bauhaus, Neoconcretism, Gutai, Constructivism, Minimalism, institutional critique, and more. Before and after Austin, and whether they had read Austin, artists in various contexts were questioning the traditional parameters of traditional aesthetic forms in painting, sculpture, theater, and dance. Importantly, the "action" in self-consciously active art incorporated and deflected the sociopolitical contexts in which artists found themselves, responding to the rise of psychoanalysis (surrealism), collectivist aspirations (Constructivism), or rising corporate capitalism and new wars (including cold ones) that defined the second half of the twentieth century. To notice that art movements invoke a term like *action* is thus not to assume that there is any equivalence among the "realities" that such performative acts seek to make.

With that caveat in mind, it is worth lingering just a bit longer on Rosenberg's text and context to notice how this emphasis on action affected the reception of the painting. For one, it redefined the relation between the artist and his work. "A painting that is an act is inseparable from the biography of the artist," said Rosenberg: "The act-painting is of the same metaphysical substance as the artist's existence. The new painting has broken down every distinction between art and life."[7] This lack of separation expanded the notion of the artist's "signature" at a presumably existential level. Viewers were encouraged to see a painting as part and parcel of an artist's existence, not simply "reading" biographical content into its imagery but, more radically, encountering the work as life itself. With this stance on the work, the artist's actions were celebrated as much as the canvases themselves; when the canvases alone were displayed, beholders were encouraged to discern the choreographic actions that produced them.

Intriguingly, Rosenberg began to use the language of the theatrical medium to describe a new kind of viewing.

> Criticism must begin by recognizing in the painting the assumptions inherent in its mode of creation. Since the painter has become an actor, the spectator has to think in a vocabulary of action: its inception, duration, direction—psychic state, concentration and relaxation of the will, passivity, alert waiting. He must become a connoisseur of the gradations between the automatic, the spontaneous, the evoked.[8]

Intriguingly, the art critic tried to discern the duration of the work's creation, imagining the gallery display as a kind of performance piece; with this kind of encounter, the painting's "beholder" took on the qualities of a theater's "audience" member. The performative gesture of action painting thus required an intermedial calibration, one that implied duration and one that reflected on the difference between gestures that were "spontaneous" and those that were "evoked." To encounter action painting meant learning from other art forms to become a different type of receiver.

Let us compare such work with another early example that exposes the intermedial and reality-making performativity of painting: Yves Klein's famous two-hundred-piece series of Anthropométrie paintings. During what would be an unfortunately short career, Klein began to produce monochrome block paintings in his beloved blues, a pursuit that was for him about accessing a life force, albeit one inflected by an unorthodox combination of Rosicrucian spiritual and existential reflection. Klein's search for "absolute freedom" in painting meant pushing the boundaries of painting itself; his language called for a spatial expansion beyond the two-dimensional: "Today anyone who paints must actually go into space to paint."[9] Klein famously went "into space" with his *Leap into the Void*, a moment of apparent flight and apparent danger captured in a photograph and circulated in a self-published journal under the intermedial title "Théâtre du Vide." The Anthropométrie paintings were another mechanism for the spatialization of painting, one whose theatrical elements were also quite pronounced. Beginning in 1958 and hiring women to serve as "living paintbrushes," Klein organized numerous salons in which spectators were invited to watch as female ensemble members immersed themselves in human-size trays of his trademark ultramarine blue, alternating who prostrated herself across a huge horizontal canvas on the floor. Looking at the canvases now, we find ourselves speculating about the choreography behind the images. We can see how the intensity of the blue varies with the intensity of the press of the three-dimensional body parts as they made contact with the canvas. The women's own acts of self-painting—the smears over the abdomen and circular swirls over their breasts—now remain on the canvas as the signature "brushstrokes" of the artist. Meanwhile, the white space of the canvas marks absent spaces where the rest of their limbs should be; their hands are isolated in negative white space, detached from their limbs and seemingly splayed in panic. The effect of the Anthropométries is thus one that recalls Rosenberg's formula; the performed painting was one in which a painter's material is "doing something" to another material, in which "the image would be the result of that encounter."[10] Knowledge of those historical actions affects how we encounter them now. The paint presses and brushstrokes are indexes of actions whose "gradations" we try to discern, speculating on the existential "biographies" of their makers as we do.

While the concept of "action painting" seems to resonate with Yves
Klein's practice, it is also important to note that Klein himself resisted this
alignment. In fact, the terms in which he rejected that alignment bring
forward other intermedial and philosophical questions.

> Many art critics claimed that via this method of painting I was
> in fact merely reenacting the technique of what has been called
> "action painting." I would like to make it clear that this endeavor
> is opposed to "action painting" in that I am actually completely
> detached from the physical work during its creation. . . . I would
> not even think of dirtying my hands with paint. Detached and
> distant, the work of art must complete itself before my eyes and
> under my command. Thus, as soon as the work is realized, I can
> stand there, present at the ceremony, spotless, calm, relaxed, wor-
> thy of it, and ready to receive it as it is born into the tangible
> world.[11]

Initially it is perhaps a little hard to reconcile Klein's desire to enter
"into space" with the assertion that in the Anthropométries he preferred
to be "detached," "distant," and "spotless." Interestingly, the apparent
contradiction uncovers another alignment with the conventions of "theater" as a practice. Unlike the action painter, who positions himself as the
instrument of action, Klein essentially delegated and ordered the actions
of others, a position very much akin to the director's role in the theater.
Moreover, he was more able to remain "calm" and to receive the work as
it unfolded by practicing the piece with his ensemble first: like any theater director, he "rehearsed." Hence, the delegated and rehearsed quality
of this performed painting did not conform to the lone and spontaneous
conventions of American action painting as Rosenberg had celebrated it, a
fact that makes a canvas like *Suaire de Mondo Cane* all the more intriguing. As a piece that was made "in rehearsal" in 1961, it is an index of a
central aspect of Klein's practice. One can thus look at the canvas and
wonder what "was automatic, spontaneous, or evoked," but one looks
simultaneously with an eye toward speculating as to what "spontaneous" acts Klein might have kept in the script. What "evocations" did he
decide to eliminate? And what elements could have been rehearsed until
they were "automatic?" More pointedly, different kinds of contemporary
receivers might find themselves reading different kinds of content into
the canvas. Certainly for a spectator asking feminist questions about the
painting's production, the imprint of the female body parts have a particular urgency. By what logic could this male artist imagine that his own
"freedom" would be expressed from such a spotless position? And what
were the stakes of that freedom for the mute, unnamed female nudes who
became his living paintbrushes?

The intermedial expansion of painting has taken many shapes. Allan Kaprow shared Rosenberg's stance on Pollock and wrote his own account of what he felt was most important in "The Legacy of Jackson Pollock."[12] Kaprow developed an array of Happenings to extend the action of action painting, positioning them as experiments that further blurred the boundaries of art and life and carried Pollock's action legacy even further into the sphere of the everyday. It is also important to recognize, however, that other artists innovated in the experimental expansion of painting—and not necessarily in the same legitimating spheres in which Rosenberg and Pollock circulated.

In 1954, in another part of the world, Japanese artists formed the Gutai Art Association to craft alternative techniques and an alternative place for the artist in postwar Japan. Invoking *gutai*, or "embodiment," as a first principle, they explored the performance of painting, developing new gestures and methods of working with paint: throwing it, applying it with their feet, spreading it with their own bodies. As actions, these artworks preceded Kaprow's Happenings and developed independently from the work of either Pollock or Klein. Staged in a Japan that had recently surrendered in World War II, the actions of artists such as Jirō Yoshihara, Saburō Murakami, and Kazuo Shiraga were deliberate attempts to create an alternative "embodiment" than the one they found in the political atmosphere of their homeland. As Ming Tiampo has argued, the regional specificity of these actions "decenters" narratives of innovation and experiment recounted from an exclusively Western modernist perspective.[13]

The frame of action painting can become more heterogeneous when we consider not only global and gender diversity outside of Euro-American exchange but also diversity within it. A great deal of visual art made by women can be helpfully understood as an extension—and often a parody—of the actions of male painters. In San Francisco in 1958, Jay DeFeo took the idea of action, art, and the everyday to different extremes when she began working on a huge canvas in her Fillmore studio. Layering white and gray paint into forms that became sculptural in their three-dimensionality, she undertook a process of scraping and relayering, turning her own actions as a painter into a daily ritual that lasted for nearly eight years. In her hands, the action of painting was not simply spontaneous but also continuous, transforming the creation of what she would eventually call *The Rose* into a durational and social relation in her studio. If a feminist rereading of the "everyday" in action painting is made possible through the example of DeFeo, feminist critique becomes more pointed and direct when considering something like Shigeko Kubota's *Vagina Painting* (1965) or Carolee Schneemann's *Interior Scroll* (1975). Whether squatting to paint a horizontal canvas with a brush secured from beneath her dress (Kubota) or displaying her naked body as a locus and container of textual authority (Schneeman), these artists addressed the gendered undercurrent of previous action experiments. For historians of feminist art of the 1970s such as Amelia Jones and Rebecca Schneider, the intermedial challenge was clear.[14] If access to "life" was going to be possible for the female paintbrush, it could happen only under her signature and when she controlled her own relationship to the canvas.

Minimalism and Its Misfires

The performative role of the addressee would become newly heated and newly debated with new sculptural movements in the 1960s and 1970s. Variously defined as "literalist art," "primary structures," or "specific objects," the term "Minimalism" became a catch-all for this turn in art and performance, one that reduced the parameters, materials, and gestures of art to provoke an expanded reflection on what it meant to be encountering it. Before jumping into these art movements and critical reception, it is important to elaborate on some other dimensions of performativity's propositions. Indeed, having concluded the previous section with examples of feminist reinterpretation, it seems important to return first to historic discussions of performative utterances. As much as connections between art and Austin can be found in the emphasis on action, a deeper investigation shows just how much the "felicity" of those acts depends on their reception. Indeed, *How to Do Things with Words* is most interesting for Austin's meditations on what he called the "uptake" of an utterance. He conceded quite early that performative utterances could not have world-making power unless they—somewhat paradoxically—also had the cooperation of the world around them: "Speaking generally, it is always necessary that the *circumstances* in which the words are uttered should be in some way, or ways, *appropriate*."[15] Such contingent circumstances empowered speech to be performative. Austin thus became fully engaged with all the inappropriate or precarious conditions that short-circuited performative efficacy, creating a vocabulary for what he called "unhappy" performatives, or "the doctrine of *the things that can be and go wrong*."[16] Elaborating on different types of "infelicity," he thought at length about the concept of the "misfire," speech that missed its mark. He explored a variety of examples in which the intended meaning of speech differed enormously from a receiver's uptake. He further distinguished the misfire from what he called an outright "abuse" of language. Abuses were not simply mistakes but utterances in which the "sincerity" of the speaker was in fact dubious. The difference between the sincere misfire and the insincere abuse prompted a great deal of anxious reflection—not unlike our most fraught debates around the effects of contemporary art.

One of Austin's most famously fraught reflections involved the theater: "a performative utterance will, for example, be *in a peculiar way* hollow or void if said by an actor on the stage, or if introduced in a poem, or spoken in a soliloquy. This applies in a similar manner to any and every utterance—a sea change in special circumstances. Language in such circumstances is in special ways—intelligibly—used not seriously, but in ways *parasitic* upon its normal use—ways which fall under the doctrine of the *etiolations* of language."[17] The idea that theatrical representation was hollow, void, and parasitic thus had intermedial implications. Certainly, it resuscitated a historic Western antitheatrical prejudice that has led commentators since Plato to worry about the effects of letting actors and poets into the arena of serious civic debate. Austin's argument on the "nonserious" nature of the-atrical language would be quoted and critiqued by a range of subsequent thinkers, including Jacques Derrida, Judith Butler, Shoshana Felman, and Eve Kosofsky Sedgwick who worried about its implications for a range of aesthetic sites at risk of being dubbed nonserious or insincere.[18] After all, the history of Western art has seen artists, poets, and actors constantly renewing their bid to gain legitimate entry into the public sphere. Mean-while, much of the recent history of late twentieth-century experimental art has given itself a more urgent charge, seeking to undo the art-life binary that would define theater—or any art—as "parasitic" in the first place. If parasitism assumes a reality that precedes it, much contemporary art and performance exposed the dependence of that reality on a language that defined it. Perhaps reality is actually the parasite.

While much of the art criticism that invokes Austin focuses on his reflections on "parasitism," there are other dimensions of his theory worth emphasizing here. In fact, in the same period that Rosenberg was writing and painters were "acting," a variety of critics were decidedly *unhappy* about this nascent performative discourse. Clement Greenberg is the powerful art critic most famous for launching analyses of Abstract Expres-sionist painting that critiqued Rosenberg's vocabulary in the strongest of terms. Keen to develop a specifically "modernist" art criticism, Greenberg found it necessary to reassert the autonomy and essentially "self-critical" qualities of modernist painting. Joining Abstract Expressionst painters with other artists he admired, he posited that the modernist strength of their paintings lay in the degree to which they *did not* reference condi-tions outside themselves; properly modernist paintings focused on their own essential "medium specificity," their two-dimensional uniqueness as a work on canvas.

> It was the stressing . . . of the ineluctable flatness of the support that remained most fundamental in the processes by which picto-rial art criticized and defined itself under Modernism. Flatness, two-dimensionality, was the only condition painting shared with no other art, and so Modernist painting oriented itself to flatness as it did to nothing else.[19]

For Greenberg, Jackson Pollock's paintings were groundbreaking not because of the actions that coincided with them and not because of the existence or life force of the painter, but because the paintings foregrounded the specificity of painting qua painting, meditating on their own essential flatness. For Greenberg and other critics, such as Michael Fried and Hilton Kramer, there was nothing intermedial about such painting. "What does he mean by the canvas 'as an arena in which to act'?" Kramer asked of Rosenberg in frustration.[20] To recall such claims and such frustrations is to remember that many disagree with the notion that "all art is performative." Moreover, as Greenberg had elaborated, a painting was a good painting when it did not depend on the uptake of the receiver. After all, properly modernist painting "criticized and defined itself."[21]

Certainly the most notorious and hence most often circulated argument against the intermedial and performative turns in contemporary art came from a former student of Greenberg's, Michael Fried. His "Art and Objecthood" is a text that is returned to again and again—some might say too often. I return to it briefly here only to remind ourselves of how the receiver figures in the text. Fried trained his attention largely on Minimalist sculpture and the influence of what he perceived to be its theatricality. His scandalized concern focused on many aspects of the work: its supposed literality, its durationality, and its "in-between-ness" as an intermedial form. But one of his prime anxieties about Minimalist sculpture had to do with its effect on the beholder—indeed, its dependence on the beholder: "For theater *has* an audience—it *exists* for one—in a way the other arts do not; in fact, this more than anything else is what Modernist sensibility finds intolerable about theater generally."[22]

While Fried found the audience relation intolerable, many Minimalist artists sought actively to cultivate it. They were interested in creating art works that encouraged viewers to avow their own relation to the work of art; receivers had to reckon with themselves in shared space with an artwork whose constitution as a work depended on them. Robert Morris's reflections on what he called "the better new work" defined this pursuit: "One is more aware than before that he himself is establishing relations as he apprehends the object from various positions and under varying conditions of light and spatial context."[23] And Morris's own work incarnated the pursuit as well. In historic solo exhibitions at the Green Gallery in 1964 and 1965, the gallery space was reorganized and even overwhelmed by the arrangement and volume of Morris's large geometric structures. Viewers had to adjust their comportment in the space, noticing yet unacknowledged spatial elements (including the corner occupied by his *Untitled (Corner Piece)* (1964) and questioning the assumed boundary between artwork and gallery space in the *Mirrored Cubes* (1965) that blurred it. Mel Bochner would join his own interest in numerical systems with the environmental expansiveness of Morris in a piece like

Measurement Room (1969). Lining walls, ceilings, and floorboards with a tabulation of the room's dimensions, Bochner called viewers' attention to the gallery as a spatial container, indeed, positing the work as coincident with the container in which it is viewed. If Minimalist art encouraged viewers to come to terms with themselves as bodies in a space, Eva Hesse pushed that embodied awareness further, transforming rigid geometries into serial presentations of soft, bulbous, spindly, and sometimes prickly materials that seemed to invite a tactile encounter.

Even if Morris, Bochner, Hesse and other formative Minimalist and post-Minimalist artists did not cite Austin explicitly, they were well aware that art was constituted in the moment of "uptake"; they conceived art that exposed its own interdependence on this primary encounter. But for Fried and other allied art critics, such a gesture was not only formally compromising but also decidedly unnerving. Fried famously analogized the encounter with Minimalist sculpture as a kind of threatening rapprochement with the "silent presence of another person." Furthermore, Minimalist art called increased attention to what Austin would have called "circumstances," an extended imagining that was, for Fried, hard to bear: "But the things that are literalist works of art must somehow *confront* the beholder—they must, one might always say be placed not just in his space but in his way. . . . It is, I think, worth remarking that 'the entire situation' means exactly that: all of it—including it seems the beholder's body. . . . Everything counts—not as part of the object, but as part of the situation in which its objecthood is established and on which that objecthood at least partly depends."[24]

Ultimately, the performative role of the addressee would be celebrated by some as vociferously as it was condemned by critics like Fried. In this reconsideration of "the crux of Minimalism," Hal Foster expressed the change in the viewer's relationship to the art object as follows: "Rather than scan the surface for topographical mapping of properties of its medium, he or she is prompted to explore the perceptual consequences of a particular intervention in a given site."[25] Although Foster was discussing a different kind of art than was Rosenberg, his terms chime with Rosenberg's account of how action painting transformed the viewing relationship. In both action painting and Minimalist work, the viewer focuses on the artist's gesture as itself an intervention. Whether standing before a canvas or in a site, she becomes a "connoisseur of the gradations" of that action, taking account of its "perceptual consequences."[26]

Looking back at this kind of thinking from the vantage point of the early twenty-first century, we know that Fried and Greenberg would not have their way. Much contemporary experiment seems an active attempt to reinforce that notion that "all art is performative," even if some artists and critics have had an interest in disavowing the degree to which this is so. Meanwhile, many developments in contemporary art are explicitly influenced by the challenge launched by Minimalism and have extended it in ways that even Minimalism's founding fathers might not have anticipated. For Paul Thek, Minimalist sculpture hardly went far enough in engaging the perceptual and political imaginary of its beholders. In the mid-1960s, frustrated by a cool geometry that did not come close to responding to the "entire situation" of the Vietnam War, Thek installed fabricated "meat pieces" inside cubic vitrines, pushing beholders to reflect upon what it meant to encounter material that looked like it could have once been alive. Decades later, Glenn Ligon took the geometry of the Minimalist block in another direction. In *To Disembark* (1994), he further literalized Fried's "silent presence" by imagining such blocks as containers of cargo of another sort, recalling the story of a former Henry "Box" Brown whose freedom came when he allowed himself to be shipped in such a box from Richmond, Virginia, to Philadelphia, Pennsylvania. The geometry of *To Disembark* thus reminded receivers that the legacies of slavery are part of the "entire situation."

Uptaking Performance and Other "Relational" Turns

Let us now return to the work of Eiko and Koma. We left them prone amid minerals, plants, and water, waiting for someone to enter the gallery space in which *Naked* was on view. It is easier to see the significance of their realization of how difficult it was to sustain *Naked* without a receiver in the room; the felicitousness of their work's performative gesture depends on the presence of an addressee. It seems fairly clear, too, that the installation violates a variety of modernist art principles and embodies much of what modernist art critics feared. If Fried was menaced by a Minimalist sculpture that came upon visitors like "the silent presence of another person," then *Naked* also literalized that supposed literalism by using silent people to create a kind of sentient structure. Like other Minimalist challenges that expanded attention to an "entire situation" and "included the beholder," Eiko and Koma's piece had an environmental reach. The floor of the gallery strategically functioned as a sound trigger when a visitor entered the room. With each step, one announced one's presence, and the artwork seemed to respond. The resulting self-consciousness in the visitor might have felt welcoming to some and distressingly "in the way" to others.

Moreover, Eiko and Koma are very aware that "uptaking" takes many forms. They know that some visitors pass relatively quickly through the gallery while others linger for multiple hours. The artists' sense of their own relation to the beholder—one that might include "the beholder's body"—expands as well. "Their eyes not only see the entire frame. They travel to some other area and back to my body part. . . . Sometimes they see one part of us, sometimes Eiko's knee. We are inviting people's gaze to travel."[27] Intriguingly, the structural pursuit of *Naked* lies in part in its ability to accommodate different types of uptaking. Rather than hoping for one particular kind of encounter, Eiko and Koma want receivers to notice how they are coconstructing the exchange: "They have to put themselves in the mind, change their conditions . . . sometimes people say 'that's enough' . . . I want to stay more but I have more important things to do.'"[28] The invitation to beholders to calibrate the conditions of beholding means that Eiko and Koma also have to respond and accept the results of those choices. The performers thus have to maintain a flexible notion of what qualifies as *felicity* in this performative encounter.

With the work of Eiko and Koma, we also get the opportunity to think about other intermedial puzzles and tensions. As Japanese expatriates influenced by Gutai's aesthetics of embodiment, they bring to their work a cultural specificity that is registered to varying degrees by receivers on the global art and performance circuit. Moreover, while *Naked* was created for a museum gallery, and perhaps appropriately understood as an expansion of the display conventions of visual art, Eiko and Koma have also conceived work for other types of venues. Their pieces are often sited in theaters, for instance, a different kind of aesthetic location that engages different horizons of expectation for its receivers. When they work "onstage," say Eiko and Koma, viewers "tend to think about one evening as a whole thing," whereas in a gallery the durational parameters of the whole are much less fixed.

Those temporal and spatial horizons widen and retract in more ways when we think of other sites in which Eiko and Koma have located their work, including schools, streets, and even a large lake outdoors. Indeed, dance critics are just as likely as art critics, if not more so, to review their work. And just as visual art critics have had to adjust the parameters of evaluating their sentient sculpture, so dance specialists have had to as well. Deborah Jowitt once argued that the pair seeks to "de-condition you for dancing," a statement that both unsettles the category of dance *and* reinstalls dance (rather than sculpture) as a compass with which their work's innovation is measured.[29] For their own part, Eiko and Koma are quite clear that different kinds of venues have "medium-specific" ways of uptaking, however intermedial any artwork or performance piece happens to be. The decision to place *Naked* not in the theater but in a gallery space was thus deliberate, a key dimension of the kind of experience that they were trying to create for receivers. Rather than taking a seat in a row within a theater setting, waiting for the curtain call before departure, gallery visitors participate in the creation of the "whole thing." As Eiko and Koma elaborate, "they have to chose which bench, where to sit . . . they make a decision to leave us."[30]

The intermedial stakes of performance-based work thus shift depending on the conventions of the venue in which they are received. This

Fig. 8. Installation view of *Dance Works I: Merce Cunningham—Robert Rauschenberg*, Walker Art Center, 2011. Photograph by Gene Pittman for Walker Art Center, Minneapolis.

contingency is an intriguing one for many of the artists gathered in the Walker's collections, especially if one considers the Walker's relationship to a history of experimental performance. Eiko and Koma are part of "the collection," says Philip Bither, the museum's head performing arts curator, because of the institution's long history with them as a commissioning partner.[31] This kind of tacking between the professional spheres of different mediums has occurred with other "performative" artists. William Kentridge's drawing videos have been displayed in the Walker's galleries, but his work with Handspring Puppet Company appeared on its stages in 2001. Merce Cunningham's company has appeared on the Walker's stages for decades—and made its own contribution to the "deconditioning" of dance. Now, however, the Cunningham company's materials will be part of its "collection" (a status, it should be said, that is much different than being part of a performance library's "archive"). This means that Robert Rauschenberg is represented in the Walker's collection not only by a discrete painting like *Trophy II* (1960) but also by his intermedial redefinition of the theatrical "set" in his work with Cunningham. Meanwhile, Trisha Brown's dance *Lateral Pass* (1985) premiered at the Walker, and her canonical choreographic work *Man Walking Down the Side of a Building* (2008) was remounted there in 2008. Moreover, pieces such as *It's a Draw-For Robert Rauschenberg* (2008) give Brown a place in the Walker's visual art collection as well.

The protocols and paradoxes of "acquiring" performance-based works create their own new puzzles that exceed the parameters of this essay. To the extent that such acquisitions are also promises on the part of art organizations to sustain a future of continued reception, it is also worth lingering on some more recent turns within the artistic history of performative encounter. Indeed, much recent conversation about "the performative" in contemporary art came about not so much to recall action painting or to embrace Minimalism's "theatricality" or to notice a history of performance curating that has been going on within visual art contexts for many decades, but to come to terms with more recent "relational" art practices. Dorothea von Hantelmann captures much of this discussion in her account of the "experiential" turn. Many contemporary artists have been creating extended events of social encounter under a variety of newer labels, and each of the terms—social practice, community engagement, participatory art, relational aesthetics—has a different resonance and different stakes. A number of artists tend to serve as indexes of more recent experimentation—including Felix Gonzalez-Torres with his "stacks" and "spills," Rirkrit Tiravanija with his cooking installations, Santiago Sierra with his disturbing installations of unemployed humans in the gallery, and many more. The phrase "relational aesthetics" is often credited to the French curator Nicolas Bourriaud, who used the term to describe a variety of work in which "intersubjectivity" functioned as the "material substrate" of the art event.[32] That is, rather than paint, clay, wire, metal, or canvas, the "material" of the art object becomes the relational exchange that it provokes. As I have argued at length elsewhere, the "new" turns of these participatory forms can certainly be found in earlier work and in a variety of mediums, including the performative encounters of performance.[33] As we have also seen thus far, the relational exchange among participants will certainly have different stakes, depending on how receivers understand the regional politics and perceptual parameters of the situation in which an encounter occurs.

The task of contextualizing, mounting, and collecting relational work comes to the fore in yet new ways when we consider the work of Tino Sehgal. A piece like *This objective of that object* (2004) differently refracts the puzzle of the performative in contemporary art. Sehgal's objectless pieces have recently received worldwide attention, in part because they actively resist the structures of both visual and performing art. Trained in economics and dance, he seeks to make work that uses no natural resources and leaves no material imprint. Previous pieces have drawn on experimental choreography, distinctive in part because he forbids documentation or any reproduction that could substitute for the live event.

This objective of that object shares company with a number of his recent pieces that make use of a game-like structure, including *This Situation* (2007), recently acquired by New York's Museum of Modern Art, and *This Progress* (2010), originally sited at ICA London and remounted at the Guggenheim Museum in New York to bemused renown. *This objective of that object* is composed of five interpreters who form a loose circle around gallery visitors with their backs turned. The interpreters breathe softly, and then each successively begins to whisper, "The objective of this work is to become the object of discussion." They repeat the phrase, as noted in the Walker's acquisition write-up, "in expectation of the visitor's response." If there is none, the interpreters will gradually lower their voices and, after pauses and moments of silence, sink to the floor, apparently undone by the fact that their performative utterance has not produced a felicitous uptake. If, however, a visitor does offer a response, the interpreters actively celebrate the apparent "happiness" of the performative encounter. There may be an exchange between a visitor and an interpreter. The interpreters may then decide at any moment to initiate a circular dance and a series of phrases and exit the room, often leaving one remaining interpreter behind to sustain conversation with the visitor. As in other works by Sehgal, the interpreter may finish by reminding the visitor of the name of the artist, the name of the work, and the year it was made, both parodying and rein-forcing visual art conventions of attributing artistic authorship.

If much late twentieth-century art has called on the receiver to avow her role in the constitution of the art object, then this piece isolates that directive in its skeletal structure. The piece is an encounter about encoun-ter, thereby making explicit the primary condition that Eiko and Koma endured. Because it uses text and language more than the other artworks described so far in this essay, the Sehgal piece also more explicitly returns our discussion of the performative to the exchange of speech. How, after Austin, is this piece doing things with words? The "objective" is the intention of an utterance as well as the intent of the work. Reciprocally self-constituting, the work is itself the "discussion" that it seeks to pro-duce; if felicitous, that exchange will be both the form and content of the work. The utterance of the work is "happy" when the "object" of the dis-cussion becomes the discussion itself. Meanwhile, the work has less than satisfying mechanisms for contending with a lack of uptake; interpreters sink to the floor until the process can start again. But the aspiration is also to induce awareness in receivers of their own role in producing the out-come. Importantly, that sense of embeddedness comes within a structure that is simultaneously the work's theme. It is an exchange about exchange whose misfires are about misfiring.

There is a kind of recursive quality to Sehgal's work—one that in turn produces recursive sentences from critics like me who are trying to come to terms with it. But it might be exactly that sense of recursion that explains the interest of so many critical theorists in Sehgal. Earlier I noted that interest in the midcentury reflections of speech-act theorists resurged as the twentieth century wore on. The recent revision of performativity theory was part of a broader effort to understand the complexities of sub-ject formation, a project that questioned the assumption that self-making was essentially a voluntary operation, regulated only by the exercise of internal will. More recent thinkers as varied as Michel Foucault, Jacques Derrida, Judith Butler, and many others began to excavate a history of critical philosophy to mount alternative conceptions, frames that took seriously the degree to which social "circumstances" in fact produce our internal perception of a voluntary will, often with particular ideological effects.[34] It was in such a context that the notion of the "performative" was revived, this time to tease out the implications of the constitutive power of language that Austin himself might not have pursued. Indeed, for many recent theorists, it is most important to consider the degree to which the primary "doing" of the performative is the ideological constitution of the doer herself.

To ground such a complex notion, let us look at one famous philosophical example that dramatized this kind of recursion—and, incidentally, served as a resource for Bourriaud's relational aesthetics. Louis Althusser's "Ideology and Ideological State Apparatuses" is a key text in this conversation, particularly for the vocabulary of "hailing" and "interpellation" that he introduced and for the example he used to describe how we participate in our own ideological formation:

> That very precise operation which I have called *interpellation* or hailing . . . can be imagined along the lines of the most commonplace everyday police (or other) hailing: "Hey, you there!" Assuming that the theoretical scene I have imagined takes place in the street, the hailed individual will turn round. By this mere one hundred and eighty degree physical conversion, he comes a *subject*. Why? Because he has recognized that the hail was "really" addressed to him, and that "it was *really him* who was hailed" (and not someone else). Experience shows that the practical telecommunication of hailings is such that they hardly ever miss their man: verbal call or whistle, the one hailed always recognizes that it is really him who is being hailed.[35]

Althusser's teachable example proved fruitful for many subsequent conversations in critical theory. It temporarily anthropomorphized "ideology" as a cop whose performative utterance sought an addressee; moreover, it was by physically and psychically allowing ourselves *to be addressed* that ideology did its work. That famous "turn" was a form of uptake that ensured the felicitousness of ideology's performative reach. Moreover, Althusser was keen to note that the process of address and uptake had a temporal coincidence: "Naturally for the convenience and clarity of my little theoretical theater I have had to present things in the form of a sequence, with a before and an after, and thus in the form of a temporal succession. . . . But in reality these things happen without any succession. The existence of ideology and the hailing or interpellation of individuals as subjects are one and the same thing."[36] Althusser thus posited interpellation *of* subjects *by* ideology as itself a recursive process, as "one and the same thing." Joining an Austinian language with an Althusserian one, Butler would attempt to tease out a degree of variability in the process of hailing: "As Althusser himself insists, this performative effort of naming can only attempt to bring its addressee into being; there is always the risk of a certain misrecognition. If one misrecognizes that effort to produce the subject, the production itself falters. The one who is hailed may fail to hear, misread the call, turn the other way, answer to another name, insist on not being addressed that way."[37] At the same time, if misfire or misrecognition is possible, it still occurs within a recursive structure that both constrains and enables the subjects it made.

It is no coincidence that some bloggers and other commentators have used the language of Althusser's "hailings" to describe the exchanges at work in Sehgal's pieces.[38] Since Sehgal is concerned with exposing the ideological nature of subject formation within museum institutions, we could say that *This objective of that object* is an interpellation about interpellation. Indeed, the choreography of the piece seems to invoke but revise the choreography of Althusser's "theoretical theater." In Sehgal's piece, in fact, the addresser's back is turned while the addressee reckons with being hailed by the piece. Any "comment" is registered as a felicitous "recruitment," prompting the addresser to instantiate its success by making her own 180-degree turn.

Moreover, the piece seems to hail participants whether they fully intend to be recruited. In von Hantelmann's accounts of the enactment of this piece, its structure accommodates a wide range of responses, even turning ringing "cell phones" or discreet "comments in a foreign language" into a felicitous uptaking. Visitors thus find themselves "hailed" despite themselves, reckoning with the process of recruitment. It is thus perhaps no wonder that accounts of Sehgal's pieces includes so many critics' chronicles of their own process of reception. We find critics using the first person more often to describe the work, as the evaluation of the work coincides with a highly personal process of exchange. (I have my own story, one that involves the effects of bringing my children to *This Situation* in Paris and watching how their presence unsettled the commentary of the players until one found a way to interpellate my son into the piece.) We also find critics trying to push the structure of the work to test its hailing capacities. In response to *This Progress* at the Guggenheim Museum in 2010, a "theoretical theater" that included structured conversations with child players, Jerry Saltz did not fully collaborate with the discursive conventions. The result was that his child interlocutor burst into tears, prompting Saltz's to write an account of "How I Made an Artwork Cry."[39]

Like all the work chronicled in this essay, Sehgal's oeuvre also brings forward intense reflection about the intermedial nature of so-called performative work. He quite actively refuses the language of theater and performance to describe his structures, using terms like "interpreter" or "player" to refer to the interlocutors he hires. At the same time, he is perceived as challenging the conventions of a visual artworld motored by the creation and purchase of material objects. As Rebecca Schneider has argued, these pieces seem to accrue a good deal of "medial panic" as artists, critics, and curators debate different frames of legitimation and delegitimation.[40]

Finally, the intermedial puzzles of contemporary art create new performative realities (and new performative problems) for receivers trying to make sense of them. If a residual "antitheatrical" discourse still influences the evaluation of self-consciously "performative art," then artists like Sehgal have an interest in making sure that no one calls their work theater. And if performing artists such as Trisha Brown, Merce Cunningham, and Eiko and Koma are to receive the legitimation of a visual artworld context, it certainly helps that they have created work for gallery spaces and produced objects that are collectible. But it also seems important to explore the possibility of recursion and reciprocity happening in more than one direction. A museum context does something to these intermedial works, but these works also do something back to the museum. They require new presenting apparatuses; they ask the institution to make new kinds of promises. It will be exciting and intriguing to see whether and how intermedial panic can be turned into intermedial transformation. The performativity of art will, in the end, perpetually transform the institution that houses it.

Notes

"Performativity and Its Addressee: Walker Art Collection" was originally published in *Living Collections Online Catalogue, Volume 1: On Performativity* (Minneapolis: Walker Art Center, 2014).

EPIGRAPH: Eiko, interview by Justin Jones, November 30, 2010, https://walkerart.org/magazine/eiko-koma-on-naked.

1. See Dorothea von Hantelmann, "The Experiential Turn," in *On Performativity*, ed. Elizabeth Carpenter, vol. 1 of *Living Collections Catalogue* (Minneapolis: Walker Art Center, 2014), https://walkerart.org/collections/publications/performativity/experiential-turn/.

2. J. L. Austin, *How to Do Things with Words*, 2nd ed. (Cambridge, MA: Harvard University Press, 1975).

3. Harold Rosenberg, "The American Action Painters," *ARTnews* 52 (January 1952), 23–39.

4. Rosenberg, "The American Action Painters," 25.

5. Rosenberg, "The American Action Painters," 25.

6. Austin, *How to Do Things*, 6.

7. Rosenberg, "The American Action Painters," 27–78.

8. Rosenberg, "The American Action Painters," 29, 10.

9. Label text for Yves Klein, *Dimanche* (1960), from the exhibition *Art in Our Time: 1950 to the Present*, Walker Art Center, Minneapolis, September 5, 1999, to September 2, 2001, https://walkerart.org/collections/artworks/dimanche.

10. Rosenberg, "The American Action Painters," 22.

11. Yves Klein, quoted in Nan Rosenthal, "Assisted Levitation: The Art of Yves Klein," *Yves Klein, 1928–1962: A Retrospective*, exhibition catalog (Houston: Rice University Institute for the Arts, 1982), 124.

12. Allan Kaprow, "The Legacy of Jackson Pollock," *ARTnews* 57 (October 1958): 24–26, 55–57.

13. See Ming Tiampo, *Gutai: Decentering Modernism* (Chicago: University of Chicago Press, 2011).

14. See Amelia Jones, *Body Art/Performing the Subject* (Minneapolis: University of Minnesota Press, 1998); and Rebecca Schneider, *The Explicit Body in Performance* (London: Routledge, 1997).

15. Austin, *How to Do Things*, 8.

16. Austin, *How to Do Things*, 14.

17. Austin, *How to Do Things*, 22, italic in the original.

18. Jacques Derrida, "Signature Event Context," trans. Samuel Weber and Jeffrey Mehlman, in *Limited Inc.* (Evanston, IL: Northwestern University Press, 1977), 1–23; Judith Butler, *Bodies That Matter* (New York: Routledge, 1993) and *The Psychic Life of Power: Theories in Subjection* (Stanford, CA: Stanford University Press, 1997); Shoshana Felman, *The Literary Speech Act* (Ithaca, NY: Cornell University Press, 1983); Eve Kosofsky Sedgwick, "Queer Performativity: Henry James's *The Art of the Novel*," *GLQ: A Journal of Lesbian and Gay Studies* 1, no. 1 (1993): 1–16.

19. Clement Greenberg, "Modernist Painting," in *The New Art: A Critical Anthology*, ed. Gregory Battcock (New York: E. P. Dutton, 1966), 68–69. The first version of the essay, using the term "support," appeared in *Forum Lectures* (Washington, DC: Voice of America, 1960).

20. Hilton Kramer, "The New American Painting," *Partisan Review* 20 (July–August 1953): 427.

21. Clement Greenberg, "Modernist Painting" [1965], in *Modern Art and Modernism: A Critical Anthology*, ed. Francis Fascina and Charles Harrison (New York: Harper and Row, 1982), 6.

22. Michael Fried, *Art and Objecthood* (Chicago: University of Chicago Press, 1998), 163.

23. Robert Morris, "Notes on Sculpture, Part II," *Artforum* 5 (October 1966): 21.

24. Fried, *Art and Objecthood*, 154–55.

25. Hal Foster, "The Crux of Minimalism," in *The Return of the Real: The Avant-Garde at the End of the Century* (Cambridge, MA: MIT Press, 1996), 38.

26. Foster, "The Crux of Minimalism," 38.

27. Eiko and Koma, interview by Justin Jones, https://walkerart.org/magazine/eiko-koma-on-naked.

28. Eiko and Koma, interview.

29. Eiko and Koma, interview.

30. Eiko and Koma, interview.

31. Eiko and Koma, interview.

32. Nicolas Bourriaud, *Relational Aesthetics*, trans. Simon Pleasance and Fronza Woods (Dijon, France: Les Presses du réel, 2002).

33. Shannon Jackson, *Social Works: Performing Art, Supporting Publics* (New York and London: Routledge, 2011).

34. Jacques Derrida, "Signature Event Context," trans. Samuel Weber and Jeffrey Mehlman, in *Limited Inc.* (Evanston, IL: Northwestern University Press, 1977), 1–23; Judith Butler, *Bodies That Matter* (New York: Routledge, 1993) and *The Psychic Life of Power: Theories in Subjection* (Stanford, CA: Stanford University Press, 1997); Shoshana Felman, *The Literary Speech Act* (Ithaca, NY: Cornell University Press, 1983); Eve Kosofsky Sedgwick, "Queer Performativity: Henry James's *The Art of the Novel*," *GLQ: A Journal of Lesbian and Gay Studies* 1, no. 1 (1993): 1–16.

35. Louis Althusser, "Ideology and Ideological State Apparatuses," in *Lenin and Philosophy and Other Essays*, trans. Ben Brewster (New York: Monthly Review Press, 1971), 162–63.

36. Althusser, "Ideology and Ideological State Apparatuses," 162–63.

37. Judith Butler, "Subjection, Resistance, Resignification: Between Freud and Foucault," in *Psychic Life of Power*, 95.

38. See, e.g., Katie Kitamura, "Tino Sehgal," *Frieze* 131 (May 2010), https://www.frieze.com/article/tino-sehgal-2.

39. Jerry Saltz, "How I Made an Artwork Cry," *New York*, February 3, 2010, http://nymag.com/arts/art/reviews/63638/.

40. Rebecca Schneider, *Performing Remains: Art and War in Times of Theatrical Reenactment* (New York: Routledge, 2011), 129.

Chapter 11

Just-in-Time

Performance and the Aesthetics of Precarity

As part of the Creative Time Summit on Living as Form, *three performers take the stage of the Skirball Center for the Performing Arts in New York. The performers are Malik Gaines, Jade Gordon, and Alexandro Segade of My Barbarian, a three-person theater company popular among curators in the expanded visual arts.[1] Each performer begins jogging in place as a synthesized soundtrack rises, punctuated by a metronomic ticking and the sound of a dog bark.*

> ALEXANDRO, JADE, MALIK:
> Morning morning morning
> In the morning
> MORNING MORNING MORNING

Each of them sings the greeting while doing stretching exercises, launching an unremarkable exchange about morning routine ("I have coffee in the morning." "I don't.") before moving in formation to embody different notions of "time."

> ALEXANDRO, JADE, MALIK:
> Cyclical time wheel within a wheel
> Historic time always galloping
> SPECTACULAR TIME NA NA NA NA

Pitching their voices aharmonically, they circle, fist pump, and briefly splay jazz hands to embody "cyclical," "historic," and "spectacular" time. They thereby indirectly introduce and credit Creative Time, the nonprofit arts organization that commissioned the piece for its 2011 annual summit. "Creative Time," they ask, "what will you do now?"

As it had before, this year's summit took place in September. But in September 2011, several blocks from the Skirball, quite a few others were beginning a different kind of doing. In the audience and backstage, all of us were checking Twitter feeds and recent posts to follow the actions of protesters who we understood to be overtaking Wall Street. Small and large groups left the summit at various points to watch and sometimes to join. As the summit and *Living as Form* exhibition continued over the long weekend, audience members spoke from the floor with reports about what was happening on Wall Street. Creative Time speakers and artists who had already planned to explore "the gift economy" or the "aesthetics of protest" saw our beloved themes illustrated and expanded by the deliberative arenas and DIY social systems that would become Occupy Wall Street.

I would like to use the conjunction of My Barbarian's performance at Creative Time next to the emergence of the Occupy movement as a kind of background that will always become foreground in my thoughts about the relation between performance and precarity. As 2011 wore on, Occupy Wall Street expanded exponentially and impossibly quickly across the United States and different parts of the globe, a floating signifier and a growing network of techniques that magnetized and morphed to meet the specific concerns of different sites. In Chile, Occupy was about free public schools; in Israel, it focused on rent prices; in Spain, it focused mostly on the high unemployment of youth; in Oakland, it was about the summary execution of Oscar Grant and racialized police violence; at the University of California, it was about the movement for public education—and then it became about police violence too.

Not everything that I hope to express about possible connections among theater, performance, and precarity can be consolidated into a meditation on the Occupy movement, much less indexed by a single performance. As a jumping-off point, however, both sites will be reminders of the paradoxical place of so-called creatives in a contemporary economy. As a term that appears in Richard Florida's disquisition on the creative class and in Daniel Pink's meditation on "right brain" leadership, as well as in nation-wide attempts to argue for the importance of the arts in society, the term "creativity" is itself a floating signifier. In the broadest contemporary discussions of work, creatives are charged with motoring innovation and the affective life of a globalizing service economy—even as they simultaneously face the precarity and atomization of being "flexible laborers."[2] The turn to affective and immaterial labor in a post-Fordist economy is one whose aesthetic and social consequences have received much attention from politicized intellectuals in the field of expanded visual art history.[3] Meanwhile, the post-Operaismo school's meditations on the subject appear in various wings of the arts, humanities, and social sciences as critics and citizens debate the consequences of the immaterial turn—its potential for

Fig. 9. Temporary Services,
*11 People 16 Spaces / How to
Guerilla Art*, 2006. Photograph
courtesy of Temporary Services.

co-optation and its potential for progressive redirection. I think that there is, however, a different kind of specificity that emerges when one looks at this turn with a theatrical eye, and with an awareness of how the history of theatrical labor has shadowed the precarious emergence of performance both as an interdisciplinary field of study *and* as the central scaffolding of a service economy.

Theater's Affects

My Barbarian performers stop their song and break into direct address to the audience. They thank us for "assembling," using a keyword that would become a contentious one as the Occupy movement gathered steam, provoking heated debate over whether the right to assemble included the right to occupation. While the contentious association in "assemble" springs from the term's agonistic call to a space for critical deliberation, this assembly was specifically a theatrical event. That is, it appeared to be more safely "festive"—or to recall too those awkward "assemblies" that all of us once endured in school.

> ALEXANDRO: Time for Morning exercises.
> JADE: The closeness of the living organism.
> MALIK: Living as form starts now!
> ALEXANDRO: Better get in shape.
> JADE: Everybody stand up.
> MALIK: Everybody stand up.
> ALEXANDRO: Everybody stand up.
> JADE: Let's stretch.

One thing that seems taken for granted about the immaterial turn is that there was indeed a *turn*. Somewhere in the 1970s—anticipated in the 1960s by Herbert Marcuse and C. Wright Mills, and by the process-based artwork of the 1960s—labor became more service oriented and engaged in the production and exchange of affect. Sociologists and cultural geographers have been announcing this turn for a while. Daniel Bell engaged in what he called "a venture in social forecasting" in 1973 when he published *The Coming of the Post-Industrial Society*. There, he invoked terms such as "communication" and "encounter" to describe shifts in working life that focused on personal and relational exchange. In contrast to an industrial form of labor that produced commodity objects, Bell articulated the essentially *interactional* quality of what would become service labor: "The fact that individuals now talk to other individuals, rather than interact with a machine, is the fundamental fact about work in the post-industrial society."[4] For the next two decades, social scientists of various stripes addressed subthemes within this pervasive and complex "turn," one that took on new qualities during the deregulating ethos of the Reagan-Thatcher '80s. By 1992 Andrew Sayer and Richard Walker's *The New Social Economy* synthesized a range of scholarship with an eye that remained keenly focused on Marxist frames of surplus value and concerned with economic justice. In addition to exploring the elusive "products" of the "brave new world of a service economy," they showed how "just-in-case" industrial systems had not so much disappeared as been replaced by new "just-in-time" systems of manufacture. This shift substituted Fordist with so-called Toyotaist models, celebrating the spontaneous and flexible in lieu of the planned and anticipated in social systems more generally.[5] If Sayer and Walker were concerned to show how the discourse of the "social turn" obscured remaining class divisions, others were more excited to instrumentalize the power of immaterial encounter. In 1999 Joseph Pine and James Gilmore assembled Harvard Business School case studies into a well-circulated handbook called *The Experience Economy*, piquing its readers with the thrilling insight that "Work Is Theater & Every Business a Stage."[6] With loose analogies about how to "set the stage," to "theme experience," and to "act your part," small and large businesses were told to "get in shape" for the experiential turn.

While this trajectory of reflection on the social economy continued apace, it was the Italian network of post-Operaismo or "workerist" philosophical reflection that captured the attention of artists, humanists, and selected social theorists more deeply in the late '90s and early 2000s. En route to widely circulated theories of "empire" and of "the multitude" as a post-Fordist revolutionary subject, Michael Hardt and Antonio Negri detailed the elements of the service economy. Employing terms such as "affective labor," "virtuosity," or "immaterial" labor, their vocabulary placed many of the preoccupations of artists and humanists at the center of their social theory. Translating Maurizio Lazzarato's concept of "immaterial labor" and Paolo Virno's meditations on "virtuosity," Hardt, Negri, Antonella Corsani, and others have propelled a robust and urgent discourse that tries to come to terms psychically and politically with a world of labor that organizes emotion to produce immaterial experiences.[7] Lazzarato's definition of immaterial labor was able to capture not only the fleeting nature of the service experience but also the wider emphases of a so-called knowledge economy, one whose immaterial products circulated as information, software, and others forms of "cognitive" innovation.[8] Hardt and Negri thought more specifically about the emotional dimension of affective labor; in this zone, an affective laborer's product is in part the affective experience of his or her client-receiver, the "feeling of ease, well-being, satisfaction, excitement, or passion" elicited in the service interaction.[9] Meanwhile, in trying to argue for the historical significance of this turn, Virno used the concept of "virtuosity" to consider precedents of immaterial production in the virtuoso of the performing artist or political orator, suggesting that these early forms of immaterial creativity were becoming democratized.[10]

Whether there is indeed revolutionary potential in this so-called turn has been heavily debated. A recent issue of *ephemera* helpfully took the pulse of such theory and complicated its puzzles, mixing case study, feminist critique, and philosophical elaboration to show how structures of class, gender, and the insecurities of temporary labor persist in spheres animated by a discourse of creativity and encounter.

> That capital today seems to rely to such an extent on an enhanced subjective and productive autonomy of labour does not eliminate, but rather intensifies [an] ambivalence. To picture immaterial labour as a new vanguard subject with an inertial potential for communism would be an attempt to foreclose by decree, in theory, what can only be resolved in practice. If and how, in what situations and in what ways, something "escapes" capture and produces

resistance is the ambivalent question par excellence, and it is only in "the real movement of things" that it can be answered.[11]

Of course, when we begin to look at this shift in production and this explosion of critical reflection with a theatrical eye, some elements look strangely familiar. Within "the real movement of things" organized by dance and theatrical labor, we might note that the signature elements of the post-Fordist economy—affect, immateriality, and atomization—certainly do not feel new at all. What are the chestnuts of theater studies if not meditations on the management of affect? Think of Diderot perplexing on the paradoxes of le comédien. Think of William Hazlitt expounding on the "flashes of lightning," in Samuel Taylor Coleridge's words, emitted by Edmund Kean or of Shakespeare's own reflections on the how-tos and wherefores of seeming.[12] When we look at these questions from the perspective of a specifically Americanist theatrical eye, we can also see the Americanist precedents for the affective turn in performance history, whether in Karen Halttunen's Confidence Men and Painted Women (1982), in Warren Susman's (1984) opining on the shift from "character" to "personality" in the history of white, male American subjectivity, or in Willy Loman's plaintive efforts to be "well-liked" as a midcentury sales culture created the conditions for a new definition of American tragedy.[13] Actors, choreographers, playwrights, and theater managers around the globe and throughout history have considered themselves in the business of organizing emotion to produce immaterial experience. Along the way, performance-makers understood themselves to be creating a feeling of "hospitality, ease, well-being, excitement, and passion" for their patrons.[14] Moreover, they have also known that the immaterial effects of theatrical labor still involved an intense degree of materiality. Theatermakers mobilize architecture, transport machinery, and install lighting; the immaterial products of theater and dance involve the staffing of tour coordinators, stage managers, and technicians. And the immaterial experiences of theater and dance require the highly material training of performers' limbs, voices, and faces. The ritual "warm-up" before every performance is a consistent reminder of the material support system needed to produce immaterial effect.

If managers, actors, and dancers are acutely aware of (if differently specialized in) the highly material apparatus supporting their immaterial products, it is not always clear where that knowledge fits within a contemporary social economy and the realms of social theory it is spawning. Take, for instance, the language of affect and consider the many different kinds of styles, techniques, and effects we have imagined under its umbrella. The "affective" coordination that is the history of theater propelled a fine-tuned vocabulary for stylized feeling. We can jostle between Konstantin

Stanislavsky's reflections on "emotion memory" and the externalized emotions of Brechtian Gestus. We can recall the state of encounter created amid the *bhava* and *rasa* of Sanskrit theater or the endless differentiations that Western theater history plots among Elizabethan acting, romantic acting, melodramatic acting, and naturalistic acting. We can remember how many auteur directors and choreographers—from Hijikata Tatsumi to Jerzy Grotowski to Pina Bausch—place affect and encounter at the very center of their aesthetic inquiries. All we do in our studios, on our stages, at our conferences, and in our workshops is talk about innovation in affective making, citing a long history of how practitioners and citizens have dealt with its immaterial effects.

But is this wide and rangy vocabulary—this theatrical awareness of a variety of emotional styles and a variety of emotional effects—of relevance to the global discussion of the affective turn? While scholars of theater and dance can be thankful for the apparent recentering of familiar questions, the finer points of how different virtuosos developed different kinds of affective skills or different ways of managing immateriality is less often recounted in the generalized analogy between performance and affective labor. What would happen if it was?

Whose Art Is Immaterial, and with What Kind of Virtuosity?

After My Barbarian performers announce that it is time to stand up, they ask everyone in the eight-hundred-seat theater to stand and engage in a collective morning exercise. Part yogic, part theater warm-up, they use the signature phrases of the exercise class—"Shake it out"—and the clichéd metaphors of bodily expansion—"Touch the ceiling . . . you can reach the lights." As the summit attendees stretch and shake—a group ready to perform the basic bodily techniques of "caring for the self" that so many call "de-materialized"—the trio embarks upon an internal dialogue.

> MALIK: Is this theater or social practice?
> ALEXANDRO: Theater is social, and requires practice.
> JADE: That's provocative at 10:17 A.M. Switch directions.
> MALIK: Theater is conservative and social practice is progressive.
> ALEXANDRO: Stop. Stretch your arms across your chest.
> JADE: As theater people, we have an understanding of social practice, Laurie Anderson and I.
> MALIK: If you rehearse, you can't be a performance artist. Sorry.
> ALEXANDRO: Art is capitalist and performance is socialist.
> JADE: I'm fine with whatever you want to call me, as long as you acknowledge that I am living.

My Barbarian's brief foray into what might be called an "interarts" discourse provides an opportunity to think about theatrical and performance metaphors not only in relation to a larger service economy but also in relation to a specifically artistic response to a presumably immaterial turn. By calling themselves (and Laurie Anderson) "theater people," My Barbarian mark themselves within a specific history of practice that "performed" long before contemporary workers and contemporary visual artists began to do so in earnest. Such a self-marking asks old questions as well as new ones about how discourses of immateriality and virtuosity figure in artistic practice. The long-term link between the immaterial turn and the domain of performance is, of course, something that the Operaists have noticed. Hardt and Negri use the performance word—and its suffixed "-ative" version—at different moments in their argument. And Virno in particular has tracked the connection in his meditations on the virtuosic, foregrounding historic analogies to performance as "unproductive labor" in Marx and as political action in the thinking of Hannah Arendt. Virno had specific reasons for thinking anew about virtuosity. In a late twentieth-century context of service labor, he found food for thought in "the special capabilities of the performance artist," elaborating that, first, "theirs is *an activity which finds its own fulfillment (that is, its own purpose) in itself . . .* and [second] *. . . is an activity which requires the presence of others.*"[15] It was the first quality that so intrigued and perplexed Marx when he tried to define labor whose "product is not separable from the act of producing."[16] And it was the second quality that underpinned Arendt's equation between the performer and the political actor: "acting men need the presence of others before whom they can appear; both need a publicly organized space for their 'work.'"[17]

Interestingly, both these qualities emphasized by Virno are distinct from the primary quality emphasized in a lay definition of virtuosity—one that would link virtuosity to "excellence," "mastery," or "exceptionalism." Virno refers to the "skilled dancer," "memorable" piano performances, and orators and priests who are "fascinating" and "never boring," but the specific skills and techniques of these immaterial makers are underemphasized to craft different principles of philosophical connection. Indeed, Virno is far keener to map the nonobject producing, other-directed element of virtuosity to a larger labor field. Virtuosity, in his reading, is a dimension of a generalized "Toyotaism" and provides a way of characterizing immaterial labor based on language and "the productive mobilization of the cognitive faculties."[18] The result is a dispersed virtuosity that uses the linguistic and cognitive "talents and qualifications" that used to be associated with "political action," but that are now incorporated into the everyday post-Fordist work force. To make this connection between virtuosity and immaterial labor, Virno sidelines the lay notion of exceptional skill; intriguingly, Virno even allows for its reversal: "Each of us is, and has always been, a virtuoso, a performing artist, at times mediocre and awkward, but, in any event, a virtuoso."[19] Virtuosity here is thus decidedly not unique and exceptional but democratized and awkward, something that all of us have the capacity to access. Indeed, in Virno's frame, you can deliver a mediocre performance and still be a virtuoso.

The provocations of such a reversal are rich and complex, but it also creates some new puzzles. If we read Virno's definition of virtuosity back across midcentury task-based choreography and apply it, as well, to various contemporary strains of "exhausted dance," we can find those performance forms clearly exposing their inseparability from the act of execution (à la Marx) and emphasizing their dependence on viewers to exist (à l'Arendt). At the same time, however, we should also remember that these artistic forms have launched impassioned *critiques* of virtuosity whose target has been the *lay* sense of virtuosity. Such critiques have sought to undo virtuosic excellence that serves "the spectacle" of consumer-society.[20] The relative coincidence of these two virtuosity discourses has created an interesting conceptual tangle, perhaps even some conceptual confusion. At times, today, we find ourselves in discursive situations where some celebrate virtuosity's immateriality (in Virno's sense) and others condemn virtuosity's exceptionalism (in the lay sense), not always realizing the degree to which the two approaches to the virtuosic are talking past each other.

Let's foreground the interarts dimension of this tangle. From the perspective of the visual arts, the turn to process art, to the production of actions in lieu of sculptures and paintings, we find an urgent match with Virno's virtuosic turn. The qualities emphasized in Virno's brand of virtuosity sounded especially compelling to midcentury artists who had heretofore been making objects (and art commodities) in the so-called Fordist mode. The turn to the experiential, to the event, to the encounter, to process, and to reciprocal interactions with spectators seemed to offer a liberation from the object, an opportunity to forgo the traditional skills and parameters of object making to produce networks of performative encounters. The immaterial, viewer-dependent results of these late twentieth-century visual art experiments (from Morris at Judson to Abramovic and Ulay in the gallery to Gran Fury in the street) developed an experiential playbook, producing works that "found their own fulfillment in themselves" and understood their dependence on "the presence of others." Framed inside Virno's philosophical history, it is no wonder that such nonobject-based, post-Minimalist, or dispersed installation practices were associated with sociopolitical action. They possessed a brand of event-based, spatially organized, cognitively framed, and spectator-savvy engagement that Arendt associated with "the political actor."

But in an interarts context it is perhaps worth rethinking how this kind of aesthetic virtuosity is plotted, especially because it is often unclear what definition of virtuosity is on the line in any given art project. This is to say that, just as twentieth-century actors and dancers and musicians were moving away from the lay definition of virtuosity to make work like John Cage's *4' 33"* (1952), Judson Church's task-based dances, or Living Theater's nonmatrixed performances, visual artists were moving toward the virtuosity that Virno encodes, developing virtuosic practices whose experiential and immaterial relationality provided a counter to the object-producing conventions of a visual art sphere. These two seemingly mutual exclusive virtuosities can be difficult to track.

What, for instance, do we make of situations where a resuscitation of virtuosity in Virno's sense coincides with a critique of virtuosity in the lay sense? For one, it can create new prescriptions and new confusions about the radical potential of an artwork. It spawns, for instance, the banal but resilient sense that "if you rehearse, you can't be a performance artist," a shibboleth that devalues the forms of theater that require "practice." Here, the development of vocal skills, bodily coordination, or non-"boring" expression is critiqued as a capitulation to a conservative sense of virtuosity as excellence; at the same time, that critique celebrates the romantically "unpracticed" as progressive (even "socialist," as if socialism does not need rehearsal). Moreover, in an interarts context, different receivers will have different barometers for what qualifies as a good "bad" performance or as a bad "good" performance. As José Esteban Muñoz has argued, My Barbarian is an example of "queer virtuosity" from one angle of vision.[21] From another angle, however, theirs is a structured use of the nonvirtuosic, or what they themselves have called "dedicated amateurism."[22] If either of them hit a musical note too well or exposed too much technical prowess in a dance move, they might endanger the aesthetic of a politically open, participatory DIY performance world. This aesthetic is also one that responds to the expanded reach of a museum-based context whose relation to "engagement" and "performance" is both enthusiastic and equivocal at once. As "theater people" who are trying to manage their own political action in the "organized space" in which they find themselves, their virtuosity partly lies in their ability to deliver an immaterial experience for an expanded visual art audience that has historically mistrusted the display of exceptional theatrical skill. Perhaps dedicated amateurism is the new naturalism, one that must also navigate a new interarts ecology that produces and presents performance.

As the script of My Barbarian indexes with strategic nonchalance, the lingering associations that philosophers and critics have attached to theater and to performance continue to inflect a wider (art)world's sense of what is progressive and regressive about it, about what is co-optation and where the potential lies for alternate affective eruption. Indeed, theatrical terms continually appear in discourses that cannot decide whether it is an agent *of* disruption or a vehicle of social constraint that needs *to be* disrupted. "Is this theater or social practice?" asks Malik as he stretches on each side. The question anticipates the binaries that will be invoked as the dialogue continues: "Theater is conservative and social practice is progressive." "Art is capitalist and performance is socialist." By declaring the binary frames, My Barbarian makes them available for critique, repeating persistent if underargued ways of thinking that still structure how certain kinds of work are received. Moreover, the elisions among different binaries expose the relational construction of every association. Performance can only be imagined as "socialist" when it is opposed to a capitalist economy of a visual art market, but presumably not when it becomes "theater."[23] Social practice's progressivism, meanwhile, is placed as the opposite of theater's conservatism, an opposition that ignores an entire history of activist theater. It should be said that this interarts, intergenre jockeying is not only a habit of an expanded visual art world. The scapegoating of theater's conservatism has buoyed arguments for the apparent progressivism of performance. One need only remember Josette Féral's meditations on the confinements of theatricality, or Baz Kershaw's elaborations on "the radical," or Richard Schechner's overly quoted (now retracted) assertion that theater was becoming "the string quartet" of our era to realize how much "theater people" have themselves relied on the rhetoric of theatrical conservatism to stage a new revolution.[24]

The interarts dialogue prompts more opportunities to reflect not only on how virtuosity is defined but also on how we locate immateriality as such. As noted above, the language of immateriality has had an important influence in a twentieth- and early twentieth-first-century visual art context. Because visual artists had primarily been in the business of making material objects, the novelty of time-based, process, embodied, and group-based works could be touted for their "dematerializing" turns. Later, others would go on to notice that a dematerialized aesthetic discourse happened to coincide with an immaterial discourse in social theory.[25] Parallel discourses underscoring the ephemerality of performance art coincided with this art historical framing.[26] Performance art may not have been clearly "socialist," but its promise to be "anticapitalist" presumably came from its resistance to object commodity status. As I have argued elsewhere, however, the perception of dematerialized dispersal often depends on a medium-specific lens.[27] The entry of the body of the artist into the space of a gallery could only feel dematerializing in a context that equated materiality with the objectness of the art and not with the embodiment of the body. From the vantage point of the theater and dance histories, these newer uses of dematerialized and immaterial labels felt both familiar and defamiliarizing at once. Once again, dance and theater workers had already inhabited the "unproductive" realm for quite some time by virtue of the fact that their products did not last, at least not in the ways that the market, the museum, or the archive understood the idea of lasting.[28] But if, after Marx, such performance labor produced a product that "is not separable from the act of producing," the labor was not so much dematerialized as differently material. The inseparability of such forms from the body of the laborer in fact made them feel hypermaterial, requiring feats of gestural, often repetitive, and kinesthetic effort to bring them continually into being.

Without minimizing the galvanizing and experimental effects of dematerialization or of the new virtuosity discourse in art, it seems important to notice that perceptions of immateriality and virtuosity are context specific and relationally produced; they are effects that emerge when local habits for defining materiality or for defining skill have been challenged. Meanwhile, those local habits also produce the sense that such challenges have radical potential. In a gallery-collector context, the violation of object-based convention produced the sense that performance could avoid art's "capitalism." But as any nineteenth-century actor-manager could have told you—and as Tino Sehgal has reproduced for a new art world—capitalist incorporation of immaterial product is not only possible but also an historic pre-post-Fordist occupation. The routinized equation between dematerialized ephemerality and "anticapitalism" was thus difficult to sustain, as a wide field of highly authored, highly monetized art experiences now makes clear. Meanwhile, the conceptual confusion produced by a critique of virtuosity as excellence and a celebration of virtuosity as immaterial has produced a new artistic niche. One need no longer cultivate exceptional performance skill; indeed, one can claim to be resisting the "conservative" social demand for consumptive spectacle in one's decision not to display virtuosic skill in the lay sense. At the same time, one can claim to have mastered virtuosity in the conceptual sense; one can secure high fees and commissions to use deskilled bodies (or to mask the skills of skilled ones) to produce an immaterial product. The result might be "mediocre or awkward"—it might even be "boring"—but it contains aesthetic value by virtue of what Virno would call the "productive mobilization of the cognitive faculty."[29] Mediocre dancing can be good conceptual art.

I happen to be intrigued by much of this contemporary, interarts practice and its virtuosic cognitive rigor. But I cannot help but notice that it has a cross-medium politics, or at least a cross-medium disingenuousness. For many highly skilled choreographers and theatermakers, the act of apparent deskilling required laborious effort (think about how hard it is to perform Yvonne Rainer's *Trio A* [1965]). But many choreographers committed to a practice that avoided the display of virtuosic exceptionalism out of particular concerns regarding spectacular and voyeuristic politics of the dance medium. To "say no to virtuosity" (in the lay sense) was to "say no to spectacle." But what happens when the deskilling directive is invoked to legitimate the work of artists who never cultivated such skills in the first place? Or more bluntly, what happens when the arena of the apparently deskilled is used to mobilize the arena of the actually unskilled? An artist can transpose the presumed political radicality of deskilled virtuosity in one art form to support the assertion that another art form's use of unskilled, immaterial virtuosity is politically radical as well. Awkward performance in the museum is radical because it is not an object, but also because it is antitheater. Mediocre movement in the gallery is radical because it is not an object, but also because it is antidance. Again, I myself enjoy coming to terms with the conceptual effects of these cognitive mobilizations. But I also find it disingenuous when high-profile critics, curators, and artists feel that they can use an antitheater or antidance stance as a kind of amulet to deflect attention from the fact that their event-based biennials, curated actions, and performative acquisitions might be more in league with what Guy Debord would have called "the spectacle" than most theater or dance productions could ever hope to be.[30]

Performance and the Precarity of Flexibility

As the performance continues, My Barbarian opens new sections with the sound of an alarm clock, a punctuation that orchestrates the creativity of their time and that also winks at the parameters of the commission. They were told to create a "fifteen-minute" performance for the summit. Around eleven minutes and twenty-eight seconds into the performance, the alarm goes off again, launching an animated preamble about "crisis" and a "song and dance" about what it means to live crisis, not as a singular event, but as an ongoing dynamic of precarity.

ALEXANDRO: There's a job crisis. People have too many jobs.
JADE: Some people don't have any.
MALIK: Some people only have one lonely sad job.

A, J, AND M *(singing)*: Wednesday morning I install art at the museum
Tuesday night I work the door at a club for beer
Saturday morning I take care of a kid in a doorman building
Thursday afternoon I work at a phone bank for a blood bank
Sunday I eat

Wednesday morning I install art at the museum
Tuesday night I work the door at a club for beer
Saturday morning I take care of a kid in a doorman building
Thursday afternoon I work at a phone bank for a blood bank
Sunday I eat brunch for free at my friend's restaurant if I wash
    the dishes

Mondays I'm the CEO of a non-profit
In between I work on my dissertation
Fridays I have off

Zero percent job growth
Zero percent job growth

In the first line of this section, My Barbarian defines the "job crisis" in a way that might initially sound peculiar: "people have too many jobs." Of course, those lines and the subsequent song make visible the pervasively itinerant element of "crisis" in a post-Fordist labor context, one that compels laborers to multitask in a field of temporary jobs and to remain perpetually on the move. The "I" of My Barbarian's song moves to a different context each day, following a calendar that knows nothing of the traditional "workweek" and that disallows the arcs of continuity that some kinds of productivity (e.g., being a "CEO of a nonprofit," "working on my dissertation") might typically require. The I of the song is thus motoring and motored by the exceedingly "flexible" labor environment that has accompanied a contemporary social economy. In the '80s and '90s, sociologist Ulrich Beck began to put a name to such systems and their affects in his elaboration of "the risk society." He tracked a deregulating trend in markets and governments that celebrated a world where individuals were free to form their own DIY biographies, unfettered by the constraints of systemic interference.[31] The paradoxical advancement of a kind of "institutional individualism" celebrated privatized models of creativity and life management, so that "risk" could become synonymous with thrill and creative speculation rather than with precarity and insecurity. Indeed, systems of security and protection were imagined only as inconveniences, in danger of encumbering the new flexible laborer if they were not helpfully taken out of the way. Such a discourse is all too compatible with the just-in-time ethos of post-Fordist manufacture, rationalizing "just-in-time" employment practices that privilege temporary, contract labor while rationalizing the dismantling of systems of social and economic security. As Beck continued to track the discursive effects of "risk" and "individualization," he painted a picture of contemporary workers that sounds now like a review of My Barbarian's performance:

> Constantly changing between different, partly incompatible logics of action, they are forced to take into their hands that which is in danger of breaking into pieces: their own lives. Modern society does not integrate them as whole persons into its functional systems; rather, it relies on the fact that individuals are not integrated but only partly and temporarily involved as they wander between different functional worlds . . . And the ubiquitous rule is that, in

order to survive the rat race, one has to become active, inventive, resourceful, to develop ideas of one's own, to be faster, nimbler, and more creative—not just on one occasion, but constantly, day after day. Individuals become actors, builders, jugglers, stage managers of their own biographies and identities.[32]

The irony, of course, is that the celebration of individual resourcefulness, of the capacity to create a "life of one's own," was received as desirable by a variety of creative laborers. Flexibility seemed, after all, to be the key to social agency. The just-in-time ethos now structures a variety of social fields, including government and employment organizations that used to be responsible for supplying "just-in-case" systems. Laborers are now "free" to juggle many jobs, construct nimbler lives, and avoid situations that offer the dubious protections of regulation, social welfare, or employment security. "Small wonder that the governments and the corporations started actively promoting a myth of flexibility," writes Brian Holmes: "The emerging 'virtual class'—including cultural producers, digital artisans, prosumers, what are now called 'immaterial laborers'—stumbled more or less blindly into it."[33] Holmes's assertion gestures to a wider point about the degree to which what we now, in 2012, call "precarity" is the other side of a coin that used to be celebrated as "flexibility." So too the "variety" and "plurality" of a mobile lifestyle has transmogrified into what many decry as the "atomization" and itinerancy of work. Indeed, in the rush to avoid becoming Marcuse's "one-dimensional man," the conformist image of the unnimble, salaried worker was something that creative laborers sought to avoid.[34] "Some people have one lonely sad job," says My Barbarian, resuscitating the condescension. But as Holmes argues, together with others such as Luc Boltanski and Eve Chiapello, the "new spirit of capitalism" has capitalized on that disdain.[35] Workers are now encouraged to find happiness in many jobs, and to be thankful not to be weighed down by regular salaries, health insurance, or the possibility of pensions. The emergence of today's precarity was thus helped along by the fact that so many of us cathected to flexibility's marketing campaign.

Of course when it comes to the new Janus-faced flexibility of this kind of post-Fordist labor, theater's field practitioners are once again all too familiar with this way of organizing labor. Theatermakers have tried various routes to avoid the itinerant destiny of a laborer working in a temporary form. Whether organizing city-to-city caravans in the Middle Ages or the post-Broadway tour in the twenty-first century, the concept of "the tour" is one that contracts the repetition of performance to sustain the life of the artist over time. Repertory models or state-theater models went another route, offering membership to a select group of performers, designers, and technicians in exchange for successively new acts of immaterial performance in a season; the life of the artist could thus be sustained not by moving but

Fig. 10. My Barbarian, *Creative Time Living as Form (10:15–10:30 A.M.): Part One: Morning Theme (10:15–10:16 A.M.)*. Creative Time Summit, Skirball Theater, New York, 2011. Photograph by Sam Horine and courtesy of Creative Time.

by serially presenting new performances in one place. Additionally, within dance and theater history, we find that performance workers turned to the "just-in-case" organizational form of the union sooner and with more consistency than visual art workers. Indeed, the naturalization and consistency of those unions mean that the significance of something like the Art Workers Coalition in 1969 looks bafflingly belated to a performance laborer's eye.[36] Of course, early union adoption within ensemble forms also meant that their practitioners accepted the trade-offs of fixity for security; they unionized discrete divisions of labor among writers, actors, set designers, stage managers, lighting designers, and choreographers whose categorical fixities baffle visually trained artists now. In our current precarious economy, many performance laborers find themselves trying to avoid getting an equity card for fear that they will become unaffordable to local theaters—or unaffordable to conceptual artists who might hire them as material in their latest installations (i.e., if union rules apply).

Ultimately, within the grand history of theatrical and dance performance, the pervasive narrative of performance labor is one of temporary contracts and itinerancy. Some countries tried to work with this model and still provide the basics of health care and unemployment benefits; France's recent debates on the future of what are all too literally and resonantly called "*les intermittents du spectacle*" (the intermittent labor of the entertainment industry) does not augur well for the future of this model.[37] And indeed, as the Eurozone countries increasingly hack away at the surviving security structures of a welfare state, more EU workers are working increasingly as *intermittents*, which is to say more like American workers who are themselves more often leading the contracted, temporary, flexibly precarious lives that American artists have known all too well. What Gregory Sholette has speculated from the perspective of expanded visual art sounds disconcertingly resonant in the expanded theatrical world:

> Perhaps, rather than an historic compromise between artistic creativity and the neoliberal economy, what has fixated neoliberalism onto the image of the artist as ideal worker is not so much her imaginative out-of-the-box thinking or restless flexibility as the way the art world as an aggregate economy successfully manages its own excessively surplus labor force, extracting value from a redundant majority of "failed" artists who in turn apparently acquiesce to this disciplinary arrangement.[38]

Sholette's reference to "out of the box" thinking invokes a wider discourse on creativity that has been instrumentalizing the arts within an experience economy. Indeed, the high irony of our current moment is that life is so precarious for creative self-biographers at a time when so many industry pundits celebrate "the creative class," call the MFA the new MBA, or declaim that "right-brainers will rule the world."[39] Richard Florida's definition of "creative" occupations is notoriously capacious, including everyone from artists to chefs to architects to hairdressers to software designers. No doubt it would also include one-day-a-week CEOs, call-center operators skilled in the "encounter" of the phone bank, as well as those who "work the door" or "install art." Creativity discourse motors hundreds of small and large sectors in an atomized service economy. What it also does, however, is obscure significant differences in how immaterial labor is structured and remunerated. In other words, and as many others have noted, the creative class discourse hardly ever mentions class difference. Florida's urban neighborhoods can be "vitalized" best when a coalition of artists, restaurant owners, and software designers occupy it. As numerous critics have noted, this discourse obscures the classed and raced lives of marginally employed neighbors who already live there.[40] Additionally, it also happens to obscure economic asymmetry within the "creative" class itself, repressing the relative precarity that some of these urban adventurers will endure over others.

It seems to me that there are other related differences obscured by the creativity discourse, obfuscations that oddly enough appear in some of the uses to which the Operaismo vocabulary is put. As noted earlier, sometimes the post-Fordist moment is defined as a "service" economy, sometimes as a "knowledge" economy. Some models refer to "cognitive" capitalism, some emphasize "affective" labor, while others focus more generally around "immaterial" labor. While knowledge and cognition, service and affect may all be immaterial, it also seems important to remember that that they are hardly equivalent terms. To concretize with My Barbarian's examples, being a CEO is different from "working the door." "Writing a dissertation" is different from "taking care of a kid." All may produce immaterial products, but the signature professions of a knowledge industry—business professional, academic professor, social-media project manager—are not equivalent to other immaterial forms, such as those requiring the affective skills of front-line personal encounter at the cash register or the emotional labor of eldercare or childcare. Perhaps this is a moment to remind ourselves how the feminist critique of labor had already begun so-called post-Fordist analyses, even if feminism continues to undergo what Dorothy Smith, following Tillie Olsen, once called a "peculiar eclipsing."[41] Indeed, in trying to come to terms with the "invisibility" of women's work, feminists were already well on their way to describing forms of labor that we might now call immaterial, affective, and service. As Kathi Weeks has argued, some early attempts were hampered by the compulsion to analogize domestic work to an industrial model, not always fully grasping that they were delineating an experiential mode of work that was becoming ubiquitous.[42] Marxist feminists' overreliance on a "separate spheres" argument not only presumed heterosexual contracts but also became increasingly untenable as the nature of work changed. That said, it seems important to note places where feminists characterized women's care and women's service as all too material compared to the frictionless "cognitive" prestige of the men they supported. Here is Dorothy Smith on the matter way back in 1987:

> The place of women, then, in relation to this mode of action is where the work is done to facilitate men's occupation of the conceptual mode of action . . . They do the clerical work, giving material form to the words or thoughts of the boss. They do the routine computer work, the interviewing for the survey, the nursing, the secretarial work. At almost every point women mediate for men the relation between the conceptual mode of action and the actual concrete forms on which it depends. Women's work is interposed between the abstracted modes and the local and particular actualities in which they are necessarily anchored. Also, women's work conceals from men acting in the abstract mode just this anchorage.[43]

Other feminists also recognized the need to delineate gendered and classed definitions of affective and cognitive skill within a generalized immaterial sphere. Feminist sociologists of labor such as Arlie Hochschild would refine Daniel Bell's language of "encounter" and "communication" to track the specific skills and specific burdens of what she called "emotion management," developing a discourse that could differentiate the gendered experience and class status of a specifically affective form of labor from more privileged forms of employment in a wider immaterial economy.[44] Gendered emotion management and gendered performance skills have "anchored" the cognitive creativity of others; affective labor has long been "women's work." And—akin to other performance laborers—gendered workers have experienced such anchoring work as deeply "material," whatever its immaterial effects and however "cognitive" their employers' labor was claimed to be.

Performance Studies as Post-Fordist

Throughout a performance whose intervals are carefully clocked, My Barbarian makes sure that there is plenty of time for affective connection. They encourage Summit attendees to create feelings of hospitality and ease in the room, suggesting collective massage, a cleansing breath, and reflection on the individuated pleasures of Life.

MALIK: Feels good doesn't it? Living as form.
ALEXANDRO: Life form.
JADE: I am a life form.
MALIK: Stop massaging.
ALEXANDRO: Take a deep breath.
JADE: Focus on your breathing . . .
MALIK: I'm not an activist, I'm a lifestyle artist, in magazines.
ALEXANDRO: That's not how I would describe you.
JADE: You need a life coach.
MALIK: Switch directions.
ALEXANDRO: I could be your life coach, if you trusted me.
JADE: I would trust you—if I didn't know you.
MALIK: What kind of politics is that?

Having tried to underscore other histories and dimensions of precarity and affective labor that preceded the current rush to quote the post-Operaismo school, it should be noted that Michael Hardt did not claim to be tracking something new, just something newly pervasive.

I do not mean to argue that affective labor is new or that the fact that affective labor produces value in some sense is new. Feminist analyses in particular have long recognized the social value of

caring labor, kin work, nurturing, and maternal activities. What
are [sic] new, on the other hand, are the extent to which it has
become generalized through wide sectors of the economy.[45]

Of course, such attributions of prescience do not always imply deep
engagement with feminist work. But if Hardt is right in recognizing that
affective labor was not so much new, as newly "generalized," then we
could say that our own intellectual spheres have become generalized along
similar lines. If laboring spheres turned to a metaphor of the performing
arts to characterize broader changes in the organization of "life" and "life-
styles," then we should note that the academy followed suit. Indeed, the
discourse of performance studies emerged and expanded across formerly
discrete disciplines to keep pace with and offer an account of this kind
of "life coaching." Performance studies emerged to track not simply life
forms of the aesthetic sphere but also life stylings of all kinds. Performance
studies scholars began to notice the operations of performance in places
far away from the stages we had once studied. We imported ritual theory
to find liminality in street behavior and *communitas* at the shopping mall.
We took Erving Goffman's frames on the performance of everyday life to
analyze the bits and pieces of quotidian existence, tracking the "backstage"
behaviors of salesclerks or the "keying" rituals of high-school reunions.[46]
Performance studies evangelists claimed to be uniquely positioned to
understand these interpersonal realms, dimly discerning that change was
afoot, perhaps not fully comprehending whether we were using or being
used by an expansion of immaterial and affective labor. In fact, we can
think of the consolidation of performance studies as itself decidedly post-
Fordist; performance studies was both a symptom of and laboratory for
the new world of affective labor. If the affective and immaterial labor of
service began to structure our contemporary global economy, performance
studies was a place to "get in shape" for such change, an eclectic training
ground that readied us to serve and/or use affective service to our advan-
tage. In pronouncing the future of performance studies in the academy,
Richard Schechner's reimagining of the "whole academic performing arts
enterprise" now all too clearly resonates with Florida's discourse of the
creative class.[47] Performance studies was an effect and a propeller of a
world where "face-management," "framing," and "keying" would become
the basic skill set of any post-Fordist laborer.

    Within that transition, it is worth lingering on how some of the cen-
tral elements of affective labor and precarity wove their way into our
syllabi under different guises. Hochschild's careful study of PSA flight
attendants tracked how women's traditional acts of staging and scene setting were adapted by airline trainers who told them to treat customers
as if they were guests in their living room. PSA's jingle assured customers
that "our smiles are not just painted on," a reference that inadvertently

evoked another historic female profession; Halttunen's "painted ladies"—
along with Tracy Davis's actresses as working women—are a reminder
that some affective skills are part of the oldest of professions.[48] These and
many more forms of emotion management encouraged the repression of
discord to maintain a pervasive sense of hospitality. Hochschild's analysis
brought forward questions about the authenticity of such emotions and
the experience of being a subject perpetually in service—is she faking it?
Hochschild wrote with a keen understanding of the skill involved and
with a degree of distress about the potential for self-alienation.

> This labor requires one to induce or suppress feeling in order to
> sustain the outward countenance that produces the proper state of
> mind in others—in this case, the sense of being cared for in a con-
> vivial and safe place. This kind of labor calls for a coordination of
> mind and feeling, and it sometimes draws on a source of self that
> we honor as deep and integral to our individuality.[49]

Hochschild was of course not the first to wonder about the integrity and
authenticity of someone whose job was to act—or to fake it. Other por-
tions of her text would worry and wonder about the difference between
"seeming" and actuality: "Seeming to 'love the job' becomes part of
the job; and actually trying to love it, and to enjoy the customers, helps
the worker in this effect. In processing people, the product is a state of
mind."[50] Throughout, her understanding of affective labor came with an
acute awareness of its immaterial product—the comfortable, satisfied
"state of mind" of the receiver. Following Virno, Marx, and Arendt, it was
a subordinated version of activity that found its fulfillment "in itself" in an
organized space and in the presence of eager observers.

But Hochschild's concerns would also receive critique at a time when
conceptions of authentic subjectivity were being questioned. As Kathi
Weeks has noted:

> the fact remains that the critique of alienation works by evoking
> a given self, our estrangement from which constitutes a compel-
> ling crisis . . . [There is thus a] tension at the heart of Hochschild's
> analysis: she insists on the social construction and malleability of
> the emotions while also positing them as fundamental to the self
> such that their alienation is a problem . . . her argument, in other
> words, is animated by an ideal of the "unmanaged heart."[51]

The critique of the concept of a "given self" would set the scene for many
more elaborations of gender and the performance of identity, critiques such
as those of Judith Butler who argued most forcefully against any model
of given, prior, unmanaged selfhood. Together figures like Hochschild and

Butler from different feminist disciplines contributed to the interdisciplinary syllabus of performance studies. They, along with many others, contributed to the sense that our favorite sites of study were becoming "generalized" and that we should take a more active role in directing the expansion, lest we be directed by it.

While the discourse of affect was already present under different verbiage, we could say that the latent discourse of precarity was as well, though its route is differently complicated. To focus on one example, consider the infatuation with the local, the resistant, and the microact in social and cultural theory of the '90s. The sussing out of such microacts of resistance was not only part of performance studies but also integral to a wider 1990s cultural-studies discourse that valued spontaneous, fleeting acts of improvised intervention. Michel de Certeau's concept of the "tactic" can serve as an index of such an ethos; his formulations have animated many a syllabi.

> The place of the tactic belongs to the other. A tactic insinuates itself into the other's place, fragmentarily, without ever taking it over in its entirety, without being able to keep it at a distance. It has at its disposal no base where it can capitalize on its advantages, prepare its expansions, and secure independence with respect to circumstances. The "proper" is a victory of space over time. On the contrary, because it does not have a place, a tactic depends upon time—it is always on the watch for opportunities that must be seized "on the wing." Whatever it wins, it does not keep. It must constantly manipulate events in order to turn them into "opportunities."[52]

De Certeau's project was a precise one, an attempt to expose a degree of agency in contexts where some sociological frames saw none. My concern is not with his project per se, but with how it became, to use Hardt's term again, "generalized" to such a degree that everyone wanted to position themselves and their sites as tactical agents. It seems to me that the celebration of de Certeauian tactics now feels a little different in an age that feels the downsides of precarity.[53] While terms such as fluid, liminal, nomadic, or tactical each emerged within an urgent social and critical milieu, their generalization risked banalization. Even as we acknowledge the precisely political goals of certain theoretical maneuvers, it is hard not also to see that such celebrations of the tactical could ease our way into post-Fordist flexibility. Most insidiously, the notion that resistant political expression happened "on the wing" prepared us to be flexible. It prepared us to decide that the "on the wing" ethos of "just-in-time" behavior was agential, a resistant act that flouted the cumbersome structures of the "just-in-case" bureaucracy.

In other words, much as we lament the loss of what Lauren Berlant recently called our "infrastructures of continuity,"[54] perhaps we also need to look in our own backyard to remember that continuity has not exactly been a high-priority item for many in the arts and critical humanities, especially amid an ethos that celebrated discontinuity wherever possible. Many academics now find it less than tenable to tout such terms when the underbelly of student debt, corporate philanthropy, high tuition, and revenue-generating certificate programs turns out to pay the salary that guarantees our freedom to teach the great goodness of flexible citizenship. My Barbarian's text hints at the precarious foundations of the academic enterprise: "I used to go to school on borrowed money," says one character. "Will they revoke my degrees for never paying it back?" Many now find it impossible to celebrate fluidity when so many terribly smart colleagues and students are enduring "dark matter" status not only in academia but also in every arts, education, and social service sector. These are individuals who might appreciate hearing about strategies as much as tactics right now, as much about stability as liminality, and who might appreciate the chance to consider holding "one sad lonely job" over the fluid freedom of holding several.

Precarious Production

After performing exercise and dialogue before the summit audience, My Barbarian reorganized the space once more. This time, they asked members of the audience to join them onstage. The assembly launched a new exercise called "Hours of the Day," a structure that continued exploration of the urgency and creativity of clocked time.

> MALIK: We'd like to invite you to place your body somewhere on the stage or in the aisles. Whichever feels more right. Trust your instincts . . .
>
> MALIK: Give yourself a little space if you can. Imagine a typical workday. Whatever that means to you. Think about what you do with your body during that day. The positions you take, the objects you manipulate, the things that go in and out of your body, the people you interact with . . .
>
> Members of the audience came up to the stage, slowly and then more quickly. While varied in gender, race, and size, unless you knew them personally little distinguished them as individuals until the exercise began.
>
> MALIK: For each hour of the day, demonstrate your technique of the body.
>
> ALEXANDRO: If you are sleeping, sleep.
>
> JADE: If you are scrubbing, scrub.

ALEXANDRO: If you are teaching, teach.

JADE: If you are fucking, fuck.

ALEXANDRO: If you are eating, just eat.

MALIK: Let's begin at 6 A.M.

My Barbarian's projected clock began ticking again as performers assumed a 6 A.M. pose, with many dropping directly to the floor to sleep. Others began jogging. Anne Pasternak, the Director of Creative Time, started brushing her teeth. By 9 A.M., most of the group was up and moving. By 10 A.M., many were typing; indeed, several of the typists did so continuously as the hours ticked, providing a stabilizing, if repetitive, choreographic base underneath the variety of other behaviors. As the hours of the day wore on, some rushed, some drove, some walked, some stood. Some paused to eat at the same time but on opposite sides of the stage, suggesting the possibility that they might join each other. As 10 P.M. arrived, some began getting ready for bed; others were dancing, alone but also together. Some kept dancing and working and drinking until all was quiet. As the last person went down early in the morning, another woke up.

Hours of the Day is a theater exercise that My Barbarian uses in their workshops, one that seemed a suitable match to the temporal themes and temporal parameters of Creative Time's orchestrated summit. It was also a different way of organizing the assembly. It was a performance before beholders who were simultaneously actors. When the task was finished, it elicited the most applause and cheers of any moment in the performance, even if all of us might have been hard-pressed to articulate its "point." It was, after all, a form of activity "whose fulfillment happened in itself." As a virtuosic performance whose effects were immaterial, it might have looked unproductive to some, but to others, it was another contemporary instance of post-Fordist making in the experiential mode. It also seemed a moment that sought to open up that kind of labor for another end. If the potential of mobile and affective post-Fordist labor can only be discerned in "the real movement of things," then Hours of the Day seemed to be a rehearsal for that discernment, or at least a kind of warm-up that allowed those in the room to take a collective audit of our behaviors. As such, it recalled the sense of possibility circulating in Sholette's dark assessment of the dark matter of precarious labor, the possibility that inheres in the "revenge of the surplus."[55] It was also an assembly that recalled the earliest of constitutional reflections on the right to assemble, one that protected the right to gather as itself expressive content, whether it had reached deliberative agreement or had already came with a clear list of demands. Like other ad-hoc, open systems assembling throughout the world under the banner of Occupy, it initiated reflection on the "real movement of things," working under the assumption that, according to John Inazu, "many group expressions are only made intelligible by the practices that give them meaning."[56]

The task here was simple: to perform the hours of one's day for and in a new context and to see what would happen when the individuated movement of one's things occurred next to other individuals who moved side-by-side. It was a miniendurance performance, self-selected, and relatively safe. It was certainly safer than the larger one taking place a few blocks away and that would transmit its behaviors, affects, knowledges, and best practices around the world. If more such rehearsals, assemblies, and performances of endurance are necessary to redirect affective labor and virtuosic action, then Occupy is a reminder that a huge sector of the population is willing to spend just that kind of time.

Notes

"Just-in-Time: Performance and the Aesthetics of Precarity" was originally published in *TDR: The Drama Review* 56, no. 4 (Winter 2012): 10–31. Reprinted courtesy of MIT Press.

1. I use this term to refer schematically to experimental, event-based, or socially oriented art practice that measures its distance from visual art traditions. More on this topic as the essay develops, but for an early attempt to reflect on how the turn from art-historical to visual-cultural models is similar and dissimilar to the turn "from" theater to performance studies, see Shannon Jackson, "Performing Show and Tell: Disciplines of Visual Culture and Performance Studies," in "Show and Tell: The State of Visual Culture Studies," ed. Martin Jay, special issue, *Journal of Visual Culture* 4, no. 2 (2005): 163–77.

2. See Richard Florida, *The Rise of the Creative Class* (New York: Basic Books, 2002); Daniel H. Pink, *A Whole New Mind: Why Right-Brainers Will Rule the Future* (New York: Riverhead Books, 2006); and Rocco Landesman interviewed by Ann McQueen, *Grantmakers in the Arts Reader* 24, no. 1 (Winter 2013), https://www.giarts.org/article/interview-rocco-landesman.

3. See Julia Bryan-Wilson, *Art Workers: Radical Practice in the Vietnam War Era* (Berkeley: University of California Press, 2011); Brian Holmes, *Unleashing the Collective Phantoms: Essays in Reverse Imagineering* (New York: Autonomedia, 2008); Gerald Raunig, *Art and Revolution: Transversal Activism in the Long Twentieth Century* (Cambridge, MA: Semiotext(e), 2007); and Gregory Sholette and Blake Stimson, *Collectivism after Modernism: The Art of Social Imagination after 1945* (Minneapolis: University of Minnesota Press, 2007).

4. Daniel Bell, *The Coming of Post-Industrial Society: A Venture in Social Forecasting* (New York: Basic Books, 1973), 163.

5. Andrew Sayer and Richard Walker, *The New Social Economy: Reworking the Division of Labor* (Cambridge, MA: Blackwell Publishers, 1992).

6. B. Joseph Pine and James H. Gilmore, *The Experience Economy: Work Is Theater and Every Business a Stage* (Boston: Harvard Business Review Press, 1999).

7. Maurizio Lazzarato, "Immaterial Labor," in *Radical Thought in Italy: A Potential Politics*, ed. Paul Virno and Michael Hardt (Minneapolis: University of

Minnesota Press, 1996), 133–50; Paolo Virno, "Virtuosity and Revolution: The Political Theory of Exodus," in Virno and Hardt, *Radical Thought in Italy*, 189–212; Michael Hardt, "Affective Labor," *boundary 2* 26, no. 2 (1999): 89–100.

8. Lazzarrato, "Immaterial Labor," 142, 138.

9. Michael Hardt and Antonio Negri, *Multitude: War and Democracy in the Age of Empire* (New York: Penguin Press, 2004), 108.

10. Virno, "Virtuosity and Revolution."

11. Emma Dowling, Rodrigo Nunes, and Ben Trott, "Immaterial and Affective Labour Explored," *ephemera* 7, no. 1 (2007): 6.

12. "Seeming" worries are varied throughout Shakespeare—*Cymbeline*, *Winter's Tale*, and *Troilus and Cressida*. See Tracy Davis, "'Reading Shakespeare by Flashes of Lightning': Challenging the Foundations of Romantic Acting Theory," *ELH* 62, no. 4 (1995): 933–54; and John D. Cox, *Seeming Knowledge: Shakespeare and Skeptical Faith* (Waco, TX: Baylor University Press, 2007).

13. Karen Halttunen, *Confidence Men and Painted Women* (New Haven, CT: Yale University Press, 1982); Warren Susman, *Culture as History: The Transformation of American Society in the Twentieth Century* (New York: Pantheon Books, 1984); Arthur Miller, *Death of a Salesman* (New York: Penguin Books [1949] 1976).

14. Michael Hardt and Antonio Negri, *Multitude: War and Democracy in the Age of Empire* (New York: Penguin Press, 2004), 108.

15. Paolo Virno, *A Grammar of the Multitude: For an Analysis of Contemporary Life Forms* (Cambridge, MA: Semiotext(e), 2004), 52, italic in the original.

16. Karl Marx, *Capital: A Critique of Political Economy, Vol. 1*, trans. Ben Fowkes (New York: Vintage Books, 1977), 1048.

17. Hannah Arendt, *Between Past and Future: Eight Exercises in Political Thought* (New York: Penguin Books, [1954] 1977), 154.

18. Virno, "Virtuosity and Revolution," 55.

19. Virno, Virtuosity and Revolution," 55.

20. See André Lepecki, *Exhausting Dance: Performance and the Politics of Movement* (New York: Routledge, 2006); and Yvonne Rainer, "Some Retrospective Notes on a Dance for 10 People and 12 Mattresses . . . ," *Tulane Drama Review* 10, no. 2 (1965): 168–78.

21. José Esteban Muñoz, *Cruising Utopia: The Then and There of Queer Futurity* (New York: New York University Press, 2009), 169.

22. Studio Museum of Harlem, *My Barbarian: The Not-So Amateur Dedicated Amateurs*, 2007–8.

23. For further explorations on how antitheater sensibilities structure visual-art performance discourse, see Rebecca Schneider, *Performing Remains: Art and War in Times of Theatrical Reenactment* (London: Routledge, 2011).

24. Josette Féral, "Theatricality: The Specificity of Theatrical Language," *SubStance* #98/99 31, no. 2–3 (2002): 94–108; Baz Kershaw, *The Radical in Performance: Between Brecht and Baudrillard* (London: Routledge, 1999); and Richard Schechner, "A New Paradigm for Theater in the Academy," *TDR: The Drama Review* 36, no. 4 (1992): 7–10, and "Theater Alive in the New Millennium," *TDR: The Drama Review* 44, no. 1 (2000): 5–6.

25. See, e.g., Bryan-Wilson, *Art Workers*; Miwon Kwon, *One Place after Another: Site-Specific Art and Locational Identity* (Cambridge, MA: MIT Press, 2002); and Lucy R. Lippard, *Six Years: The Dematerialization of the Art Object from 1966 to 1972* (Berkeley: University of California Press, 1997).

26. See, e.g., Peggy Phelan, *Unmarked: The Politics of Performance* (London: Routledge, 1993).

27. See Shannon Jackson, *Social Works* (London: Routledge, 2011), particularly chap. 3, "High Maintenance: The Sanitation Aesthetics of Mierle Laderman Ukeles."

28. For an extended discussion of exactly this issue, see Schneider, *Performing Remains*.

29. Virno, *Grammar of the Multitude*, 55.

30. The critical back-and-forth surrounding Performa 2011 exemplifies this dynamic but requires another essay to treat it thoroughly.

31. See, e.g., Ulrich Beck, *Risk Society: Towards a New Modernity* (SAGE Publications, 1992), and *World Risk Society* (Cambridge: Polity, 1999).

32. Ulrich Beck and Elisabeth Beck-Gernsheim, *Individualization* (London: Sage Publications, 2002), 23.

33. Holmes, *Unleashing the Collective Phantoms*, 19, 21.

34. Herbert Marcuse, *One-Dimensional Man: Studies in the Ideology of Advanced Industrial Society* (Boston: Beacon Press, [1964] 1991).

35. Luc Boltanski and Eve Chiapello, *The New Spirit of Capitalism* (New York: Verso, 2005).

36. On the Art Workers Coalition, see, e.g., Alexander Alberro and Sabeth Buchmann, eds., *Art after Conceptual Art* (Cambridge, MA: MIT Press, 2006).

37. Pierre-Michel Menger, *Les intermittents du spectacle* (Paris: Éditions de l'École des hautes études en sciences sociales, 2005).

38. Gregory Sholette, *Dark Matter: Art and Politics in an Age of Enterprise Culture* (New York: Pluto Press, 2010), 134.

39. See, e.g., Florida, *Rise of the Creative Class*; and Pink, *A Whole New Mind*.

40. See, e.g., Jamie Peck, *Workfare States* (New York: Guilford Press, 2001).

41. Dorothy Smith, "A Peculiar Eclipsing: Women's Exclusion from Man's Culture," *Women's Studies International Quarterly* 1 (1978): 281–95; and Tillie Olsen, "One out of twelve: Women who are writers in our century," *College English* 34, no. 1 (Oct. 1972): 6–17.

42. Kathi Weeks's excellent retrospective essay on the subject should be required reading for anyone working with these questions. See Kathi Weeks, "Life within and against Work: Affective Labor, Feminist Critique, and Post-Fordist Politics," *ephemera* 7, no. (2007): 233–49.

43. Dorothy E. Smith, *The Everyday World as Problematic: A Feminist Sociology* (Boston: Northeastern University Press, 1987), 83–84.

44. Arlie R. Hochschild, *The Managed Heart: Commercialization of Human Feeling* (Berkeley: University of California Press, 1983); Bell, *Coming of Post-Industrial Society*.

45. Michael Hardt, "Affective Labor," *boundary 2* 26, no. 2 (1999): 97.

46. Erving Goffman, *The Presentation of Self in Everyday Life* (New York: Anchor Books, 1959), and *Forms of Talk* (Philadelphia: University of Pennsylvania Press, 1981).

47. Richard Schechner, "Performance Studies: The Broad Spectrum Approach," *TDR: The Drama Review* 32, no. 3 (1988): 4–6.

48. Halttunen, *Confidence Men and Painted Women*; Tracy Davis, *Actresses as Working Women: Their Social Identity in Victorian Culture* (London: Routledge, 1991).

49. Hochschild, *Managed Heart*, 7.

50. Hochschild, *Managed Heart*, 5–6.

51. Weeks, "Life within and against Work," 244.

52. Michel de Certeau, *The Practice of Everyday Life*, trans. Steven Rendall (Berkeley: University of California Press, 1984), xix.

53. For differently situated arguments that sound a similar concern, see Lila Abu-Lughod, "The Romance of Resistance: Tracing Transformations of Power through Bedouin Women," *American Ethnologist* 17 (1990): 41–55; Brad Epps, "The Fetish of Fluidity," in *Homosexuality and Psychoanalysis*, ed. Tim Dean and Christopher Lane (Chicago: University of Chicago Press, 2001), 412–43; and Jon McKenzie, *Perform or Else: From Discipline to Performance* (London: Routledge, 2001).

54. I was struck by this phrase because it resonates with terminology that is important to me in *Social Works* (2011). Berlant invoked this phrase at a salon hosted at Barnard in 2011 and is developing it for a new project. See http://www.youtube.com/watch?v=rlOeWTa_M0U.

55. Sholette, *Dark Matter*, 19–22.

56. John D. Inazu, "The Forgotten Freedom of Assembly," *Tulane Law Review* 84 (2010): 567.

Chapter 12

✦

Seven Ways to Look at *Windows*

Harrell Fletcher

Harrell Fletcher's collaboration with the Exploratorium's Center for Art and Inquiry, *The Best Things in Museums Are the Windows* (2013), is a project that brings forward a range of questions. At base, it starts with a deceptively simple one: What if we could go directly from the Exploratorium to the top of Mount Diablo, which is across the San Francisco Bay and visible from the windows of the museum's new space at Pier 15 (see fig. 12.1)? The implications of executing such an idea, however, are far more complex, logistically and conceptually; that mixture propels the work as a whole. Ultimately, *The Windows* draws from various genealogies in art, science, education, and community practice. In trying to come to terms with its context and its effects, I found myself exploring a few different domains of comparison.

Proposition 1: This Is a Social Practice Artwork

It is not a coincidence that the Exploratorium's Center for Art and Inquiry has recently focused its attention on the work of artists identified with a so-called social turn in the arts. Such artistic practices are defined by a range of labels such as relational aesthetics, social practice, poststudio art, community art, participatory art, and public art. Those terms all come with slightly different orientations. Within the visual art field, however, the embrace of the social is partly characterized as an embrace of the relational—that is, an embrace of person-to-person encounter as a material aspect of the art object. Rather than conceiving of art as a thing bound by a frame or balanced atop a pedestal, art becomes most interesting as a structure for enabling interaction among those who engage with it; in such social practice artwork, the nature of that interaction is itself the form and central matter under question. Harrell Fletcher's *The Best Thing in Museums Are the Windows* thus joins a vast and ever-growing roster of

Fig. 11. Harrell Fletcher, *The Best Things in Museums Are the Windows*, 2013.
Photograph courtesy of the artist.

expanded art events conceived as relational explorations. We could place
it in a network of internationally renowned—if highly differentiated—
contemporary works, ranging from the perpetually eroding and perpetually
replenished stacks and candy spills of Felix Gonzalez-Torres to the service
art pieces of Christine Hill to the discursive choreographies of Tino Sehgal
to the collaboratively coordinated environmental interventions of Frances
Alÿs. In these and thousands of related pieces conceived at museums, biennials, and strategically chosen off-site locations, artists are still mobilizing
material—candy, dirt, lumber, paper, and bodies—as well as the staff and
institutional resources of an art context to produce actions, processes,
encounters, and alternative social spaces.[1] Indeed, the art requires action
and encounter to become itself and, to some ways of thinking, requires
continued action to remain itself. Perhaps because of its environmental
ethos, perhaps because of its allegiances to a number of social movements,
the West Coast of the United States has become an important site of innovation in this field—whether in the feminist happenings of Suzanne Lacy,
the sustainable food experiments of Suzanne Cockrell and Ted Purves, the
prison data pieces of Sharon Daniel, or the interactive wish systems of
Miranda July and Harrell Fletcher himself. Each of these artists is affiliated with degree-granting programs in the social practice field, in graduate
art practice programs in San Diego, Los Angeles, San Francisco, Santa
Cruz, and Portland—an index of how much the traditional MFA is being
redefined on the West Coast by artists' interest in framing, engaging, and
reimagining social systems.

Like any purported "turn" in a given intellectual, artistic, or political movement, this turn is not properly understood as new. It is an ethos
that remembers and occasionally forgets lineages in the Constructivist
experiments in the early twentieth century and the Happenings of the mid-
twentieth century.[2] While community art histories may not have had the
same formal preoccupations with "relationality" as such, the art movements of the Works Progress Administration through other federal and

community-sponsored initiatives certainly share the impulse to make art from social interaction. Finally, many quite rightly question whether sociality can ever be imagined as a new element in any art object. Art objects framed as paintings, staged as theater, or upheld by pedestals all initiate encounters of various sorts. *Pace* modernist critics who might have argued otherwise, art has always required process and always activated interpersonal exchange. Perhaps these social turns are not so much adding a new material as foregrounding a relational dimension that was always there.

Proposition 2: This Is an Exploratorium Exhibit

The Best Things in Museums Are the Windows included exercises that investigated the speed of sound, lectures about radioactivity, animal-dissection demonstrations, and explorations of human movement. Exploratorium educators, exhibit developers, scientists, curators, and explainers animated the trail, setting up their wares and exposing the scientific undercurrents of the everyday. Meanwhile, the structure of the project enabled and required exhibition and demonstration from a host of community organizations along the trail—a sailing organization for the disabled, a local farm, a music school, a community garden, and more. The project arguably is a full-scale continuation of the goals and identity of the Exploratorium, questing forward to find new ways to produce "eye-opening, always changing, and playful place(s) to explore and tinker."[3] The Exploratorium is arguably already quite "social" and participatory in its techniques and goals. As an organization that is part of a much longer history of a specific museum practice, one that is usually differentiated from the history of art museum practice, it joins a host of a history museums and science museums that began working much earlier to liberate the object from its bounded place on the pedestal. It is not as if this museum genealogy does not have its problems. Whether recalling the fraught colonizing ethos of early anthropology museums or the Cold War science museums erected to celebrate a nation's scientific prowess, early "learning centers" certainly placed constraints on the frames and goals of what could be learned. Arguably, however, the exhibition models of most science museums were already propelled by a principle of encounter, even if that encounter was less than reciprocal. Objects were displayed not only to induce contemplation but also to impart information and provoke a different kind of awareness about the functioning of the world. As such, art museums are now realizing how much there is to learn from science museums.

As a twentieth-first-century science museum–turned-learning center, the Exploratorium has redefined itself with an awareness of the nationalist critiques—and sketchy factualisms—that structured the dramaturgy of science and history museums of the past. (Not much taxidermy to be found here.) Reimagining itself soon after its founding in 1969 as a new triumvirate—"a museum of science, art, and human perception"—the focus would seem to be on mobilizing the mutually redefining potential of each of these terms. Bonnard's flash of recognition about windows being the best things in museums here becomes clear.[4] It is not that one longs to escape the museum by looking out the window—or by jumping through it. The window is a lens to look through and to look with; it is a prosthetic that frames encounters and produces new ones. The window might be found in a mirror that changes the shapes of the beings it reflects or in the projector that disperses them across an environment; the window might be a magnifying glass, the transparent wall of a terrarium, or a pool of water whose surface reflects the faces of the children who look down upon it. These and other "windows" offer access to a kind of knowledge and an awareness of how that knowledge is made. Here human perception is activated but also under question. We are in a space of investigation that asks us to think, not only about what we know but also about how we know what we think we know. Such an ethos exposes the conceptual rigor that has redefined the fields of art and science in the late twentieth century, underscoring the shared impatience of both domains with perceptual habits that accept the "givenness" of the world before us. Ultimately, then, it is not simply that the best things in the museums are the windows, but that the museum's windows might be the best windows that there are.

Proposition 3: This Is an Alternative Classroom

If the museum's windows are striking for the lenses on the world that they provide, then this project tried to see whether such windows could be imported, resituated, and extended to a world beyond the Exploratorium's physical site. As such, it is perhaps another instance of a wide and rangy movement in progressive pedagogy, one that explores the effectiveness of learning environments beyond the traditional school. Whether recalling the tacit learning of Tolstoy's agrarian villages, the experiential democracies imagined by John Dewey, or Paolo Freire's disquisitions against the stifling practices of "banking" education, alternative education movements develop new practices for hands-on, inquiry-based learning—and seek out exterior places and hands-on environments in which to site it.[5] Contemporary researchers such as Jean Lave tout the importance of LPP— Legitimate Peripheral Participation—documenting the effectiveness of learning in sites that are peripheral to the formal classroom. [6] Throughout the *Windows* project, Fletcher recalled a favorite story of Exploratorium founder Frank Oppenheimer, one that told of a woman who reportedly came home after a visit to the Exploratorium and rewired a broken lamp. How might others be emboldened to use the lessons of the museum in spaces outside of it?

The Exploratorium is, of course, already an LPP; it is already a place where teachers, families, and professional organizations reap the educational benefits of participating in the Legitimate Peripheral sphere. *The Best Things in Museums Are the Windows* thus challenged the Exploratorium to peripheralize the periphery, or to alter our sense of where lines between center and periphery are drawn by resiting its exhibits in the natural and urban landscape of the Bay Area. We as participants would learn about the physics of wind on a sailboat and about radioactivity on a (formerly?) radioactive island. We learned about historic train systems on streets where the rails were buried and about the effects of drought in the middle of a forest. Recalling the ethos of the alternative classroom, the educational efficacy was heightened by placing the encounter on a site were relevant issues and histories were palpable.

As such, *The Windows* also joined and advanced a pedagogical turn within the contemporary art networks of social practice described earlier. Indeed, many artists have been quick to realize that the social turn is not only not new to art but also not new to other arenas of inquiry. Mining the field of education for alternative models—A. S. Neill's Summerhill School, the unschooling of John Holt, Jonathan Kozol's "free schools"—art collectives such as the Center for Land Use Interpretation, Chto Delat, the Center for Urban Pedagogy, or WochenKlausur, as well as individual artists such as Sharon Hayes, Pablo Helguera, and many more, model their practices on pedagogical ones.[7] There is thus a very interesting chiasmus between artistic domains and educational domains in our present moment. While educators are redefining schooling by making it more like art, artists are redefining aesthetics by making it more like school. In this space of mutual appropriation, a different hybrid arises. Artists and teachers both create think tanks, devise group exercises, install projects, distribute assignments, and welcome failure, eliciting opportunities for reflective interaction on the workings of art and the environment around them. At its best, art's conceptual framing loosens the predestined instrumentalization of education, while the educational pursuit places inquiry and sociality at the center of the artistic sphere.

Proposition 4: This Is a Work of Institutional Critique

The phrase "institutional critique" was coined in the 1980s to characterize a range of art practices that took the institution, specifically the art institution, as a central medium and object of reflection.[8] Andrea Fraser famously constructed alternative docent tours and an alternative docent

persona—Jane Castleton—to expose the inner workings and inner economies of the museum space. Inspired by the institutionally targeted work of
Hans Haacke, extended by the counterexhibition strategies of Fred Wilson, artists who identified with institutional critique developed practices
for mining and rendering visible the operational structures of the exhibition space. Elmgreen & Dragset, Mierle Laderman Ukeles, Tino Sehgal,
and many others have incorporated security guard staff into their artworks. These artists along with others such as Josh Greene, Mark Dion,
Pierre Huyghe, and many more have displayed curatorial offices and curator's bodies inside their exhibition practices, turning the museum space
inside out. More recent social practices have extended institutional reflection, though often they involve museum staff less as objects and more as
interlocutors in a shared space of reflection. For example, Portland artist
and Harrell Fletcher's student Lexa Walsh exemplified such a mode as an
education artist-in-residence with her *Meal Ticket* system for gathering
staff from across the institution.

The Windows was a variant of this variant. The Exploratorium is a
space that, to some degree, already makes transparent the workings of its
operations. In its new space, visitors are invited to see into the workshops
and laboratories that create its exhibits. Upon visiting the Exploratorium,
Fletcher was increasingly interested in the people who kept the museum
running and contributed to its learning. These are the people charged with
sustaining a learning space, art space, and dynamic space for thousands
of daily visitors of various regions and generations. What would it mean
to draw these makers further out into the open? To place them in a different natural habitat while also giving them the opportunity to engage with
each other?

If *The Best Thing in Museums Are the Windows* was, in part, an extension of the Exploratorium's status as a venue of LPP, it also legitimated
such peripheral participation for the museum's staff. It was a group experience filled with challenges, frustrations, bonding moments, and learning
moments for a group of employees. It was a retreat activity carried out by
those who usually tend to the retreats of others. Non-Exploratorium participants thus found ourselves engaging with a specific group of employees
throughout the trip; people like Julie Hartford and I would find ourselves
in conversation but just as often we were spectators to conversations
among staff members that seemed to have been going on for a while.
Many team members knew the names of each other's partners and kids,
and the illnesses that they were recovering from. They knew what projects
each was putting on hold to be there and how much work was piling
up in their offices as we walked. They knew each other's taste in music,
food preferences, and social foibles. In seeing these institutional representatives interacting with each other, I felt surrounded by people who were
likely the smartest kids in school—though not necessarily the most well

behaved. They questioned each other at every turn, layering query upon query, twisting devices that I didn't think we were supposed to touch, interrupting each other, teasing each other, turning someone's demo into a debate. As producers of one of our city's notable "off-site" experiences, these staff members were having their own "off-site," relying on a history of trust as they followed a series of structured activities. But they were also testing that trust and, hopefully, strengthening it. *The Windows* allowed Exploratorium staff to do their own exploring as well.

Proposition 5: This Is a Walking Art Piece

If social practice can describe a range of expanded forms in contemporary art, then "walking art" is both a variant and a precedent of such a turn. As Jason Groves chronicles in his essay in this catalogue, walking has always been a source of inspiration for the artist, philosopher, and everyday citizen.[9] While a range of thinkers elaborated on the imaginative effects and physical benefits of walking—whether for clearing or activating the mind, accessing the natural world, or reencountering an urban one—numerous artists over the course of the twentieth and twentieth-first centuries have incorporated the act of walking as an artistic material. Surrealists created chance excursions—or "deambulations"—that spontaneously explored the city and wider outskirts of Paris, translating the concept of "automatic writing" into a moving, corporeal form. Later, Situationists sought to politicize the act of alternative walking, developing the practice of the "derive," which more self-consciously sought to upset or resist the spatial habits of urban space in order to imagine new psychogeographical relationships.[10] Such practices were extended in the sphere of site-based choreography, whether in Lucinda Childs's *Street Dance* (1964), Trisha Brown's sculptural dance *The Stream* (1970), or Yvonne Rainer's deployment of *Street Action (M-Walk)* (1970) to protest the American invasion of Cambodia. Walking has extended the practice of endurance art, expanding the act of walking into days, weeks, and even years to test and redefine the experience of embodiment and temporality. Some walking art pieces posited literal and symbolic destinations, such as Ulay and Marina Abramovic's decision to end their relationship after walking the Great Wall of China. Others such as Tehching Hsieh's *One Year Performance 1981–82 (Outdoor Piece)*, ended undramatically; in that piece, walking was a mundane vehicle for eluding sheltered space and its conventions of social interaction.

The Windows partakes of some of the genealogies suggested above, mixing chance spatial encounters with deliberately planned spatial alternatives. And the peak of Mount Diablo gave this walk a focused sense of destination. As a four-day event, it also required a degree of endurance, and some Exploratorium staff members wondered whether they would endure and enjoy the psychic drain and alternative imagining that often accompanies long excursions. The artist whom Fletcher most explicitly cites as inspiration, however, is Richard Long. Living outside Bristol, England, Long famously devised walks and perambulations that conformed to—or suddenly surfaced—geometries that were both precise and new. Integrating the act of walking with the act of "marking" (to quote a recent retrospective), Long entered the terrain of the natural world to denaturalize his (and our) relationship to it. *Turf Sculpture* (1967) and *Turf Circle* (1966) marked the landscape at right angles or in perfect circumferences. His famous *A Line Made By Walking* (1967) photographed the trace left by repeatedly walking in a grassy field near his home. The geometrically precise line stands out as an all too human intervention in a natural landscape, simultaneously invoking reflection on the delicacy, focus, and once presentness of the figure who made it. *The Windows* plots its own unexpected geometry, even if its "line" was made not only by walking but also by sailing. Indeed, as anticipated and documented in the Exploratorium's map of the work, the thrill and chutzpah of this piece partly resides in its desire to conform to an imagined line, one that runs as due east as possible from Pier 15, through Oakland and Berkeley, to the top of Mount Diablo. The step-by-step endurance of this walk was thus often experienced in relation to this imagined line, attempting to reconcile the material and the ideal, the lateral view and the bird's eye view, with each progression across water and ground.

Proposition 6: This Is a Contemporary Artwork by Harrell Fletcher

At the beginning of this essay and throughout, I have referred to *The Best Things in Museums Are the Windows* as a piece "by" Harrell Fletcher. As a work commissioned by the Exploratorium's Center for Art and Inquiry, this highly collaborative work indeed simultaneously exists as a piece, idea, and proposition conceived by Harrell Fletcher. Its structure recalls other works associated with this name, such as *A Walk to Pike's Peak* in Colorado. Moreover, many of Fletcher's pieces have created structures that include the desires and knowledge of everyday people, heightening our awareness of the everyday expertise of the amateur (such as in *The People's Biennial*, cocurated with Jens Hoffman) or extending our experience of everyday intimacy (such as *Learning to Love You More* [2002–9] created with Miranda July). *The Best Things in Museums Are the Windows* will have his signature, and it will join the history of other pieces "by" Fletcher—those proposed and theoretically authored by him.

Proposition 7: This Is Not a Contemporary Artwork by Harrell Fletcher

As a social practice piece, however, this is a work that is not exclusively understood as one conceived by a single artist. While his artistic proposition galvanized Exploratorium curators, staff, and community partners, it was simultaneously conceived as a piece that featured others' expertise and counted on the trust of the team it assembled. It was made by the staff members who planned demonstrations along the path and by those who coordinated sailors, historians, and trackers in advance. It was made by the group who first stepped on the Bay Area Association of Disabled Sailors sailboat and by those who joined at various points along the way. Moreover, the piece now lives as a proposition whose simplicity and complexity can be an invitation for others in the future, others who decide to imagine their own creative walks and follow unorthodox geometries across the landscape. In the end, *The Best Things in Museums are the Windows* is a vehicle for exposing the expertise and creativity, not only of Harrell Fletcher, but also of an Exploratorium that is already here, there, and everywhere.

Notes

"Seven Ways to Look at *Windows*: Harrell Fletcher" was originally published in *The Best Things in Museums Are the Windows*, ed. Harrell Fletcher (San Francisco: Exploratorium Center for Art and Inquiry, 2014), 18–25.

1. For more context on a range of contemporary social art experiments and exhibitions, see, e.g., Nicolas Bourriaud, *Relational Aesthetics*, trans. Simon Pleasance and Fronza Woods (Dijon, France: Les Presses du réel, 2002); Grant Kester, *Conversation Pieces* (Berkeley: University of California Press, 2004) and *The One and the Many: Contemporary Collaborative Art in a Global Context* (Durham, NC: Duke University Press, 2011); Shannon Jackson, *Social Works: Performing Art, Supporting Publics* (New York and London: Routledge, 2011); Nato Thompson, *Living as Form: Socially Engaged Art from 1991–2011* (Cambridge, MA: MIT Press, 2012); Claire Bishop, *Artificial Hells: Participatory Art and the Politics of Spectatorship* (London: Verso, 2012); Ted Purves, ed., *What We Want Is Free: Generosity and Exchange in Recent Art* (Albany: State University of New York Press, 2004); and Tom Finklepearl, *What We Made: Conversations on Art and Social Cooperation* (Durham, NC: Duke University Press, 2013).

2. For more on these genealogies, see, e.g., Maria Gough, *The Artist as Producer: Russian Constructivism in Revolution* (Farmington Hills, MI: Thomson Gale, 2006); Christina Kiaer, *Imagine No Possessions: The Socialist Objects of Russian Constructivism* (Cambridge, MA: MIT Press, 2005); Jeff Kelley, *Childsplay: The Art of Allan Kaprow* (Berkeley: University of California Press, 2007); and Judith Rodenbeck, *Radical Prototypes* (Cambridge, MA: MIT Press, 2011).

3. "About the Exploratorium," The Exploratorium, https://www
.exploratorium.edu/about-us.

4. Harrell Fletcher, "The Best Things in Museums Are the Windows," The Exploratorium, https://www.exploratorium.edu/arts/works/the-windows, accessed November 2021.

5. For more background on these genealogies, see, e.g., Leo Tolstoy, "The School at Yasnaya Polyana," in *Tolstoy as Teacher: Leo Tolstoy's Writings on Education* (New York: Teachers and Writers Collaborative, 2000); John Dewey, *Art as Experience* (New York: Perigee Books, [1934] 1980); and Paolo Freire, *The Pedagogy of the Oppressed* (New York: Penguin, 2017).

6. See Jean Lave, *Situated Learning: Legitimate Peripheral Participation* (Cambridge: Cambridge University Press, 1991).

7. In addition to texts already mentioned, related reading on this nexus includes A. S. Neill, *Summerhill: A Radical Approach to Child Rearing* (New York: Hart Publishing, 1960); John Holt, *How Children Fail* (New York: Pitman, 1964); Jonathan Kozol, *Free Schools* (New York: Houghton Mifflin, 1972); and Pablo Helguera, *Education for Socially Engaged Art* (New York: Jorge Pinto Books, 2011).

8. See, e.g., Alexander Alberro and Blake Stimson, eds., *Institutional Critique: An Anthology of Artists' Writings* (Cambridge, MA: MIT Press, 2009).

9. Jason Groves, "A View from the Edge: The Peripatetic Perspective," in *The Best Things in Museums Are the Windows* (San Francisco: Exploratorium Museum, 2014).

10. See André Breton, "The First Manifesto of Surrealism," in Charles Harrison and Paul Wood, eds., *Art in Theory, 1900–1990* (Oxford: Blackwell, 1992): 432–39; and Guy Debord, "Theory of the Dérive," in Ken Knabb, ed. and trans., *Situationst International Anthology* (Berkeley, CA: Bureau of Public Secrets, 1981), 62–66.

Chapter 13

✦

Countercarnival in a
Performance-Friendly World

En Mas'

In coming to terms with *En Mas'*—a platform, parade, and provocation staged by Claire Tancons and Krista Thompson—I find myself in the midst of a deliciously conceptual puzzle. Here we have a project that promises to overturn and call the bluff of several political and artistic assumptions, challenging at every turn binaries that would oppose stasis and duration, object and action, local and global, visual art and performing art, populist and elite. Of course, it has historically been the job of carnival to upend conventional categories. Mikhail Bakhtin famously chronicled the carnivalesque as a buoyant and temporary space where roles are reversed, where the high play low and the low play high.[1] Throughout *En Mas'*, I find artists recalling François Rabelais's famous salute—"Bottoms Up"—only this time I hear more distinctly what might be called the *formal* challenge of the exhortation.[2] Throughout this project, artists, curators, and citizens deploy carnival as aesthetic and social material. Yes, these works unsettle divisions between high and low, but they also flout a range of contemporary conventions and formulas, exposing blind spots and reinvented wheels within site-specific, performative, and relational discourses of the artworld. *En Mas'* does not simply ride the wave of new art experiment; rather it reveals the longer and deeper histories of what some still think is "new." In what follows, I offer some reflections on contexts and concepts that I see informing and unforming within the *En Mas'* platform; these works suggest that today's contemporary artworld "turns" both repeat and repress carnivalesque histories to which they are unwittingly indebted.

I. The Performance of the Black Atlantic: Motion and Music

The forms assembled under *En Mas'* are not so much the products of a region as the movements of a circuit. Paul Gilroy famously opened his disquisition on the Black Atlantic with a reminder of how the forced migratory patterns of the transatlantic spurred the creation of new hybrid ensembles: "The cultures of this group have been produced in a syncretic pattern in which the styles and forms of the Caribbean, the United States, and Africa have been reworked and reinscribed in the novel context of modern Britain's [and modern Europe's] own untidy ensemble of regional and class-oriented conflicts."[3] An *En Mas'* artist like Lorraine O'Grady references that ensemble in her search for forms and formats that allow the exploration of her "Caribbean–New England–European bohemian life."[4] O'Grady is one of many who assembles new syncretic forms from the cultures and conventions of a transatlantic circuit, allowing diverse and sometimes contradictory symbols to coexist and unsettle each other.

Carnival steps in to hold this diasporic untidiness, quite literally stepping, advancing, meandering, moving across the byways and waterways that have transported and produced transnational Black identities. Conceptually, this means supplanting an analytic fixation on the products of culture with an analytic that values the movements of culture. Carnival is a form in motion from both macro- and microperspectives. It is the propulsive site where the transatlantic migratory patterns of the diaspora collide; at the same time, it is its own local form, an aesthetic action on the ground that parades within the communities that it simultaneously forms. The *En Mas'* platform follows this migration and strategically "calls" at historic sites of carnival creativity, anchoring in Santiago de los Caballeros, Port of Spain, Fort-de-France, Kingston, New Orleans, Notting Hill, Brooklyn, and finally Nassau. At such sites, we find the ebullience and detritus of the parade as form, one that indexes the "routes" followed and forged by traveling bodies. Carnival's commitment to the parade route mimics, repeats, claims, and reperforms the primary mobility of diasporic subjectivity. Such an orientation unsettles artistic conventions and requires a different kind of a curatorial emphasis. Consider Christopher Cozier's recalling of Peter Minshall's carnival aesthetics, substituting the language of artwork with that of roadwork: "Since many of the activities surrounding our lives are street activities I thought it interesting to replace the word art with road."[5] Claire Tancons herself has subsequently asked, "How might the epistemological shift articulated by Cozier from artwork to roadwork affect the way in which Carnival is conceived of and, by extension, curated?"[6] and seems to have found an answer in *En Mas'*. In such an aesthetic, travel is not the dead space between two end points but is itself the place to be. The roadworks of carnival use streets and sidewalks instead of galleries and stages, turning exhibition into procession, putting theater on the march. Moreover, the legacy of carnival exposes a racial and colonial history within the canons of avant-garde experimentation, one that precedes the perambulations of the Surrealists and the psychogeographic motions of the Situationists. The parade is an ancestor to and unexpected collaborator with legions of artists and art groups for whom "walking" became an aesthetic practice.[7]

If Gilroy's emphasis on the diasporic routes of the Black Atlantic points to carnival as an exemplary index and site, other elements of his argument give us different ways to think about its symbolic productivity. As a sociologist and cultural critic, Gilroy was keen to emphasize the necessity of focusing on the nonliterary or extratextual dimensions of Black cultural expression. He focuses on "music" as a domain and figure within an interpretive frame that values sound, image, and gesture: "The power of music in developing black struggles by communicating information, organizing consciousness, and testing out or deploying the forms of subjectivity which are required by political agency, whether individual or collective, defensive or transformational, demands attention to both the formal attributes of this expressive culture and its distinctive *moral* basis."[8] Black music is thus a syncretic form that contains and propels the ambivalent experience and transfigurative hopes of modernist Black subjectivity. For Gilroy, "The politics of fulfillment is mostly content to play occidental rationality at its own game. It necessitates a hermeneutic orientation that can assimilate the semiotic, verbal, and textual. The politics of transfiguration strives in pursuit of the sublime, struggling to repeat the unrepeatable, to present the unpresentable. Its rather different hermeneutic focus pushes towards the mimetic, dramatic, and performative."[9] While some might question the ease with which Gilroy elided musical, choreographic, and theatrical forms under banner of the "nontextual," his emphasis legitimated the hermeneutic of scholars and artists who worked with such forms and positioned themselves within the cultural genealogies of the Black Atlantic. Performance studies scholar Joseph Roach set the bar high with *Cities of the Dead*, a study of circum-Atlantic performance as a "busy intersection" and "behavioral vortex where cultural transmission may be detoured, deflected, or displaced."[10] Fred Moten and other scholars coming from the fields of performance studies, sound studies, dance, musicology, and theater found in the Black Atlantic a hermeneutic that transformed a geographic lens on cultural creativity while offering an intermedial expansion of where such creativity could be found.[11]

If Black Atlantic identity is less a site than a trajectory, less an object than a performative, then the artists of *En Mas'* represent various configurations from vortices of behavior that circumnavigate the Atlantic. It includes English-speaking circuits from London to Kingston, such as the "actor boys" recalled in Chris Campbell's replaying of Jonkonnu traditions. Nicolás Dumit Estévez offers a safe place in which to reenact the memories and gestures of the Dominican Republic, "to co-enact personal fears, taboos, fantasies, and desires."[12] This gathering also includes French postcolonials who live under the "big sun" on islands such as those of the Guadeloupe archipelago or Martinique, where Christophe Chassol shot his eponymous film, still affected by France's casual and persistent racism. Chassol uses the tradition of monkey masquerade in the Fort-de-France carnival to stage a potent and ambivalent comeback on behalf of French Justice Minister Christiane Taubira of French Guiana.[13] But the monkey-masked performers also find themselves lodged within a video and sound installation that revels in Black musical powers of transfiguration. Chassol's provocatively rich soundscape layers and braids musical traditions of Europe within those of the Caribbean, including the everyday sounds of the marketplace and the homeplace, including the bird calls and animal cries of a natural landscape that offer new vehicles for human self-figuration.

If Chassol reclaims but relocates a European musical idiom within a potent vortex of intercultural and interspecies interaction, Cauleen Smith is called by a sound sequence that is even more unexpected. She reclaims and relocates the mass cultural tones of Steven Spielberg's *Close Encounters of the Third Kind*, citing and siting its familiar dips across the scale within the bodies and instruments, the buildings and streets of New Orleans. Citizen-musicians play tuba and trombone, bassoon and cello, allowing the familiar sounds to reverberate differently within each instrument, sometimes gently extending its vibrations with the swing and sting of second-line tones. Indeed, the piece seems to disassemble the component parts of a New Orleans funeral. It stays true to the complexity of that performance form as Roach has elaborated it, "a moment in which the community joyously affirms its renewal in the very act of marking the passing of one of its own."[14] But if the funeral parade is about motion, the motion of this parade is made when a camera moves across an array of largely stationary individuals. The camera connects individual citizens on street corners and sidewalks, near overgrown gardens, before fenced-in schools, past houses in various states of repair, asking us to decide where and when "joy" or "community" might be found. It pans across a river that has been the source of so much fraught and productive connection, and into the bayous where other kinds of magic happen. The compelling oddity of the refrain echoes Gilroy's elaboration of the "low frequency" at which black political expression must often operate.

> Created under the very nose of the overseers, the utopian desires which fuel the complementary politics of transfiguration must be invoked by other, more deliberately opaque means. This politics exists on a lower frequency where it is played, danced, and acted, as well as sung and sung about, because words, even words stretched by melisma and supplemented or mutated by the screams which still index the conspicuous power of the slave sublime, will never by enough to communicate its unsayable claims to truth. The willfully damaged signs which betray the resolutely utopian

Fig. 12. Cauleen Smith, *H-E-L-L-O*, 2014. Video still. Location Congo Square. Sousaphone: Kirk Joseph. Cinematography by William Sabourin, 2014.

> politics of transfiguration therefore partially transcend modernity, constructing both an imaginary anti-modern past and a postmodern yet-to-come.[15]

Indeed, the opacity of conceptual art practice is here given a different spin, joined to a practice whose politics are not overtly referential but are nevertheless affectively urgent. Smith extends the syncretism of Black cultural production to a Hollywood soundtrack, turning it over and giving it back as plaintive memorial and tenuous invitation.

II. Many-Headed Hybrid Art

Many contemporary artists experiment across forms, and their experimentation travels under many terms—*interdisciplinary, intermedial, collaborative, group art, relational aesthetics, hybrid art*. Some terms specify the terms of experimentation—*time-based art, photo-based art*—and some hybridize those terms into compound phrases—*video installation, social sculpture, site-specific performance*. Once again, the carnival tradition tells a story of hybrid art experimentation that precedes contemporary gestures, even as those contemporary gestures would seem to offer a welcoming context for remembering them. By mining what historian Peter Linebaugh called the "many-headed hydra" of Caribbean politics, contemporary artists have a chance to remember hybrid aesthetics differently.[16] *En Mas'* comes at a time when there is, arguably, a renewal of artworld interest in the phenomenon of performance. Museums are curating performance within the interior of major exhibitions, not only in a nightly series or at the opening donor event. Biennials and art fairs offer an array of ticketed and unticketed experiences next to a traditional display of objects, frames, and pedestals. Modern art museums are creating new spaces in which to house performative work; the Whitney moved into its new building; MoMA loves its atrium, and the Tate Modern opened the Tanks next to Turbine Hall to offer "permanent" space for the presentation of "temporary" works. As Claire Tancons herself has asked, "what more propitious a time could there be for the advancement of the debate on the place of, not just Carnival, but of performance in general within contemporary Caribbean art practice when so-called performance art dominates the mainstream contemporary art discourse?"[17]

Indeed, the time seems quite propitious in part because of the varied kinds of performance that we find in galleries of late. Increasingly, we find museums siting artists that hail not simply from the Euro-American canons of "performance art" but also from the older traditions of the "performing arts." Trained choreographers now regularly appear inside major exhibitions; Sarah Michelson made history for being the first choreographer to win the Whitney's Bucksbaum Award for the best work in that biennial.[18] And Ralph Lemon has sited his dances and curated dance himself within a variety of spaces—Harlem Studio and MoMA—and has been in constant discussion about what it means for art institutions to "acquire" his work.[19] Curators and concept artists are placing trained opera singers inside their work, featuring pianists as sculpture, asking puppeteers to circumnavigate the gallery, and asking actors to rehearse inside it. While minor interventions and major retrospectives of body art, live art, and performance art continue, the performing arts are making a strange kind of comeback within spaces that once ignored or excluded them.

This kind of context would seem ripe for reconnection with the older performing art form of carnival. *En mas'* practitioner and historian Peter Minshall was quick to position carnival as an early version of a hybrid art form: "To evaluate the place of the Carnival in Caribbean culture and art, it is helpful to realize that Carnival incorporates a broad range of forms and activities. Carnival in Trinidad includes: lyrical songs (calypso and soca), instrumental music (steel bands and brass orchestras), and costumed masquerade along with the dance and movement by which it is presented (mas'). . . . The most visual of these forms is what we call mas': the tradition of costumed masquerade in the Trinidad Carnival."[20] Notably, however, Minshall found the need to account for gaps within this apparent connection, realizing that an artworld interest in hybrid art still circumscribed the terms of hybridity. The rearrival of carnival now thus promises to incarnate contemporary desires for experience, motion, interaction, and embodiment in art; at the same time, its rearrival threatens to unhinge the explicit and implicit parameters of a "performative turn." It turns up genealogies of mask, theater, ritual, parade, and dance that might be inconveniently at odds with the hermeticism of the gallery, threatening to circumnavigate the space in patterns decidedly off the grid. Once again, carnival calls the bluff and, to mix the metaphor, exposes the blind spot of artworld interests in performance.

It should also be said, however, that carnival cannot reenter differently without also reckoning with the internal hierarchies within performing art histories. Minshall's move also meant reckoning with the classed conventions not only of performance art, but also of discrete performing-art forms: "Though it is performance, mas does not easily fit into the mold of any one of the more conventional performing arts. It is theatrical, but it is necessarily broader of stroke, more symbolic, simpler than conventional narrative theater. It involves dance, but this dance is often more spontaneous than choreographed; or, it is dance that is aimed at articulating the mas that is worn, more than the body that is wearing it. It is most akin to what has become known as simply 'performance' or 'performance art,' yet the mas had these characteristics, naively and unselfconsciously, long before the term 'performance art' was coined."[21] In many ways, the field of performance studies was formed to critique classed thinking about performing-art forms, expressly borrowing from anthropological and folkloric fields to expand the parameters of performance. This move in turn unsettled assumptions about the parameters of "dance" or "narrative theater." The dialectic of high and low, of choreographed and spontaneous, has been at the center of discussion within performance studies; so too are assumptions about why we call some forms broad, naïve, and unselfconscious. The interdisciplinary opportunity of this expansion is also its danger. When carnival—and allied forms such as ritual or festival—come into the performance orbit via an anthropological lens, a certain discursive habit might deemphasize aesthetics to foreground tradition; within such a shift, one is supposedly no longer thinking formally but only sociologically. Once again, this is the danger and opportunity of performance studies. On the one hand, an anthropological frame widened the parameters of what qualified as performance beyond the Euro-American tradition of the performing arts. On the other hand, such a widening risked defining certain forms as sites where anthropologically marked community members made performances spontaneously, reproducing tradition self-consciously in shapes too broad and unrefined to qualify as aesthetic acts.

The curation of carnival thus can seem oddly overdetermined. While it has been excluded from artworld thinking, the terms of reincorporation can create new problems and constraints. And yet, *En Mas'* artists venture into this fraught territory, devising hybrid art forms and formats that allow them to navigate this volatile terrain. In Santiago, Nicolás Dumit Estévez creates *C-Room*, a refuge and research space in which to assemble carnival memories. Participants were invited to meet at Museo Folklórico Don Tomas Morel, a site founded by a visionary folklorist and collector who preserved vernacular objects of everyday life and the intricate masks and costumes of Santiago carnival. The museum recalled but redefined the conventions of the anthropological museum. Sited in a small space within the city of Santiago, echoing the counteranthropology of Zora Neale Hurston, the collection was a living enactment of a living archive before its precious detritus was pillaged.[22] Entering through the backdoor of this once vibrant site, Estévez's participants now find a roundabout route in which to reinhabit carnival. Paradoxically, their reenactments of the fears and taboos of this public form occur in a quasi-privatized space. Here they can reconnect with forms, images, and gestures that might get called primitive under an anthropological frame; here they can explore the topsy-turvy identities and sexualities of carnival's contribution to queer performance historiography. At a time when many artists maintain an interest in "relational aesthetics," C-Room exposes carnival's deep knowledge of the form, navigating modes of intersubjective exchange that are generous and buoyant but that also have their threats and dangers.[23] Moreover, the fundamental turns within the relation—a turn to the everyday, the ordinary, and the participatory—hardly feel like "turns" within a carnival practice that has been going on for hundreds of years. A "relational" aesthetics of "the ordinary" turns out to be embedded within the populist politics of the Black diaspora where, as C. L. R. James declared, "The greatest artists of our day have been people who somehow have found themselves in circumstances in which they did not write or work for the educated intellectual public, as all these other writers do, but found themselves compelled to appear to the ordinary citizen."[24] Finally, at a time when many artists tout a commitment to research-based practice, Estévez alters the form and format of research. His work provides a safe space to air fears, taboos, and memories, positioning the vernacular not only as object of study but also as method of study. C-Room offers a flexible space in which to experiment with their reenactment, delicately reviving a performance archive that needs care and protection to live at all.

Throughout En Mas', we find artists mining the cross-disciplinary art of carnival, positioning this many-headed hybrid art as precursor and challenge to contemporary performance curation. If artworlds now claim an interest in the figures and forms of the performing arts, Charles Campbell recalls countertheater of the "Actor Boy," a Jonkonnu character from Jamaican slave celebration. Mixing Victorian boots and costume with the ebullient headdress of Jonkonnu, the Actor Boy is an intercultural embodiment of diasporic identity. More pointedly, however, the strategic mixture of contextual references—from Europe, Africa, and the Americas—empowers a trickster figure to enact the Black Atlantic politics of hybridity. Not content simply to "mix," Actor Boy signifies with and

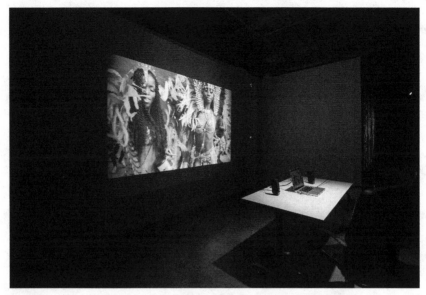

Fig. 13. Lorraine O'Grady, *Looking for a Headdress*, 2014. Installation view, Contemporary Arts Center New Orleans, 2015. Courtesy of Alexander Gray Associates, New York. © 2021 Lorraine O'Grady / Artists Rights Society, New York.

on loaded cultural symbols, asking participants to question the boundaries that presumably divide continents, cultures, and classes. The political exploration of Black Atlantic hybridity receives a different airing in Lorraine O'Grady's "Looking for a Headdress," a space where O'Grady first imagined a "three-ring circus where aspects of the protagonist's Caribbean–New England–European bohemian life happened simultaneously."[25] Foiled by the exigencies of money and labor that prevent the timely arrival of the headdress in question, her work documents a contemporary search for a form adequate to the memories and cultures of diasporic carnival traditions. She recalls her own explicitly theatrical character, Mlle. Bourgeoise Noire, a feminine counterpoint to Actor Boy. The search also takes us along carnival's routes—from Toronto to Brooklyn to Brazil to Trinidad to New Orleans—embodying the diasporic roadworks, and roads worked, by a tradition perpetually on the move.

Indeed, these and so many other pieces explore the productivity and tension of exhibited performance, recalling once again Minshall's advocacy for the form: "Mas is a performance art. It is not merely visual; a mas costume displayed on a mannequin is not mas . . . The field of art 'performance' has been described as a natural searching in response to the growing irrelevance of conventional object-oriented art to the dynamic modern world. Mas can offer the same opportunity to transcend the object in favor of the experience, yet in a manner that is not elite and inaccessible, but by its nature popular and participatory."[26] The turn "from" objects to "experience," however, is not without its difficulties, and the exhibition strategies of *En Mas'* will no doubt confront many of them. Fortunately, Bahamian artist John Beadle provides another space in which to meditate on the perils of combining object and experience, stasis and duration, display and action, within a museum space. With *Inside-out, Outside-in*, Beadle asks what it means to place a parade inside a box, facing rather than disavowing the oddity of bringing a street performance into a white cube. On the one hand, the enclosure gives focus and a formal attention to vernacular practices and Black Atlantic readymades; on the other, it asks a question about why we had to wait for artworld attention to notice the political potency of a form that lives just outside the museum's door.

III. Countercarnivalizing Carnival

One might ask why we see a renewed artworld interest in performance at this particular moment of the twenty-first century. One kind of answer would position this interest within an overall socioeconomic shift, a shift from a Fordist economic emphasis in the production of objects to a post-Fordist emphasis on the production of services. From this view, the curating of performance, carnival, and festival responds to the prevailing ethos of the experience economy, one that quenches a consumer thirst for unique experiences and specialized encounters. Within this post-Fordist world, performance practices and performance metaphors abound. Indeed, as elaborated in their much-cited handbook for new businesses, *The Experience Economy: Work Is Theater and Every Business a Stage*, B. Joseph Pine and James H. Gilmore, like other promoters of the experience economy, encourage businesses to "set the stage" and "act our parts well," all toward motoring a contemporary economy focused less on the production of commodities—or static objects—and more on the production of experiences.[27] The spirit of performance is both symptom of and a canny response to a globalizing world. Its language also finds its way into geographic and urban planning discourses. When would-be cosmopolitan cities make a bid for global status as a "world city" or "city of culture," international festivals and biennials are key to their playbook.[28] Urban festivals ostensibly consolidate and promote the unique identity of the city; major biennials transform lesser-known cities into international destination points. Carnival itself has been expanded across the Caribbean and more widely by governments seeking more tourists and returning residents: the Bahamas, which has introduced carnival this year (despite its own vibrant Jonkonnu tradition), is the latest example.[29] For many, this post-Fordist context underpins the contemporary interest in performance curating.

And of course, for many, this context reveals the insidious collusion of artists and artworlds in the inequities of a global service economy as well. Oft-cited, post-Operaismo philosophers such as Antonio Negri, Michael Hardt, Maurizio Lazzarato, Paolo Virno, and others critique the effects of post-Fordist practices on contemporary labor spheres; in such sites, performance is not a site of resistance but a mode of compulsory participation.[30] Workers are told *to perform*, that is, to reorient and retrain their labor to provide immaterial "experiences," "services," and "affective" relations as a primary product. Without excavating in full the twists, turns, and blind spots of post-Fordist social theory on the experience economy, it is hard not to notice that this supposed "turn to service" has found its way into the event-based ecology of the museum and various domains where civic leaders curate their city. Whether in festivals on the streets or interventions in the gallery, event-based programming seems to encourage dynamic participation *and* to heed the call of an event-based service economy. The act of curated performance thus potentially occupies the same plane as other post-Fordist labor spheres that understand themselves to be marketing experiences and encounters. This conjunction forces us to look anew at the resistant impulses behind performance experiments of the twentieth century as well as the celebrated return of carnival now. What were and are all these attempts to use embodied and time-based work to resist the static art object? To what degree are such resistances of objectness in fact propellers of eventness, enabling an immaterial turn that seems fully in consort with the latest capitalist iteration? Is performance being channeled to encourage our cathexis to—rather than our resistance of—an experience economy that has been propelling us along?

So much for airing the latest conspiracy theories about how the new spirit of capitalism embeds itself within the very forms that seek to critique it. In many aesthetic and social theory circles, the celebration of the experiential is quickly followed by a critique of the experiential. That relay now has formed a deep groove in habitual critical theorizing about the contemporary role of performance. In such a context, the curating of carnival would seem overdetermined, a symptom of an experiential turn that is simply domination with a friendly face. Indeed, this twenty-first-century argument resuscitates Bakhtinian critiques, recalling earlier "release valve" theories in which the temporary topsy-turvydom of carnival actually maintains social hierarchies while seeming to resist them. Before capitulating to this critique of capitulation, however, it seems important to notice the internally complex strategies of *En Mas'* artists, those who explore whether a performative ethos can be deployed and redirected for politically potent effects.

We can start by reminding ourselves of the long, deep, and complex history of performance, which means that there is a huge constituency of performance laborers for whom the so-called performative turn is hardly a turn at all. Long before a post-Fordist economy, indeed, long before a Fordist economy, performers in various cultures have been using a variety of forms to create "immaterial encounters" for their communities. What the artworld might experience as a "turn" is something that these laborers experience as continuity; more pointedly, the performative turn feels more like a strange appropriation of forms that historically had more potent things to do than to play handmaiden to a newly spirited service economy. Recall Gilroy's disquisition on the "low frequency" of the "slave sublime" in Black Atlantic musical performance, as well as its "utopian politics of transfiguration." The soundscapes created by Cauleen Smith are, among other things, reminders of that deeper history; even as she disassembles carnival's component parts, she searches for an equitable space where they might be put back together again. Indeed, in explaining her use of the *Close Encounters* theme, Smith recalls Gilroy's sonic phrasing while also critiquing a post-Fordist performative turn that paradoxically keeps performers from performing:

> This message, offered to humans on their home planet by unknown alien visitors, seems apt in the face of the challenges currently facing a city rapidly absorbing newcomers into re-habilitated neighborhoods even while creating insurmountable obstacles for the return of the population that produces and performs the culture that has made New Orleans one of the most significant cultural intersections on earth. The infrastructure/infrasound of culture is more fragile than the people who embody it. It's my hope that a friendly and hospitable (although sometimes plaintive) infrastructure/infrasound (Hello) might be a tactic worth considering.[31]

Smith's piece disallows the ebullient celebration of Mardi Gras by recalling the politics and aesthetics of the Second Line simultaneously calling to us in a low frequency that remembers the place and power of transfiguration. As such, she revives an internal critique within an experiential performance form; she interrupts a service economy with what might be called funeral service economy, one that knows the politics of pleasure clubs and the urgency of social aid.

A similar strategy of countercarnivalization can be found in Ebony Patterson's *Invisible Presences: Bling Memories*, a re-creation of the bling funeral, as well as in Charles Campbell's *Actor Boy: Fractal Engagements*.[32] In the latter, Campbell intervenes in a Kingston civic sphere that has packaged and rebranded the historic masquerade festival of Jonkonnu in favor of a Trinidad-styled carnival. Following the movements and entering the spaces of excluded citizens, his alternate routes subvert the contemporary festival. Ebony Patterson reappropriates an appropriated tradition to create the decorative coffins of a funereal form that elevates lost loved ones. In this case, however, the parade form is launched in the face of city-curated carnivals and parades from which they are now excluded. Staged on the periphery of a "festivalized city," Patterson's krewe creates a counterfestival, deploying a carnivalesque idiom against the carnivalization of their city, collectively shouting, "we don't want it, wup wup," in the face of civic leadership. As Joseph Roach has said of the deep politics of Mardi Gras in New Orleans, these works "become a performance machine for celebrating the occult origin of their exclusion."[33] Akin to what Claire Tancons has called the "anti-spectacular spectacle," Patterson's and Campbell's performances critique a contemporary society of the spectacle, but also launch a critique of knee-jerk antispectacle critiques as well. Like Cauleen Smith, Patterson and Campbell criticize a performative turn that paradoxically disempowers historic carnival performers, critiquing a festivalized city that now banks on traditions that it no longer remembers. At the same time, this work responds to those who are quick to disparage the experience economy of a performative turn, reminding artworld critics that performance has always been and can still be more than a post-Fordist symptom.

If these contemporary artists find it necessary to detach and deconstruct the carnival form to recall its political traditions, artists such as Hew Locke and Marlon Griffith foreground the internal aggressions within contemporary carnival politics. Extending a practice of countercarnivalization, both artists intervene in festivalized cities that have rebranded carnival traditions, this time focusing our attention on the surveillance and policing practices built into so-called civic celebration. Griffith's POSITIONS+POWER adapts Michel Foucault's insights on the panopticon to demonstrate the spatial power of particular positionalities, including those who survey carnival from the literal and metaphor heights of police power.[34] Griffith further underscores the historic connection between these practices and the surveillance systems built throughout the slave history of the Black Atlantic, explicitly using the word *overseer* to define both the contemporary policeman and his "dog." Hew Locke extends this investigation into what dance scholar, André Lepecki, has called the "choreopolicing" of protest forms.[35] In *Give and Take*, part of *Up Hill Down Hall: An Indoor Carnival* curated by Tancons for Tate Modern and coproduced for *En Mas'*, Locke also reappropriates an appropriated tradition, this time focusing on carnivals within London's Notting Hill neighborhood that repress the possibility of diasporic connection.[36] Sited within the Turbine Hall—the site of many relational and immaterial art encounters—Locke critiques the forces of gentrification that have evicted the descendants of a carnival tradition. Performers wear body shields with images of rehabbed condominiums, combatting physical intrusion with this potent symbol of private property. Perhaps most interesting, however, is the combination of affects, gestures, and props

assembled in its police parade. The performers are ambiguous characters, sometimes encouraging the audience to join with them in celebration
and sometimes turning on them, herding them and restricting movement
around the architecture of the hall. Marlon Griffith's contribution to *Up
Hill Down Hall, No Black in the Union Jack*—not part of *En Mas'*—offers
a parallel instance of counter-choreopolicing. His performers carry large
mirrors that reflect citizens back to themselves. At the same time, the mirrors double as police shields and even treble as musical instruments. So too
their batons simultaneously function as weapons and as drumming instruments; police whistles sound an alarm and then occasionally venture into
truncated melodies. If the shield, baton, and whistle are conventionally
understood as objects that corral the carnival event, which operate outside
the event to control it, Locke and Griffith take these props inside the performance event. They signify upon the tools of the overseer, interiorizing
its exterior, carnivalesquing an apparatus that sought to control carnival.
Moreover, the Notting Hill carnival signifies on the Turbine Hall, producing a Notting Hall where relational encounters are staged along with their
internal antagonisms. Mixing the celebratory ethos of the performative
turn with the choreoharassment of police aggression, Locke interrupts the
hospitable fulfillment of art's service economy.

En Mas' unravels many conventions of the artworld, including its conventions for breaking convention. Carnival recalls a performing art history
and many-headed hydra art that exceeds national spaces and precedes
the diffuse and mobile forms of contemporary hybrid art. It questions
contemporary definitions of the new by recalling inconvenient precedents,
creating countercarnivals against carnivalization, and calling the bluff of a
post-Fordist experience economy that unwittingly invites a political form
it simultaneously endeavors to exclude. Bottoms up, indeed.

Notes

"Countercarnival in a Performance-Friendly World: *En Mas'*" was originally
published in *En Mas': Carnival and Performance Art of the Caribbean*, ed.
Claire Tancons and Krista Thompson (New York: ICI Press, 2015), 46–57.

1. Mikhail Bakhtin, *Rabelais and His World*, trans. Hélène Iswolsky
(Bloomington: Indiana University Press, 2009).

2. Bakhtin, *Rabelais and His World*, 411.

3. Paul Gilroy, *The Black Atlantic: Modernity and Double-Consciousness*
(Cambridge, MA: Harvard University Press, 1995), 3.

4. Lorraine O'Grady, project description for *Looking for a Headdress*, Sum-
mer/Fall 2014, https://lorraineogrady.com/tag/looking-for-a-headdress/.

5. Christopher Cozier quoted in Claire Tancons, "Curating Carnival: Performance in Contemporary Caribbean Art," in *Curating in the Caribbean*,
ed. David A. Bailey, Alissandra Cummins, Axel Lapp, and Allison Thompson
(Berlin: Green Box, 2012), 50.

6. Tancons, "Curating Carnival," 50.

7. Examples of artists who have explored walking as practice include André Breton and Tristan Tzara, *Excursions & Visites Dada/Première Visite* (1921); Stanley Brouwn *Pedestrian Footsteps on Paper (1960)*; Richard Long, *A Line Made By Walking* (1967); Daniel Buren, *Sandwich Men* (1968); Vito Acconci, *Following Piece* (1969) and his lesser known work *Anchors* (1977); Yvonne Rainer, *M-Walk* (1970); Asco, *Walking Mural* (1972); Tehching Hsieh, *One Year Performance* (1980–81); Marina Abramović and Ulay, *The Lovers—The Great Wall Walk* (1988); and Francis Alÿs, who said, "Walking, in particular drifting, or strolling, is already—with the speed culture of our time—a kind of resistance . . . a very immediate method for unfolding stories." Alÿs's projects include *Ambulantes* (1992–2006), *Duett* in collaboration with Honoré d'O (1999), *The Collector* in collaboration with Felipe Sanabria (1991–2006), and *The Green Line* (1995). See also Hamish Fulton, *Slowalk (in support of Ai Weiwei)* (2011); Juan Betancurth and Todd Shalom, *4Ever21* (2012), Amara Tabor-Smith, *He moved swiftly but gently down the not too crowded street: Ed Mock and Other True Tales . . .* (2013); and Harrell Fletcher, *The Best Thing in the Museums Are the Windows* (2013). For analyses of walking, please see Michel de Certeau, *Practice of Everyday Life* (Berkeley: University of California Press, 2011); Tom McDonough, ed., *The Situationists and the City* (London: Verso, 2010); Francesco Careri, *Walkscapes: Walking as an Aesthetic Practice* (Barcelona: Editorial Gustavo Gili, SL, 2002); Merlin Coverley, *Psychogeography* (Harpenden, England: Oldcastle Books, 2010) and *The Art of Wandering* (Harpenden, England: Oldcastle Books, 2012); David Pinder, "Arts of Urban Exploration," *Cultural Geographies* 12 (2005): 383–41; and Rebecca Solnit, *Wanderlust: A History of Walking* (New York: Penguin Books, 2001), 29, which includes, "Walking shares with making and working that crucial element of engagement of the body and the mind with the world, of knowing the world through the body and the body through the world."

8. Gilroy, *Black Atlantic*, 36, italic in the original.

9. Gilroy, *Black Atlantic*, 38.

10. Joseph Roach, *Cities of the Dead: Circum-Atlantic Performance* (New York: Columbia University Press, 1996), 29.

11. Fred Moten, *In the Break: The Aesthetics of the Black Radical Tradition* (Minneapolis: University of Minnesota Press, 2003); Thomas DeFrantz, *Dancing Many Drums: Excavations in African American Dance* (Madison: University of Wisconsin Press, 2001); Daphne Brooks, *Bodies in Dissent: Spectacular Performances of Race and Freedom (1850–1910)* (Durham, NC: Duke University Press, 2006).

12. Nicolás Dumit Estévez, project description for *C-Room*, Santiago de los Treinta Caballeros, Dominican Republic, 2014, https://www.clairetancons.com/curating/en-mas-carnival-and-performance-art-of-the-caribbean-2/.

13. For more information about Christiane Taubira, please see Agnès Poirier, "How the Maverick Christiane Taubira Is Transforming French Politics," *Guardian*, August 14, 2013, http://www.theguardian.com/commentisfree/2013/aug/14/christiane-taubira-french-politics.

14. Roach, *Cities of the Dead*, 61.

15. Gilroy, *Black Atlantic*, 37.

16. Peter Linebaugh and Marcus Rediker, *The Many-Headed Hydra: Sailors, Slaves, Commoners, and the Hidden History of the Revolutionary Atlantic* (Boston: Beacon Press, 2000).

17. Tancons, "Curating Carnival," 42.

18. Whitney Museum of American Art, "Sarah Michelson Receives 2012 Bucksbaum Award," April 9, 2012, http://whitney.org/2012BucksbaumAwardToSarahMichelson.

19. Ralph Lemon, interview by David Velasco, "Ralph Lemon Talks about 'Some sweet day,'" *Artforum*, October 18, 2012, http://artforum.com/words/id=35891.

20. Peter Minshall quoted in Tancons, "Curating Carnival," 35.

21. Minshall quoted in Tancons, "Curating Carnival," 36.

22. For discussion of Zora Neale Hurston, please see Anthea Kraut, *Choreographing the Folk* (Minneapolis: University of Minnesota Press, 2008); and Robert E. Hemenway, *Zora Neale Hurston: A Literary Biography* (Champaign: University of Illinois Press, 1980).

23. For sample analyses of "relational aesthetics," see Nicolas Bourriaud, *Relational Aesthetics*, trans. Simon Pleasance and Fronza Woods (Dijon, France: Les Presses du réel, 2002); Shannon Jackson, *Social Works: Performing Art, Supporting Publics* (New York and London: Routledge, 2011); Claire Bishop, *Artificial Hells: Participatory Art and the Politics of Spectatorship* (London: Verso, 2012); Grant Kester, *The One and the Many: Contemporary Collaborative Art in a Global Context* (Durham, NC: Duke University Press, 2011); and Nato Thompson, *Living as Form: Socially Engaged Art from 1991–2011* (Cambridge, MA: MIT Press, 2012).

24. Quoted in Paul Ortiz, "C. L. R. James' Visionary Legacy," *Against the Current* 156 (Jan./Feb. 2012), https://againstthecurrent.org/atc156/p3494/.

25. O'Grady, project description for *Looking for a Headdress*.

26. Minshall quoted in Tancons, "Curating Carnival," 36–37.

27. B. Joseph Pine II and James H. Gilmore, *The Experience Economy: Work Is Theater and Every Business a Stage* (Boston: Harvard Business School Press, 1999). See also Jens Christensen, *Global Experience Industries: The Business of the Experience Economy* (Oakville, CT: Aarhus University Press, 2009); Brian Lonsway, *Making Leisure Work: Architecture and the Experience Economy* (New York and London: Routledge, 2009); J. Robert Rossman, *Designing Experiences* (New York: Columbia Business School Publishing, 2019); Bernd Schmitt, *Experiential Marketing: How to Get Customers to Sense, Feel, Think, Act, and Relate to Your Company and Brands* (New York: Free Press, 1999).

28. See Stanley Waterman, "Carnivals for Elites? The Cultural Politics of Arts Festivals," *Progress in Human Geography* 22, no. 1 (February 1998): 54–74; Jeannine Tang, "Biennialization and Its Discontents?" *Red Hook Journal*, April 8, 2013; Caroline A. Jones, "Biennial Culture: A Longer History," in *The Biennial Reader*, ed. Elena Filipovic, Marieke van Hal, and Solveig Øvstebø (Bergen, Norway: Bergen Kunsthall, 2010), 66–87, and Thierry de Duve, "The Glocal and the Singuniversal," *Third Text* 21, no 6 (November 2007): 681–88.

29. See also Philip W. Scher, *Carnival and the Formation of a Caribbean Transition* (Gainesville: University Press of Florida, 2003); and Garth L. Green

and Philip W. Scher, *Trinidad Carnival: The Cultural Politics of a Transnational Festival* (Bloomington: Indiana University Press, 2007).

30. See Michael Hardt and Antonio Negri, *Multitude: War and Democracy in the Age of Empire* (New York: Penguin, 2004); Paolo Virno, *A Grammar of the Multitude: For an Analysis of Contemporary Life Forms* [Cambridge, MA: Semiotext(e), 2004]; and Michael Hardt, "Immaterial Labor and Artistic Production," *Rethinking Marxism: A Journal of Economics, Culture & Society* 17, no. 2 (2005): 175–77.

31. Cauleen Smith, project description for *H-E-L-L-O (Infra-Sound/Structure)*, New Orleans, June 7, 2014, https://curatorsintl.org/special-projects/en-mas/performances/cauleen-smith/.

32. Other projects working to highlight how the "turn" is not a turn to those who have been doing it for a while include Marlon Griffith's *Runaway/Reaction* (2008), part of *SPRING*, a processional performance curated by Claire Tancons for the seventh Gwangju Biennale.

33. Roach, *Cities of the Dead*, 14.

34. For analysis of the panopticon, see Michel Foucault, *Discipline and Punish: The Birth of the Prison* (London: Verso, 1995).

35. André Lepecki, "Choreopolice and Choreopolitics; or, The Task of the Dancer," *TDR: The Drama Review* 57, no. 4 (Winter 2013): 13–27.

36. Coincidentally, Tancons was invited by Tate Modern to curate a project about carnival in the Turbine Hall during the weekend of the Notting Hill Carnival to which Locke's *En Mas'* project was integrated. Griffith, one of the artists for *En Mas'*, also contributed a project to the Tate event, though it was, unlike Locke's, not part of *En Mas'*.

Chapter 14

✦

Utopian Operating Systems

Theaster Gates's Way of Working

The nomination for the Vera List Prize in socially engaged art was due in the summer of 2012, and at that point, Theaster Gates's career had gone "through the roof," to quote my earlier chapter (and Bamuthi) at the time. But a year later, after he was picked to receive the prize and the ceremonial award was bestowed, the roof had been further blown up and blown apart, its pieces reassembled into new shapes to be sold at art fairs to raise money to build more roofs back home. With hundreds of art reviews, awards, and blockbuster openings to his credit, with major curators and major politicians seeking a moment of his time, this is an artist whose influence is felt and deployed in a range of powerful systems.

Indeed, one finds now that critics, curators, and everyday spectators have an increasingly shared understanding of where the innovations of Gates's practice lie, with nearly every review or feature article touching on similar themes, moments, and systems. While an artworld perspective might worry about routinization, an urban-planning perspective might welcome such dissemination as the circulation and scaling up of a body of "best practices." But of course what is not resolved is the significance of a practice that addresses so many "perspectives"—as well as the future of a practice that seems still to depend on the charisma, tirelessness, and unattached attachments of the what he himself calls "the silly charismatic magic man," that artist associated with the signature, Theaster Gates Jr.[1]

So what do we think we know about the person associated with this signature? We can say that he is a potter, cross-media artist, urban planner, community organizer, and DIY policy wonk whose work engages concepts of home, spirituality, and neighborhood, with a particular focus on the history of African American cultural life. Part installation, part relational aesthetics, and part urban revitalization, *Dorchester Projects* has come to exemplify a wide-ranging practice while simultaneously providing the ground from which new work emerges.

Fig. 14. *Dorchester Projects, Archive and Listening House*, Chicago, Illinois, 2013.
Photograph by Sara Pooley. Courtesy of Rebuild Foundation.

With multiple degrees in art, religious studies, and urban planning, as
well as a varied professional career, Gates's background pushes the concept of "interdisciplinary." He is a trained ceramicist whose objects appear
in major collections. He grew up singing in the gospel choir of his local
church and later launched the Black Monks of Mississippi, a group that
regularly sings and plays inside his installations, reminding the artworld of
performing art histories that exceed the category of performance art. He
is an urban planner who devised an art program for the Chicago Transit
Authority (CTA; and is now transforming the CTA into a public art project of its own) and who rehabilitates found buildings with the combined
imagination of a sculptor, social worker, and public historian. He is also an
artist whose international reputation has skyrocketed in the last few years,
with commissions from the 2010 Whitney Biennial, the 2011 Miami Basel,
the 2012 Armory Show, and the 2012 Documenta 13, as well as retrospectives and solo exhibitions at high-profile museums in Seattle, New York,
Minneapolis, Milwaukee, Los Angeles, Chicago, and more. And now he is
the first to receive what will be a biennial prize from the Vera List Center
for Art and Politics.

Let's recall some of the basic history of the *Dorchester Projects*, an
art project that began opportunistically in 2006 with Gates residing in a
South Side Chicago neighborhood at 69th street and Dorchester Avenue.
Watching his neighbors threatened with eviction or foreclosure in a neighborhood where forty percent of the buildings were already abandoned, he

purchased leftover structures and began to reimagine their social use. He began with a house next door, rehabilitating it and filling it with books and "outmoded" glass lantern slides procured from the art history department of the University of Chicago, just before they were about to give them away. Collecting more houses, a former candy shop, and—more recently—a bank, he has repaired and altered their interior and exterior to devise more social spaces—a kitchen for collective cooking and eating (Soul Food Pavilion), another restored first floor for video watching (Black Cinema House), and a space for secular worship (carrying forward the *Temple Exercises* that first appeared at the Museum of Contemporary Art, Chicago, when he was still an "emerging artist"). He calls his own residence "Listening House," as it doubles as a place for storing and playing preserved vinyl recordings. Gates used funds he received from commissions and sales to repair these structures, as well as to create collective support systems for the maintenance, gardening, security, and sidewalk repair of neighbors on his block. He has been compared consistently to artists like Houston-based Rick Lowe who have committed to rebuilding local infrastructure. Like Lowe, Gates frames *Dorchester Projects* as a commitment to the art of "staying": "Like I could live in other places . . . but the impact that I could have on Dorchester is so much more substantial . . . I can help my whole block get fences by the end of the year . . . For the cost of one year's condominium fees, anything might happen."[2] Gates thus also joins a growing group of high-profile artists (Paul Chan, Vik Munoz, and more) who have created short- and long-term systems of redistribution between artworld markets and underresourced regions of the planet.[3]

Within the sphere of community-engaged art or social practice aesthetics, artists face many occupational hazards. And the work of Gates and his team compels, in part, for the way it skirts those hazards and scoffs at those who want to make it accountable to certain kinds of binary framing. Take, for instance, the presumed risk of "instrumentalization," the accusation that socially oriented art subordinates its forms to the predetermined values and "outcomes" of a given context. Managing that risk in turn opens one to other kinds of accusation, the concern that "aestheticization" will only create spectacles, escape, or elitist panaceas that neutralize revolutionary thinking. But what happens, really, when a work boot is retrieved, dipped in tar, and lined up with its fellows? What happens, really, when the vinyl of the record and the glass of the lantern are placed in relation to a candy store that has become home? The acts, and so many others like them, seem invitations to think about the aesthetics of the instrument, repurposing the heretofore purposeless and divesting the same forms (say, the fire hose) of its most horrific historical function. Indeed, the riveting effect of *Dorchester Project*'s rivet making seems to come from a willingness, not only to challenge categorical boundaries, but also to force an awareness of how differently positioned receivers conceive categories like form and function, product and process, artist and neighbor, instrumental and artistic, in the first place. To those binaries, we might add others that are continually antagonized in the process of making a project like *Dorchester Project*:

Form/Content
Background/Foreground
Inside/Outside
Autonomy/Heteronomy
Art/Apparatus
Text/Context
Form/Function
Figure/Ground
Medium/Support

I myself have meditated quite a bit on all the above, especially that last pairing, recalling as it does the formal experiments of the twentieth century that exposed the art medium's dependence on the frames, walls, spectators, and buildings that support it. If we recall those art histories of institutional critique, and the site-specific practices that questioned our ability to cordon off the ground and the surround, then we have with the *Dorchester Projects* an unexpected extension and lateralization of the omnipresence of aesthetic support. Here, the art object isn't separable from the pedestal that holds it, which itself is not separate from the floor that supports it, or from the wood furnished to make the floor, or from the people who furnished the wood and built the structure upon which that floor was laid. The radical outside of the thing we understand to be inside is matched, in reverse, by the radical interiority of that which we all thought was most comfortable outside. This means bringing the exterior inside the artistic frame, where the fence is the art, and where the "found" wall can be framed or stacked or varnished, or reformed with quotation marks into objects that can be sold to rich people. How much farther can we move aesthetically into the outside? How much of the outside can we allow in? And how does every one of Gates's answers trouble the assumptions behind such questions?

> I was drawn to the use of metaphor and specifically the use of the word "niche." In biological terms a niche is generated and sustained by the very things it supports. In the case of stem cell niches, the stem cells secrete growth factors and biopolymers that create scaffolds that serve as depots for these factors that can be accessed at specific times in response to environmental cues.[4]

Other binaries are undone and confounded in this work, say, for instance, those that would oppose the ameliorative effects of a socially engaged work from the conceptually "negative" edge of a socially antagonistic work. As those embedded in contemporary movements for art and social justice know too well, this oppositional frame dogs many current debates in the field of social practice art. In social practice discourse, the affects mobilized and produced are varied, but they are often framed in polarizing terms that propose a choice between the consensus-building, harmony-seeking emotions of some projects next to the disturbing, "antagonistic" emotions of others. To some scholars,[5] socially engaged art only does the deep work of aesthetics when it maintains discomfort and tension, a twenty-first-century version of aesthetic refusal that recalls Theodor Adorno's modernist critiques of "committed" art.[6] In fact, the phrase social practice and the concept of antagonism have another history that is worth remembering now, one associated with a particular Marxist and post-Marxist tangle of critical puzzles. Karl Marx's notoriously complex but notoriously generative introduction to the *Grundrisse* exposed what he called the "relationality" of persons, worlds, and things that appear to be given, natural, and autonomous.[7] Marx's stance on the commodity, laborer, and all varieties of beings and objects was to expose their sociality, their spatiotemporal connection to other beings and objects on which their self-definition depended. The effort here was to show a thing to be a relation, a person to be a social practice. The trick of capitalism and of other constraining forces was that they prompted us to repress that relationality, repress the social practice that is a person, to sublimate the social practice that is a thing. That repression and sublimation, that alienation, worked its magic to create the sense of a world where individuals and objects were discrete, rather than embedded in an interdependent relation of capital, labor, or a variety of other hierarchies and social systems. Marx wrote, "The reciprocal and all-sided dependence of individuals who are indifferent to one another forms their social connection."[8] This kind of alienation needed to be combated by thinking and making that foregrounded our repressed, connective relationality, that showed the object's contingency in a social system, and revealed the interdependence of persons who thought of themselves as independent. This then is social practice in social theory. Social practice denoted a way of seeing and making that exposed the contingency and interdependence of our world.

Following Marx, Louis Althusser, Antonio Gramsci, Stuart Hall, and many others, Ernesto Laclau and Chantal Mouffe advanced post-Marxist thinking through the concept of antagonism.[9] Here Marx's conception of social practice as contingent relationality informed Laclau and Mouffe's resonant elaboration of "antagonism" as a potent conceptual challenge to a naturalized world. Laclau and Mouffe were careful to emphasize that antagonism is not about "opposition" or any of the other simpler synonyms with which it is aligned:

antagonism cannot be a *real* opposition. There is nothing antagonistic in a crash between two vehicles: it is a material fact obeying
positive physical laws. To apply the same principles to the social
terrain would be tantamount to saying that what is antagonistic
in class struggle is the physical act by which a policeman hits a
worker militant, or the shouts of a group in Parliament which
prevent a member of an opposing sector from speaking . . . It is
because a physical force *is* a physical force that a countervailing
force leads it to rest; in contrast, it is because a peasant *cannot be*
a peasant that an antagonism exists with the landowner expelling
him . . . Real opposition is an objective relation . . . antagonism
constitutes the limits of every objectivity.[10]

In Mouffe and Laclau's frame, then, antagonism is the dimension and process that would question the givenness of a human being, the givenness
of a peasant or landowner, rather than the social relation that constitutes
both. To antagonize would be to expose the contingency of this supposed
objectivity, to engage with humans and things as social practice, in social
practice. Antagonism has a degree of compatibility with a conceptual art
practice; it finds ways to question the conventions that produce persons
and objects as given and natural and discrete. Most importantly, antagonism is not just about being edgy, ironic, or uncomfortable, but about
initiating thinking and making that expose the constructedness of spaces
whose identities and divisions are naturalized and experienced as given
and normal. Antagonism thus might have a range of affects, sometimes
those of doubt and distress, but also those that elicit compassion, sincerity,
or earnestness. Antagonism exists in the denaturalizing social effect of a
gesture or affect, not in the attributes of the affect itself.

   This kind of reframing seems essential to understanding the affective
world of Gates. It seems partly necessary to understand the personal post-
secularism of his practice, one that knows that a degree of social privilege
often undergirds the capacity to trash those who believe, one that suspects that the ratification of perpetual doubt actually has a class politics.
It seems necessary to understand the radically equalizing power of the
Dorchester Projects's domestic welcome, one that takes in and smiles
equally at a table of persons and things that usually receive differential
treatment. What Fred Moten has elsewhere called "radical hospitality" can
feel quite insecure in both artworld and academic circles; it requires one
to risk a degree of earnestness or trust.[11] But its oddity in spaces unused
to the idiom might provoke its own antagonisms, even a compassionate
antagonism that disrupts the habitual conventions by offering sincerity at
a moment that one least suspects it. "There's an earnestness that almost
comes from a naive vantage point," says his friend, curator Hamza Walker.
"Some of the moves I would look and say, 'I can't believe you would do

that—or anybody' . . . there's something else on his mind that didn't get beat down."[12] Such commentary exemplifies once again the range of perspectives and sensibilities Gates's work invites and manages. The "naive vantage point" in one circle is accepted, ordinary knowledge in another. One person's earnestness might be another's capitulation. One receiver's antagonism is another's do-gooderism. One person's form is another's function. Some aesthetic sensibilities might worry about the hyperearnestness or hyperpragmatism of Gates's practice, but to other urban planners, Gates's work seems utopian, hardly pragmatic at all. "It's important that the utopian choose a greater and more clever operating system," writes Gates in response to this conceptual challenge, one that does not seek to disenchant utopian hopes so much as to allow enchantment and disenchantment to coexist. "It is first vision and a hope so quiet and precious that I could never tell that art world its importance."[13] Without full disclosure to the artworld or, for that matter, to the policy world, these practices alter what it means to rehabilitate, refresh, or rejuvenate a space by exposing the antagonism within every effort to do so. I think about this next to Gates's own visual representation of what he calls "Utopian Tension."[14] The zigzagging lines reverberate within a tensely affective sphere, a movement that vacillates from side to side as it presses forward, a simultaneous inhabiting of opposing spaces. The zigzag exposes promises made and not kept; it occupies the unlikeliness of actual redress at the same moment that it repairs a door and shares a meal.

> Demystification is an indispensable tool in a democratic, pluralist politics that seeks to hold officials accountable to the rule of law . . . But there are limits to its political efficacy . . . What is more, ethical political action on the part of humans seems to require not only vigilant critique of existing institutions but also positive even utopian alternatives . . . Demystification tends to screen from view the vitality of matter and to reduce political agency to human agency. Those are the tendencies I resist. The capacity to detect the presence of impersonal affect requires that one is caught up in it. One needs, at least for a while, to suspect suspicion and adapt a more open-ended comportment. If we think we already know what is out there, we will almost surely miss much of it.[15]

New Materialist scholar Jane Bennett's directive to "suspect suspicion" resonates in Gates's domain, as does her admission that a vitalist stance sometimes requires a "willingness to appear naive or foolish."[16] To me, such affective complexity also helps to understand a key element of Theaster's practice that is oft-remarked and less often analyzed, that is, his performative capacities as a speaker and an interlocutor who knows how to sing. When asked about his performances in museum galleries, Gates eschewed

any connection to the practice of performance art.[17] Gospel, blues, and
jazz performances—whether from local choirs or from the Black Monks
of Mississippi—foreground a wide history of the performing arts, one
sourced from Black Atlantic genealogies of creativity and oppression.[18]
The intervention defamiliarizes the visual art space both politically and
formally; the radical interventions of performance art suddenly look like
easy accommodations of the museum's white cube. Gates has created similar effects not only with his ensembles but also as a soloist. Consider his
performance of David Drake—or Dave the Potter—an African American
slave whose pots bear his signature and who Gates embodies in song and
laboring gesture. Consider also Gates's capacities not only as a singer but
also as a trickster speaker whose voice channels the tones and rhythms of
the urban planner, the artworld snob, the testy neighbor, the radical activist, and more. "Gates is possessed of a flexible speaking voice that . . . can
embody half a dozen characters," wrote John Colapinto in the New Yorker
after following Gates around on his many appearances.[19] In his public lectures and impromptu conversations, Gates's flexible voice deftly embodies
a range of demographic positions. The polyphony offers a twenty-first-
century iteration of what Mikhail Bakhtin might have called heteroglossia,
a representation of a society's double-voicedness that will not achieve
Hegelian resolution but that lives in perpetual, dialogic tension.[20] It also
makes potent use of what J. L. Austin described as the performative power
of the speech act, soliciting a range of receivers who may hear themselves
in his phrases and tones, implicating receivers who have to manage their
own responses to his locutions.[21] At a time when "performance" is celebrated and condemned for its capitulations to the pleasures and thrills
of a so-called experience economy, it seems important to emphasize the
antagonistic power of such performances as well.[22] Many of us have been
in the room when audiences ask Gates to sing, and he actively seems not
to hear the request, as if he knows that what the room wants is not what
the room needs. At other times, we have heard him suddenly begin to
harmonize during someone else's lecture, turning the speaker's words
into an unexpected melody. These and other heteroglossic performances
zigzag across social spaces and perspectives, transforming the sound by
giving voice to content and forms that are in fact already there. Sometimes,
such performances puncture liberal pluralist harmony with inconvenient
reminders of structural racism; other times, they transform the dry and
sedate into unexpected opportunities for vitalist connection.

> Let's consider Theaster's entire practice a form of pottery. Like the
> basic form of clay, his project is essentially a vessel that contains
> as it omits, that absorbs as it pours. Whatever is inside is defined
> by what is outside, and the work's meaning and impact lie in the
> beautiful, exquisite and visionary sweet spot where the crossing

> happens between what is inside and what is outside, between inte-
> rior and exterior systems, of exchanges across and through the
> porous, metaphorical and literal skin.[23]

Carin Kuoni's elaboration in this volume offers a link between vital materialism and the systemic interdependence of artistic form and its supporting
apparatus. Indeed, Kuoni's sense of this "sweet spot" echoes the insights
of thing theorist, Bill Brown, who mined the links between Gates's practice
and the fictive Yamaguchi's influence.

> If you want to say that Theaster Gates has his hands all over every-
> thing, you should recognize those hands as potter's hands . . . Of
> course Yamaguchi had to object to any idea of a start to the pro-
> cess that does not originate in matter. At the origin, "you gather the
> clay," he taught: With hands held as though poised for prayer, you
> gently squeeze in and then press down, squeeze and press down,
> before the thumb finally begins to hollow the "void that holds."[24]

In this metaphor of the "void that holds," we have an image that sustains
a range of necessary paradoxes. The prayerful press of the hands defines
the interior of the object that holds them. At the same time, the press of
the hand announces its dependence on an outside, on the body of the
laborer and the apparatus of the wheel; unlike other aesthetic objects,
the craft object has rarely felt it necessary to disavow that dependence, a
position that goes in and out of favor. Indeed, as craft historians such as
Glenn Adamson and Valerie Cassel Oliver argue, the presumably static
craft object has been both enlivened and devalued by its attachment to
the laboring bodies who make and use it.[25] Whether remembering the
"live demonstration" that typically accompanies the display of craft or the
utilitarian ethos that places the craft object "below" the art object, craft's
association with bodily enactment are now in favor, reminding us of yet
another performing art history that exceeds the canon of performance art.

In Gates' hands, the materiality of clay and pottery has a materialist
politics that remembers the vitality of craft *and* the inequities of systems;
such hands propel an integrated practice that is in perpetual tension with
itself.[26] When asked by Carolyn Christov-Bakargiev about his focus on
matter and materiality at a time when there is so much focus on so-called
immaterial information, he told the story of a set of glass lantern slides
that were no longer useful to the University of Chicago.

> I realized that what I was interested in was not only found objects
> but also discarded knowledge—that there was a relationship. I
> was willing to take on the burden of not only the material waste
> but also the knowledge waste that so disposable. The knowledge

was disposable because it was on archaic material. . . . I think
that one of the great travesties of this world we will get to is that
people will forget how to touch things, and they will forget how
things looks and feel in three dimensions.[27]

In that same interview, Gates made a connection between pottery and
urban renewal, between the materialist politics of the tactile object and the
materialist politics of an urban economy: "I think that studying clay helped
me understand that ugly things, muddy things, or things that are unformed
are just waiting for the right set of hands. So, in a way, maybe clay became
a metaphor that helped me understand the rest of the world."[28] Taking the
epistemology of the pot to "the rest of the world" means seeing potential
in "muddy" structures, in abandoned buildings and streets, in places that
get labeled "blight." But "the right set of hands" needs to connect the dots
among humans and things with an aesthetic stance and a political stance
that undo the damage done by past programs of urban renewal. It seems
for that reason that Gates is interested in the material vitality of social systems, the affective power of alternative policy: "Restoring the buildings is
important, but that is the beginning of the work. Some larger transaction
needs to continue to occur between the structures that have been reactivated and the ether. I want karmic consequence and ineffable results, not
just sound, but things that start with 'trans-.' "[29]

It is here, of course, that trickster politics get even trickier. Indeed, the
aesthetic of the "large transaction" is now a key element of the practice
attached to the signature of Theaster Gates Jr. Julia Foulkes gives the name
"Theastering" to this merger of signature and system; he "combines the
emphasis on community-based arts that emerged in the 1970s with the
promotion of 'creative economies' in city centers starting in the 1990s.
He moves the creative sector to the peripheral neighborhood."[30] Indeed,
taking a cue from a field that used to call itself "nonprofit management"
and now calls itself "social entrepreneurship," Theastering means combining the energies and resources of heretofore distinct nonprofit, for-profit,
and public sectors. As the prices for Gates's art objects increased, it meant
using the profits to fund the purchase of neighborhood buildings before
they were torn down, and now that those prices have rose all the more,
it means overtly scaling up object production for a hungry art market to generate revenue for Gates's nonprofit, the Rebuild Foundation.
Gates keeps no secret about his DIY model of redistribution: "I wanted
people in my neighborhood to benefit from all of this cultural, physical
activity that was happening around my art practice. If I was intentional
about that, a new revenue stream would be a by-product of an art happening."[31] And elsewhere, he is even clearer about the highly inequitable
system with which he works; in speaking of his connections to wealthy
art collectors, he admits to deciding "to leverage the fuck out of them as

they were leveraging me."[32] For some, a Robin Hood practice can't do anything but corrupt the person at the center of it. For others, it is a strategic redirection from within, channeling pleasure, material, and money to "work the system," in Bill Brown's words, "to pervert it." Fred Moten also addresses Gates's enmeshment in "the kinds of ominous public/private partnerships—the corporate entanglements and mercantile impurities—that stripe and striate modernity and its erstwhile subjects/citizens." And at the same time, Moten spies, or asks if others can spy something else: "Or is Gates's work productive of precisely that rich insistent, anti-racist, common, communist meditation on 'the interpretive significance of slaves having themselves once been commodities'?"[33] In the answer to this dangling generative question, Gates, the *Dorchester Projects*, and all the persons and things that surround the work offer the possibility of joining an economic materialism, to use one language, to a vital materialism, to use another. The accusation of market impurity must confront the face of someone whose ancestors and neighbors have already been placed violently inside it. When Gates frames "money" as a kind of material or speaks of deploying his "clay" and his "cash," he occupies the zigzagging space between appropriating and being appropriated, leveraging and being leveraged. Far more radically, his practice suggests that the confident ability to differentiate those polarities comes with racial privilege; so too, the impulse to declare mercantile impurity is more breezily exercised by those who are not descendants of slaves.

Urban planning taught me to make big projects," said Gates of the scale and infrastructural imagination required now to mobilize all forms of cultural, economic, human, and social capital. And to all of us would-be artists and organizers who worry about scale, being leveraged, and who is being appropriated by whom, he cites the Bible for wisdom. Channeling all at once the values and know-how of the Shepherd and the Charlatan, the Homebuilder and the Hustler, he declares:

"Be Not Afraid."[34]

Notes

"Utopian Operating Systems: Theaster Gates's Way of Working" was first published in *Entry Points*, ed. Carin Kuoni and Chelsea Haines, Vera List Center Field Guide on Art and Social Justice 1 (New York and Durham, NC: Vera List Center for Art and Politics in association with Duke University Press, 2015), 214–29.

1. Theaster Gates, *12 Ballads for Huguenot House* (Cologne: Walther König, 2012), 34.

2. Maura Guyote, "Theaster Gates' Dorchester Art + Housing Collaborative Offers Affordable Housing and Art Space in Chicago," *Creative Capital*, Aug. 29, 2014, https://creative-capital.org/2014/08/29/theaster-gates-dorchester -arthousing-collaborative-offers-affordable-housing-community-space -chicago/, accessed January 2015. Gates told an interviewer, "By 2009 I

realized that not only would I live there but I would try to make a substantial impact on the place where I lived. And so it started to feel like a project five years ago . . . If we think not only about these artist housing units but also start to think about other types of spaces that might grow up over the next couple of years to support artists who live in a larger community, and that larger community that wants culture to be part of it, then not only are we making a good housing project but we are building and transforming a community . . . The buildings had old joists and were in bad shape. But we were able to capture those joists and then they were reclaimed to make shelving, countertops and baseboards, and some of the crawl spaces. So we were really mindful of what materials were available locally that could go back into the building; and even if they can't be structural members as they had been, how can we use the materials to make these apartments even more special than they were."

3. See Shannon Jackson, *Social Works: Performing Art, Supporting Publics* (New York and London: Routledge, 2011).

4. See Katayoun Chamay, "The Meaning of Domain," in *Entry Points: The Vera List Center Field Guide on Art and Social Justice, No. 1*, ed. Carin Kuoni and Chelsea Haines (Durham, NC: Duke University Press, 2015), 254–55.

5. See, e.g., Claire Bishop, "Antagonism and Relational Aesthetics," *October* 110 (Fall 2004): 51–79.

6. Theodor Adorno, "Commitment," in *The Essential Frankfurt School Reader*, ed. Andrew Arato and Eike Gebhardt (New York: Continuum, 1982), 300–318.

7. Karl Marx, *Grundrisse: Foundations of the Critique of Political Economy*, trans. Martin Nicolaus (London: Penguin Books, 1993), 83–112.

8. Marx, *Grundrisse*, 156.

9. Elements of this argument were first articulated in my "Social Turns: In Theory and across the Arts," in *The Routledge Companion to Art and Politics*, ed. Randy Martin (New York: Routledge, 2015), 104–13.

10. Ernesto Laclau and Chantal Mouffe, *Hegemony and Socialist Strategy: Towards a Radical Democratic Politics* (London: Verso, 1990), 122–25.

11. Fred Moten and Stefano Harvey, *The Undercommons: Fugitive Planning and Black Study* (New York: Autonomedia, 2013); and the exhibition *Feast: An Exhibition of Radical Hospitality* at the Smart Museum of Art, University of Chicago, February 16 to June 10, 2012.

12. Hamza Walker quoted in John Colapinto, "The Real-Estate Artist," *New Yorker*, January 20, 2014, http://www.newyorker.com/magazine/2014/01/20/the-real-estate-artist.

13. Gates, "Visual Thoughts," in *12 Ballads*, 42.

14. Gates, "Visual Thoughts," in *12 Ballads*, 30.

15. Jane Bennett, *Vibrant Matter: A Political Ecology of Things* (Durham, NC: Duke University Press, 2010), xiv–xv.

16. Bennett, *Vibrant Matter*, xiii ("willingness to appear naive or foolish, to affirm what Adorno called his 'clownish traits' ").

17. See Colapinto, "Real-Estate Artist."

18. See Paul Gilroy, *The Black Atlantic: Modernity and Double Consciousness* (Cambridge, MA: Harvard University Press, 1995); and Fred Moten, *In*

the Break: The Aesthetics of the Black Radical Tradition (Minneapolis: University of Minnesota Press, 2003).

19. Colapinto, "Real-Estate Artist." Full quote: "Gates is possessed of a flexible speaking voice that, to suit his message and the mood of his audience, can embody half a dozen characters: a trash-talking homeboy who grew up on the city's tough West Side; a rarefied academic, who refers to Derrida and Sontag; an inspirational leader whose voice swells in the Baptist-church cadences he heard as a child; or an opaque modem artist who speaks in koans."

20. Mikhail Bakhtin, *The Dialogic Imagination: Four Essays*, ed. Michael Holquist, trans. Caryl Emerson and Michael Holquist (Austin: University of Texas Press, 1981), 324–27.

21. J. L. Austin, *How to Do Things with Words*, 2nd ed. (Cambridge, MA: Harvard University Press, 1975), 1–11.

22. B. Joseph Pine and James H. Gilmore, *The Experience Economy: Work Is Theater and Every Business a Stage* (Boston: Harvard Business School, 1999).

23. See Carin Kuoni, "Gates Gatherings," in *Entry Points: The Vera List Center Field Guide on Art and Social Justice, No. 1*, ed. Carin Kuoni and Chelsea Haines (Durham, NC: Duke University Press, 2015), 260–61.

24. Bill Brown, "Redemptive Reification (Theaster Gates, Gathering)," in *My Labor Is My Protest*, exh. cat. (London: White Cube, 2013), 36–37.

25. Glen Adamson, "Craft and the Romance of the Studio," *American Art* 21, no. 1 (Spring 2007): 14–18; Valerie Cassel Oliver, "Craft Out of Action," *Hand + Made: The Performative Impulse in Art and Craft* (Houston: Contemporary Art Museum Houston, 2010), 5.

26. See Adamson, "Craft and the Romance of the Studio," 14–18.

27. Theaster Gates, interview by Carolyn Christov-Bakargiev, *12 Ballads*, 14.

28. Gates, interview by Christov-Bakargiev, 13.

29. Gates, interview by Christov-Bakargiev, 48.

30. Julia Foulkes, "Learning from Chicago: Responses to Dorchester Projects from The New School Faculty," in *Entry Points: The Vera List Center Field Guide on Art and Social Justice, No. 1*, ed. Carin Kuoni and Chelsea Haines (Durham, NC: Duke University Press, 2015), 263–71.

31. Gates, interviewed by Carolyn Christov-Bakargiev, 14.

32. Colapinto, "The Real-Estate Artist."

33. Moten, *My Labor Is My Protest*, 5. Moten is quoting Paul Gilroy, *Darker than Blue: On the Moral Economies of Black Atlantic Culture* (Cambridge: Cambridge University Press, 1997), 5.

34. Gates, "Visual Thoughts," in *12 Ballads*, 29.

Chapter 15

✦

Trusting Publics

Paul Ramírez Jonas

"You are faithful in the execution of any public trust."

Have you read that phrase somewhere? Heard it somewhere? It beckons, with its solicitous second-person mode of address. It elevates with its grand, anachronistic vocabulary. It belongs on a plaque or on a government building engraved in stone. It might be embedded in the script of a ceremony or performed by an official charged with a swearing in. Of course, its present tense—you *are*—could either be projective or commemorative, descriptive or performative. Perhaps the faithfulness of the "you" is to be tested. Or perhaps that faithfulness has already been demonstrated and is being honored by a ritual speech act.

In fact, I found the expression almost a decade ago in a fortune cookie, imprinted on a tiny piece of paper that I later attached to my office door. Ruffled at the corners around yellowing tape, it is affixed to a door in a building designed by the architect of California's first public university. The building is old. Its furnace is loud and creaky; its pipes are fragile, and its doors and floors need replacement and repair. The maintenance of this building has been deferred, as has much of the infrastructure of public education in California (where I work) and in New York (where Paul Ramírez Jonas works). One could say that the erosion of a public-education building demonstrates that public trust has been violated, but one could also ask if the public cared to maintain that trust. One could ask if such trust is something that the public knew was theirs.

I open with this paean to a fortune cookie to remind myself that messages of grave importance can be found in the smallest of things. That reminder seems important as one approaches the work of Paul Ramírez Jonas, an artist who endows small objects and gestures with the systemic meanings that they deserve.

Atlas, Plural, Monumental—a noun and two modifiers, lateralized in sequence to invite speculation on their relationship. As a grand cartographic representation of the world, the aspirations of an atlas are

comprehensive; so too ambition defines the monument, as a nationalist glorifier of history and collective memory. But these terms, casually
linked by the word *plural*, are also fragile, their force undone as represented worlds change and as represented publics propagate. As one travels
through Ramírez Jonas's world, one finds residues of atlas-like ambitions
along with representations that counter that grandiosity: the epic itinerary
of the sixteenth-century explorer Ferdinand Magellan is only indirectly
reproduced (1995) and the adventure traveler's urge to reach the "top of
the world" is simultaneously acknowledged and parodied (1997). These
investigations of global representation are also records of global positioning that explore the explorer's attempt to account for the world and to
place the self (usually *him*self) within or outside it. Ramírez Jonas's repro-
ductions of kites and early prototypes for flying machines likewise survey
the navigational impulse, honoring a history of scientific experimentation
but also hacking that history in ways that anticipate its future (1994). The
alarm-clock triggering system embedded in his kites take pictures of the
ground below; we now might read these contraptions as jerrybuilt drones,
recording the global position of the artist who flies the kite while subjected
to its surveillance. Other projects mimic the meteoric and the cosmic,
in videos that record a "longer day" (1997) and assemble the times of
"another day" in sunrises throughout the world (2003). Still others reach
for the moon, on wax records (1998) and on paper (2008).

As a critic preoccupied with public trust, Ramírez Jonas's musings on
the "pluralized monumental" is what most absorbs me. He is an artist who
relentlessly mines the forms and values attached to the word *public*. If
such a project is riddled with disavowed contradiction, it is also buoyed by
hope—hope that might be ironic at times, comic at others. His early collaboration (with Spencer Finch) *Masterpieces without the Director* (1991),
which offered an unofficial audio guide packaged in a mock tomato can to
the Metropolitan Museum of Art, anticipated much of what would follow.
Instead of offering the customary authoritarian "expert" point of view, the
artists "canned" the public response to the museum's "masterpieces." The
project thus emerged without a central, singular mastermind; rather its
making occurred only through public engagement. Moreover, by implying
that such masterpieces would normally need a director—not a painter,
sculptor, or author—Ramírez Jonas implied that the piece was not only a
physical art object but also scenic and collective. Whether the work was
filmic or theatrical, the masterpiece unfolded in time, with an ensemble, in
expanded space. That sense of assembly—of processes, people, spaces, and
objects—would inform much of Ramírez Jonas's future practice.

Whether described as pluralized, relational, public, or social, Ramírez
Jonas is one of a large coterie of globally connected artists identified under
the rubrics of social practice and socially engaged art. While Ramírez
Jonas is committed to sculpture, his diverse body of work also relies on

arrangements of materials and environments that elicit novel and unorthodox interaction. It is no coincidence that theatrical metaphors recur in his practice, prompting us to pay attention to the gestures and dialogues that surround them. As critic Nicolas Bourriaud argues in his oft-quoted writing on relational aesthetics, such works position intersubjective exchange not as background or aftereffect of artistic encounter but as an element of the artwork itself. Félix González-Torres—a central figure for both Bourriaud and Ramírez Jonas—famously placed stacks of paper and mounds of candy on the floors of galleries, inviting spectators to take one away with them.[1] Such artworks propel action and reflection; beholders decide whether to partake and then are more likely to consider their connection to the people who came before and those who will come after.

While social practice artists often reject any connection to "public art"—or so-called Plop art—such relational and pluralized practices arguably coincide more forcefully with contemporary debates about the public. Recall Jürgen Habermas's classic elaborations on the public sphere as a domain of "talk," or dialogue and debate. Recall Richard Sennett's lament over the "fall of public man," where he extolled the public realm as a space of interaction among strangers.[2] As critics such as Nancy Fraser and Michael Warner have argued, however, Habermas did not fully fathom the exclusions these parameters created, presuming as it did educated white male property owners for whom the issues of women or of slaves were private matters unworthy of public deliberation.[3] Such an intragroup model of public relations misrecognizes what for Sennett is key to any dynamic conception of the public: a willingness to engage a public of strangers, a commitment to sustain the lives of people unlike us and whom we may never know.[4] In these and the many feminist and postcolonial critiques that have followed, publicness comes into being through exchange; it is a set of actions as much or more than a physical space. Art projects that self-consciously organize exchange thus resonate with public-sphere theory. To take seriously the aesthetics of encounter is to experiment with publicness. To pluralize a monument is to make public art . . . more public.

But to create a pluralized monument often means using unexpected materials, maybe small objects like keys and cans, maybe anachronistic ones such as alarm clocks and kites. It is striking to read Ramírez Jonas's own medium lists, which often deviate from museum standards. Reading across the entries, we find not only canvas, wood, ink, metal, and single-channel video but also tin cans, clocks, a music stand, an illustrated lecture, and a phonograph. His pluralization also embraces dematerialized material, including the actions, language, and sounds of people. Sometimes the representation of sound appears as an object (a phonograph), and sometimes it enters the register as a song ("The Battle Hymn of the Republic"). As the dates of production advance chronologically, Ramírez Jonas's medium seems to open into the domain of speculation. *Paper*

Moon (I Create as I Speak) (2008) has a music stand and microphone, but the artist also desires "the public's voice" as material. The tendency to specify the contributions of audience members has increased as Ramírez Jonas's social practice has developed: *Dictar y Recordar* (2010) includes ten typists and "your appreciated participation." His inventory of media thus functions as social invitation.

Even with these speculative expressions, many pieces transpire in interactions whose words, emotions, gestures, twists, and turns cannot be fully specified or anticipated by the registrarial list, of course. And it is in the interactions between art and audience where the public work of "stranger exchange" unfolds. Here I mean *stranger* in both its senses, as adjective and noun. On one hand, the strange and unexpected exchanges elicited by these works give us a new angle on the reality before us. On the other hand, these unexpected interactions occur among strangers, giving us parameters with which to inhabit space shared with people we do not know. They require the medium of talk among strangers, as Habermas or Sennett might propose, but they also become laboratories for examining the effects of the dramas that they provoke. Indeed, at a time when an ethic of democratic participation has been made banal by the participatory compulsions of late capitalism, opportunities for delicate and nuanced attention seem rare.[5] How does an artist or any citizen create a dialogue? How can you get people to talk to you? And, from the other side, how do you orient yourself toward an artwork that is going to trigger a response from you? How do you fight the urge to run away?

To understand both the political stakes and subtle underpinnings of such public dramas, the keen ears and eyes of philosophers and sociologists might be helpful. I think of Erving Goffman's theatrical sociology, its micro-attention to self-presentation within shifting dynamics of "frontstage" and "backstage." Goffman tracked how individuals and groups instantiate and shift among behavioral codes appropriate to various scenarios. People key into new situations, sometimes suspending certain social codes to allow for the playful reframing of a context. In such cases, Goffman observed, "participants . . . are meant to know and to openly acknowledge that a systematic alteration is involved, one that will radically reconstitute what it is, for them, that is going on."[6] One could say that the promise of public exchange exists in this kind of keying and, more importantly, that public art becomes socially responsive when it allows for such keying and rekeying. Public art can rekey our movements through the world, creating safe parameters for inviting new forms of exchange among strangers. If, in Goffman's terms, "keyings seem to vary according to the degree of transformation they produce," the transformative possibilities of public art depend on such keyings—that is, on an imaginative aesthetics of encounter.[7]

Ramírez Jonas's work is in dialogue with a history of public art, as well as a history of its willingness and unwillingness to respond to such social possibilities. Several works particularly focus on a history of nationalist public art, finding new social possibilities in monuments, which might otherwise appear inert and bounded. For the work *His Truth is Marching On* (1993), the patriotic American anthem "Battle Hymn of the Republic" can literally be rekeyed, if played by viewers on eighty wine bottles with the provided mallet. *The Commons* (2011), an oversize monument not cast in bronze but made of cork, likewise rekeys the nationalist convention of the equestrian statue. Beholders do not simply perambulate reverently around it but are invited to tack notes to its torso. Ramírez Jonas demonstrates that the so-called monument has always been more social and more porous than either its nationalist celebrants or its counternationalist retractors have acknowledged. *The Commons* is a testament to the fragility of monuments, as well as to the instability of the identities that need them. The debated flags, statues, and insignias are places where individuals and publics consolidate; as such, they are artifacts to be examined, to be rekeyed, and to be unified as spaces of temporary connection among strangers in a shared (re)public.

Returning to small things and their capacity to hold messages of grave and systemic importance, we find the key in Ramírez Jonas's world newly literalized and socialized, conjoining the small and the large, the local and the systemic and reframing the physical and perceptual boundaries of these polarities. Ramírez Jonas's keys have traveled to several domains—and provoked varied instances of "system alteration."

In *Mi Casa, Su Casa* (2005) the artist invited such reframing by exploring the symbolic function of locks and doors. Audience members were asked to allow a copy of any key on their keychain to be exchanged for one designed by the artist. Sited in San Diego and Tijuana, the work confronted the United States–Mexico border; the word *casa* in its title, representing a private house and a bordered country, provoked a self-reflexive awareness of how and when we shut our doors. The literal key thus metaphorically rekeyed this perceived division between private and public, simultaneously exposing self-differentiations and self-identifications across national borders.

Taylor Square (2005) was sited in Cambridge, Massachusetts, on what was a nondescript triangle at a three-way intersection in an area of New England where there are already many squares—Porter Square, Inman Square, Davis Square, and Harvard Square. Ramírez Jonas was commissioned by Cambridge's city council to do a public artwork; he scoured the designated area before finding a strip of land whose curb was crumbling. Smiles circulated among civic leaders who found Ramírez Jonas's proposition quite convenient, as they had been meaning to repair the site anyway. They could get a twofer out of the process: a public-art project and a speedy overhaul of this tiny bit of Cambridge's infrastructure. Ramírez Jonas ended up constructing what he called a park, a tiny one at a tiny square. A small bench and wrought-steel fence, with a lock on the outside that is always open from the inside, was installed. Like other key pieces, this project invokes the work of González-Torres, channeling and expanding the potential of small objects to induce stranger exchanges for public purposes. Ramírez Jonas manufactured five thousand individual keys to the lock on this park, giving one to each of the nearby neighbors. The gift of the key came with a note:

> Here is your key. It is one of 5000 keys that open Taylor Square, Cambridge's newest park. The park and the keys are a work of public art that I made for you. The park has barely enough room for a bench and a flagpole; please accept this key as its monument. Add it to your key chain along with the keys that open your home, vehicle or workplace. You now have a key to a space that has always been yours. Copy it and give away to neighbors, friends, and visitors. Your sharing will keep the park truly open.[8]

The deployment of the diminutive park with its tiny key is just one example of how Ramírez Jonas has heralded breakthrough modes of embedding microinteractions within large-scale public scenarios. The sentence, "You now have a key to a space that has always been yours," resonates as a delicate attempt to expose a commons that remains available to citizens who may or may not reckon with their own relationship to its erosion. Paradoxically, it had to be the key—the mechanism that both defines and undoes the boundary between inside and outside, my property and yours—that prompts an awareness of something that had been theirs, yours, ours, and mine all along.

With a similar goal, *Key to the City* (2010)—executed in New York City and elsewhere—encouraged city residents to explore the civic landscape and reflect on their role in its collective ownership. Civic leadership passed on to everyday citizens "keys" to unusual public and privately maintained sites. While the political right and left disavow their relationship to public institutions, this project aimed to invent a safe conduit for repairing that sense of connection. Ramírez Jonas's "medium" for this piece includes a telling mix of objects, spaces, and people: twenty-four thousand keys, twenty-four sites, one hundred fifty-five collaborators, and the mayor.

If public art is in fact a field of practice, its history precedes the creation of the term. One can track genealogies across eras and regions of the world, finding public impulses in the graphic symbols of cave paintings, the statuary monuments of ancient civilizations, the commissioned frescos of cathedrals, the memorials of historical battles, and all varieties of artful expression subsidized by rulers, conquerors, and civic officials charged with addressing—and thereby constituting—a public through art. In the twentieth century, the term became more ubiquitous among the citizens of cities whose (usually elected) officeholders graced civic spaces

Fig. 15. Participants in Paul Ramírez Jonas, *Key to the City*, 2010. Photograph courtesy of the artist.

with sculptural works that promised beauty, contemplation, and collective uplift. Adjacently, however, artists, curators, and citizens find themselves encountering works whose parameters differ. If one model finds the artist working hermetically in her studio, releasing a finished work onto and into a public, other models now start with the site of arrival. Practicing what Suzanne Lacy has called "new genre public art," artists are now trained to excavate the material, historical, and sociological conditions of the commissioning site, crafting public artworks that respond to the local conditions that they find.[9] For many artists, those conditions include volatile political and economic factors that might exceed the values and original intentions of the commissioning body. Indeed, as the public-art historian Rosalyn Deutsche has demonstrated, the ever-expanding parameters of public art have exposed the fragility and inequity of so-called public space.[10]

And they expose the fragility and inequity of what we might call public trust. Indeed, we find so many of the genealogies, materials, and theatricalities of Ramírez Jonas's practice colliding in his recent work aptly titled *Public Trust* (2016). In this project—sited in three public squares in the Boston area—Ramírez Jonas, with a trained team of interlocutors, installed stations that invited citizens to make a promise, publicly. As visitors walked through the plaza, they lingered at tables assembled for conversation and fabrication. Behind them, a large dynamic billboard displayed a series of promises collected from the daily news and from their

Fig. 16. Individual posing with promises from Paul Ramírez
Jonas, *Public Trust*, 2016. Photograph courtesy of the artist.

fellow citizens on the ground. "MBTA pledges to keep stations clean."
"Saudi Arabia promises to protect pilgrims." "I promise to visit my grand-
parents more." "Chelsea Clinton vows to stay friends with Ivanka Trump."
"I promise I will never have cosmetic surgery."

As individuals considered the possibilities of promise making, they also
faced the question of what it meant to share it publicly. Would that public sharing make them more accountable to their own speech act? How,
furthermore, would the public receive their promise? Would it inspire or
confuse them? Would they welcome it or laugh at it? Could the promisers
trust the public, and could the public trust them? Meanwhile, Ramírez
Jonas's team worked materially and immaterially to seal the promise.
Recalling classic mechanisms of binding a trust—the plaque, the hand-
shake, the pledge over the Bible or other sacred text—citizens were invited
to choose a means of solidifying their pledge, say by shaking the hand
of an interlocutor-stranger or by signing a rubbing of it. Once again, the

intimacy of a personal gesture found its way into a structure for reactivating public assembly.

Public Trust, like so much of Ramírez Jonas's works, asked the question of whether a public comes into being in the encounter that may or may not be defined as "art." It considered whether that encounter depends on a square, a pier, a plaza, or a park; on cleaned sidewalks or billboards; or on the imprimatur of an art organization. It proposed that publicness depends on physical and verbal interactions that might ask citizens to tell us what they value and who they trust. It happens when they are asked to give up their keys and when they are given the opportunity to make a promise to the world. From theaters without directors to reanimations of public trust, Ramírez Jonas's public keys and keyings do what Goffman's keys and keyings almost did. To key and rekey is not to manage one's vacillation between the actually private realm and the actually public realm. Rather those keyings—in song, in objects, in interactions—are invitations to examine the instability and necessity of trust. They ask us to confront not only the unstable boundary between private and public but also the necessity of joining my private and public with yours.

Notes

"Trusting Publics: Paul Ramírez Jonas" was first published in *Atlas, Plural, Monumental: Paul Ramírez Jonas*, ed. Dean Daderko, Karen Kelly, and Barbara Schroeder, 71–109 (New York: Dancing Foxes Press, 2017).

1. Nicolas Bourriaud, *Relational Aesthetics*, trans. Simon Pleasance and Fronza Woods (Dijon, France: Les Presses du réel, 2002).

2. Jürgen Habermas, *Democracy and the Public Sphere*, trans. Luke Goode (Ann Arbor, MI: Pluto Press, 2005); Richard Sennett, *The Fall of Public Man* (New York: Knopf, 1977).

3. See Nancy Fraser, "Rethinking the Public Sphere: A Contribution to the Critique of Actually Existing Democracy," *Social Text* 25/26 (1990): 56–80; and Michael Warner, "*Publics and Counterpublics*" in *Public Culture* 14, no. 1 (Winter 2002): 49–90.

4. See Sennett, *Fall of Public Man*.

5. See Joseph Pine and James H. Gilmore, *The Experience Economy: Work Is Theater and Every Business a Stage* (Boston: Harvard Business School Press, 1999); and Luc Boltanski and Eve Chiapello, *The New Spirit of Capitalism*, trans. Gregory Elliott (New York: Verso, 2005).

6. Erving Goffman, *Frame Analysis: An Essay on the Organization of Experience* (New York: Harper and Row, 1974), 45.

7. Goffman, *Frame Analysis*, 78.

8. Paul Ramírez Jonas, "Taylor Square, 2005," http://www.paulramirezjonas.com/selected/new_index.php#15&26_2005&sub152&04_TaylorSquare.

9. Suzanne Lacy, ed., *Mapping the Terrain: New Genre Public Art* (Seattle, WA: Bay Press, 1994).

10. Rosalyn Deutsche, *Evictions: Art and Spatial Politics* (Cambridge, MA: MIT Press, 1998).

Part 3

✦

Restagings

Chapter 16

The Way We Perform Now

This piece is adapted from a lecture delivered in the Performing Institutions series curated by Artists Space with the 2012 Whitney Biennial. The event also included David Velasco of Artforum *as well as Sarah Michelson, who had just become the first choreographer to win the Bucksbaum Award for the best work presented at the Whitney Biennial. Artists Space represented the Performing Institutions series in the following terms: "Taking as its starting point the 2012 Whitney Biennial's allocation of the fourth floor Emily Fischer Landau Galleries as a performance space for music, dance, theater, and participatory programming, this series of talks consider the status of performance and 'virtuosity' within the parameters of an institutional public sphere. Does this turn toward 'activity without end product' potentially shift entrenched relations between institution and artist, artwork and viewer, or reinforce a contemporary experience of totalizing social production?"*

Terms of Engagement

I would like to group some thoughts under the title "The Way We Perform Now" in part to have a chance to think about each component part of such a phrase. So first, I would actually like to break down and complicate what we think we might mean by "The Way," "We," "Perform," and "Perform Now." In the second part, I'd like to review some thinking that I see so many others doing about this question, particularly in the last year, and to see if we can abstract some key concerns and occupational hazards of affiliating with so-called performing institutions in our current moment.

So to begin. "The Way" invokes larger and broader questions of medium, technique, skill, and material as they interface with different conceptions of duration, spectacle, amateurism, virtuosity, conceptualism, experience, pleasure, and rigor. These various ways of making art and culture also interact with different conceptions of what we think that the way used to be. Did the way used to mean the making of objects in a studio or did it mean the making of dance movement in a different kind of studio? Did the way used to mean creating commodity art for selling to collectors or has the way referred to the rehearsing of ticketed plays for subscriber audiences? Did the way used to be public plop art that has now been replaced by dispersed performative practices?

Those differing notions of what the way might be obviously exposes vastly different notions of who the "We" might be, based again on who you think that the we once was and whether you ever thought you were part of it. Is the we former art-school students, people for whom performance inhabited a side pursuit in an underresourced studio where one experimented with liberating oneself from the object before returning to proper object making in the better-resourced studios of the rest of the school? Is the we former theater students, people for whom performance meant accessing the diaphragm, learning scansion, developing emotion memory, and experimenting with all varieties of objectives and obstacles to create believable characters? Is the we former dance students, those who perched limbs atop bars and bodies before mirrors, submitting themselves to Balanchinian discipline so that they could produce feats of virtuosic excellence that made it look like they weren't suffering, only to realize that over there—in another studio, another gallery, under some different artists' signatures, or MoMA PS1—the frank exposure of suffering in performance had become an aesthetic long before?

Perhaps the we is a set of museum curators—those trained in a wide and varied set of rigorous visual art histories, those who navigate that turmoil of setting up an exhibition while being responsive to an artist's bidding, those who now find themselves cajoled and sometimes pressured to install performance-based activity whose precedents and purpose remain equivocal in a museum context hurtling ever more toward what this program's announcement called "the experience of totalizing social production." Perhaps the We is the group of performance curators who have been making performance happen for a while, people like Philip Bither at Walker Art Center in Minneapolis or Peter Taub at the Museum of Contemporary Art in Chicago who might see themselves in a longer lineage of performance enablers—the descendants of someone like Gertrude Lippincott who staged the first dance event at the Walker in 1940. Are these individuals called performance curators, performance coordinators, engagement specialists, or "event" schedulers at the museum? Such individuals might be called artistic directors at places like Danspace or The Public Theater or the Metropolitan Opera. If you descend from the longer and varied history of that We, it can be odd and defamiliarizing to learn that the performing art forms that your performing institutions have historically supported are those now associated with "the experience of totalizing social production."[1] Conversely, you may have a more sanguine reaction to the news that so many museums now want to make themselves performance ready, transforming galleries into spaces for music, dance, theater, and participatory programming.

Finally, is the We the receiver of this Performance Now: the one who thought of herself as a beholder at one venue and as an audience member at another venue, the one who sat in rows in the theater and who roamed in four-second–per-work intervals in the museum, the one who is now struggling to figure out the terms of her engagement with hybrid work? She finds herself propping her back against a gallery wall or muscling in on the lone bench, struggling to catch a glimpse of a gesture only barely seeable across the gallery floor. When she goes to the theater, that same person now finds herself asked to get out of her comfortable seat in the theater to roam and circle sculptural objects that used to be called sets or, even more disconcertingly, told to "participate" or to "interact" with them. For the we that is an art receiver, what art literacies and art habits were functionally suspended in some places and reactivated at others? What literacies and habits now seem to need complete recalibration with every newly encountered work?

And what do we make of the word *perform* in my title or even the double phrase "perform now," which sounds so menacingly familiar as a directive, a command, and a twenty-first-century compulsion? "Perform . . . now." It sounds like a marketing campaign for an investment firm, a luxury car, or a high-end laser printer. On the one hand, the way we perform now is not so different from some of the ways that some members of this we performed then. This is hardly the first era that has seen performance in the museum; as David Velasco has said as well, it is hardly the first time it has happened at the Whitney.[2]

But even if we might want to counter the presentism of Performance Now by reminding us of the then, I do think it is worth speculating on what we think is different about now. Why is the conversation about performance institutions and "virtuosity" happening in this now with a different kind of urgency or with a different inflection than it had at various moments of performance past? Certainly, one answer to the question has to do with the threat of "the experience of totalizing social production" and the fact that the compulsion to Perform Now is such a ubiquitous marketing campaign.[3] Because Artists Space used this language, and also is worrying and wondering about the role of "activity without end product," it seems to me that yours is a venue that has been thinking about contemporary theories of immaterial and affective labor, so I thought I might address some aspects of that conceptual question. Indeed, in what philosophers such as Antonio Negri, Michael Hardt, Maurizio Lazzarato, Paolo Virno and others now call a post-Fordist service economy, labor spheres, both aesthetic and otherwise, are told *to perform*, that is, to reorient and retrain their labor force to provide "experiences," "services," and "affective" relations as a primary product.

We hear now about the necessity of creating so-called immaterial encounters as a key to success in a globalized labor sphere, one that has supposedly transitioned away from the industrial, the so-called Fordist, model of material, object-based, commodity making. We might all be, as we should be, suspicious of any celebration of a generalized immateriality that represses the material labor of sweatshops, call centers, and Foxconns that produce our immaterial experiences. Indeed, one function of some contemporary performance might actually be to remind us of the performing bodies who—like Nicole Mannarino, whose sweat-drenched costume received so much chronicling[4]—do the physical labor and material work that produces immaterial experiences for their receiver-consumers. But while being suspicious of the newness or the comprehensiveness of an "immaterial turn," it is hard not to notice that the pressure to Perform Now in the museum is an index of a more pervasive social and cultural pressure. If, under Glenn Lowry's leadership, MoMA has made "public programming" a central goal, some may feel he is embracing a performance-friendly context for museum participation.[5] But some might worry that he is also moving the museum toward the same experiential service idiom that informs so much else in our lives right now: the service training of the Hertz employee, the conversational banter of the Westin hotel receptionist, the cosmopolitan manners of the tech support system, or the hospitality aesthetic of the biennial caterer. The museum, along with the hotel and car-rental company, thus sometimes seem to occupy the same plane as that of other post-Fordist cultural laborers who understand themselves to be marketing experiences, encounters, and—to quote this event's promotional material once again—"activities without end product" that actually end up advancing a "totalizing experience" economy.

So this is to acknowledge that thinking about the way we perform now is to think about how it is embedded in the kind of landscape explored by a variety of contemporary social theorists, including those in the Workerist or post-Operaismo School of Italian theorists who have recounted the "turns" from agricultural to industrial economies and now to the "turn" to the service economy that we currently occupy. It should be acknowledged, however, that this supposed turn looks different to those who have been revising traditional performing arts fields than it does to those who have been revising visual art object-making fields. For those who descend from the dancers, singers, actors, chorines, touring troupes, actor-managers, and stage managers that populate theater, opera, music, and dance history, the creation of affect and the design of experience has been central to our and their very long labor history; they have been coordinating affect and experience long before any post-Fordist moment. Other visual artists may have been making objects—activity *with* an end product—but the history of theater, dance, opera, and music is in part a very long history of "activity without end product."[6] Indeed, that is precisely why Marx turned to these performer-laborers with such perplexity and why people like Paolo

Virno or Michael Hardt recall these immaterial makers to understand the nature of affective, immaterial labor now.[7] But at least let's notice that those who descend from the performing-arts fields do not experience this turn in the same way, that they have been in existence long before the experience-based economy discovered them. They also might happen to feel that their practices have resources beyond those that reify the "society of the spectacle" or that capitulate to totalizing social production.[8] Indeed, the specter of such capitulation notwithstanding, touting its threat can also seem like just another way of harboring quite old modernist antithe-atrical prejudices under a new frame.

Occupational Hazard and Alternate Possibilities

Alright, having done some scene setting around the terms of engagement, our ways, our we's, and how they perform now, I want also to try to find a way to be functional at this particular now, that is, the now of May 26, 2012, on the eve of the closing of the 2012 Whitney Biennial, which itself has generated so much interesting conversation and debate about the questions above. This is also a year—I'm on the academic calendar—that included Performa 2011 and its defining and, for some, its deforming of the terms of engagement. Performa renewed and reinforced the category of some-thing called "visual art performance" category, eliciting a flurry of engaged responses from Roberta Smith, Claire Bishop, Andrew Horwitz, Gia Kour-las, Claudia La Rocco, Caden Manson, and others about what that could possibly mean. A symposium organized by the Under the Radar Festival called "Performance and Context: The Black Box and The White Cube" was not sure that it meant much, but the presentations offered learned and sometimes hilarious disquisitions that made clear that the stakes for making it mean are urgent for some.[9] Subsequently, Mårten Spångberg reportedly annoyed and inspired artists and critics of all varieties when he declared that this new cross-arts ecology was an opportunity of a lifetime for those who want to Perform Now.[10] Meanwhile, lots of non–New York-based art-ists and curators have been approaching those stakes from different angles. Compatriots at the Walker in Minneapolis are trying to figure out what it means to be "collecting" Merce Cunningham's costumes, and meanwhile, the Fusebox Festival in Austin was founded in 2005 to provide a platform for questioning these boundaries across art disciplines to shift the context of discussion entirely.[11] Yvonne Rainer and members of Marina Abramović's ensemble at Museum of Contemporary Art in Los Angeles tried to figure out what they were doing at that much-vetted, if not exactly feted, donor event—whether it was a capitulation to or an interruption of the museum's experience economy.[12] In the United Kingdom, Siobhan Davies has hosted her Parallel Voices seminars to ask why visual art conversations and dance conversations rarely converge.[13] Some of us have hosted our own gatherings to advance conversation—I have at Berkeley under the rubrics of "Making Time" and "Curating People"—as has Artists Space, The Kitchen, Tate Modern, MoMA, the Pew Center for Art and Heritage, and many more.[14]

All these events, dustups, kerfuffles, clarifying conversations, and transformative, and not-so transformative art pieces have generated a great deal of engaged thinking. So rather than reproduce that thinking, I wonder if it might be time to take a kind of collective audit—to take the temperature of where we are now with the way we perform now. Herewith, then, is a brief, reductive, and overlapping list of my top ten occupational hazards faced in the "context-swap" that we are in—a way of identifying recurrent habits in order, I hope, to encourage a sense of adventure as well as a sense of humility going forward.

I. Disciplinary Barometers Affect Our Encounters with Interdisciplinary Art Forms

When I first began making this argument, I used to say that "medium-specific histories affect our encounters with un-medium-specific work," but then theater and dance people began to ask me what "medium specific" meant. That is to say that I had unwittingly made my own point. Even if we all claim to be interested in hybrid artmaking, the forms that we have experienced will affect how we gauge the innovation of a cross-arts experiment. It will also affect what reference points and vocabularies we use—and do not use—to compare it, and what traditions of interdisciplinary art works remain blind to us due to our own artistic itineraries.

Furthermore, once we try to learn more about what we do not know, the frames that we use to parse these new knowledges can create their own exclusions. Indeed, we can find ourselves turning to the next point.

II. Binaries Produce Blind Spots

This happens when we find ourselves in, for instance, gatherings that think about the relationship between visual arts and performance, and realize that a huge range of heterogeneity is reduced and rendered equivalent by such an opposition. When that heterogeneity is reduced in discussion, we end up with a limited conception of distinctive traditions and movements *within* forms, differences that in turn offer alternate points of connection across other forms and produce different points of conflict. Dance is actually enjoying a special kind of incorporation in the art museum at present in a way that theater is not; we cannot begin to notice the difference without noticing the historic tussles and tangles that exist within and across dance and theater, or dance-theater, as forms. Similarly, visual art is a baggy and largely unhelpful term for an enormous variety; painting's relationship to action or environment or to flatness will connect the dots to performance differently than those that connect it to (or disconnect it from) the parameters of sculpture. I think too even of the symposium that was framed as a discussion of the black box and the white cube as a way of binarizing the visual art and theatrical trajectories. The opposition might keep us from noticing the specificity of the history of the white cube within a longer, not always white, history of museum display; the polarization also reduces the specificity of the cube—whether white or some other color—as a specific object that tried to open the door to other modes of self-conscious (performative) engagement with the viewer. Meanwhile, it undernotices that the black box is a form of theatrical space that reacted against the theatrical proscenium; the black box is not equivalent to theater but a variant of theatrical experimentation. And of course that opposition also won't track the quite different associations and projections at work when the black box becomes a figure for the cinema. So the shorthand is helpful, but it also produces blind spots right at the place where productive connections across and within art forms have been made.

I am sure that it is the case that all of us are vigilant enough about such habits; so we already know strenuously to avoid or combat them. Once we all remain committed to exploring and enabling cross-arts experiment, it is interesting to begin to notice anew the places where it has already occurred. In my own work, I cannot help but notice that, occasionally . . .

III. The Deconstruction of One Form Involves the Reconstruction of Another

One begins to notice this dynamic when one compares a work in relation to one artistic barometer and thinks about what it means to measure it from another. So while I delight in analyzing Andrea Fraser's institutionally critical interventions in the space of the museum,[15] I cannot help but notice the traditionally theatrical conventions that she uses to do it: a costume, a script, and the creation of a persona. On the one hand, Fraser is dematerializing the visual art space; on the other hand—and from the perspective of the performing arts—Fraser is also acting.

Some can end up being suspicious about the appropriation of one form to stage the disruption of another. And some might be even more suspicious of the fact that few people notice this reuse. In fact, please see the next point.

IV. Innovation to Some Can Look like a Reinvented Wheel to Another

I always try to not use examples too much when I am talking about these hazards, but let's consider, for instance, something like dance critic Gina Kourlas's critical response to Michael Clark's *Who's Zoo* (2012): "For one, he forages deeply through the costuming and movement language of Merce Cunningham, even showcasing one of his former dancers. It's awkward to watch such repurposing of the Cunningham aesthetic, with its skittering feet, impossible balances and quivering muscles under Spandex."[16] So we have here a situation where one set of eyes is seeing the reproduction of a tradition where another pair of eyes may have assumed invention. And Kourlas seems to be objecting to the idea that this repurposing will not register to those for whom such movement is new. (It's kind of like what NBC used to say when it ran the *Friends* reruns for so many years to an audience that it hoped hadn't seen all of them; it is after all "new to you.") Meanwhile, when I made this point in front of Stefan Kalmár at Artists Space, he assured me that Kourlas is the one who is misreading Clark's self-conscious appropriation: "She didn't get it," he assured me.

Indeed, this way of articulating the hazard of swapped contexts has, I think, become more persistent in the last year of critical response as critics, viewers, and fellow artists are weighing in with more intensity about what they see and don't. I myself tend to phrase the problem in these terms, where like David Levine, I wonder why "bad theater" ends up being received as "good art," as well as why "good theater" is often received as "bad art"—or as Andy Horwitz said in one of his pieces, why the visual art world considers so much theater "laughable."[17] So I think it is worth going a level deeper in this discussion about good and bad, innovation and repurposed tradition, and also being clear about how elements such as execution and concept, amateurism and virtuosity, skilling and deskilling actually have a more complicated cross-arts history. To invoke a term in Artists Space contextualization of this event . . .

V. What Happens When Virtuosity as Technical and Physical Skill Meets Virtuosity as Conceptual and Cognitive Skill?

It seems so basic to review this—and I realize that I am creating a new binary. At the same time, it really seems to me that tussles around this relationship are key toward understanding why differently positioned viewers and artworlds will find the same work beautiful from one angle and lame from another, conceptually rigorous from one position and like the emperor's new clothes from another. Depending on one's answer to this question, virtuosity can look like a capitulation to totalizing social production from one angle of vision or like the interruption of that totality from yet another.

While they use different labels, all varieties of twentieth- and twenty-first-century art forms have had their conversations around what might be called a conceptual turn. To be brief but reductive, we can generalize and say that the so-called conceptual orientation on art making focused on decentering the execution of identifiable skill—whether skill was understood to lie in the stroke of a paintbrush or in the height of a leap—to focus on the art object as an exploration of an idea. In its most cynical form, this is when art put itself in quotation marks, provoking, in a less cynical reading, a critical form of reflection on the parameters and definition of art itself. Within different art forms, there rose growing suspicion of virtuosic skill as traditionally executed. The internal critique of these art forms—and the critique of their relation to social systems, economies, and culture industries—needed to happen in an environment that sidelined the appeal and pleasure of virtuosic skill to focus the artistic encounter on the idea, the idea of movement, the idea of task, the idea of exchange, or objecthood, of the body, museum, studio, theater, or screen.

I think we end up with difficulty sometimes when such conceptual pursuits partake of experimentation across art forms. Without more solid immersion in the trajectory of conceptual practice that got us to different points, whether conceptual visual art, or Minimalist dance, postdramatic theater, or expanded cinema, we might still have different ways of deciding where the idea is and where the skill is. When is a piece appropriately understood as virtuosic in the lay sense of the term, that is, as executing exceptional skill? And when is a piece appropriately understood as virtuosic in the sense forwarded by Paolo Virno, as immaterial cognitive virtuosity in the conceptual sense?[18] For Stefan Kalmár, Gia Kourlas "did not get" that Michael Clark was putting the Cunningham aesthetic into quotation marks, not so much cluelessly repurposing Merce but conceptually exploring "the idea of Merce." Sometimes rigor in the conceptual sense of virtuosity looks amateur in the lay sense of virtuosity—and vice versa. Is it helpful to invoke the quotation mark effect to think critically? At the same time, when do the quotation marks seem not to provide enough traction? Put another way, when does the invocation of the conceptual turn seem to be rationalizing the fact that certain artists never learned any skills in the first place?

Indeed, this brings me to another complication in a growing list of occupational hazards, the case of hijacked deskilling.

VI. Hijacked Deskilling

The history of deskilling in conceptual art and performance occurred when artists trained in a variety of forms actively masked that skill, marshaling a series of conceptual questions to interrogate and perhaps explode the art traditions from whence they came. This actually can be hard to do; hard for Jackson Pollock to do, hard for Yvonne Rainer. But I think we can breed distrust when we find those internal critiques of virtuosity used to celebrate work that might be, dare I say, mediocre or even banal. The specific parameters of artists' decision to mask or self-deskill assumed that they had the skills in the first place, a formulation that may sound odd until you think of the number of ways that critiques of virtuosity in one context are hijacked to rationalize experimentation that does not have to make itself accountable to the form it says that it is rejecting. Forgive me for not sharing an example here.

But we can also say that the reverse situation can also be a hazard. In a landscape where we might have different barometers and tolerances for gauging the relationship between virtuosity as concept and virtuosity as skill, we can also find that a new exposure to some techniques and forms might look suspiciously virtuosic, like capitulations to older traditions of art and beauty. So while unfamiliar conceptual forms can appear curiously unskilled, they can also look egregiously proficient—too good or too beautiful in that lay sense of virtuosity to have any conceptual value. Indeed, some forms look to some eyes . . .

VII. Suspiciously Overskilled

Certainly this suspicion shadows performance in the museum, especially dance performance, especially beautiful dance performance. Indeed, at our Making Time gathering in April 2012 in Berkeley, Sabine Breitwieser acknowledged that, in her conversations with museum trustees, part of what appeals to them about this trend in dance curating is the idea that beauty and skill are being brought back into the museum gallery after so much conceptual art disallowed it.

So that makes it suspicious to some, and perhaps we can talk about the possible misrecognitions and missed opportunities that befall any context that capitulates to it—or any context that is too quick to reject the possibility that alternate beauties and alternate uses of skill sets might make a critical intervention. If the homogenizing of the heterogeneity of performance has meant that too many understand performance only to be itself when it is live, spontaneous, unrehearsed, and everyday, then we find not only dance people but also theater people needing to explain why some kinds of interventions might need rehearsal. Consider Richard Maxwell's statement on his Whitney experience, where he almost needed to apologize to articulate the alternate rigor that comes from rehearsal:

> Rehearsal is getting used to the idea of repeating. It feels more honest to say to the people that are going to watch a theatrical production, "Look, we know we've repeated this. We're not going to put any energy into pretending that this is the first time it's happened." I think about rehearsal as a way of reckoning with the fact that we're going to repeat . . . I feel like repetition also has something to do with being the best that you can be . . . It's something tangible that you can master . . . I don't know if I can defend that. Maybe by saying, we can do it, so let's do it, let's master that.[19]

Again, rehearsal and mastery can sound suspicious in a context that is worrying about beauty and skill being smuggled back into the art institution under the guise of performance. But we can also back up and be suspicious of that suspicion, asking if there is a binary opposing the conceptual deskilled traditions of visual art to the virtuosic (but presumably less-conceptual) traditions of dance and theater that is creating new blind spots of its own.

Earlier I asked why this kind of cross-arts conversation is happening now and with a different framing and urgency than it has happened before. In acknowledging that it seems to have something to do with the threat of a post-Fordist labor context bent on the affective and immaterial totalized social experience, I think that we can also acknowledge that a huge part of why all these hazards seem to matter is that they are occurring in a power field. Indeed, they are being worked out in an apparently asymmetrical power field, one where donor dollars, collector interests, ticket prices, union rules, and the availability of day jobs all seem to swirl in an anxious mess. In this mess, we can find ourselves enduring what many experience as the following . . .

VIII. The Provincialism of the Elite

This is the way that certain powerful organizations can position themselves suddenly as discover-adventurers, even as they pluck what Claudia La Rocco called "blue-chip" specimens into their curatorial vision—or fly preanointed British bad boys from one context to another, akin to what happened to German opera's former bad boy Christoph Schlingensief before all the biennials and art critics discovered him.[20] When that habit is paired with the other habit, that is, the offer of a performance commission to the friend of a friend who sat next to you at dinner, some cry foul, feeling that whole reams of practice and generations of artists are being pushed to the sidelines despite the apparent gesture of incorporation. And, of course, once one is offered the chance to swap contexts, especially in one where the new context is perceived to be more powerful than another, one might not necessarily find that the resources and know-how provided match the status of the space. Do installers at the art museum have any sense of where to store props, direct lighting, or provide performers with a way to go the bathroom?

That kind of frustration seems to be exacerbated by a pervasive sense that is the power relation between visual artworlds and performing artworlds is asymmetrical and nonreciprocal.

IX. There Always Seems to Be More Power Elsewhere

Claudia La Rocco says that visual artists aren't jostling for recognition at Danspace to the same degree that choreographers are hoping for a spot at MoMA.[21] Or that the Guggenheim would never ask Sarah Michelson to paint a painting, even if the performance world might be chasing after David Hockney to get him to make an opera. To some dance and experimental theater artists, there is a sense that visual art institutions and celebrity visual artists occupy the powerful, totalizing, donor-driven, speculative sphere. But of course visual artists happen to feel themselves to be a part of a critical history that distanced itself from the all-powerful culture industry, the "culture of the celebrity" more readily associated with the brainwashing function of the performing-arts fields. The sense that power is always elsewhere will inevitably boomerang back to the recognition that power is also right here at home.

That sense that the grass is greener, and that sense that its greenness must mean it is artificial turf, fuels finger-pointing that might keep us from noticing the larger issue: economic concerns around live art are embedded in larger questions of how artists will be able to stay alive.

X. Live Art and a Living W.A.G.E.

Older forms of jealousy among fellow artists can become exacerbated as one learns about the economic models of other forms and wonders about further corruption. Performing artists who never sold documentation suddenly are. Visual artists who never sold tickets to experience their work suddenly are. Are you selling out more if you sign up with a gallery, or more if you decide to choreograph a Gap advertisement? But it seems to me that economic distrust, cynicism, and longing bespeak a much larger question about the economic models that will sustain culture workers of all varieties, the subject that I understand to be that of another Artist Space gathering with Working Artists and the Greater Economy (W.A.G.E). My hope would be that the questions we are asking today might be joined to the questions you are asking in those upcoming forums. Only then might we extract ourselves from the distress and cynicism maladroitly doled out on each other. Only then might we join in a shared discussion about how such finger-pointing keeps this cross-arts context-swapping from being a new opportunity to imagine cultural labor together more imaginatively.

Conclusion

Indeed, each of the hazards that I list above contains within them another way to be, think, and question ourselves and each other. I think it is useful to try to imagine the same work from the headspace of another, to measure its distance from forms that are different from the ones that you habitually, perhaps even unconsciously, use. Even as I worry about the hijacking of deskilled discourses to rationalize "mediocre" work, I also ask my students and colleagues to think more about the effects of the quotation marks.

What happens when a dancer's moves are defamiliarized by being placed inside a gallery's cube? Or when theater's conventions of realistic acting are made into an endurance performance on the gallery floor? And what happens when the defamiliarization happens in the other direction, when a dancer's moves frame, quote, and tilt what we think a museum is? Finally, all art forms have their celebrity artists, distributing opportunities and resources inequitably and sometimes without logic. But sometimes there is a logic, one discernible when we all make time to talk about how we perform now. It might be even more discernible when we make time about how we want to perform later, to talk about how we might like to perform later, for each other and for a future where artists and artistic experiments still live.

Notes

"The Way We Perform Now" was first published in *Dance Research Journal* 46, no. 3 (2014): 51–61.

1. "Performing Institution," Artists Space, https://artistsspace.org/programs/performing-institution#announcement.

2. David Velasco, "Performing Institution," symposia presented by Artists Space, May 26 and 29, 2012, https://artistsspace.org/programs/performing-institution.

3. "Performing Institution," Artists Space, https://artistsspace.org/programs/performing-institution#announcement.

4. Deborah Jowitt, "Walking Backward in Devotion," *DanceBeat*, March 3, 2012, http://www.artsjournal.com/dancebeat/2012/03/walking-backward-in-devotion/; Claudia La Rocco, "Ode to Sweat," *Performance Club*, March 15, 2012, https://claudialarocco.com/the-performance-club/.

5. Jane Levere, "MoMA Expands Again," *ARTnews* 105, no. 10 (2006): 67.

6. "Performing Institution," Artists Space, https://artistsspace.org/programs/performing-institution#announcement.

7. Karl Marx, *Capital: A Critique of Political Economy* (London: Penguin Books, 1991); Paolo Virno, *A Grammar of the Multitude: For an Analysis of Contemporary Life Forms* (Cambridge, MA: Semiotext(e), 2004); Michael Hardt, "Immaterial Labor and Artistic Production," *Rethinking Marxism: A Journal of Economics, Culture and Society* 17, no. 2 (2005): 175–77.

8. "Performing Institution," Artists Space, https://artistsspace.org/programs/performing-institution#announcement.

9. The Under the Radar Festival, NYC, 2012, "Performance and Context: The Black Box and the White Cube." See https://www.culturebot.org/2011/12/11981/culturebot-conversations-at-under-the-radar/, accessed 12/1/2021.

10. Claudia La Rocco, "Do a Little Dance, Make a Little Love," *Performance Club*, March 6, 2012, http://web.archive.org/web/20120309015731/http://theperformanceclub.org/2012/03/do-a-little-dance-make-a-little-love/.

11. Abigail Sebaly, "Cold Storage and New Brightness: The Merce Cunningham Acquisition at the Walker Art Center," *Brooklyn Rail*, December 10, 2010, http://www.brooklynrail.org/2011/12/dance/cold-storage-and-new-brightness-the-merce-cunningham-acquisition-at-the-walker-art-center;

Robert Faires, "Fusebox Festival: All Shook Up," *Austin Chronicle*, April 27, 2012, http://www.austinchronicle.com/arts/2012-04-27/fusebox-festival/.

12. Claudia La Rocco, "Yvonne Rainer Blasts Marina Abramovic at MOCA LA," *Performance Club*, November 11, 2011, http://web.archive .org/web/20120111103205/http://theperformanceclub.org/2011/11/yvonne -rainer-douglas-crimp-and-taisha-paggett-blast-marina-abramovic-and-moca -la/.

13. Siobhan Davies, "Parallel Voices," 2010, https://archive.siobhandavies .com/work/parallel-voices/.

14. "Curating People," UC Berkeley Arts Research Center, April 2011; "Making Time: Art Across Galler, Screen, and Stage," UC Berkeley Arts Research Center, April 2012; "Performing Institution," Artists Space, May 2012; "Performance at Tate: Into the Space of Art," Tate Modern, 2016; "Performance at Tate: Collecting, Archiving, and Sharing Performance and the Performative," Tate Modern, October 2014–September 2016; "In Terms of Performance," The Pew Center for Arts and Heritage and UC Berkeley, 2016–present.

15. Shannon Jackson, *Social Works: Performing Art, Supporting Publics* (New York and London: Routledge, 2011).

16. Gia Kourlas, "Do Not Feed or Annoy the Dancers," *New York Times*, April 1, 2012, http://www.nytimes.com/2012/04/02/arts/dance/michael-clarks -whos-zoo-at-whitney-biennial-2012.html.

17. David Levine, "Bad Art & Objecthood," *Art/US* no. 13, May/June 2006, reprinted in *Performance Club*, September 11, 2012, http://theperformanceclub .org/2012/09/reprint-bad-art-objecthood/; Andy Horwitz, "Visual Art Perfor- mance vs. Contemporary Performance," *Culturebot*, November 25, 2011, http:// www.culturebot.org/2011/11/11663/visual-art-performance-vscontemporary -performance/.

18. Paolo Virno, "Virtuosity and Revolution: The Political Theory of Exo- dus," in *Radical Thought in Italy: A Potential Politics*, ed. Michael Hardt and Paolo Virno (Minneapolis: University of Minnesota Press, 1996), 13–37.

19. Richard Maxwell, interview by David Velasco, *Artforum*, April 25, 2012, http://artforum.com/words/id=30817.

20. Claudia La Rocco, "Mothers in Search of a Child," *New York Times*, May 18, 2012, http://theater.nytimes.com/2012/05/19/theater/reviews/there -we-will-be-buried-at-the-whitney-biennial.html.

21. Claudia La Rocco, "All Things Seen: Claudia La Rocco in Conversation with Marissa Perel," Movement Research Critical Correspondence, April 19, 2012, https://movementresearch.org/publications/critical-correspondence/all -things-seen-claudia-la-rocco-in-conversation-with-marissa-perel.

Chapter 17

Drama and Other Time-Based Arts

At the time of the invitation to deliver a Spencer Lecture in Drama, Martin Puchner gave me wide brief in selecting a topic; he told me in an email that *drama*, he has decided, really is "Harvard lingo for theater/dance/performance/installation art. No one objects. So don't feel constrained at all." It was of course lovely to have this kind of expansive permission, since the relationships among theater/dance/performance and the visual art practices that produce installation art, relational art, process art, and more have been a preoccupation for me in recent years. Hence, you will see me using this as an opportunity to share with you some of the experimental art contexts in which I have found myself. At the same time, I thought it might be an interesting idea to think about drama after all, to use this invitation to think with you about what the "the dramatic" might say back to this expansive assembly theater/dance/performance/installation art. What follows is a conceptual exercise to unsettle some habits of thought. At the end, I also find the exercise helpful to understand a peculiar group of contemporary art works where, indeed, something like "drama" and say something like "installation art" collide. This essay unfolds in three parts, the first being a scene setting about some of the contemporary art experiments that, for some, make the curating of people in art an urgent, contemporary question. I will then recall some older lexicons around drama and time in art, bringing forward some chestnuts of dramatic and aesthetic theory to see how they set off, and are set off by, juxtaposition with those contemporary experiments. And finally, I turn to three artists for whom the question of drama in time-based art is not simply a conceptual exercise but functions as central material and motivating propeller in much of their work.

The Way We Perform Now

Over the last decade, we saw what some feel to be a new or newly redefined interest in performance in the visual art space. I will offer some exemplary touchstones of this maybe not so new version of an old preoccupation (recalling moments shared in the previous chapter and throughout this book. In fall of 2011, Rosalee Goldberg declared Performa 11 to be a biennial devoted to the question of "theater" in the visual art landscape, an interest declared in part because she actually cannot stand theater and wanted to put forward and reinforce the specific category of visual art performance. That challenge intersected with other ones coordinated by experimental performance festivals like Under the Radar or American Realness, as well as with a flurry of engaged responses from Roberta Smith, Claire Bishop, Andrew Horwitz, Gia Kourlas, Claudia La Rocco, Caden Manson, and others about what that visual art performance could possibly mean. A symposium organized at Under the Radar called "Black Box versus White Cube" was not sure that "visual art performance" meant much, but the presentations offered learned and sometimes hilarious disquisitions that made clear that the stakes for making it mean are urgent for some. Artists trained in theater and dance eyed with wariness and excitement this apparently welcoming visual arts context, hoping to find alternative sites for supporting their experiments.

Artists trained in visual art practices watched, chiasmatically, from the other side of the fence, trying to decide if a performance turn was a dynamization or a corruption of their field of practice. Mårten Spångberg reportedly annoyed and inspired artists and critics of all varieties when he declared that this new cross-arts ecology was an opportunity of a lifetime for choreographers and theater-makers who had never fit easily into art-market speculation. As recalled in this book's introduction, in the spring of 2012, Jay Sanders and Elizabeth Sussman offered a Whitney Biennial that was celebrated in part for the performances curated inside it, including Wu Tsang's *Green Room*, Michael Clark's *Who's Zoo*, Richard Maxwell's installed rehearsals, and, of course, Sarah Michelson's *Devotion Study #1—The American Dancer*, which made history for being the first choreographic work, made by a trained choreographer, to win the Whitney's Bucksbaum Award. By fall of 2012, the Museum of Modern Art (MoMA) was commissioning all varieties of performances—from the maybe parodic, maybe activist, maybe earnest "events" of Grand Openings to the siting of, not simply "movement in the gallery," but trained choreographers like Ralph Lemon, Steve Paxton, and Faustin Linyekula making dances with other trained choreographers on subjects that engaged the fundamentals of dance history. Meanwhile, lots of non–New York–based activity has been approaching those interart stakes from different angles. As I noted in chapter 16, compatriots at the Walker Art Center in Minneapolis are trying to figure out what it means to be "collecting" Merce Cunningham's costumes and those at the Fusebox Festival in Austin tried to shift the context of discussion entirely. Members of Marina Abramović's performance at Museum of Contemporary Art (MOCA) in Los Angeles tried to figure out what they were doing at that much vetted, if not exactly feted, donor

Fig. 17. Anne Teresa De Keersmaeker, *Work/Travail/Arbeid*, 2015. Museum of Modern Art, New York. Copyright Anne Van Aerschot.

event—whether it was a capitulation to or an interruption of the museum's experience economy; meanwhile, Yvonne Rainer and numerous other Los Angeles–based curators, artists, and scholars have tried to help them figure it out as well. In the United Kingdom, Tate Modern has opened its Tanks, committing "permanent" space to the presentation and exhibition of "temporary" and "ephemeral" art forms. Siobhan Davies has hosted her Parallel Voices seminars that reckon with how often visual art conversations and dance conversations run in parallel universes, the disciplinary habits that continue to structure interdisciplinary conversation. Some of us have hosted our own gatherings to advance conversation—I have at Berkeley under the rubric of "Making Time" and "Curating People"—as has Artists Space, The Kitchen, MoMA, and Culturebot, and recently the Pew Center for Art and Heritage has committed to a series of convenings and publications that seek to guide artists and audiences through murky interarts waters.[1]

So this is a bit of scene setting for thinking about the way we perform now, where "the way" does indeed seem a curious and not entirely coherent enmeshment of theater/dance/performance/installation art. However—unlike at Harvard perhaps—we find that lots of people object. The objections when raised revolve around whether particular individuals accept and welcome "this way," or these ways, or these ways and means of being time-based art. Indeed, if we just unpack for a bit the way and

the "we" of "performing now," we can see what objections, or least confusions, emerge. After all, the way invokes larger and broader questions
of medium, technique, skill, and material as they interface with different
we's, these we's who also share different conceptions of duration, spectacle, amateurism, virtuosity, conceptualism, experience, pleasure, and
rigor. What looks conceptually rigorous to one group looks exceptionally
unskilled or like a reinvented wheel to another. What looks like virtuosic skill to another group looks like the brainwashed capitulation to the
entertainment industry to yet another. These various ways also interact
with different conceptions of what we think that the way used to be and
whether we were ever part of the we who did it. Did the way used to
mean the making of objects for gallery exhibition or the making of dance
pieces for international tours? Did the way used to mean the rehearsing
of ticketed plays for subscriber audiences or did it used to mean creating
commodity art for selling to collectors? Did the we used to be playwrights,
who now find authorship decentered in place of a model that sees them
writing "textual material" for others to manipulate? Perhaps the we is a
set of museum curators, those trained in a wide and varied set of rigorous
visual art histories but who now find themselves cajoled and sometimes
pressured to install performance-based activity that feels equivocal and
uneasy in a museum context hurtling ever more toward what those symposia at MoMA and Artists Space called the event-based culture of the
post-Fordist "experience economy." Perhaps the we is the group of performance presenters who have been enabling performance to happen for a
while, individuals who might be called artistic directors in theaters or performance curators in museums. For those of us who descend from these
we's, this contemporary turn to performance can look curious, if interestingly so. For those who descend from the chorines, the touring troupes,
the actor-managers, and the stage managers who populate theater, opera,
music, and dance history, this turn hardly feels new but descends from a
much longer labor history. And when they hear of the anxiety of those
who worry about performance as a propeller of the event-based immateriality of a contemporary service economy, they might find this scene even
more curious, gently suggesting that it is inappropriate to see the resources
of "theater" and "dance" and the history of performing arts simply as
vehicles for propelling the visual art museum's capitulation to a twenty-
first-century, post-Fordist event-based economy.

Finally, the we refers to the receivers of these performances now and
our means of making sense of them. I'm thinking of the receiver who once
thought of herself as an audience member at one venue and as a beholder
at another venue, the one who sat in rows in the theater and who roamed
in three-second-per-work intervals in the museum, the one who is now
struggling to find a place to prop her back against a wall or to perch on
the lone bench in order to glimpse a gesture only dimly seeable across the

museum gallery floor? This we is also a specialized group of academics and critics who find ourselves in a perpetual state of reskilling, people like me who enter the museum scene anxiously reminding everyone that I know that I am not an art historian, or people like Carrie Lambert-Beatty who dare to write on Yvonne Rainer while assuring people that she knows that she isn't a dance historian.[2] For the we that is an art receiver or the art critic, what art literacies and art habits were functionally suspended in some places and reactivated at others?

Drama and/as Time-Based Art

If varieties of frames, keywords, values, and anxieties now circulate around the way we perform now, then terms like "drama" and "time-based art" are two of the many, many terms that might be deployed to make sense of them. What happens when we place these terms in conversation? By inserting these terms—one quite old, one relatively new—into the discussion, I do not mean to suggest that they have stable referents. Indeed, the referents for these terms morph and change in response to opportunistic projections and curious bouts of amnesia. This exercise is in attempt to juxtapose the ambiguous and changing associations of both terms with those of the other, hoping that it clarifies something about contemporary predilections and artistic sensibilities that circulate now. What Gerard Genette and others have said about the history of "genre" categories—such as drama—applies in our contemporary scene as well. Genette famously argued that the history of genre classification is always a contemporary exercise, one that often mistakes a network of modes and conventions derived inductively from contemporary observation for deductively determined, hard and fast genre categories perceived to function securely for all time.[3] Surely the contemporary tussle over the way we perform now is the latest iteration of this analytic impurity in a long history of attempts to classify and disentangle genres, modes, and conventions across art forms.

So, without saying what time-based art is, I will start with what others have claimed for the term. Varieties of sites and individuals claim credit for coining this hyphenated phrase. The British artist and master teacher David Hall tells one story that begins with him, one that has him working across media, in sculpture and photography, while installed through the Artist Placement Group in a Scottish TV station. There, pieces like *TV Interruptions* (1971) or *60 TV Sets* (1972) positioned television itself as artistic material, one whose screens, modified liveness, and associated industrial systems exploded conventional boundaries of the static museum object. For Hall and others afterward, time-based art referred to the alternative use of then-new media technologies; importantly, however, this sense that time-based meant technologically based coincided with a much broader questioning of painting and sculpture more generally. As sixties Minimalist experiments quickly prompted new ones in so-called process art, Happenings, and events, time-based experiments were part of a much larger effort, sometimes formal, sometimes political, sometimes both, to "dematerialize" conventions of object making in visual art institutions. Hall recalled his sculpture workshops for undergraduates at the University of Kent in 1971 and attendant realization of where the students wanted to go: "In discussion it became clear that some students were becoming interested in producing works which were non-object-based, consistent with 'the developing "fringe" element of late sixties art . . . which was already engaged in the essential "dematerialization" of the object.'"[4] This genealogy of time-based art is thus very familiar to contemporary art historians, charting as it does the late twentieth-century transition of so many modern and contemporary art museums whose collections, buildings, and curatorial divisions of labor underwent significant transformation in response to both a wide and not always differentiated array of media art and processual/performance art. The thing that unifies this motley and heterogeneous assembly is that they are all "nonobjects." Time-based art is thus fairly clearly a term coined by a particular we and particular notion of how the way used to be, that is, a group of artists and art organizations whose art had not yet been "based in time."

If David Hall sought in his signature writings what he called then an "autonomous practice" for video art, he might not necessarily have appreciated or at least foreseen how very widely that category would expand to include a range of nonobject forms. When Kristy Edmunds started the Time-Based Art Festival in Portland, Oregon, she and her curators included a range of forms that were not only "based" in video and then new technologies but also derived from, if also measuring their distance from, normatively time-based forms such as theater, dance, and music, as well as normatively static forms such as painting and sculpture. Perhaps as a conscious decision to be more inclusive, perhaps with an awareness that the time-based art term might provide a way to repackage experimental theater and experimental choreography, the Time-Based Art Festival and its allies curated temporal art forms that would elsewhere be categorized as dance (if site-specific dance), music (if avantgarde music), theater (if postdramatic theater), body art (of the sculptural variety), and now a range of relational and social works where intersubjective exchange was the primary medium and material of the art event.

Now let me turn to drama. As a student of drama and theater, I had not thought myself to be a student of time-based art forms until a visual art historian told me that I was. It was an early version of many defamiliarizing conversations that eventually led to the publication of *Social Works*, as well as a number of journal and catalogue essays that have explored, to varying degrees, the disciplinarity of so-called interdisciplinary scholarship and art making.[5] But is drama a time-based art? On the one hand, the answer is a most obvious "yes," almost too obvious to be very interesting. Drama is linked to the temporal art of poetry; it is a form and genre that depends on something like narrative or, even more precisely, plot. And the fact that the task of the dramatic writer has been centrally concerned with something like the management of duration would suggest that it is a time-based art form, indeed already one for quite some time. On the other hand, there are ways of answering "no." Perhaps the first form of "no" would come in the form of an unprocessed reaction that recoils at the link between this old category and one that was meant to mark the new. Drama is classical, and time-based art is avant-garde. Drama maintains tradition; time-based art breaks from it. Of course, this reaction also assumes that the object-based tradition is the one from which the "we" is trying to break free. As I have noted elsewhere, it is always unsettling when the avant-garde interruption of one form—the way of one form— turns out to perpetuate the traditional ways and means of another form.

But there are other, perhaps more interesting, reasons to respond "no," or at least "not quite," in answer to the question of whether drama is a time-based art. One avenue would in fact emphasize drama's link to plot and propose that plot is exactly what time-based art bypasses, extends, or thwarts. Let's recall Aristotle's disquisition on the subject of plot in tragedy, or what he calls "the required qualities of the structure of events." Consider his directive that they include robust and clear beginnings, middles, and ends, patterned with what the Stephen Halliwell translation calls "appropriate magnitude."

> Beauty consists in magnitude and order, which is why there could not be a beautiful animal which was either minuscule (as contemplation of it, occurring in an almost imperceptible moment, has no distinctness) or gigantic (as contemplation of it has no cohesion, but those who contemplate it lose a sense of unity and wholeness), say an animal a thousand miles long. So just with our bodies and with animals, beauty requires magnitude, but magnitude that allows coherent perception, likewise plots require length, but length that can be coherently remembered.[6]

If we decide to foreground such a conception of plot within the category of drama, we are then confronted, not simply with temporality or time-basedness as such, but with a specific structure for managing temporality. With the directive that it be neither minuscule nor gigantic, we have a prescription for a temporal arc that is arguably inadequate for understanding time-based experiment. Single actions such as sweeping, dispersed interventions in corners and barely perceptible shifts of light, temperature, or sound have been hallmarks of time-based or process art, actions that strategically withdrew marks of "distinctness" to provoke reflection on how formal and aesthetic distinction was perceived in the first place. Meanwhile, we could say that other kinds of highly extended time-based art practices partake of the gigantic. Consider the endurance performances of Marina Abramović, whether of eight or twenty-four hours, or of Abramović and Ulay as they traversed the Great Wall of China, or Tehching Hsieh and Linda Montano, or Hsieh on his own. Certainly, the public reception of those pieces tried to place discernible beginnings, middles, and ends on them, resorting to the ready-made plots of masochism or, say, marriage to do so. But the pursuit of these and other less spectacular works was to endure beyond the durationality of a recognizable and "coherently remembered" plot, to endure past the point of a seeable end to experience time at the point that it loses its "sense of unity and wholeness."[7] We can take this question of plot back to the technologically mediated domain of Hall's time-based art where we find video and film "installed" more often than screened; such installation are less likely to follow the ups, downs, and resolutions of plot and are more often likely to follow the repeated structure of "the loop." Whether driven by concept or by the open-all-day parameters of the museum and gallery space, such time-based art assumes that a receiver that will enter at any time; the art unfurls frame after frame until the loop starts again for each hour after hour until closing. So between the endurance of performance art and the loop of time-based media, we have forms based in time that do not necessarily conform to drama's time, approaching as they do the expansions and uncontemplatability of an animal a thousand miles long.

We can certainly invoke other resources for understanding the historical stakes of temporality in aesthetic discourse. When someone like Gotthold Ephraim Lessing offered his discourse on time, he did so in part to delineate among different art forms that are now so ubiquitously mixed (as theater/dance/performance/installation art) now. In his own time, Lessing went to great pains to delineate the temporal arts from the static ones to celebrate the peculiar potency of each. His vocabulary could become entangled and tautological at once.

> If it is true that in its imitations painting uses completely different means or signs than does poetry, namely figures and colors in space rather than articulated sounds in time, and if these signs must indisputably bear a suitable relation to the thing signified, then signs existing in space can express only objects whose wholes or parts coexist, while signs that follow one another can express only objects whose wholes are parts are consecutive.[8]

From such premises, he deduced other ones, arguing that it was because of this difference in means that the painter expressed subjects in juxtaposition by using "bodies" and that the poet expressed subjects consecutively by using "actions." As numerous critics such as David Wellberry and later W. J. T. Mitchell have shown, Lessing's delineations were themselves unstable, as his impulses to self-qualify certainly revealed. It is also safe to say that theorists of the theater have wondered about theater's relation to Lessing's time and space categories. The wholes and parts of the theater used both actions and bodies in ways that were both juxtapositive and successive; this interart combination of separate "departments" is not radical from the perspective of theater history, but fairly normal, carrying forward a combination that Aristotle might have called, with different associations, plot and spectacle.

If it is now de rigueur to say that we don't believe Lessing, it would seem anachronistic to return to him. At the same time, it occurs to me that the anachronistic delineations are, not only teachable, but also persistent delineations that still structure the ways in which aesthetic experiment is understood by differently positioned we's. Despite skepticism or confusion at different historical moments, visual art criticism's perpetuation of these delineations proceeded apace, expanding with unique eloquence on the peculiar effects of painting's juxtapositive techniques. In his classic *Discourses on Art* (1771), Joshua Reynolds elaborated on the perils of working in static visual forms, in particular the perception that the visual artist had but a singular and fleeting chance to convey his aesthetic impact, not being able to rely on the temporality of unfolding encounter to recuperate him. "He has but one sentence to utter, but one moment to exhibit," said Reynolds of the painter. "He cannot, like the poet or historian, expatiate. Poetry having a more extensive power than our art exerts its influence over almost all the passions; amongst those can be reckoned one of the most prevalent dispositions, anxiety for the future."[9] If the safety net of expatiation belonged only to those in the time-based arts of poetry, visual artists had only a singular moment to produce the unique effects of parts and wholes juxtaposed in space since, for Reynolds, "What is done by Painting, must be done at one blow; curiosity has received at once all the satisfaction it can ever have."[10]

This kind of eighteenth-century generalization—one that argued that the visual art experience occurred "all at once" and "at one blow"—would have its twentieth-century ratification in modernist art criticism. In the wake of visual art expansion in Minimalist, dematerialized, and time-based art to which I referred above, there was a simultaneous effort to shore up the expanse and argue for the importance of autonomy and medium specificity in art, in particular in visual art whose dalliance with "theatricality" imperiled it. Recall the oft-quoted statements of Clement Greenberg on the flatness of modernist painting, or Michael Fried's antitheatrical disquisitions, which Martin Puchner has rightly argued always seem to keep theater motoring along.[11] Many know only too well that modernist, anti-Minimalist narrative that tried to keep the proper departments of static visual art apart from the encroachments of time-based media. For modernist critics, properly modernist painting meditated on flatness to achieve the ultimate incarnation of the all-at-once encounter. For Greenberg, such "medium specificity" delivered its one blow; for Fried, that blow distinguished the "presentness" that is grace from the ongoing "presence" of theatricality. In Fried's view, the problem with theatrical and temporally expanding forms was that theater "defeated" art in time, that is, in "succession," blow by blow by blow by blow.[12]

By this point, it should be clear that I do not think that a "yes" or "no" answer to the unmodified question of drama as a time-based art is possible. But I do think that it can become interesting when we ask ourselves what parameters allow us to answer "yes," and what parameters might prompt us to answer "no." By thinking through ideas of plot or the blow-by-blow debates about the proper departments of poetry and painting, we might expose the parameters, puzzles, and blind spots of approaching drama and time-based art as categories in the first place. But, before moving on, it should also be noted that drama has other associations in addition to its temporal ones, associations that foreground the mode of representation in which this temporal art unfolds. From the perspective of literary genre history, there is far more than one temporal poetic art form. What if we consider drama as one among a few temporal "genres," that is, as a genre conventionally delineated from say the lyric or the epic? This triad is also hardly a stable one; it is not necessarily as explicit in classical poetics as Northrup Frye might have assumed but, if you believe Gerard Genette, was a generic invention of the Romantic period.[13] At the same time, it is interesting to think about how this triad shifts the axis of comparison, so that slightly different qualities become emphasized in the category of the dramatic. Recall the lyric's association with first-person expression and its link to a form of a personal revelation. Recall the epic's association with narrative, often third-person narrative that recounts and contains the capacity to traverse identifications and time periods. From this angle of vision, drama comes forward most specifically as a dialogic genre based in mimetic substitution, where actors stand-in for characters who take part in a particular form of structured exchange. Or, as Genette would say, where the artist speaks through characters who appear to speak for themselves. By delineating among temporal poetic genres like the lyric, dramatic, and epic, we might find ourselves wondering if different classic genres offer more traction for understanding some time-based experiments than others. Karen Finley and a host of other feminist performance artists are perhaps interestingly understood within the parameters of the lyric. Meanwhile, the strategies of Sharon Hayes or Andrea Fraser might be best understood within the parameters of the epic—or what Aristotle would have called the "mixed" epic-dramatic mode; such a link strengthens the one that Benjamin Buchloh and others have made among

Benjaminian and Brechtian epic theater and the goals of institutional critique in visual art practice.[14] Finally, noticing how the epic and lyric are differentiated gives us different perspectives on "the dramatic." At the very least, this angle on the dramatic allows us, not only to emphasize the specific parameters of temporality understood to be dramatic (tragic) plot, but also to think rhetorically and poetically about the very different modes of first-, second-, and third-person address installed in different performance and time-based art forms.

In fact, my sense is that much of what passes for innovation in event-based, relational, process art, or performance art now, is more often linked to the lyric or the epic than it is to the dramatic. Indeed, it often seems that there is something about the dramatic, something about a form that is linked to "coherently remembered" plots and to a form that appears to need the mimetic substitution of actors inside the scripted confines of second-person dialogue, which makes it less easily absorbed or celebrated in visual art venues that otherwise seem so thirsty for performance. One could decide how firmly to stand behind that assertion, but it is interesting to see it emerge from the conceptual exercise of this essay; in part, it helps me to understand why "theater" remains an equivocal and ambivalent form within visual art contexts, even when they understand themselves to be well past Fried's disdain for theatricality.

Installing Drama

At this point, I would like to think further about the way we perform now, at least in art venues, next to these tangles around drama, plot, acting, and time-based art in relation to a few artists. I have chosen those who seem both to ride and to challenge an antidramatic sensibility within the protheatrical turns of contemporary visual art practice. Significantly, my examples also happen to draw from an experimental performing arts scene—in one case, a so-called postdramatic theater scene—that seems to care, however fitfully, about what contemporary visual art circles think of them. They are thus a particular we within the we.

Richard Maxwell is one of the most well-known postdramatic practitioners in the United States, identified as he is with the downtown New York experimental theater scene, positioned within a generational narrative that plots his influences, and his likenesses and unlikenesses, to figures like Mac Wellman or Liz LeCompte, as well as a host of second- (or is it third-) generation theatrical experimenters. He has also been included within a cohort of experimenters whose techniques some feel are approaching exhaustion; they are at least indexes of what Shawn-Marie Garrett called the "awkward age" of New York theater, one that has retreated from political engagement, is embarrassed by bold gestures, and has regularized the "whatever" aesthetic that keeps small houses relatively full in the maybe postironic, but not necessarily earnest, age of early twenty-first-century theatermaking.[15] Maxwell is a former member of Cook County Theater Company in Chicago who became artistic director and a guiding figure for New York City Players. His style of textual arrangement in the service of performance was honed in more than twenty plays; some of them, such as *House, Showy Lady Slipper, Boxing 2000, Caveman, Drummer Wanted,* and many more have circulated widely on the European experimental theater stage that often identifies, before American audiences do, what our most interesting American theater artists are up to. A more recent piece, *Neutral Hero*, appeared at The Kitchen, despite Hurricane Sandy, after appearances throughout France, Switzerland, Belgium, Germany, Canada, and elsewhere. Also in 2012, he installed a piece at the Whitney Biennial, a rehearsal of a play about a witch hunt written as textual material expressly for the commission and listed as an untitled "piece for Whitney Biennial" in his biography.

It is now cliché for commentators to refer to the signature "deadpan" style that Maxwell cultivates in his actors—and for such commentary quickly to follow with qualifications about how much he rejects such characterizations. It is almost as common for his celebrators to laud the effects of his practices of excision, claiming that the withdrawal of, not only spectacle, but also the honed skills of actorly mimetic substitution restores players and receivers of the theatrical event to a shared experience of "presence." It is a mode of argument that is also quickly followed by qualifications that debate, usually on Derridean autopilot, the metaphysical naiveté of such a pursuit. When Garrett invokes Maxwell in her frustrated meditation on the idiom of awkwardness, this mode, this style of enunciation, is invoked as an element that is redefining, or potentially deskilling, the genre of drama.

> What happened to virtuosity? Or is this its new incarnation, artful artlessness? . . . Welcome to New York experimental theater at the end of the century. Banality, disorientation, and nerditude are what American culture offers us these days, so young theater makers are finding ways of theatricalizing these developments . . . These subterranean feelings come through most eloquently in song, dance and movement, rather than language. Words in this new work are dead on arrival, voiced with deadpan vapidity—even numbers are more lively. Forms, too, have been around the block a few times: the plays shamble along an Aristotelian arc, merely going through the motions of all of the goings-on. "I tell now," a character called Mike in Richard Maxwell's *House* reports in monotone to the audience, "I'm looking for the guy who killed my brother and get the revenge for my brother's killing." Got it?[16]

There are many elements to debate about Maxwell's work within the landscape of experimental theater, but I am putting him forward as an exhibit for my conceptual exercise and the categorical explosions that arise when we consider drama within time-based practice more generally. I have been interested to try to understand what it meant for Maxwell to navigate his status as a kind of exception that used to prove the rule to which I referred earlier, the general rule that performance forms other than theater have been more easily assimilated by a contemporary visual artworld hungry for the experiential programming. Maxwell was the one theater representative selected for installation in the 2012 Whitney Biennial, a positioning that added an *Artforum*-esque stream of critical reflection on his work to the critical responses already heaped by critics of experimental theater. What I find myself wondering is how the careful modulation—and sometimes even rejection—of certain ways of theater-making facilitated his entry into the art-biennial space. We might ask if it is precisely the "awkwardness" of the performance style or the "no color" withdrawal of virtuosic actorly skill that made his work more palatable to a contemporary artworld that has historically distrusted virtuosity (at least of the theatrical variety), or for whom the creation of something like "dramatic character" was at least vaguely uncomfortable and often an embarrassment to be avoided. We might further consider how he handled the temporal parameters of the installation, electing not to present a piece at a specific theatrical time but instead to install a rehearsal process on the gallery floor. According to Maxwell, "We didn't want just to do a show on the Whitney's fourth floor. It didn't make sense to carry over the trappings of theater into a museum structure. It would be a forced fit. In my work, I embrace the environment and circumstances. . . . I talk with actors about being in a place of readiness, to not deny or ignore the room."[17] The decision to rehearse thus also handled the temporal parameters of the museum, allowing for the arrival and exit of visitors at different points during the day, effectively using the rehearsal conceit to match the unbounded conventions of the "loop" so often linked to time-based art. It is also interesting to listen to the accompanying Whitney audio guide when Maxwell opines further on his pursuit of something like "neutrality" in performance and ends up sounding like an installation artist:

> I had a disagreement with an actor once that ultimately led to us parting ways. At the end of the first rehearsal, she was troubled. After much discussion she asked me, does it ever get beyond zero. I said no. My answer was disingenuous but served its purpose, because she left the project. I said no because not getting beyond zero has to be OK. And my answer is disingenuous because when you stop and think about all that is going on—what she would wear, what she would sing, what she would play, what the others

in combination with her would do, what the addition of a whole audience can do, what the room's architecture will yield, what the temperature will be, what the lights and set would look like, what it could mean—how could it possibly ever be zero? The venture quickly is a dizzying array of limitless possibilities, and we have just begun.[18]

Maxwell's pursuit of "neutrality" at the Whitney and in his play *Neutral Hero* thus elicit prose that can be reheard by receivers well-schooled in the goals and philosophical pursuits of installation art, a practice that itself creates structures ultimately for exposing the futility of neutrality given the contingent encumbrances—architecture, light, and temperature—of the environment in which the art appears.

But it is also interesting to notice that even this notion of rehearsal, *la répétition*, needs a particular kind of conceptual justification as "installed drama" in order for this theatrical practice not to be perceived as a "forced fit" in the space of the museum. "Rehearsal," says Maxwell,

is about getting used to the idea of repeating. I think if we only had to do this once—say the story was written and somehow we were able to present this as a one-time event—my shows would look a lot different. Not just because of the time factor, but because of the way that performers behave. There's something to this fact that we have to repeat something. I don't have a problem with realism—of trying to pretend you're someone else, this character written on a page—if it's only going to happen one time. . . . But it really is more honest to say to the people that are going to watch a theatrical production, 'look, we know we've repeated this. We're not going to put any energy into pretending that this is the first time it's happened.' I think about rehearsal as a way of reckoning the fact that we're going to repeat."[19]

It isn't simply about honing mimetic skills at acting (a theatrical value, a virtuosic value?) but more interestingly for him about the avowal of the need to repeat. Arguably, however, Maxwell cops to his theatrical training when he also admits that rehearsal is not only about a conceptual notion of repetition but also an act rooted in a theatrical value of virtuosity. It is a surprising line for someone touted as postdramatic theater's appropriately awkward answer to the critique of virtuosity's power. For Maxwell, "I feel like repetition also has something to do with being the best that you can be. . . . In storytelling, it's nicer to watch people who know their lines than those reading from a page. I don't know if I can defend that. Maybe saying, we can do it, so let's do it, let's master that."[20] But what if it is, and does he need to apologize if he can't quite defend it? What we celebrate mastery in this installed form of theatricality? And before whom does the-atrical mastery need to be defended?

This question around the need to defend or apologize for the traditional skills of theater making brings me to the work of David Levine. Levine did graduate work in English at Harvard and in directing at Columbia (before returning to the faculty at Harvard). Fairly soon into his post-graduate life, he forsook theater, at least temporarily, to establish a career as a visual artist, but one whose visual art engagements use the stuff of the drama as primary material. There is thus a specific theater-like sense about his time-based work, another approach to the installation of drama that differs from the generalized theatricality that modernism deplored or that postmodernism seemed to celebrate. Consider a piece like *2 Forms of Endurance* (2007) in which two theater students reenacted Abramovic and Ulay's *Light/Dark* (1977), reenacting its signature gestures, testing the bounds of trust, but placed within a compendium of theater exercises. Reenacted performance art is here turned into an odd kind of theater-like scene study. In *Bauerntheater* (2007), Levine cast an American actor as a character in a Heiner Muller play, requiring him to till potato fields for ten hours a day for a month. Elsewhere, he has framed the vexed rela-tionship between the mimetic dramatic form of acting and other forms of time-based labor. In *Actors at Work* (2007), Levine paid actors to do their day jobs, casting them with Equity contracts as "administrative assis-tants," "poster distributors," "messengers," and "waiters." The move both prompted a reflection about where the lines between acting and nonact-ing were drawn, but more intensely exposed the fragile, surrogated, and temporary service economy on which actors rely. It also defamiliarized the professional protocols of acting as a form of time-based labor.

If the above are a few examples of what it might mean to "install drama," Levine's project *Habit* (2012) offered new ways to think about its puzzles. *Habit* received a workshop premiere at the Massachusetts Museum of Modern Art (Mass MoCA), its full premiere at the Luminato Festival, and was reinstalled in the Essex Market in New York City as part of the Cross-ing the Line Festival, interestingly reviewed in both the theater and visual art press. The piece consists of a house-like structure constructed hyperreal-istically and installed in a gallery space. Lights "really" turn on, and water "really" runs through its pipes. Enclosed on all sides except for windows and doors, three actors inhabit the rooms to perform a three-person play. The play is performed continuously, in a loop, for nine hours, the amount of time that the gallery remains open. The intensity of that loop thus trans-forms the "coherently remembered" plot of a simple play into the less easily contemplated temporal experience of the "gigantic" endurance form. The script performed inside the house is not titled "Habit" but "Children of Kings," a script written by Jason Grote on a commission from Levine. Marsha Ginsberg drew the drawings for the set, also on commission from

Fig. 18. Installation shot of David Levine's *Habit*, performed at Essex Market in New York as part of the Crossing the Line Festival, 2012. Photograph by Julieta Cervantes.

Levine. The actors supply material, too, committing to play out the scenes of an excruciating twenty-something love triangle, complete with Cain and Abel–like brothers and a female who is Madonna, whore, coke addict, and a student of semiotics all at once. "The aim," says Levine, "was to commission an absolutely anonymous, if heartfelt, piece of contemporary conventional American realism (because realism is one of our habits)."[21] Interestingly, we have a discourse around anonymity and habit that echoes the language invoked by Maxwell. While I might want to argue about how necessary the laconic form of Gen X sexism was to depicting the habit of realism—hardly feels anonymous or habitual to me—the other conventions of acting it out certainly were. And these conventions of realistic acting are a central part of what Levine installs. The play was written to allow the creativity and structures and choices of actors to unfold as a central drama of the piece; the pleasures of scene study are thus brought into the gallery. Says Levine, "the play is that it has *really flexible beats*; beats that actors can ride, modify, flex and surf."[22] In other words, the mimetic practices of surrogated dialogic exchange—here the realistic genre of drama—have been brought into the gallery, despite its forced fit.

Notably, some of the press and critical response emphasized how the piece activated the gallery experience; as one piece wrote: "it subverts the typical relationship between audience and performance. Like those of the actors, the viewers' options are varied and unscripted: They can hover

Fig. 19. David Levine, *Habit*, 2010–12. Photograph by Marsha Ginsberg.

over the actors, just inches away from an intimate scene; follow a character from room to room; or sit on a bench to watch what comes within their
field of vision."[23] This kind of interpretive frame recalls conventional ways
of writing about the break in convention that has spawned so much post-
Minimalist process art, the way in which the beholder becomes activated
by the entry of a temporal form into a space that traditionally presented
static ones. The heretofore static conventions of juxtaposed space are disrupted by an action that unfolds, as Lessing might have said, consecutively.
But there are a few things that this analytic perspective—from a particular
we about a particular way—misses. For one, it does not quite track the
effects of how time and space are redelineated from another direction,
that is, what it does to the temporal event of the dramatic when moved
into the gallery space of static encounter. In other words, it is not just
that theatrical time activates space, but that sometimes the gallery space
stops time. At the very least, it stops, interrupts, or stalls the conventional
temporality with which theater is typically received, taking the arc out
of the play by having it repeat, making the action of acting available for
reflection, exposing the action of acting as form of creative and skilled
labor. Notably it was this defamiliarization of dramatic acting that Ben
Brantley—a different we—most emphasized in his encounter. This was an
endurance performance that isn't performance art. It is an endurance performance that is also a job, an acting job that is a day job, an acting job

that is, in fact, an all-day day job. In this plaintive and captivating world, the creativity and precarity of mimetic acting comes forward not because it is staged but because it is in-stalled. And I do mean stalled. For the space of this piece, maybe just maybe, drama was enlivened precisely because it had been arrested, in-stalled by the space of visual art.

So if drama is a form that is associated or measures its distance from "plot" and is associated or measures its distance from the dialogic form—wherein the artist speaks through characters who appear to speak as themselves—then the thrill and embarrassment of this surrogated relationship is something carefully navigated in drama's installation. If Maxwell withdraws from drama's mimetic substitutions and its "color," Levine commits to its enactment in order to install it. By foregrounding the embarrassments of drama's worst forms, his project simultaneously allows himself and his receivers to revel in the elements that make it so compelling. Both these strategies involve a degree of commitment to something earnest—to presence or to the habitual appeal of realistic acting—while modulating that earnestness with some kind of mediating detachment—the direct address in deadpan style or the gallery installation as an eccentric frame. Both these techniques allow the artistic to speak "dramatically" through characters who appear to speak for themselves; at the same time, these techniques also allow the artist to avoid secure belief in or capitulation to drama's generic possibility.

As a final example, let me turn to an artist whose reputation was first burnished in the visual artworld but whose connection to the dramatic, to acting, and to theater—if of the epic variety—has been a recurrent motif. The motif does not mean that he necessarily measures his distance from theater, quite the opposite. Indeed, Gerard Byrne's work has been primarily measured from the barometer of photography and then the serial presentation of photography known as film and video. As someone whose time-based photography transmogrified into video installation, he might more firmly fit the practice David Hall had in mind when he invoked the term time-based art. But Byrne's pursuits have always been regularly accompanied by an engagement with the temporal and presentational forms of drama and theater. In a lengthy essay on Byrne called "The Storyteller," George Baker appropriated Walter Benjamin's title to foreground, not only the narrative pressure felt in Byrne's photography, but also a connection that, Baker suggested, Benjamin might have made between the effects of Brecht's epic theater and the effects of Byrne's photo practice.[24] This was a connection made all too explicitly by Byrne himself, in photographs like *Street Scene* where the composition is significant for the didactic Byrne places under it, one that quotes Brecht's famous account of demonstration in the recounting of an accident in the street. Of course, Byrne's self-conscious preoccupation with Brecht sounds, from the perspective of theater history, like an engagement not with the dramatic but with the epic theater form that distanced itself from drama's plots and its mimetic surrogated structure. Brecht famously opposed epic theater to Aristotelean dramatic theater in polarizing charts that are highly unstable (if oh so very teachable). But Baker—again part of a visual artworld's we—cares less about the epic-dramatic dyad than he does about a more general deployment of theater, in whatever form, in contemporary visual art practice. But in passing over—or not really needing to care—about an epic-dramatic opposition, he is allowed to make other connections to create a roomier umbrella. He explores Byrne's Brechtian preoccupation with theater forms that are not themselves "Brechtian" as texts, but whose deployments in contemporary art, photography, and video installation create Brechtian effects. Byrne photographs, for instance, the jury chamber of the set of the play *Twelve Angry Men* while a "loquacious" caption from the *Irish Times* lauds the success of the "formula" of locking a "group of people in an enclosed space" and letting "them strip each other down."[25] *Twelve Angry Men* is not exactly a Brechtian play, but Baker argues that this photographic documentation achieves what he calls the "realization" of a Brechtianism cued to our contemporary moment.

> As photographed by Byrne, this stage set hardly seems a theatrical space at all—an outmoded or even historical space perhaps, with its dated fan, wooden furniture, and multiple ashtrays, but not necessarily false in its visual connotation. . . . here a theatrical construction seems elevated by the photography into the illusion of a somewhat banal reality. . . . the documentary power of the photograph . . . makes the theatrical space somehow more real. And of course, theater sets are 'real' sites in social space, hardly mere constructed fictions for the camera. Since this moment, the *In the News* photographs of the production of *Twelve Angry Men* have spawned an entirely new sequence of in Byrne's work, a series of untitled photographs of theatrical spaces and objects, including Beckett, Pinter, and Ionesco. In all of them, as photography documents the theater, it seems to produce the 'realization' of its object, providing photography with the power of enactment that theater once held on its own.[26]

Other works of Byrne's defamiliarize or, we could say, alienate the fundamentals of modern drama and twentieth-century theater in sculptural rather than photographic form. For instance, his 2004 and 2006 *In Repertory* creates an environmental installation, claiming to transform the white cube into a black box, and arranging iconic stage props and set pieces of modern drama—the forlorn tree of *Waiting for Godot*, the covered cart of *Mother Courage*, and a painted backdrop of Rogers and Hammerstein's *Oklahoma!*

But I am most interested in projects like *A Man and a Woman Make Love* (2012), which premiered at Documenta 13; the latter has a high octane, multichanneled chutzpah in its installation of videos of actors acting found dialogue, that is presenting the dramatic exchange of the group interview in the mode (or perhaps genre) of mimetic acting. One can see connections to Byrne's earlier work, including *1984 and Beyond* (2005–7) in which Dutch actors perform a *Playboy* conversation published in 1963 where a group of luminaries was assembled to contemplate the future. Byrne sites the conversation within a modernist architectural space, which in turn was projected in the space of a gallery on television screens atop plinths, recalling time-based media's familiar scene of address.[27]

The production values, spatial reach, and continued investigation of the nonneutral neutralities of heterosexual masculinity of this installed drama expanded further in *A Man and a Woman Make Love*. There an assembly of male actors performs the text of a discussion about sex convened by André Breton in 1928; the actors occupy a men's club of sorts, with wood paneling and upholstered sofas, along with the requisite ashtrays. They recount then shocking escapades and pose truth or dare questions of each other's sexual proclivities, using the plummy tones and jocular flourishes of a masculine exchange teetering, as this one will be, on the wires and fragile pedestals that connect and support an angled collection of video screens while projections ricochet across the room. The frames also eventually include tantalizing images that gradually zoom out and up to reveal the video apparatus documenting the acting scene, as well as the efforts of the mixer mixing the sound and the technician lighting it; we also see the vaguely distracted audience who appears to be watching the scene unfold, recorded as they sit in their theater seats, projected to the roaming visitors to Documenta galleries (and later Whitechapel galleries).

What to make of these actors acting? While others have to withdraw or parody or in some formal way ensure their distance from the acting of the actor, why is Byrne celebrated for works that incorporate actors so spectacularly? The mode of acting is not clearly Brechtian, and indeed the mode of acting is far from the experimental; it does not adhere to an ethos of detachment or irony so endemic to what so many postdramatic theatermakers understand to be avant-garde. By what agreement is Byrne permitted these romps into committed, nearly earnest, acting? It seems partly to come from the ricochet across screens that both propels and interrupts the conventional ricochet of dramatic dialogue. The dramatic is tolerated conceptually in part because of how intolerable it becomes affectively. The oddity and cheesiness of the earnest actor is made palatable, even renewed, by the vague irritation of being in-stalled, that is, sited and stalled, by the highly crafted and choreographed conventions of time-based media installation. Finally, we might ask whether the video documentation of the acting is doing what Baker felt that photography was doing to the stage set, that is, "providing it with a power of enactment that theater once held on its own."[28] Or conversely, we might ask whether the practice of installing drama gives us an alibi to indulge in the power of dramatic enactment, despite the supposedly tired, old, anachronistic nature of the genre. Perhaps installed drama allows us to indulge in a power of enactment that theater, not only still has on its own, but also agrees to lend to others for their own surrogated use. Installation gives drama the status of a time-based art.

Notes

1. In fact, based on a mutual interest in the varied terms, techniques, and histories engaged, if often misrecognized, in this scene of cross-arts experimentation, Pew's Executive Director Paula Marincola and I commissioned forty-five contemporary artists, curators, and scholars to produce texts on debated "keywords" in this minefield. Shannon Jackson and Paula Marincola, *In Terms of Performance*, Pew Center for Arts and Heritage, Philadelphia, 2016, http://www.intermsofperformance.site.

2. Carrie Lambert-Beatty, *Being Watched: Yvonne Rainer and the 1960s* (Cambridge, MA: MIT Press, 2008).

3. Gerard Genette, "The Architext," in *Modern Genre Theory*, ed. David Duff (New York: Longman, 2000), 210–18; and in the same volume, Northrup Frye, "The Mythos of Summer; Romance," 98–117.

4. Joanna Heatwole, "Media of Now: An Interview with David Hall," *Afterimage* 36, no. 1 (2008): 14–17.

5. Shannon Jackson, *Social Works: Performing Art, Supporting Publics* (New York and London: Routledge, 2011).

6. *Aristotle's Poetics*, trans. Stephen Halliwell (London: Bloomsbury, 1998), VII.

7. *Aristotle's Poetics*, VII.

8. Gotthold Ephraim Lessing, *Laocoön: An Essay on the Limits of Poetry and Painting*, trans. Edward Allen McCormick (Baltimore: Johns Hopkins University Press, 1984), 78.

9. Joshua Reynolds, *Discourses on Art* (New Haven, CT: Yale University Press, 1975), 60.

10. Reynolds, *Discourses on Art*, 146.

11. Michael Fried, "Art and Objecthood," *Artforum* 5 (1967): 12–23; Martin Puchner, *Stage Fright: Modernism, Anti-Theatricality, and Drama* (Baltimore: Johns Hopkins University Press, 2011).

12. Fried, "Art and Objecthood"; Clement Greenberg, "Modernist Painting," in *The New Art: A Critical Anthology*, ed. Gregory Battcock (New York: E. P. Dutton, 1973), 68–69.

13. Genette, "The Architext," 210–18; Frye, "The Mythos of Summer," 98–117.

14. Benjamin H. D. Buchloh, "Conceptual Art, 1962–1969: From the Aesthetic of Administration to the Critique of Institutions," *October* 55 (1990): 105–43; *Aristotle's Poetics*, VII.

15. Shawn-Marie Garrett, "The Awkward Age: New York's New Experimental Theater," *Theater* 31, no. 2 (May 2001): 45–53.

16. Garrett, "The Awkward Age," 45–46.

17. Richard Maxwell, "Richard Maxwell (Interview)," interview by David Velasco, *Artforum*, April 25, 2012, https://www.artforum.com/interviews /richard-maxwell-talks-about-his-new-work-in-the-2012-whitney-biennial -30817.

18. Richard Maxwell in residence at Whitney, "Untitled," audio guide, April 25, 2012.

19. Maxwell, "Richard Maxwell (Interview)."

20. Maxwell, "Richard Maxwell (Interview)."

21. David Levine, Marsha Ginsberg, Jason Grote, and Amy Holzapfel, "The Habit of Realism (Interview)," *Theater* 42, no. 1 (2012): 95–107.

22. Levine et al., "The Habit of Realism," 99.

23. Tresca Weinstein, "David Levine's 'Habit' at Mass Moca," *Times Union*, February 26, 2011, https://blog.timesunion.com/localarts/david-levine%E2 %80%99s-%E2%80%9Chabit%E2%80%9D-mass-moca-22611/15156/.

24. George Baker, "The Storyteller: Notes on the Work of Gerard Byrne," in *Gerard Byrne: Books, Magazines, and Newspapers* (New York: Lukas and Sternberg, 2003), 7–88.

25. Baker, "Storyteller."

26. Baker, "Storyteller," 33–34.

27. *Gerard Byrne: A State of Neutral Pleasure*, Whitechapel Gallery, January 7 to March 18, 2013, http://www.whitechapelgallery.org/exhibitions /gerard-byrne.

28. Baker, "Storyteller."

Chapter 18

Assemblies

Public Participation, Heteronomous Worlds

This chapter's title sounds a range of keywords that might be reassembled in various ways. Public. Assembly. Participation. Heteronomy. World. One might experiment with different ways of deciding which could be adjectives that modify which nouns. My hope is to reflect on concepts of public assembly, setting them off against human-centered and other-than-human–centered ideas of how the arts address a heteronomous world. As is likely clear by this point in the collection, such an interest comes from a range of sources—from an earlier artistic life in the performing arts, from past work on social reform, from my ongoing interest in the relation between aesthetics and politics, and now, more recently, from a range of climate and health struggles on a global scale. Extending the central themes of *Back Stages*, this chapter once again reengages two broad scholarly arenas: (1) The so-called interarts conversation, that is, what it means to place performance within and across visual arts, installation, film, and new media;[1] (2) The social conversation, that is, whether and how the arts can activate a complicated commitment to social justice and the public good. Such political contexts give the theme of assembly a different kind of urgency. As other contributions to this collection make clear, such social and political questions are of course urgent for a range of regions and nations outside the United States as citizens grapple with the changing understandings of what the "public" in public sector might be. Those questions also remain vital and thorny for artistic worlds. They reload inherited debates about the autonomy of the arts, about whether social turns instrumentalize and neutralize art's capacity to imagine otherwise. Questions about sociality and assembly vivify more contemporary debates as well, about whether participatory turns newly activate artistic worlds or whether they evidence art's absorption by the ethos of post-Fordist service. I will start with a renewed meditation on performance as an interart topic and then move into an excavation of the keyword "assembly." From there, I will endeavor to join both trajectories in some reflections on public participation as a structure for socially engaged art practice, moving to the theatrical art project *City Council Meetings* as a case study. Having focused on the limited agency of human political actors, I will then turn to another site and a new assemblage, the posthumanist challenge of climate aesthetics, using projects from the 2019 Venice Biennial to focus discussion. Throughout, an emphasis on performance allows us to foreground aesthetic process as well as the world-making power of assemblage; moreover, those made worlds—public, private, civic, and environmental—depend on the productive power of enactment and reenactment to come into being. That said, a turn to climate exposes anthropocentric conceptions of performance, especially the human-centered assumptions of its enactment. Shared worlds depend on politically deliberative gathering, but they also depend on other kinds of responsive enactments when toxic assemblages arise unbidden on the sentient inhabitants of the planet. Artistic responses in all these situations will often walk fine lines between the functional and the formal, the activist and the abstract, the intelligible and the eccentric. Performance's future life might well hinge on the ability to walk that walk.

Performance and Assembly

Throughout *Back Stages* I have placed my thinking amid a large group of scholars who think continually about bodies, language, spectacle, sound, time, and space in ever new combinations. That context has become newly energized and estranged by performance experiments that are sited not only in theaters but also in visual art galleries, biennials, museums, installations, plazas, parks, community centers, and other site-specific locations. As those contexts have proliferated, we have seen tremendous variance in how such practices are produced and received. Former sculptors have different assumptions than do theater practitioners about what it means to mobilize bodies, language, spectacle, sound, time, and space. Painters differ from choreographers in their approach to time. Meanwhile, the curators and producers of all these forms have learned new skill sets to support hybrid experiments—aesthetically, institutionally, politically.

In exploring keywords and phrases in this chapter, we have an opportunity to broach issues of art, participation, social justice, and publicness with renewed emphasis. But this chapter also allows a climate perspective to unsettle humanistic assumptions of volition and autonomy that have undergirded my conceptions of performance for most of my career. Let's start a keyword excavation. First, we might note that the keywords "assembly" and "assemblage" have a range of etymological associations. I'll foreground seven.

1. A bringing or coming together
2. A gathering of persons for the purposes of deliberation and decision

3. A work of art consisting of miscellaneous objects fastened together
4. In a line, a series of workers and machines in a factory by which a
   succession of identical items is progressively assembled
5. In schools, a general gathering of staff and pupils
6. An archaeological site of found fossils
7. A posthuman biopolitical formation developed in the context of
   critical theory

These associations are wide and varied and provide a range of prompts for refining our understanding of how performance assembles and propels the social world. Such worlds are of course interested in knowing (to take number one) how to bring people and things together, or how to endure their coming together in ways that are often unexpected. We might consider in number three, the artistic genealogy of assembly; assemblage—from Jean Dubuffet to Robert Rauschenberg to Romare Bearden to Betye Saar—denotes an aesthetic practice of combination and juxtaposition, a way of bringing multiple perspectives and forms into the same space. As such, assemblage undergirds a genealogy of modern and contemporary aesthetics. Pushing ahead, "the assembly line" is a central image from industrial labor history. It brings to mind an image of work that has arguably been changed by a postindustrial shift in the nature of labor; the purported shift from Fordism to post-Fordism tracks a move from the production of commodity objects to the monetization of services and experiences. As such, the twenty-first-century assembly line of experiential labor coincides with a supposed turn to participation and immaterial service. Meanwhile, the school assembly—a general gathering of staff and pupils for teaching, disciplining, training, and perhaps inspiring—is also a familiar image, one being defamiliarized now as the nature of "school" is reassembled by twentieth-first-century pedagogies, online technologies, and privatization strategies. The associations of the archaeological assemblage of found fossils recall earlier chapters on the historiographical act, as well as on what it means to reenact the past. Finally, the more recent theoretical elaboration of assemblage in climate aesthetics and biopolitical scholarship threatens to upend the formal and phenomenological assumptions of all the above—more on that upending in the last part of this essay.

All those associations are resonant, but it is the second association on which I will linger first, as it foregrounds the social and political dimensions of assembly. A *gathering* of persons for the purposes of *deliberation* and *decision*. Here of course is the definition most associated with the long tradition of democratic social theory. Such democratic assemblies might take shape as protest (a space of gathering), as the public sphere (a space of deliberation), or in governmental bodies (a place of decision). Indeed, when I first started to think about public (re)assembly, I wanted to explore the relation between protest and governance. What does it mean to assemble in public in the twentieth-first century (pre- and post-COVID)? Furthermore, what does it mean to assemble public-sector systems? The first question is not obviously related to the second. One might ask if and when there is a relation between the public appearance of the former and the systematic operations of the latter. To take up the first question is to invoke the long history of reflection about protest and the public sphere, especially about the physical appearance and arrangement of bodies in real time and copresent public space. Within social theory, to assemble in public is to recall both the *embrace* and the *condemnation* of this appearance, embraced as a key element of so-called democratic process and condemned as an unruly take-over by the "masses."[2] In her *Notes Toward a Performative Theory of Assembly*, Judith Butler recalls the ambivalence among thinkers of all political persuasions about whether and how such assemblies index "the people" and whether they index a "populism" to be celebrated or a "populism" to be castigated.[3] Butler cites Ernesto Laclau and Chantal Mouffe to reinforce her argument that any appeal to "the people" as such depends on a "constitutive exclusion" of who is not recognized within the assembly or who is rightly or wrongly represented by said assembly.[4] So too attributions of "democracy" or the "democratic power" of any gathering shift depending on one's tacit alignment with the principles and symbols of the gathering; what looks like brainwashed populism from one vantage point is heralded as democracy in action from another. For Butler, however, an assembly is most specifically "performative" in a different sense, that is, by virtue of its power as an "act of delimitation," an act of both exclusion and inclusion. The performativity of assembly "establishes a fundamental problem of democracy even as—or precisely when—it furnishes its key term, 'the people.'" Like an Austinian speech act that does things with words,[5] Butler highlights the world-making power of assembly to produce a "people" that it simultaneously appears to describe and which it can never fully include.

But assemblies are performative in other ways that invoke not only the rhetorical sense of the performative but also the physical and aesthetic sense of performance. This means returning to the physicality of assembly, the appearance of bodies in real time and space, with roles assigned or assumed, sometimes with appropriate infrastructure for managing safety, crowd flow, and sightlines, as well as its durational unfolding. In my past work on the relationship between performance and socially engaged art, this infrastructural sense of performance is what I often emphasized. Notably, Butler brings this orientation to bear on her understanding of what it means to "assemble in public," an orientation that takes seriously the physicality of "a concerted bodily enactment" next to their rhetorical effects.[6] Here it is worth sharing a longer quote:

> After all, there is an indexical force of the body that arrives with
> other bodies in a zone visible to media coverage: it is *this* body,
> and *these* bodies, that require employment, shelter, health care,
> and food, as well as a sense of a future that is not the future of
> unpayable debt; it is *this* body, or *these* bodies, or bodies *like* this
> body or these bodies, that live the condition of an imperiled liveli-
> hood, decimated infrastructure, accelerating precarity.[7]

I linger on this passage from Butler because here we might find a possible
answer to my earlier questions. Once again, "What does it mean to assemble in public in our present moment? And what does it mean to assemble
public-sector systems? Is there a relation between the public appearance
of the former and the systematic operations of the latter?" Here Butler
suggests that there is an acute and urgent relationship between the former
and the latter. The bodily assembly in public in fact provokes awareness
of public sector systems, the need for access to such systems to sustain
the lives of those bodies. The immediate, physical appearance signals its
dependence on social systems, the need for access to them. As someone
who has devoted a substantial portion of her scholarly and administrative
career to isolating such moments of systemic awareness, this perceived
link is music to my ears. If only it were always true that bodily assembly
provoked awareness in fellow citizens about everyone's need for access
to health care, employment, shelter, food, and free education. But does
it? Does it always? Indeed, for many, is not the arrival of bodily assembly
greeted with shock (and awe), disdain, even disgust, and, at the very least,
annoyed feelings of inconvenience? Do they really have to block my way
to work?, asks the inconvenienced citizen (who has a job). Do they really
have to stop my path to the grocery store, school, or the doctor? (Are they
at risk of contaminating me, asks the COVID-sheltered citizen, one who
might also be deciding whether to join or to repudiate local and global
gatherings for racial equality and social justice?)

Let's return one more time to other parts of this definition.
Having thought about the performativity of gathering, the middle term—
deliberation—connects assembly to the goals of the liberal public sphere,
as Jürgen Habermas and his critics elaborated it.[8] It suggests that the
assembled gathering is indeed a place to share perspectives and disagree-
ments, and to reconcile the aspirations and demands of varied citizens and
varied constituents. Decision, however, takes us elsewhere, certainly when
set within the context of democratic governance. In such a context, decision might imply the institution of a new process, new law, new regulation,
new binding agreement. And, once again, this is where we also find an
interesting dialectic between the act of assembling in public and the act of
assembling (and implementing) public-sector systems. For Butler, there is
a recursive and transitory relationship between the physical assembly and

the decisions and power they have on something like "government." In speaking about the Occupy movement or Arab Spring, she notes:

> such enactments are invariably transitory when they remain extra-parliamentary. And when they realize new parliamentary forms, they risk losing their character as the popular will . . . [further] . . . As the popular will persists in the forms it institutes, it must fail to lose itself in those forms if it is to retain the right to withdraw its support from any political form that fails to maintain legitimacy.[9]

Dissatisfaction with the law or governmental processes—whether the laxity of its regulation or the restrictions of its regulation—prompt the desire to assemble, which in turn might evolve a new law or governmental processes, which in turn might create new dissatisfactions, which might in turn prompt new acts of public assembly, new strikes, new lockouts. However abstract, the effort is to ensure that the popular will not "lose itself" in its "instituted" forms. But what does that mean? When citizens worry about losing themselves in institutions, that concern is often read as a concern to avoid one's own bureaucratization, to ensure that the spirited expression of the people's will remains alive and lively *against* governmental regulation. Understanding and largely appreciating that interpretation, I myself have been more interested to explore how the people's will might remain alive and lively *in* regulation—that is, in the public forms they institute. When and how do people see themselves in their instituted public forms? And is it possible for them to see themselves there more?

For me, this is the moment that art comes in; this is where performance comes in. Many of my past preoccupations can be recast as participatory projects that use the arts to enliven our relation to the institutions that keep us alive; such publicly engaged art projects have a chance of resensitizing citizens to their public systems, to the "will" behind and within their instituted forms. This is space where the heteronomous condition of the embedded citizen becomes a problem of form. In *Social Works,* I shared some of my favorite examples of such publicly reassembled art and performance work.[10] For instance, feminist artist Mierle Laderman Ukeles began her artistic career washing museums to foreground the labor that kept a museum running; she then went on to become a semi-permanent artist-in-residence with New York's sanitation department to foreground the labor that keeps the city running. In *Touch Sanitation* (1979–80) she shook the hands of all five thousand sanitation workers in New York City's five boroughs saying, "thank you for keeping New York City alive." Or in *Social Mirror* (1983) she perched a mirror on the side of a moving garbage truck, inviting fellow citizens to see themselves reflected, literally, in their public-sector system. Over the last decade, of course, we have seen a variety of new participatory genres with complex political stakes. The forms and formats of Occupy were most resonant for how they instilled liveliness within newly instituted forms, including the general assembly and its human microphone, as well as DIY social institutions—pop-up public kitchens, libraries, and daycares—that doubled as public art.

In addition to exploring artists who enter systems of public service, we could also cite examples of public servants who deploy aesthetic practices. Take the feted career of the former mayor of Bogotá, Antanas Mockus. This mathematician, philosopher, and son of an artist ran for mayor, won, and proceeded to engage the city as, he said, "a 6.5 million person classroom."[11] At the time, the corruption, violence, and incivility of Bogotá was perceived by some to be on the verge of chaos, unfixable. Mockus responded by using aesthetic humor to activate a different citizen consciousness. He put on a Superman costume and acted as a superhero: "Supercitizen." Faced with extreme traffic, gridlock, accidents, Mockus responded by hiring 420 mimes to control traffic in dangerous streets. Mimes poked fun at reckless drivers. Mimes followed pedestrians who ignored stoplights, shaking their fingers and mocking their every move. Mockus called his cultural strategy "a pacifist counterweight . . . with neither words nor weapons, the mimes were doubly unarmed. My goal was to show the importance of cultural regulations."[12] And, as he further described, "in a society where human life has lost value, there cannot be greater priority than reestablishing respect for life as the main right and duty of citizens."[13] Traffic fatalities dropped by more than half during this period. Another time, Mockus asked citizens to put their civic power to use with 350,000 "thumbs-up" and "thumbs-down" cards, distributed by his office to the populace. The cards were meant to approve or disapprove of other citizens' behavior; people actively and peacefully used them in the streets. Such mechanisms allowed individual citizens to leverage their relationship to law and government in exchanges with each other; that is, it allowed citizens to reconsider their living relation to "instituted forms." It dispersed that power to a range of people, turning everyday events into miniassemblies, that is, minigatherings for tacit and explicit deliberation. This participatory form had systemic stakes, allowing citizens to reconfirm or object to societal decision-making over the norms by which individuals would interact with each other. Mockus's ideas of citizenship culture exemplifies of course a normative tendency. But in his participatory culture, the attempt was to restitch something like the popular "will" of the people—their emotions and desires—to public governance. Extraparliamentary practices did not simply offer a counter to parliamentarian process; they served as a vehicle for reperforming and negotiating regulation, spontaneously and eccentrically. Participatory aesthetics were deployed by "the people" as a vehicle for reckoning with the effectiveness or not of the "forms they had instituted."

Civic Participation

They, I mean we, meet every two months in the large assembly room inside the offices of the Berkeley Unified School District. They, I mean we, start to trickle in to find a seat among the rows of folding chairs placed on lino-leum floors under fluorescent lights while in front of us they—though it could be we—take their seats in front of the tables placed on the portable stage set up for the evening. They don't look at us, even though we look at them, as they arrange their papers and microphones and as the clerk calls the meeting to order. And the meeting is off and running, or off and stumbling, as minutes are shared, as motions to approve are seconded, as the group, on and off the portable stage, recalls the finer parts of Robert's Rules of Order.[14] *"Point of order," someone might call from the sidelines. "Excuse me, you can't call point of order now," says someone else. And we putter along, managed by the city council "agenda" and its underwhelm-ing plot plodding along, punctuated by occasional thumps of a gavel when a motion is carried. As if something happened, as if the motion carried us, as if the motion has changed us in some way, a decision made that has changed our ways of operating in the world.*

I'm there—we are there—for the big event which is a vote to install a 1% tax on private development to support the arts in the city of Berkeley. When the agenda tells us that it's time to deliberate, I, and others not on the portable stage, line up as we planned to do in front of a microphone. Two go ahead of me and speak to express quickly their support of the measure—and then cede the rest of their three minutes to me. By the time I get up, I have five extra minutes attached to my three to share a prepared statement about the importance of the arts to the vitality of the city. I attempt to make eye contact with those on the portable stage. Two stare at their paperwork, and I try to will them to look up as I speak. I feel like I'm doing a scene study in acting class. I have my objective, and they are my obstacle.

I recall this scene as an exhibit in the mundane process of public assem-bly in part because I was prompted to recall this kind of scene when I first learned about Mallory Catlett, Jim Findlay, and Aaron Landsman's *City Council Meeting* series. Thereafter, I always recalled their project, every time I returned to the scene of my own city council meetings (I was a cultural commissioner for the City of Berkeley for five years). *City Council Meeting* reenacted transcripts from actual city council meetings in each US city it toured—including New York, Tempe, Houston, and San Francisco. In advance of arriving, they created a team of participants to decide on the arc of the evening, welcoming a larger audience to become participants in a wider process of local engagement. I am interested in this project not necessarily because it is the most exciting performance one

Fig. 20. Aaron Landsman, *City Council Meeting*, HERE Arts Center, New York, 2013.
Photograph by David A Brown / dabfoto creativ.

could imagine, but to ask about the speculative effects of this reenacted
process. What happens when the abstracting, conceptual frames of reenactment are brought to the daily rituals and civic systems? What happens
when the critical consciousness of a reenactment frame is brought to the
mundane and repetitively unfurling operations of public life, of public sector life? These are public sector and civic processes that sustain our lives,
keep our parks going, or distribute resources. What is the role, one might
ask, of role-play in this process, especially when those on each side of a
council meeting's portable stage assume the position of those on the other?

City Council Meeting are performance spaces where participants reenact and sometimes reinterpret the behaviors and rituals of city governance.
To describe in brief, the performed reenactments of *City Council Meeting*
are divided into three parts. Participants first enter an anteroom, where an
orientation video mimics the ritual entry of US courts and governmental
venues: one hears instructions about showing identification, where to line
up, how to prepare, etc. Instead of those instrumental instructions, in *City
Council Meeting* audience members are introduced to theories of democracy from Plato to Aristotle, informed by a bit of Jacques Rancière. In the
second section, everyday citizens are cast as council-meeting characters,
reading from the scripted transcripts from actual government meetings.
The final section opens the dialogue to create opportunities for reflecting
on what was just performed; it is conceived differently each time with

local artists and collaborating community members. When viewers arrive, they are given a choice of what role they want to play, that is, how they want to participate. They can be a counselor and read the meeting; they can be a speaker and say a piece of testimony ("I have a claim"); they can be a supporter who does not necessarily have to say anything; or they can be a bystander. Once the meeting starts, a local group of artists (the staffers) push the performance along. Staffers act as a kind of run crew throughout the performance and also keep performers on book as they go.

This project came about because Aaron Landsman was asked by a friend to attend a city hall meeting—or, as he said, he was "dragged" to it. He was told that the council would discuss a zoning issue that was going to be "really hot." In the midst of the mundanity, fumblings, and passing of the papers, an event arose that, for Landsman, exemplified the political theatricality of civic assembly: a man came forward to complain about the state of the park in which he was living. He dumped the contents of a bag on the stage before the city council members; it was filled with drug paraphernalia, used condoms, and trash that he had picked up on the park's playground. There was a flurry of activity and shock among council members who asked to have the stage cleaned and for the man to leave. Council members decided to suspend the meeting because he had created a public health hazard. To this, the visiting citizen responded, "thank you for making my point better than I could have." It was in this moment that Landsman decided to "create some theater" out of civic processes, deploying the theatricality of artistic assembly to redynamize connection to political assembly. For Landsman, "It seemed as if every city and almost every meeting, there is some apparently innocuous issue that gives way to more fundamental rifts, which start to come forward and energize a community to think about how it wants to be regulated."[15] Akin to Mockus's citizenship culture, Landsman sought to enliven the relation to instituted forms.

The revelation provides one kind of answer to my earlier questions—about the possible connection between assembling in public and the assembly of public-sector systems, and about how to ensure that the "extraparliamentary" popular will does not "lose itself" in parliamentary forms. If *City Council Meeting*'s theatrical reenactments propelled a process of reenergizing the popular will in relation to its instituted forms, it did so via the form of participatory role-play. "The issues we use in our transcripts are often chosen in order to make sure that people think about the form."[16] The form and, as Landsman also says, the "structures of participation," are reactivated so that people become differently attentive to those forms. Participants might find themselves reconnecting affectively, and oddly, with *Robert's Rules of Order*, or other protocols for deliberation and decision-making. Civic meetings, collective bargaining, public deliberation, collective agreements—all those public processes have their protocols, repeated again and again over time. They become so familiar that citizens stop noticing their formal character. In swapping roles and in staging reenactments, however, the ritual of assembly, became newly visible, newly urgent. Said one participant: "I found the experience of being mayor for one hour empowering. We can feel so defeated by the world around us, thinking we are powerless to change our environment. Taking a careful serious look at how the guts of a city work is a good thing to do. These are the very politics that matter most to our lives."[17] That is one testimonial, but it is useful next to concepts of political governance. Reenactment allowed an enlivened relation to a civic culture of participation, in part by reminding us that anyone could play anyone else's role. Robert's Rules. Motions made, motions carried. Interruptions and points of order. Whether reenacting the civic or reassembling the public sector, such practices shared in the attempt to animate the hardened repetitions of public systems, reminding us that such systems were and might be central to the maintenance of an equitable and democratic life. Can the "popular will" still see itself in the collective organizing, civic meetings, traffic regulation, and the parliamentary regulations it institutes? Can "the people" engage in a process for reimagining these processes anew? By joining performance to the productive repetitions of participatory assembly, such heteronomously conceived public art might provide vehicles for future speculation, for imagining the life cycle of public systems and for participating in systems that keep us alive.

Performance, Climate, Assemblage

Systems that keep us alive. As noted in my introduction to *Back Stages*, so much of my work—as scholar, teacher, administrator, and public servant—has focused on art's capacity to bring public systems to visibility. I continue to believe in the necessity of enlivened engagement with such systems. And yet, as the effects of climate degradation unfurl, as barely perceptible viruses expose the tangles of global connection (and contagion), one has to ask anew what systemic visibility actual entails. How to conceive relations among public decision-making, private behavior, and the vast temporal and spatial scales of an eroding planet? How to propel accountability in a situation where the interface between human responsibility and geological process shifts each day? In her critique of Judith Butler's conception of assembly, McKenzie Wark tacitly proposes such questions, worrying that a focus on the activation of "the people" risks excluding posthuman forms of agential action. "Is there a way to let in the co-presence of non-humans," asks Wark, "even the non-living?"[18] How, after the Anthropocene, does one conceive agency within a space that requires a decentering of inflated conceptions of human agency? It becomes a challenge to sensitize humans to their planetary embeddedness when the scale of that embedding is barely fathomable, much less affectively available.

Here I am in October 2019 in Berkeley, writing in anticipation of November 2019 in Berlin. Or, trying to write. Along with the usual temptations to procrastination—a slew of unanswered emails, list making, household chores—I have other obstacles that keep me from writing. Dry winds and hot fires spiral near me and my perch in Berkeley, California. PG&E— Pacific Gas and Electric—has serially turned off power in selected regions of Northern and Southern California. The threat to cut off service, the trees outside, the power lines outside, my daughter inside, my dog inside, the fiction of an inside and outside to the house I own, or think I own (with a bank); my work, my paralysis in the face of work—all conspire to produce a curious assemblage around me, with me, inside of me, occupying and preoccupying me.

My daughter and I brace ourselves, trying not to open the refrigerator, doing one last load of laundry, downloading documents that won't be accessible when we lose WiFi. But miraculously, and oddly, the power does not go out in our house—we are told it will go out in six hours, then twelve hours, then tomorrow. It is a curious state to be in, poised over a cooktop that could turn off any minute; fingers lingering over keys on a computer that has a little time left. I keep thinking I need to be extra productive for my last few minutes of power, a last few minutes that keep on . . . lasting. I cook, wash, and sometimes write with a strange sense of guilt, shame that I can still do these tasks, shame that I am not doing more. How could one procrastinate in a state of impending emergency? It was a curious kind of survivor's guilt; what would I do with the undeserved time I had, with my undeserved power. How could I not have the energy to work when I still had a supply of energy, undeservedly, from PG&E?

The assemblage prompts me to recall another moment when I felt this odd mix of dread and guilt, of cozy pleasure inside sequestered from a harsh landscape outside. Another moment that reproduced the fiction of inside and outside. It was upon entering a former military hanger in Venice, the eccentric site of the Lithuanian Pavilion's artificial beach, which invited the question whether and how we know a beach to be natural. Skilled singers lay prone on the beach, alternating between choral and ballad songs in international English. Part religious hymn, part gossipy aria, part sunscreen advertisement, part parodic climate science news, the

Fig. 21. Performance of the opera *Sun_Sea (Marina)* by Rugilė Barzdžiukaitė, Vaiva Grainytė, and Lina Lapelytė, 2019. Lithuanian Pavilion at the fifty-eighth Venice Biennial. Photograph by Andrej Vasilenko. © courtesy of the artists.

libretto of *Sun & Sea (Marina)* (2019) rose up the rafters as an ode to a warming planet. I was one of many viewers who waited in a long line outside to watch this opera from above. Laconic relationality observed from on high, compounding the sanctioned voyeurism of the beach. *Sun & Sea (Marina)* made climate politics disconcertingly palatable. An assemblage of bodies, song, props, set, stones, and time, a happening at a high-end biennial, off-site but still near the Prada store, adjacent to all the large cruise ships dripping oil in the Mediterranean Sea under the Mediterranean sun. A combination of feelings arose here at *Sun & Sea (Marina)*—feelings of guilt and dread, threat and comfort; of time eroding and time stolen; of energy extracted, of energy withdrawn, energy wasted, and energy undeservedly expelled. Insidious pleasure on the exhausted earth. My friend and I lingered for a long time, like everyone else who had waited hours to see this piece. Our fellow attendees were crying, sniffling, sighing around me. I didn't cry, but I was moved. Later that afternoon, my friend and I kept our plan to go to the beach, to the Lido, lying amid a torrent of blue umbrellas so numerous it was hard to see the sand of that artificial beach. More insidious pleasure on an exhausted earth. We felt badly about it.

I now carry both these scenes with me to reflect about the paradoxes of assemblage aesthetics, especially as it upends inherited ideas of autonomy (descended from a philosophical concept of self-governance) as opposed to those of heteronomy (associated with functional forms governed by external rules). This conjunction has connotations outside the realm of aesthetics, of course, in the lay conception of the autonomous individual and even the democratic citizen—the one who thinks she is an autonomous, self-governing property owner of her own house (with a bank). She lives amid its insides and outsides, installed on the California land of the native Ohlone people with trees and streets, quakes and fires, and power—power outages and power lines, economic power and political power—all around her. Continuing on, we can then hear this formal debate continue in the second, artworld scene, the context of an historic blockbuster biennial that traffics fitfully around discourses of autonomous art, one that motors and is motored by the heteronomy of the art market's interest in buyable artwork, even if the biennial form, and certainly the forms at the Lithuanian Pavilion, deploy expanded art practices that are hard to hang on a wall. *Sun & Sea (Marina)* is certainly hard to hang on a wall, and in such a context, an eight-hour performance installation seems relatively heteronomous in its expansiveness and in the range of external rules it navigates.

I now want to think about these assemblies and scene settings, these sun-shining and sun-setting scenes, next to a larger question of what happens when climate politics and climate art are placed inside (and outside) our conceptions of autonomy and assembly. When moving ideas of assembly to this expanded if inconsistently fathomable context, I find myself wondering about the effects of aesthetic recombination, especially since climate scholars increasingly use the language of assemblage to name ecological recombination. How specifically does the climate question interface with the ongoing efforts to join aesthetics and politics? How, moreover, does climate assemblage expose the limits of a human-centered model of political agency in any theory of democratic assembly?

Let's start a new scene then, one that is admittedly inseparable from the previous one, by trotting through some of the key turns and key sites in an ever-expanding discourse of climate aesthetics, environmental art, ecological art. In the United States, T. J. Demos is a leading figure called on to make and remake a genealogy of practice and thinking. He often starts with the American context in the 1960s and 1970s, including Hans Haacke's *Grass Grows* (1969); Newton Harrison's *The Slow Birth and Death of a Lily Cell* (1968); and Alan Sonfist's *Time Landscape of New York City* (proposed in 1965 and realized in 1978). A pivotal exhibition moment came in 1969 at Cornell University's gallery, one that included land art by Hans Haacke, Robert Smithson, Dennis Oppenheim, and Robert Morris. Such art practices coincided with discursive practices, including those that joined reflections on the earth's life systems with critiques of US politics on Vietnam, race relations, and gender relations, such as Rachel Carson's *Silent Spring* (1962) and Paul Ehrlich's *The Population Bomb* (1968). Most of this making and thinking engaged in a kind of restorationist eco-aesthetics, art that attempted to repair damaged habitats or to revive degraded ecosystems. In Sonfist's *Time Landscape of New York City*, Helen and Newton Harrisons' *Portable Orchard* (1972), Haacke's *Rhinewater Purification Plant* (1972), Agnes Denes's *Wheatfield—A Confrontation* (1982), Joseph Beuys's *7000 Oaks* (1982), and Mel Chin's *Revival Field* (1990), each of these pieces variously attempted to rescue natural environments from polluted conditions. Demos credits Gregory Bateson with complicating a discourse that threatened to objectify or romanticize a threatened nature in his 1972 book *Steps to an Ecology of Mind*.[19] There, Bateson argued that ecology is natural, but also social and technological, wherein ecological "health" is understood to be dependent on civilization. We might note on the side that Bateson is also a key socioanthropological interlocutor for the field of performance studies, a reminder that perhaps our field has been growing a tacit climate discourse for some time.

Bateson's idea of "systems ecology" echoes those of others who have developed climate discourses and climate art practices that join the technological, political, natural, cultural, and scientific into eco-aesthetic interventions. Indeed, one can start to plot a tangled genealogy of climate practice that increasingly pulls and pushes vectors of power and sectors of practice, pulling and pushing what may appear to be discreet and autonomous disciplinary practice into new combinations. Such combinations juxtapose social issues like migration with geological trends such as rising sea levels. Such combinations remind us, as Kathryn Yusoff says in *A Billion Black Anthropocenes or None*, that the institution of slavery and the wide-scale practice of resource extraction share the same origin moment.[20] Whether in matters of housing, transportation, labor policies, gender relations, or generational relations, it is increasingly understood that climate is part and parcel of every identifiable sociopolitical issue, undergirding it, surrounding it, inside it. This is where the language of assemblage starts to appear—not only to mark the assembly of media and perspective—but also the assemblage of sectors and the collapse of perceptual divisions between background and foreground, up and down.

Since I have been interested in recombining sectors, disciplines, objects, people, power throughout *Back Stages*, let's press further on how climate discourse and eco-art engage in hyperpractices of recombination, using the word *assemblage* now with a twentieth-first-century tuning of what that keywords means. Assemblage is a word loosely associated with new materialism and biopolitical critique, often used in contexts critical of neoliberalism and climate destruction. It signals a dispersed relation, a molecular aesthetics, a condition of involuntary and voluntary political horizontality, and a lateralized network of connection among things, species, systems, and the sentient entities often still known as "humans." Let me share here some reductive but teachable frames that I often use to convey aesthetically the conceptual shift such assemblages might entail. One would be to focus on the critique of the Anthropocene and the formal upheaval that such a critique implies. One formal upheaval appears when we consider the figure-ground relation, that is, a dialectic that elevates the primacy of the human figure in relation to a background (or backstage) relation. As art historians and performance historians such as Alan Braddock and Laura Levin have elaborated, the naturalization of that centralized and powerful human figure has environmental, feminist, and native implications.[21] It installs a viewer into a particular mode of apprehension, one that elevates culture over nature, human over nonhuman, people over planet, and the individuated figure over all forms of ground. If, however, a critique of the Anthropocene seeks to decenter the human as the central figure in a frame, it has the cascading effect of unhinging and dispersing all conceptions of ground. When that thought structure dissolves, what else dissolves with it? What happens when that human figure comes to understand her porosity and interdependence with the background and all systems that she erroneously assumed to be outside herself?

Another teachable way of framing this thought structure, and its unstructuring, is to remind ourselves of the Family of Man, or the phylogenic tree. Arguably, this absurd hierarchy undergirds our perceptions of reality, which is to say that it undergirds our perceptions of what it means to be a democratic citizen engaged with the world, what it means to be pragmatic and committed, what it means to be "functional" in the world. And yet, what do we do when this tacitly experienced hierarchy dissolves and disperses underneath us, around us, inside of us? Wark asks a similar question of Butler's human-centered theories of ethical assembly: "This line of thought tends from the human toward the Gods. It doesn't much tend in the other direction. The unchosen ethical obligation starts with the human and might be extended to other forms of life. And the ethical call of other forms of life is modeled on that of human life."[22] How to model an ethical call differently? If ethics and equity have tacitly modeled themselves on a hierarchy that places humans in league with the gods, we will likely need artists, thinkers, organizers, and everyday citizens to imagine, however eccentrically, a lateral relationship among the elements of what can no longer be an upright tree. What does it mean to make art from— and a daily life from—an imagination that sees the previously feted human in a lateral relationship with the insects or the stone? To see the monkey next to, not above, a layer of lichen? What happens when we take all these vaguely sentient and lively elements of the planet and hoist our sails (and wings) to those of the angels? Imagine placing an ant next to an angel for a recalibrating, reassembling, conversation. If this is the recalibration of reality that a climate politics requires, then eco-art might provide the shifting ground for staging that conversation.

And indeed, turning to the philosophical discourses of climate and eco-art from the late twentieth to the twentieth-first century, we see a constant lateralizing of what social theorists conventionally thought hierarchical, horizontalizing so much of what is often fathomed as vertical. Start with Felix Guattari along with Bruno Latour nearby. We could remind ourselves that in Guattari's *Three Ecologies* (1986) he imagined reassembly as transversality; Guattari perceived a general rift between "deterritorializing revolutions linked to scientific, technical, and artistic development," and "a compulsion toward subjective reterritorialization."[23] Through new technological advances, he foresaw "new emancipatory social practices and, above all, alternative assemblages of subjective production capable of connecting—on a mode different than that of conservative reterritorialization—to the molecular revolutions of our era."[24] It was in this text that Guattari referred to a concept of a "generalized ecology." And then, of course, we have Latour at his side, winning new accolades in that supporting role, to elaborate the concept of the thing, where a thing is described as a collective or "assemblage of relations, interests, values and human—as well as non-human—actors," a "leveling of the so-called human and non-human."[25] Latour has more recently asked us to dissolve the ideological and geological perspective that we feel and see when we continue to imagine our Earth as a blue sphere, a flat blue sphere, and to realize that this functional, pragmatic visualization of our world is actually a two-dimensional abstraction. Latour has asked for a different abstraction of our planet to do the very belated work of repairing it.

Repair. Hmmm, that sounds quite functional, possibly volitional, possibly necessary for parliamentary and extraparliamentary process. Would we even know what that could be? Probably not yet, but for now let's list an abridged inventory of the many conceptual moves made by climate philosophers who have evolved an assemblage imagination, a domain in which autonomous systems converge and where intelligible modes of apprehending it are dispelled. Let's see what happens when heteronomous social practice propels the goals of autonomous, artistic thinking. What words do critics give to a dispersal of forms in lateral rather than hierarchical relation? We find Mike Davis calling for an aestheticized geology in *Dead Cities and Other Tales*; Isabelle Stengers discussing an "ecology of practices" on *Cosmopolitics*; Manuel DeLanda rebuilding political theory as "assemblage theory and social complexity"; Jane Bennett building a new career as a political scientist preoccupied with the "assemblages" of

Vibrant Matter; Nabil Ahmed opining on the entanglements of an "Entangled Earth"; Timothy Morton offering "Mesh" as a netted metaphor in *Ecological Thought* that lateralizes that phylogenic tree; Gustav Metzger recalling the experiments of the 1960s and 1970s in new form to propel a repertoire of "auto-destructive happenings."[26] All these metaphors take the idea of assemblage to new heights, or new lows, or new axes for imagining dispersal and recombination; reality reordered.

That dispersal and recombination informs aesthetic practices as well—and it has for a while. Jean Dubuffet, the painter known for formal variations of assemblage painting, used to call his assemblage pieces "texturologies," aspiring to paint with the weather. If we explore eco-art practiced throughout the world—often supported by international air travel, such forms mix hemispheric conversations with local ones, mixing media and foregrounding the heteronomous conditions of material. Ice, of course, is a favored material, appearing to disappear in eco-art around the world, and a genre featured to blockbuster effect in Olafur Eliasson's *Ice Watch* (2015) at COP 21, the United Nations Climate Change Conference held in Paris in 2015. Oil is also a favored material, saturating and motoring global art institutions like the Tate, a condition made visceral by Liberate Tate's *Floe Piece* (2012) or *Licence to Spill* (2010). Ursula Biemann's collaboratively conceived platform exemplifies the medium-unspecific swirl of climate reassembly. In *World of Matter* (2013 to present), she and her collaborators seek to produce a database of cases, media clips, and cartographical combinations, ensuring that "video clips . . . can be reconfigured and interlinked to one another, rendering new insights into relations between seemingly distinct resource issues and locations."[27] In this "intricately entangled ecology of things, places and species interactions," *World of Matter* tracks the forces and tendencies and recombinations of a world working against itself.[28]

In taking the temperature, literally, of these warming, rising climate discourses, Emily Apter has to my mind created the most lucid, if ironically underplayed, attempt at a literature review, one that forces a geologic review. Apter adopts the phrase "planetary dysphoria" to describe the linguistic proliferation, mix of metaphors, and grammatically defamiliarized sentences that accompany descriptions of environmental assemblage and reassemblage. Upending figure and ground amid the choking life of a dispersed phylogenic tree, she finds in these tendencies a habit of joining the interscalic disciplines of the geologic with the intimate interpersonal disciplines of the psychoanalytic. She surveys a range of philosophical genealogies, especially German ones, to find a tacit climate discourse awaiting explicit revelation. From German Romanticism through to its leading philosophical lights, she finds this insidious glow, reminding us of Immanuel Kant's graduate thesis on fire, the twists and turns of *Naturphilosophie*, Peter Sloterdijk thinking "psycho-cosmologically,"

Eugene Thacker's *Ungrund* (undergroundedness), Ray Brassier's "vital eschatology" in *Nihil Unbound*.[29] She also surfaces other leading, non-German lights such as Jean-François Lyotard and his anticipation of "solar catastrophe"; Jacques Derrida on "geo-psycho-analysis," Nick Land's "geocosmic theory of trauma," and Robin Mackay's idea of "geo-trauma."[30] The idea of planetary dysphoria describes the effects of a kind of geological melancholia, a splitting of insides and outsides at various scales, of psychic splintering that coincides with the material splintering of rock and the leak of oil. Indeed, says Apter, "Planetary dysphoria captures the geo-psychoanalytic state of the world at its most depressed and *unruhig*, awaiting the triumphant revenge of acid, oil and dust. These elements demonstrate a certain agency: they are sentient materials even if they are not fully licensed subjectivized subjects."[31] Taking these effects back to some of the aesthetic-political queries of *Back Stages*, we might suggest that the heteronomy of planetary catastrophe undoes forms on which a theory of autonomy does not always know it depends. At the same time, an aesthetic theory of autonomy questions received patterns for understanding the world that climate science does not always know it needs. Notably, Apter turns to Wark for a final image of the planet's finale. Referencing Wark's equally defamiliarizing notion of Cyclonopedia, she focuses on what I will call, for my own purposes, the nonfunctional aesthetic qualities of our climate's functional future. Says Wark, "Our permanent legacy will not be architectural, but chemical. After the last dam bursts, after the concrete monoliths crumble into the lone and level sands, modernity will leave behind a chemical signature, in everything from radioactive waste to atmospheric carbon. This work will be abstract, not figurative."[32] Note here that our future will not be imagined or even enacted as an intelligible or referential representation of a destroyed world. Rather it will have the "abstract" look that only a "chemical signature"—not a volitional artist's signature—can provide.

Participatory Performance and the Artworld's Climate

With that inconvenient thought in mind, let's go back to the beach, the space of laconic pleasure and of gossipy denial, where the sand artificially lays in drifts beneath the bodies of hired performers, mixed with the occasional volunteer. Up above, viewer-voyeurs find pleasure and pain in the bodies flattened below. They sniffle in ambiguous grief; they walk devoutly from one side of the balcony to another with a vaguely liturgic gait. This opera-cum-installation-cum-happening was first developed and shown in Lithuania in 2017 in the National Gallery of Art in Vilnius. The work then traveled to Germany, where it was shown in a former movie theater as part of the Staatsschauspiel Dresden theater's repertoire. As a piece that moved from gallery to theater to site-specific biennial, it is thus a performance piece that exemplifies interart interaction, that is, one that is de- and recontextualized by the venue (visual art or theatrical arts) in which it is housed. The key artists are Rugilė Barzdžiukaitė, a filmmaker and theatermaker who serves as director and scenographer for this piece; Vaiva Grainytė, who serves as composer, and Lina Lapelytė as librettist. These three artists work collectively and independently depending on the project. Their earlier hybrid work—*"Have a Good Day!"*—was installed in a grocery/shopping mall in New York City and other places, focusing on the performance of customer service. Each artist has solo projects too; in fact, Barzdžiukaitė's next project is a film on cormorants; perhaps she will eventually stage the ants in song with the angels.

In *Sun & Sea (Marina)*, those sentient beings called humans do the singing, alternating among solo ballads and choral-ensemble scores as this beach day unfolds. Different characters inhabit the beach: curious children, romantic couples, fighting couples, wealthy bourgeois women, entitled male baritones. There are also two dogs; one well behaved and one not. A *Frieze* review is as good as any to dramatize the arc and variation within this performed assembly.

> They sing of passing thoughts, personal tribulations, lovers' conversations, and prophetic warnings of climate change's toll on the earth. . . . "What a relief that the Great Barrier Reef has a restaurant and hotel!" she sings. "We sat down to sip our piña coladas—included in the price!" . . . Their songs of cocktails and sunscreen soon become laced with threat and tragedy: the woman singing her "Song of Complaint" wonders at the lack of snow over Christmas, while a man caught up in a "Philosopher's Commentary" reflects on the Chinese factories that have produced the swimming suits they wear. A pair of identical twins cry over the disappearance of coral life, the extinction of the fish and bees, and muse over the possibilities of a 3D-printed future. Operatic lightness blooms into a transcendental final chorus, bleeding with fantastical imagery and ecological anxiety: "This year the sea is as green as a forest. Eutrophication! Botanical gardens are flourishing in the sea. The water blooms. Our bodies are covered with a slippery green fleece. Our swimsuits are filling up with algae."[33]

While taking in the sun and sea of *Sun and Sea (Marina)* from the frontstage above, more intrigue unfolds in the so-called backstage below, that is, the heteronomous domain of the socioeconomic. As a piece installed at an art biennial outside a theatrical venue, its artists were required to supply a theatrical infrastructure on their own. That infrastructure included set and lights but also the bodies, musically trained bodies reclining on the ground. Unlike the paint, wood, stone, screens, wires, frames, and pedestals of other biennial art, these embodied materials needed housing, food, and a basic wage to compensate for their time. With no funding to support these sentient bodies, the team did what any institutionally autonomous artist group does in our neoliberal era: they started a crowdfunding campaign to do their "project work." Circulated on Indiegogo, the pitch differentiated their work from the biennial's visual art focus, that is, they foregrounded the formal variation of the autonomy-heteronomy dialectic:

> The Biennale usually features static art works (sculptures, paintings, drawings, videos or installations), which require thorough preparation before the opening, and then stay as they are. Our case is different. We are working with a team of over than 30 people and the performers are already learning and practicing their parts. With your support they could sing live at the pavilion from the opening of the Biennale in early May to the end of October.[34]

As funds came in, the pitch became more refined, further ironizing the financialization by calculating the cost of each languishing minute:

> We have calculated that one minute of appearance of *Sun & Sea (Marina)* costs $3 (€2,65), not including the rent of the Pavilion, technical assistance and preparatory expenses. If the equivalent of a cup of coffee would turn into a support by 12,000 people, it would secure the salaries for the singers throughout the duration of the Biennale.[35]

This kind of time-based art had a different kind of pricing; time is money after all. By the time the biennial opened, they had secured enough funds to be able to perform the opera one day a week; every Saturday, the artificial beach included a cast of singing bathers. Upon winning the Golden Lion award, they and a broader public found no small irony in the fact that a blockbuster success could only be fully experienced once a week, so the Indiegogo campaign started up again, eventually allowing them to add a Wednesday performance to the run. Moreover, they found other ways to populate that beach without recourse to extra cash. Using another neoliberal move of a post-Fordist experience economy, they invited volunteer visitors to be part of a "participatory" art event. The invitation read like this:

> If you'd like to be implicated even more literally, you have the chance to participate in the production, . . . organizers are inviting the public lay on the beach alongside the performers. All you need to do is fill out a registration form, select a three-hour time

window, and show up with a bathing suit and towel . . . We will
provide free WiFi and good reading light, the website advises . . .
You are welcome to bring your kids and pets along.[36]

For the rest of the run, trained singers languished next to volunteer performers with their suits and towels. Every other day of the week, the
beach was quiet. Participatory performance thus intermittently enlivened
spectators' relation to the climate politics it staged, and it did so via the
participatory strategies of postindustrial service. The performance walked
on and around some very fine lines—those that divide and join function
and form, intelligibility and abstraction, activation and extraction.

So why was this climate performance piece the climactic success of the
Venice Biennial? And what does that "success" have to say back to the
themes of aesthetics, politics, and assemblage, as they implicated and are
implicated by the dysphoria of environmental politics? Let's start by looking at the dynamics of its reception. Consider how often the piece was
lauded for not adhering to the perceived conventions of climate art, or
more specifically for not capitulating to the literalizing functionality of
climate aesthetics. Reviews contrasted this piece from "ecologically oriented art [that] tends to amplify our sensations in order to enable us to
hear more sharply and see more clearly the scale of the climate crisis and
ecological collapse," celebrating its orientation toward "the quotidian, the
banal."[37] An explicitly and directly titled review made the case for this
work's implicit and indirect aesthetic sensibility. In "It's Hard to Make
Good Art about Climate Change. The Lithuanian Pavilion at the Venice
Biennale Is a Powerful Exception," the reviewer Julia Halperin opined: "So
much art about climate change is bad. It's preachy, literal, unimaginative,
and hung up on aerial shots of floods or topographical maps. By contrast,
Lithuania's pavilion at the Venice Biennale, titled *Sun & Sea (Marina)*, is
a revelation. . . . Unlike most works about climate change, which attempt
to scare you into action but often simply paralyze you with the vastness
of the problem, this performance sinks in by focusing on the mundane."[38]
In other words, this piece was lauded because of its recommitment to
being uncommitted, to refusing the apparent intelligibility of classic eco-
art pieces in favor of oblique aesthetic effects. The piece's curator, Lucia
Pietroiusti, also head of the Serpentine Gallery's climate platform on General Ecology, emphasized this effect, recalling an Adornoian discourse
when she said that aesthetics offers a welcome and essential "nonmoral"
sensibility into what can otherwise be a didactic climate discourse.[39]

Interestingly, though, next to that uncommitted allegiance to the steely
legacies of aesthetic autonomy, the stories of this piece's reception were
emotionally ebullient, sighing, sniffling, weeping, crying, keening in oper-
atic tones that bespeak the attachment, not detachment, of receivers
invested in the piece. Lucia Pietroiusti was struck by that as well, amid the

laconic, ironic performance of noncommitment, audience members were curiously, affectively committed. "Oh my gosh, the art world is having a nervous breakdown," said Pietroiusti. "Why is everyone coming out crying?"[40] And then she and others began to elaborate on what might be undergirding this breakdown: "And then I started to think, 'What do we hold stuck at the back of our throats so close to being released that the tiniest gesture brings it all out?' . . . Why do we hold so much, so close to tears? . . . It's a testament to what art can still do in staying with the trouble, what art can still do in terms of bridging gaps of understanding, gaps of cognition."[41]

Understanding the reaction to this piece must mean understanding this peculiar form of "breakdown." The mix of affect and detachment, anxiety and pleasure, sonic resonance next to cognitive dissonance. Recalling the conceptual tendencies of an assemblage imagination, we might frame *Sun & Sea (Marina)*'s affective landscape as the explosion of geotrauma, a place whether planetary systems and psychoanalytic systems met at the back of the throat. Following Apter, the work and the work's participants found themselves splintered, enduring the breakdown and reassembly of psyche, stone, hearts, and dust that afflict those living with planetary dysphoria. Well, maybe. At the very least, the piece occasioned the mix of metaphors, affects, critiques, and behaviors that seem to appear when a climate consciousness undoes our cognitive mapping, mocking our inherited tools for apprehending the world. In so doing, such forms of eco-art navigate the autonomy-heteronomy dialectic in twentieth-first-century form, deploying art's ability to stay "close with the trouble" and detached from the trouble in the same gasping breath.

Of course, before indulging in what Apter calls the "Goth spiritualism" of such a rhetorical moment, we might also remind ourselves that such a reaction is still dependent on the epistemological, formal, and institutional conditions in which the work is produced. Recalling the hyperembeddedness of performance and "context art," we might consider how the mix of form and medium produces such site-specific effects, especially the siting of a performance ecology in an art ecology. By placing an endurance performance in the midst of an art biennial that "usually features static art," *Sun & Sea (Marina)* created the medium-unspecific conditions of heteronomous rupture. Indeed, perhaps the relative heteronomy of the performance, sited materially and psychically in a scene of historically laconic detachment, in fact produced this geotraumatic ebullience. In doing so, it rode a new habit of artworld celebration as the art biennial grapples with this mixture; this has happened before—in biennials and museums around the world where the embodied, temporal, collective, and emotional forms of performance are received as novel, exceptional, sacrificial. Two years earlier in 2017, the Golden Lion went to Anne Imhoff's German Pavilion, one populated with dancers who crawled and jumped above and below audience members, receivers who waited in long lines to be undone. Later in 2019 at the Lithuanian Pavilion, the enactment of geo-trauma was made possible via medium-unspecific juxtaposition; arguably, medium heteronomy underwrote the perception of this work's strength, lending that strength to the sensitizing goals of climate art. An aesthetic assemblage of "miscellaneous parts" catalyzed the affective imagination of spectators embedded in the toxic assemblages of an eroding planet.

Finally, without overcelebrating or overcritiquing, without romanticiz-ing or raining chemical rain on this parade, the eruption of bodies and affects amid the stones of a military hangar bespeaks the geopsychological effects of eco-art's assemblages. This piece was saturated by the motors of neoliberal economics, including those motoring the large cruise ships docked in the Venice harbor nearby. The volunteer labor of its own par-ticipatory aesthetics is right in line, walking the line. Inviting participants to "implicate" themselves by voluntarily performing as beach-comers, the piece extracted free labor, offering the thrill of participation with the benign dread of self-implication to sustain the performance event. And we were welcome to bring our kids and pets along. Offering another case study in the long Wagnerian and Brechtian debates about culinary and critical effects of a total work of art, the piece also offered us the chance to think more deeply about how the autonomy-heteronomy dialectic oper-ates on different registers in the scene of a warming planet. After all, the eco-imagination here, as well as in the practices and discourses I glossed above, does reframe patterns of intelligibility. Conceptions of dysphoric assemblage are undoing perceptions of up and down, figure and ground, inside and outside, and much more through different reorganizations. We might understand climate assemblages as the heteronomous undo-ing of that which we thought was autonomous. They replace fathomable conceptions of time and origin with geologic temporality; they unhinge received divisions between figure and ground, self and world. They chal-lenge, à la Latour, the spherical visualization of a planet that humans only recently learned to think was round. They deploy a sentient abstraction and a geologic opacity within these rearrangements, thereby enacting the epistemological promise of aesthetic autonomy in eco-forms responsive to the opacities and hyperobjects of the poisoned world we share.

Finally, and to repeat, the heteronomy of planetary catastrophe undoes forms on which a theory of autonomy does not always know it depends. At the same time, an aesthetic theory of autonomy questions received pat-terns for understanding the world that climate science does not always know it needs. This is a needing, this is a keening, that erupts as we approach the abstraction of the chemical signature, where bad feelings coincide with guilty pleasures coincide with sentient dust. All of it, all of us, hurdle around, atop, and inside a no longer round planet, producing run-on prose like the prose I am offering to you now where subjects and predicates flow into nongrammatically. Lie on the beach that lies on you, a beach that is always already lying to you. Feel badly about it.

Notes

"Assemblies: Public Participation, Heteronomous Worlds" was previously published as "Performance, Public (Re)assembly and Civic Reenactment," in *Cultures of Participation: Arts, Digital Media and Cultural Institutions*, ed. Birgit Eriksson, Carsten Stage, and Bjarki Valtysson, 13–29 (New York: Routledge, 2020).

1. The "linguistic turn" of the 1970s has been, since at least the mid-1990s, the performative turn; some may argue we are still in the midst of this turn, if we take subsequent turns, including the affective, the participatory, and so forth to be constitutive elements of the initial turn toward the performance based. This "turn" has been examined in numerous works over the last twenty years; to name just a few chestnuts from this diverse body of materials: Andrew Parker and Eve Kosofsky Sedgwick, eds., *Performativity and Performance* (New York: Routledge, 1995); Nicolas Bourriaud, *Relational Aesthetics*, trans. Simon Pleasance and Fronza Woods (Dijon, France: Les Presses du réel, 2002); and Erika Fischer-Lichte, *The Transformative Power of Performance: A New Aesthetics*, trans. Saskya Iris Jain (New York: Routledge, 2008).

2. See, e.g., Hannah Arendt, *On Revolution* (New York: Penguin Books, 2006); Jürgen Habermas, *The Structural Transformation of the Public Sphere: An Inquiry into a Category of Bourgeois Society*, trans. Thomas Burger (Cambridge, MA: MIT Press, 1991), and the more recent *Democracy and the Public Sphere*, trans. Luke Goode (Ann Arbor, MI: Pluto Press, 2005); Nancy Fraser, "Rethinking The Public Sphere: A Contribution to the Critique of Actually Existing Democracy," *Social Text* 25/26 (1990): 56–80; and Michael Warner, "Publics and Counterpublics," *Public Culture* 14, no. 1 (Winter 2002): 49–90.

3. Judith Butler, *Notes Toward a Performative Theory of Assembly* (Cambridge, MA: Harvard University Press, 2015).

4. Ernesto Laclau and Chantal Mouffe quoted in Butler, *Notes Toward a Performative Theory of Assembly*, 4.

5. Butler, *Notes Toward a Performative Theory of Assembly*, 4. See J. L. Austin, *How to Do Things with Words*, 2nd ed. (Cambridge, MA: Harvard University Press, 1975).

6. Butler, *Notes Toward a Performative Theory of Assembly*, 8.

7. Butler, *Notes Toward a Performative Theory of Assembly*, 10, italic in the original.

8. Habermas, *The Structural Transformation of the Public Sphere*; Jürgen Habermas, *Democracy and the Public Sphere*, trans. Luke Goode (Ann Arbor, MI: Pluto Press, 2005).

9. Butler, *Notes Toward a Performative Theory of Assembly*, 7.

10. Shannon Jackson, *Social Works: Performing Art, Supporting Publics* (New York and London: Routledge, 2011).

11. María Cristina Caballero, "Academic Turns City into a Social Experiment," *Harvard Gazette*, March 11, 2004, https://news.harvard.edu/gazette/story/2004/03/academic-turns-city-into-a-social-experiment-2/.

12. Caballero, "Academic Turns City into a Social Experiment."

13. Caballero, "Academic Turns City into a Social Experiment."

14. Henry M. Robert III, et al., *Robert's Rules of Order Newly Revised* (Philadelphia: Da Capo Press, 2011).

15. Aaron Landsman and Mallory Catlett, "Introduction to *City Council Meeting*," *Theater* 43, no. 3 (2013): 57.

16. Landsman and Catlett, "Introduction to *City Council Meeting*," 58.

17. Landsman and Catlett, "Introduction to City Council Meeting."

18. McKenzie Wark, "What the Performative Can't Perform: On Judith Butler," *Public Seminar*, June 8, 2016, http://publicseminar.org/2016/06/butler/.

19. Gregory Bateson, *Steps to an Ecology of Mind* (Chicago: University of Chicago Press, 2000).

20. Kathryn Yusoff, *A Billion Black Anthropocenes or None* (Minneapolis: University of Minnesota Press, 2019).

21. Laura Levin, *Performing Ground: Space, Camouflage and the Art of Blending* (London: Palgrave Macmillan, 2014); Alan C. Braddock and Christoph Irmsher, eds., *A Keener Perception: Ecocritical Studies in American Art History* (Tuscaloosa: University of Alabama Press, 2009); Alan C. Braddock and Karl Kusserow, *Nature's Nation: American Art and Environment* (New Haven, CT: Yale University Press, 2018).

22. Wark, "What the Performative Can't Perform."

23. Félix Guattari, *Soft Subversions: Texts and Interviews 1977–1985*, ed. Sylvère Lothringer (Los Angeles: Semiotext(e), 2009), 292–93.

24. Guattari, *Soft Subversions*, 293.

25. Bruno Latour, "From Realpolitik to Dingpolitik, or How to Make Things Public in Making Things Public," in *Making Things Public: Atmospheres of Democracy*, ed. Bruno Latour and Peter Weibel (Karlsruhe, Germany: ZKM Center for Art and Media, 2005), 14–41.

26. Mike Davis, *Dead Cities: And Other Tales* (New York: New Press, 2003); Isabelle Stengers, *Cosmopolitics I* (Minneapolis: University of Minnesota Press, 2010); Manuel DeLanda, *A New Philosophy of Society: Assemblage Theory and Social Complexity* (New York: Continuum, 2006); Jane Bennett, *Vibrant Matter: A Political Ecology of Things* (Durham, NC: Duke University Press, 2010); Nabil Ahmed, "Entangled Earth," *Third Text* 27, no. 1 (2013): 44–53; Timothy Morton, *The Ecological Thought* (Cambridge, MA: Harvard University Press, 2012); Gary Carrion-Murayari and Gioni Massimiliano, eds., *Gustav Metzger* (New York: New Museum, 2011).

27. Ursula Biemann, Peter Mörtenböck, and Helge Mooshammer, "From Supply Lines to Resource Ecologies: World of Matter," *Third Text* 27, no. 1 (2013): 76–94.

28. Biemann et al., "From Supply Lines to Resource Ecologies," 78.

29. Immanuel Kant, "Succinct Exposition of Some Meditations on Fire," [1755] in Eric Watkins, ed., *Immanuel Kant: Natural Science* (Cambridge: Cambridge University Press, 2012), 309–26. Peter Slotoerdijk, *Foams, Spheres Volume III: Plural Spherology* (Cambridge, MA: MIT Press, 2016); Eugene Thacker, *In the Dust of this Planet: Horror of Philosophy, Volume 1* (Winchester, England: Zero Books, 2011); Ray Brassier, *Nihil Unbound: Enlightenment and Extinction* (London: Palgrave Macmillan, 2007).

30. Jean-François Lyotard, *The Inhuman: Reflections on Time*, trans. Geoffrey Bennington and Rachel Bowlby (Stanford, CA: Stanford University Press, 1992); Jacques Derrida, "Geopsychoanalysis," trans. D. Nicholson-Smith, *American Imago* 48, no. 2 (1991): 199–231; Nick Land, *The Thirst for Annihilation: Georges Bataille and Virulent Nihilism* (New York: Routledge, 1990); and Robin Mackay, "A Brief History of Geotrauma," in Ed Keller et al., eds., *Leper Creativity: Cyclonopedia Symposium* (Brooklyn: Punctum, 2012): 16-20.

31. Emily Apter, "Planetary Dysphoria," *Third Text* 27, no. 1 (2013): 140.

32. Mackenzie Wark cited in Emily Apter, "Planetary Dysphoria," 140.

33. En Liang Khong, "How a Beach Opera at the 58th Venice Biennale Quietly Contends with Climate Change Catastrophe," *Frieze*, May 17, 2019, https://frieze.com/article/how-beach-opera-58th-venice-biennale-quietly-contends-climate-change-catastrophe.

34. "Sun & Sea," IndieGogo, https://www.indiegogo.com/projects/saule-ir-jura-sun-sea#/.

35. "Sun & Sea," IndieGogo.

36. Julia Halperin, "It's Hard to Make Good Art about Climate Change: The Lithuanian Pavilion at the Venice Biennale Is a Powerful Exception," *Art-Net*, May 10, 2019, https://news.artnet.com/exhibitions/lithuanian-pavilion-1543168.

37. Inesa Brasiske, "Sun and Sea in Venice, Lithuania's Prize-Winning Pavilion at the 2019 Venice Biennale," *CAA News*, July 25, 2019, https://www.collegeart.org/news/2019/07/25/international-review-sun-and-sea-2019-venice-biennale/.

38. Halperin, "It's Hard to Make Good Art about Climate Change."

39. Melanie Gerlis, "How Do Art Fairs Contribute to the Climate Crisis?" *Financial Times*, June 6, 2019, https://www.ft.com/content/c8f21a30-8386-11e9-a7f0-77d3101896ec.

40. Guy Mackinnon-Little, "Interview: Lucia Pietroiusti," *TANK Magazine* 80 (2019), https://tankmagazine.com/issue-80/talks/lucia-pietroiusti/.

41. Guy Mackinnon-Little, "Interview: Lucia Pietroiusti."

Epilogue

Essential Labor and Proximate Performance

Datedness is an occupational hazard of a retrospective collection like this one. Each piece was written at a particular time and place. The republication of each piece thus becomes a kind of historical exercise. Readers have to imagine the context in which the text was originally situated, even as they test the possibilities of its recontextualization to a new moment and a new situation. As I conclude this book with some final thoughts hatched at a particular time and place—my shelter-in-place in early 2021—I am acutely aware that this epilogue will also become dated, is becoming dated with every minute of writing. COVID-19 has altered my and others' assumptions about the experience of time and the medium of performance. It is thus with a sense of anticipation and concern that I wonder and worry about the future of performance's powerful proximity.

The assembly of this collection coincided with the rise of COVID-19 and its lethal circulation across the globe. As its effects unfolded, each week revealed new understandings of its properties and new protocols for its management. From handwashing to fist bumping to mask wearing to "social" distancing, from prohibitions against travel to exhortations to shelter, we all adopted, refined, and expanded our COVID behaviors and our COVID vocabularies for naming what we were enduring. Many asked why we had not anticipated the arrival of a lethal virus. Why, indeed, did a virus have to become a pandemic? Meanwhile, this immediate pandemic made more visible another four-hundred-year pandemic, the one rooted in the transatlantic slave trade and whose "afterlives" persist in the inequities of governance systems, health systems, and patterns of everyday life.[1] In and beyond the United States, COVID-19 coincided with a new rise in #BlackLivesMatter activism that exposed the connection between health and race, between the medical sector and all sectors committed (or not) to social equity.

Life in the time of COVID thus meant asking a range of questions around a set of intersectional themes. For many of us privileged to have shelter and to remain healthy, it meant having way too much time to ask them. The enormity of global and activist crises coincided with the monotony of everyday life, prompting existential and often Kafkaesque questions about how to spend our time. For many of us, again privileged to have jobs and broadband, it meant moving our work and our social work online, filling our calendars with Zoom links and our screens with gridded images of our fellow coworkers, collaborators, activists, family members, students, artists, and friends. Entirely new protocols of politesse emerged as we navigated a different kind of multimedia existence—when to mute, when to self-display, when to screen-share, and when to sit quietly anonymous . . . the unseen but seeing spectator in a digitally dispersed cinematic apparatus. Indeed, the time-based form of digital engagement became a different kind of medium during this period. The dual associations of that word *viral*—viral as digital circulation, viral as lethal contagion—had never felt quite so resonantly connected, as if the viral expansion of our digital life necessarily fed on the viral threat of our physical vulnerability.

Many of us in the arts also found ourselves asking a new series of questions. Why did the cultural sector have to collapse so dramatically with the spread of the pandemic? Why the furloughs and the layoffs of our arts colleagues? How to rebuild? And how could we join an antiracist ethos to the equitable rebuilding of that cultural sector? But of course we also found ourselves noticing a new kind of response to these questions, and a new kind of energy in methods of engagement. Like every other sector, we found cultural organizations worldwide moving their work online, and in that movement, we found museums, theaters, fairs, and festivals newly interested in the medium of the screen. Whether the freemium model of the #MuseumFromHome or the subscription model of Broadway HD, it is fair to say that COVID began to change perceptions of how citizens accessed the life of culture.[2] As such, it is also fair to say that the time of COVID has produced a new interest in screen-based media—as backstage infrastructure and frontstage interaction, as the vehicle for delivering art and as the object of artistic intervention. Video artists who normally required their work to be physically installed agreed (tentatively) to cloud-based dissemination. Those same video artists who normally sold work in limited editions conceded to streaming their work (temporarily) in limited blocks of time. One sample case responded to the online compulsion with an offline awareness of the importance of antiracist activism: Arthur Jafa's never-before streamed work was streamed. *Love Is the Message, The Message Is Death* (2016) streamed for forty-eight hours in a networked collaboration with thirteen arts institutions, including the Hirschhorn, Dallas Museum of Art, Museum of Contemporary Art in Los Angeles, Studio Museum of Harlem, Tate Modern, Palazzo Grassi of the Pinault Collection, and more. While COVID produced a renewed interest in time-based media—expanding our sense of art's *medium*, including its *base* of operations as well as the *time* it seeks to fill—it also challenged definitions of live performance. Indeed, every day underscored the difference among the associations attached to that word *live*—liveness as copresent space or liveness as copresent time. The dominance of the digital was felt acutely in our efforts to remain in contact with loved ones, to stay up-to-date with news, to continue working over the wires and wirelessly. Those of us in the arts felt acutely the paradox of digital liveness, as institutions furloughed employees while simultaneously scrambling to move cultural production online. Perched at our #MuseumsFromHome, dialed into podcasts, Audibles, and YouTube channels, we encountered virtual exhibitions, symphonies, and plays performed to empty houses.

The *onlineness* of everything forced the question of whether the digital sphere is an extension of or a deflation of everything that we most value about the place, people, props, and life propulsions of performance. Consider the bodies of performance artists, the embodied motion of dancers, the enacted characters of theater, as well as the collaborative forms that gather bodies in casts, ensembles, assemblies, collectives, rituals, protests, and other highly populated (highly "peopled") forms. What did those assemblies become when redefined by the absence of people as a sentient element? And what about performance's reciprocal commitment to defining and being defined by shared place? What to make of our experience of spatial emptiness during this period? We witnessed renowned cultural venues—churches, museums, stadiums, and theaters—without people, already quasi-ruins. As we return to those public spaces—staggering, tentative—new choreographies emerge. Museums—like grocery stores—place distanced diagrams on the floor. Office workers separate desks, and audience members space themselves in the all-too-proximate seats of a dedicated theater. The virus is reorganizing the relation among elements such as bodies, places, props, and life propulsion, repositioning performance labor as a shaper of relations. Indeed, the virus reminded us of the lack of boundaries among those elements that we once experienced as separate from each other, a conceptual reminder of the porous, microbial, and indiscrete relationship among spaces, objects, environments, people, and species.

While reckoning with new performance practices technologically, phenomenologically, and psychically, we are also in the midst of an institutional reckoning. Indeed, keeping up with reports on COVID's institutional effects on the cultural sector has been its own kind of sprint and marathon—with datedness being a continual occupational hazard. The projections of losses in the US nonprofit arts sector continued to rise—with occasional modifications as stimulus packages came, went, and came back again. Very early on in 2020, museums in Europe were reporting losses of 75–80 percent of their earned income each week. Museums in the United States were reported to be losing thirty-three million dollars a day.[3] Some institutions laid-off staff, while others furloughed. Some implemented salary cuts across the board. Some committed to paying employees up to certain dates. As those promises approached expiration, they and more adopted a mix of strategies. And of course too many institutions have already announced permanent closures. Indeed, even within the United States, it was hard to keep up with the news, though a range of sites tried. From *Hyperallergic*'s Coronavirus Daily Report to *The Art Newspaper*, from the Association for Performing Arts Professionals to *Playbill* to Live for Live Music, from Creative Capital to lostmygig.com, crowdsourced sites kept track of the loss. (As an aside, COVID prognosticating was another domain in which it was hard to maintain an interarts perspective in the face of siloed professional networks and reporting.)

Meanwhile, in the hasty process of categorizing the essential service worker, the laborers in the arts were not included. In the United States, essential workers were defined as those who maintained the critical infrastructure of the country. When the federal government's Cybersecurity & Infrastructure Security Agency (CISA) established critical categories, they mostly corresponded to a particular definition of basic needs in healthcare, food and agriculture; water; dams; nuclear reactors, materials and waste; water; and chemical.[4] Such a list echoes the ideology embedded in Maslow's Hierarchy of Needs in which food and shelter constitute the foundation of the basic needs of physiology and safety, with the more evolved and paradoxically more expendable needs of love, esteem, or self-actualization on the less basic top of the hierarchy. Lest this analogy ring too much of twentieth-first-century motivational entrepreneurialism, we can also note that the concept of essential infrastructure corresponds to Karl Marx's hierarchies as well, one that would distinguish between the basic work of the base as opposed the ideological work of the superstructure. CISA's definition of essential service does, of course, have a twentieth-first-century ring as well, one echoed in the addition of the word *cybersecurity* to an agency in charge of the country's infrastructure. In addition to services that address the material, physiological maintenance of its citizens, the spheres of "informational technology" and "communication" were also deemed essential. In amplifying these spheres, the US Department of Homeland Security elaborated: "Reliance on technology and just-in-time supply chains means that certain workers must be able to access certain sites, facilities, and assets to ensure continuity of functions."[5] Here the cognitive spheres of digital communication and information technology entered into the realm of the essential, an entrance propelled by a post-Fordist discourse that appeals to just-in-time delivery as basic necessity. COVID's practice of naming labor thus became another place that navigated the so-called division between material and immaterial labor, a place that ultimately revealed the intersection with ideological expediency at the federal level, an intersection that did not need a performance studies scholar to force it.

This context thus prompted and continues to prompt more questions about the nature of artistic labor. First, what would it take for the arts to be categorized as essential? And second, did we really want that designation? In answer to the first, it is clear that arts organizations and artist groups nationally and globally were all trying hard to demonstrate their and our essential force. How many times did we see new marketing campaigns declaring the "arts" to be "essential" in 2020? And as noted above, organizations flipped themselves into digital platforms to demonstrate the argument. The cascade of online cultural content was extraordinary, inspiring, overwhelming, and sometimes concerning. Virtual tours—some using virtual reality—abounded in the museum world. Sequestered collections, now digitized, were available to browse. Film festivals became fully accessible online. The theater industry tried out a range of models and streaming memberships, and with small and midsize theaters putting samplers of quasi-cancelled seasons online. The economic sustainability of culture online—already a question before—thus became more acute. Much of this content was immediately offered in a freemium model; some of it required paid ticketing or subscription; some used online cultural engagement to raise money for artists' relief. All the easily accessible online programming begged the question: if our cultural life could be deemed essential—individually or federally—would people pay for what should be free?

Those questions obviously brought up other ones—conceptual, political, and even physiological—about the limits, opportunities, contradictions, and ambivalences of "the essential" as a category. From one insidious line of thought, the online life of arts organizations bespeaks a kind of creative speedup in the midst of economic turndown. The impulse to create—and to create and create and create—was not simply an internal impulse but an external compulsion. Even with all this extra time, the just-in-time pace of the digital assembly line sped up, and artists and arts organizations had to be competitive by remaining in sync with the speed of the stream. A belief in arts essential status also seemed to drive heart-warming stories of its appearance throughout the United States and the globe. Artists decorated ICUs; musicians played for hospital workers; and, of course, very early on, Italians played instruments on balconies—performances that went viral with this virus as our hearts bore witness to the irrepressible spirit of human creativity. Art in some of these stories felt like a public service, even a public health service, and therefore essential to the critical infrastructure of the nation and the globe. At the same time, we might also question this attribution of art as an essential instrument. For in these misty, affectively compelling moments of aesthetic eruption, the appeal often seemed to come from a luminously nonessential place, a place that could not be and did not want to be fully integrated into the instrumental. Updating Adorno for the COVID moment meant embracing the essential nature of art's nonessential service.

There are actually other reasons to question artists' inclusion in the essential category, at least as it was defined and mobilized in a global labor

sphere. The fact is that so many essential workers were proximate performers in the most dangerous sense, from health to food sales to delivery.
The "essential" moniker started to become not a marker of social value but
a kind of compulsory social exhortation. Essential workers had no choice
but to work. What if artistic service was deemed essential in this material,
physiological, and compulsory sense? What if we doubled down as performance people on the real-time, copresent nature of our favorite medium
and advocated for its delivery offline and not just online. What if no-touch
dances on people's doorstep were obligated rather than voluntary; pop-up
musical performances in a cul-de-sac; theater scenes performed on a roof
top, with face masks? Essential art might start to feel like an inverted Sche-
herazade, where the authoritarian directive *to be creative*—onsite, just in
time—would actually put the artist's life at risk rather than keep her alive.

The question deepens other ones about artistic labor and cultural economics, because the question remains whether we can square a global
citizenry's impulse to celebrate Italians on balconies with their concomi-
tant lack of concern for the closing of symphonies and the furloughing of
musicians. Perhaps this is just another example of the ambivalent mix of
celebration and indifference that shadows societal attitudes toward the
arts, the embrace and withdrawal routinely endured by those who create
art that everyone wants for free. Will the celebration of creativity's necessity translate into a reinvestment in creativity's institutions and in systems
that keep creatives alive?

Having got to this point in my thinking from my shelter in early 2021,
I'll close by exploring these intersections from the other direction, that
is, to see how we can imagine the future labor of art by reconciling it
with a performative discourse on the art of labor, which brings us back to
thoughts shared in my introduction. Consider once again those analogies
between the work of creatives and the work of information technology, communication, casinos, airlines, or restaurants. Notably, this is a
discourse where the time-based, so-called ephemeral, qualities of performance are invoked to dramatize the world of postindustrial service.
The post-Fordist discourse that circulated throughout this book returned
anew in a COVID-inflected discourse on the essence of essential service.
To recall, the fundamental premise in post-Fordist theories of performance is that its artistic practices, both in the performing arts and in the
participatory "turns" of contemporary art, are coinciding with a wider
turn to the performative, participatory, and experiential in a late capitalist
economy. Recall Bojana Cvejić, Ana Vujanović, and post-Operaist thinkers
who theorized a turn from material commodity production to the production of immaterial services, a turn that valued "cultural-informational
content—standards, norms, tastes, and (most important strategically)
public opinion—by means of cooperation and communication as the
basic work activities . . . Art thereby gains a new political position, and

performance has a special role to play there . . . workers are no longer
obliged merely to get the job done, but also to be virtuoso performers:
eloquent, open, and communicative."[6] Recall too that, while this thesis
"is mostly taken as promising for the politicality of the contemporary
Art World," they and many others argued that such optimism is misunderstood and misplaced, noting that performance should be talked about
less as a political practice and more "as a model of production."[7] Recall
finally that, in the face of the precarious and intermittent conditions of
artistic labor (now endured in so many other forms of essential service),
these writers called for a different kind of public education: "The question
would be how to act upon the material conditions, to no longer compose
or negotiate with them, but to reclaim art as a public good in political
and economic terms, which requires reconfiguring relations between the
state, the public sphere and the sphere of the private capital. To do this,
critical thought from within performance practice itself will not suffice,
but in fact, performance practitioners will need to politically reeducate
themselves as citizens in the public sphere."[8] By this point in the collection, and surely by the time of this writing in a COVID-ridden world, we
have had an unexpected public reeducation, one that has taught us new
lessons about what the performance workplace can be. It has become all
too clear that this aesthetic reeducation sits alongside a reeducation in all
kinds of so-called immaterial service sectors—communications, informational technology, restaurants, casinos, airlines, and just-in-time delivery
service. In the United States in 2021 under a new Biden administration,
arguably that public reeducation includes a redefinition of public infrastructure, finally referencing a range of "soft, "immaterial," but essential
social support systems. As a performance scholar who has been arguing
for an expanded concept of infrastructure since the early 2000s, this seems
like a welcome moment.

Our current situation thus underscores and further ironizes some of
the other key paradoxes of this immaterial turn to service, paradoxes earlier elaborated in Operaismo discourse and diagnosed subsequently. Keti
Chukhrov's contribution to an earlier *e-flux* special issue titled "Are you
working too much?" offers one helpful summary:

> As labor is dematerialized and the division of labor in industrial
> production erodes, capital not only occupies the working hours
> during which products or goods (and its surplus value) are pro-
> duced; it absorbs all of the worker's time, as well as his or her
> existence, thoughts, and creative desires. . . . Labor coincides
> increasingly with the creative maneuvers of a virtuosic performer,
> with active memory and an engagement with knowledge. . . .
> In this way, productive activity occupies life, social and societal
> space, the intellect, the "soul."[9]

In other words, in the postindustrial universe and its fractured gig economy, laborers are encouraged to work like artists—to follow their passions and to embrace the freedom of a flexible workplace, one unfettered by job security, reliable wages, or comprehensive health care. Moreover, this entrepreneurial takeover of the worker's soul is packaged for her as freedom and self-actualization, as the opportunity to design her own life, creatively, flexibly, autonomously. This is a context where the apparent DIY ethos of crowdsourcing, kickstartering, and flexible self-entrepreneurialism also depend on a do-it-to-yourself practice of self-exploitation. It is a context where the flexibility of a digital economy distributes excess risk onto individual workers while extracting their surplus value. And it is a context where even, and especially, cultural laborers willingly submit to hours of unremunerated labor for the "love" of their work, a passionately immaterial labor that compensates (wittingly or not) for the ongoing gigification of the cultural sector.

In the midst of this irrepressibility, those of us invested in the discourse and practice of performance might review once again the contradictions and hazards of being defined as immaterial. How do workers' own physiological experience of their lives chime with, or not, the purported dematerialization of the economy? Is the immaterial labor of an informational technology company analogous to the immaterial labor of a restaurant worker or of an actor? In fact there is no clear shift in this turn from object to service, or in the turn from the so-called material to the so-called immaterial. Even the frictionless sphere of the Internet depends on objects, people, infrastructure, routers, and grids; the apparently unfettered experience of digitally powered delivery is ridden with an urgent materiality. In several of the essays compiled in this book, I have questioned the integrity of this lumpy immaterial category; that questioning was expedited—along with my own political reeducation—during the time of COVID. Recall the US federal decree: "Reliance on technology and just-in-time supply chains means that *certain workers* must be able to access certain sites, facilities, and assets to ensure continuity of functions."[10] Those workers include Uber drivers, cashiers, Instacart workers, and Amazon deliverers whose contact-heavy labor revealed the risky materiality undergirding the digital consumer's "no touch" service experience. The Gig Workers Collective open letter on the subject dramatized the predicament of the essentially expendable, the surplus from which a postindustrial tech sector extracts value: "Instacart [is] profiting astronomically off of us literally risking our lives, all while refusing to provide us with effective protection, meaningful pay, and meaningful benefits."[11] Moreover, the definition of the immaterial category became even shakier upon confronting the wide range of economic positions it includes. It covers the so-called cognitive labor of the tech executive as well as the emotional labor of the nursing-home worker. It includes online Zoomers and offline service workers. It includes the performing artists who used to work day jobs (and night jobs) in restaurants until all jobs, onstage and offstage, were suspended. As part of our reeducation, COVID thus foregrounded the tacit materiality as well as the economic inequity already embedded in the immaterial class category. The definition of immaterial work cannot hold up when reckoning with the impurity of immaterial life. You are always touching someone, and someone is always touching you.

I opened *Back Stages* with an image of me as an audience member on the floor; some bodies sat next to me, other bodies crawled past me, a few bodies touched me. COVID dated that image. After a year of habituated distancing, it was shocking to recall that assembly of proximate bodies. My hope is that by the time this book sees publication that shock is also dated. My hope is that this book's readers have reentered a world of proximate performance—in art, in everyday life, on the frontstage, in the backstage, and in the zone that recognizes the porousness and interdependence of all these domains. Alongside this hope is of course a larger wish that the lessons of COVID stick with us—that the racial health disparities it revealed are addressed (and redressed) and that the precarities and asymmetries of twentieth-first-century labor are addressed as well. If there is a chance of revitalizing the power of performance as the rest of the twentieth-first-century unfolds, it will require a good deal of work materially and psychologically, systemically as well as aesthetically. I continue to hope, as I write. You can decide where hopes lie as you read.

Notes

1. Saidiya Hartman, *Lose Your Mother: A Journey along the Atlantic Slave Route* (New York: Farrar, Straus, and Giroux, 2007).

2. Broadway HD is a subscription-based streaming platform for Broadway stage productions: https://www.broadwayhd.com/.

3. See Network of European Museum Organizations, "NEMO publishes initial results of survey on the impact of the corona crisis on museums in Europe," July 4, 2020, https://www.ne-mo.org/news/article/nemo/nemo -publishes-results-of-survey-on-the-impact-of-the-corona-crisis-on-museums -in-europe.html; and Alliance of American Museums Appeals to Congress for $4 Billion in COVID-19 Relief," *Artforum*, March 20, 2020, https://www .artforum.com/news/alliance-of-american-museums-appeals-to-congress-for -4-billion-in-covid-19-relief-82502.

4. CISA, "Guidance on the Essential Critical Infrastructure Workforce," March 19, 2020, https://www.cisa.gov/publication/guidance-essential-critical -infrastructure-workforce.

5. See United States Cybersecurity and Infrastructure Security Agency, "Guidance on the Essential Critical Infrastructure Workforce," https://www .cisa.gov/publication/guidance-essential-critical-infrastructure-workforce.

6. Jasbir Puar, Lauren Berlant, Judith Butler, Bojana Cvejić, Isabell Lorey, and Ana Vujanović, "Precarity Talk: A Virtual Roundtable with Lauren Berlant,

Judith Butler, Bojana Cvejić, Isabell Lorey, Jasbir Puar, and Ana Vujanović," *TDR: The Drama Review* 56, no. 4 (2012): 175, muse.jhu.edu/article/491900.

7. Puar et al., "Precarity Talk," 175.

8. Puar et al., "Precarity Talk," 176.

9. Keti Chukhrov, "Towards the Space of the General: On Labor Beyond Materiality and Immateriality," in *Are You Working Too Much? Post-Fordism, Precarity, and the Labor of Art*, ed. Julieta Aranda, Brian Juan Wood, and Anton Vidokle (Berlin: Sternberg Press, 2011), 94–111.

10. See United States Cybersecurity and Infrastructure Security Agency, "Guidance."

11. Gig Workers Collective, "Instacart Emergency Walk Off," March 27, 2020, https://gigworkerscollective.medium.com/instacart-emergency-walk-off-ebdf11b6995a.

BIBLIOGRAPHY

Abu-Lughod, Lila. "The Romance of Resistance: Tracing Transformations of Power through Bedouin Women." *American Ethnologist* 17 (1990): 41–55.

Adamson, Glen. "Craft and the Romance of the Studio." *American Art* 21, no. 1 (Spring 2007): 14–18.

Addams, Jane. *The Spirit of Youth in the City Streets*. New York: Macmillan, 1909.

———. *Twenty Years at Hull-House*. New York: Penguin, 1981.

Adorno, Theodor W. *Aesthetic Theory*. Translated by Robert Hullor-Kentor. Minneapolis: University of Minnesota Press, 1998.

———. "Commitment." In *The Essential Frankfurt School Reader*. Edited by Andrew Arato and Eike Gebhardt, 300–318. New York: Continuum, 1982.

Ahmed, Nabil. "Entangled Earth." *Third Text* 27, no. 1 (2013): 44–53.

Alberro, Alexander, and Sabeth Buchmann, eds. *Art after Conceptual Art*. Cambridge, MA: MIT Press, 2006.

Alberro, Alexander, and Blake Stimson, eds. *Institutional Critique: An Anthology of Artists' Writings*. Cambridge, MA: MIT Press, 2009.

Alliance of American Museums. "Alliance of American Museums Appeals to Congress for $4 Billion in COVID-19 Relief." *Artforum*, March 20, 2020. https://www.artforum.com/news/alliance-of-american-museums-appeals-to -congress-for-4-billion-in-covid-19-relief-82502.

Alpers, Svetlana, et al. "Visual Culture Questionnaire." *October* 77 (1996): 25–70. doi:10.2307/778959.

Althusser, Louis. "Ideology and Ideological State Apparatuses." In *Lenin and Philosophy and Other Essays*, trans. Ben Brewster, 162–63. New York: Monthly Review Press, 1971.

Anderson, Benedict. *Imagined Communities*. London: Verso, 1983.

Apter, Emily. "Planetary Dysphoria." *Third Text* 27, no. 1 (2013): 131–40.

Arendt, Hannah. *Between Past and Future: Eight Exercises in Political Thought*. New York: Penguin Books, [1954] 1977.

———. *On Revolution*. New York: Penguin Books, 2006.

Arlen, Shelley, ed. *The Cambridge Ritualists: An Annotated Bibliography of the Works by and about Jane Ellen Harrison, Gilbert Murray, Francis M. Cornford, and Arthur Bernard Cook*. Metuchen, NJ: Scarecrow Press, 1990.

Asad, Talal. "The Concept of Cultural Translation in British Social Anthropology." In *Writing Culture*, edited by James Clifford and George Marcus, 141–64. Santa Fe, NM: School of American Research, 1986.

Auslander, Philip. *From Acting to Performance: Essays in Modernism and Post-Modernism*. London: Routledge, 1997.

Austin, J. L. *How to Do Things with Words*. 2nd ed. Cambridge, MA: Harvard University Press, 1975.

Bacon, Wallace A. *The Art of Interpretation*. New York: Holt, Rinehart and Winston, 1979.

Baker, George. "The Storyteller: Notes on the Work of Gerard Byrne." In *Gerard Byrne: Books, Magazines, and Newspapers*, 7–88. New York: Lukas and Sternberg, 2003.

Bakhtin, Mikhail. *The Dialogic Imagination: Four Essays*. Edited by Michael Holquist. Translated by Caryl Emerson and Michael Holquist. Austin: University of Texas Press, 1981.

———. *Rabelais and His World*. Translated by Hélène Iswolsky. Bloomington: Indiana University Press, 2009.

Bal, Mieke, and Bryan Gonzales, eds. *The Practice of Cultural Analysis: Exposing Interdisciplinary Interpretation*. Stanford, CA: Stanford University Press, 1999.

Bateson, Gregory. *Steps to an Ecology of Mind*. Chicago: University of Chicago Press, 2000. First published 1972 by Ballantine Books.

Beadle, Richard, ed. *The Cambridge Companion to Medieval English Theater*. Cambridge: Cambridge University Press, 1994.

Beck, Ulrich. *Risk Society: Towards a New Modernity*. London: SAGE Publications, 1992.

———. *World Risk Society*. Cambridge: Polity, 1999.

Beck, Ulrich, and Elisabeth Beck-Gernsheim. *Individualization*. London: Sage Publications, 2002).

Bell, Daniel. *The Coming of Post-Industrial Society: A Venture in Social Forecasting*. New York: Basic Books, 1973.

Benjamin, Walter. *Illuminations: Essays and Reflections*. Edited by Hannah Arendt, translated Harry Zohn. New York: Schocken, 1968.

Bennett, Jane. *Vibrant Matter: A Political Ecology of Things*. Durham, NC: Duke University Press, 2010.

Benson, Susan Porter, Stephen Brier, and Roy Rosenzweig, eds. *Presenting the Past: Essays on History and the Public*. Philadelphia: Temple University Press, 1986.

Biemann, Ursula, Peter Mörtenböck, and Helge Mooshammer. "From Supply Lines to Resource Ecologies: *World of Matter*." *Third Text* 27, no. 1 (2013): 76–94.

Birnbaum, Daniel. "White on White." *Artforum* (April 2002): 98–101.

Bishop, Claire. "Antagonism and Relational Aesthetics." *October* 110 (Fall 2004): 51–79.

———. *Artificial Hells: Participatory Art and the Politics of Spectatorship*. London: Verso, 2012.

———. "The Social Turn: Collaboration and its Discontents." *Artforum* (February 2006). https://www.artforum.com/print/200602/the-social-turn-collaboration-and-its-discontents-10274.

Blocker, Jane. *What the Body Cost: Desire, History, and Performance*. Minneapolis: University of Minnesota Press, 2004.

Boal, Augusto. *Theater of the Oppressed*. Translated by Charles and Maria-Odilia Leal McBridge. N.p.: Theater Communications Group, 1985.

Boltanski, Luc, and Eve Chiapello. *The New Spirit of Capitalism*. New York: Verso, 2005.

Bourdieu, Pierre. *Homo Academicus*. Paris: Éditions de Minuit, 1984.

Bourriaud, Nicolas. *Esthétique relationnelle*. Dijon, France: Les Presses du réel, 1998.

Boyer, Paul. *Urban Masses and Moral Order in America, 1820–1920*. Cambridge, MA: Harvard University Press, 1978.

Braddock, Alan C., and Christoph Irmsher, eds. *A Keener Perception: Ecocritical Studies in American Art History*. Tuscaloosa: University of Alabama Press, 2009.

Braddock, Alan C., and Karl Kusserow. *Nature's Nation: American Art and Environment*. New Haven, CT: Yale University Press, 2018.

Brasiske, Inesa. "Sun and Sea in Venice, Lithuania's Prize-Winning Pavilion at the 2019 Venice Biennale." *CAA News*, July 25, 2019. https://www.collegeart.org/news/2019/07/25/international-review-sun-and-sea-2019-venice-biennale/.

Brassier, Ray. *Nihil Unbound: Enlightenment and Extinction*. London: Palgrave Macmillan, 2007.

Brecht, Bertolt. *Brecht on Theater*. Edited by John Willet. New York: Hill and Wang, 1964.

———. "Short Description of a New Technique of Acting Which Produces an Alienation Effect." In *Brecht on Theater: The Development of an Aesthetic*, translated by J. Willett, 136–47. New York: Hill and Wang, 1992.

Breton, André. "The First Manifesto of Surrealism." In *Art in Theory, 1900–1990*, edited by Charles Harrison and Paul Wood, 432–39. Oxford: Blackwell, 1992.

Brooks, Daphne. *Bodies in Dissent: Spectacular Performances of Race and Freedom (1850–1910)*. Durham, NC: Duke University Press, 2006.

Brown, Bill. "Redemptive Reification (Theaster Gates, Gathering)." In *My Labor Is My Protest*, 36–37. Exhibition catalogue. London: White Cube, 2013.

Bryan-Wilson, Julia. *Art Workers: Radical Practice in the Vietnam War Era*. Berkeley: University of California Press, 2011.

Buchloh, Benjamin H. D. "Conceptual Art 1962–1969: From the Aesthetic of Administration to the Critique of Institutions." *October 55* (1990): 105–43.

———. *Neo-Avantgarde and Culture Industry: Essays on European and American Art from 1955 to 1975*. Cambridge, MA: MIT Press, 2000.

Bullard, Robert D., ed. *Unequal Protection: Environmental Justice and Communities of Color*. San Francisco: Sierra Club, 1994.

Burton, Johanna, Shannon Jackson, and Dominic Willsdon, eds., *Public Servants*. Cambridge, MA: MIT Press, 2016.

Butler, Judith. "Against Proper Objects." In *Feminism Meets Queer Theory*, edited by Elizabeth Weed and Naomi Schor, 1–30. Bloomington: Indiana University Press, 1997.

———. *Bodies That Matter: On the Discursive Limits of "Sex."* New York: Routledge, 1993.

———. *Gender Trouble: Feminism and the Subversion of Identity*. New York: Routledge, 2000.

————. *Notes Toward a Performative Theory of Assembly*. Cambridge, MA: Harvard University Press, 2015.

————. *The Psychic Life of Power: Theories in Subjection*. Stanford, CA: Stanford University Press, 1997.

————. "What Is Critique? An Essay on Foucault's Virtues." In *The Judith Butler Reader*, edited by Sara Silah and Judith Butler, 302–21. London: Blackwell Publishing, 2004.

Caballero, María Cristina. "Academic Turns City into a Social Experiment." *Harvard Gazette*, March 11, 2004. https://news.harvard.edu/gazette/story /2004/03/academic-turns-city-into-a-social-experiment-2/.

Careri, Francesco. *Walkscapes: Walking as an Aesthetic Practice*. Barcelona: Editorial Gustavo Gili, SL, 2002.

Carlson, Marvin A. *Places of Performance: The Semiotics of Theater Architecture*. Ithaca, NY: Cornell University Press, 1989.

————. *Theories of the Theater: A Historical and Critical Survey from the Greeks to the Present*. Expanded ed. Ithaca, NY: Cornell University Press, 1993.

————. "The Theatre *ici*." In *Performance and the Politics of Space: Theatre and Topology*. Edited by Erika Fischer-Lichte and Benjamin Wihstutz. New York: Routledge, 2013:15-30.

Case, Sue-Ellen. *The Domain Matrix*. Bloomington: Indiana University Press, 1996.

————. "Toward a Butch-Femme Aesthetic." In *Making a Spectacle*, edited by Lynda Hart, 282–99. Ann Arbor: University of Michigan Press, 1989.

Chamay, Katayoun. "The Meaning of Domain." In *Entry Points: The Vera List Center Field Guide on Art and Social Justice, No. 1*, edited by Carin Kuoni and Chelsea Haines, 254–55. Durham, NC: Duke University Press, 2015.

Chambers, E. K. *The Medieval Stage*. London: Oxford University Press, 1903.

Chandler, John, and Lucy Lippard. "The Dematerialization of Art." *Art International* (February 20, 1968): 31–36.

Chang, Aimee. "The Artist and the City: New Models for Creative Public Practice." In *Transforma: 2005–10*, 11–24. New Orleans: Transforma, 2010. https://www.transformaprojects.org/pdfs/transformaChang.pdf.

Chavis, Benjamin. Foreword to *Confronting Environmental Racism: Voices from the Grassroots*, edited by Robert D. Bullard, 3–36. Boston: South End Press, 1993.

Chukhrov, Keti. "Towards the Space of the General: On Labor Beyond Materiality and Immateriality." In *Are You Working Too Much? Post-Fordism, Precarity, and the Labor of Art*, edited by Julieta Aranda, Brian Juan Wood and Anton Vidokle, 94–111. Berlin: Sternberg Press, 2011.

Clark, T. J. *Farewell to an Idea: Episodes from a History of Modernism*. New Haven, CT: Yale University Press, 1999.

Clifford, James. "On Ethnographic Authority." *Representations* 1, no .2 (Spring 1983): 118–46.

————. *The Predicament of Culture: Twentieth-Century Ethnography, Literature, and Art*. Cambridge, MA: Harvard University Press, 1988.

Clifford, James, and George Marcus, eds. *Writing Culture: The Poetics and Politics of Ethnography*. Berkeley: University of California Press, 1986.

Cohen-Cruz, Jan. *Local Acts: Community-Based Performance in the United States*. New Brunswick, NJ: Rutgers University Press, 2005.

Conquergood, Dwight. "Literacy and Oral Performance in Anglo-Saxon England: Conflict and Confluence of Traditions." In *Performance of Literature in Historical Perspective*, edited by David W. Thompson, 107–45. Lanham, MD: University Press of America, 1983.

———. "Performing as a Moral Act: Ethical Dimensions of the Ethnography of Performance." *Literature in Performance* 5 (April 1985): 1–13.

Coverley, Merlin. *The Art of Wandering*. Harpenden, England: Oldcastle Books, 2012.

———. *Psychogeography*. Harpenden, England: Oldcastle Books, 2010.

Cox, John D. *Seeing Knowledge: Shakespeare and Skeptical Faith*. Waco, TX: Baylor University Press, 2007.

Cvejić, Bojana. "Trickstering, Hallucinating, and Exhausting Production: The Blackmarket for Useful Knowledge and Non-Knowledge." In *Knowledge in Motion: Perspectives of Artistic and Scientific Research in Dance*, ed. Sabine Gehm, Pirrko Husemann, and Katharina von Wilcke, 49–58. Bielefeld, Germany: Transcript Verlag, 2007.

Davies, Siobhan. "Parallel Voices," 2010. https://archive.siobhandavies.com /work/parallel-voices/.

Davis, Allen. *Spearheads for Reform*. New Brunswick, NJ: Rutgers University Press, 1967.

Davis, Mike. *Dead Cities: And Other Tales*. New York: New Press, 2003.

Davis, Tracy. *Actresses as Working Women: Their Social Identity in Victorian Culture*. London: Routledge, 1991.

———. "'Reading Shakespeare by Flashes of Lightning': Challenging the Foundations of Romantic Acting Theory." *ELH* 62, no. 4 (1995): 933–54.

Debord, Guy. *Society of the Spectacle*. Translated by Ken Knabb. Berkeley, CA: Bureau of Public Secrets, 2014.

———. "Theory of the Dérive." In *Situationst International Anthology*, edited and translated by Ken Knabb, 62–66. Berkeley, CA: Bureau of Public Secrets, 1981.

De Certeau, Michel. *The Practice of Everyday Life*. Translated by Steven Rendall. Berkeley: University of California Press, 1984.

———. *The Writing of History*. Translated by Tom Conley. New York: Columbia University Press, 1988.

DeFrantz, Thomas. *Dancing Many Drums: Excavations in African American Dance*. Madison: University of Wisconsin Press, 2001.

DeLanda, Manuel. *A New Philosophy of Society: Assemblage Theory and Social Complexity*. New York: Continuum, 2006.

Densu, Kwasi. "Theoretical and Historical Perspectives on Agroecology and African American Farmers." In *Land & Power: Sustainable Agriculture and African Americans*, edited by Jeffrey Jordan, Jerry Pennick, Walter Hill, and Robert Zabawa, 93–107. College Park, MD: SARE, 2007.

Derrida, Jacques. *Of Grammatology*. Translated by Gayatri Chakravorty Spivak. Baltimore: Johns Hopkins University Press, 1976.

———. "Geopsychoanalysis." Translated by D. Nicholson-Smith. *American Imago* 48, no. 2 (1991): 199-231.

———. "Signature Event Context." Translated by Samuel Weber and Jeffrey Mehlman. In *Limited Inc.*, 1–23. Evanston, IL: Northwestern University Press, 1977.

Deutsche, Rosalyn. *Evictions: Art and Spatial Politics*. Cambridge, MA: MIT Press, 1998.

Dewey, John. *Art as Experience*. New York: Perigee Books, [1934] 1980.

Diamond, Elin. "Brechtian Theory/Feminist Theory." *TDR: The Drama Review* 32, no. 1 (1988): 82–94.

———. *Unmaking Mimesis: Essays on Feminism and Theater*. New York: Routledge, 1997.

Doane, Mary Ann. "Film and Masquerade: Theorizing the Female Spectator." *Screen* 23, nos. 3–4 (1982): 74–88.

Dollimore, Jonathan, and Alan Sinfield. *Political Shakespeare: New Essays in Cultural Materialism*. Manchester: Manchester University Press, 1985.

Dowling, Emma, Rodrigo Nunes, and Ben Trott. "Immaterial and Affective Labour Explored." *ephemera* 7, no. 1 (2007): 1–7.

Dupuis, Chris. "In the Move from Stage to Museum, a Dance Becomes Performance Art." *Hyperallergic*, April 27, 2015. https://hyperallergic.com/202056/in-the-move-from-stage-to-museum-a-dance-becomes-performance-art/.

Duve, Thierry de. "The Glocal and the Singuniversal." *Third Text* 21, no. 6 (November 2007): 681–88.

———. *Kant after Duchamp*. Cambridge, MA: MIT Press, 1996.

Dworkin, Andrea. "Prostitution and Male Supremacy." *Michigan Journal of Gender and Law* 1 (1993): 1–12.

Edwards, Paul. "Unstoried: Teaching Literature in the Age of Performance Studies." *Theater Annual: A Journal of Performance Studies* 52 (1999): 1–147.

Ehrenreich, Barbara, and John Ehrenreich. "The Professional-Managerial Class." In *Between Labor and Capital*, ed. Pat Walker, 5–48. Montreal: Black Rose Press, 1979.

Elam, Keir. *The Semiotics of Theater and Drama*. London: Methuen, 1980.

Epps, Brad. "The Fetish of Fluidity." In *Homosexuality and Psychoanalysis*, edited by Tim Dean and Christopher Lane, 412–43. Chicago: University of Chicago Press, 2001.

Erickson, Jon. *The Fate of the Object: From Modern Object to Postmodern Sign in Performance, Art, and Poetry*. Ann Arbor: University of Michigan Press, 1995.

Etchells, Tim. "More Drama." August 12, 2008. https://timetchells.com/more-drama/.

Fabian, Johannes. *Time and the Other: How Anthropology Makes Its Object*. New York: Columbia University Press, 1983.

Faires, Robert. "Fusebox Festival: All Shook Up." *Austin Chronicle*, April 27, 2012. http://www.austinchronicle.com/arts/2012-04-27/fusebox-festival/.

Felman, Shoshana. *The Literary Speech Act*. Ithaca, NY: Cornell University Press, 1983.

Féral, Josette. "Theatricality: The Specificity of Theatrical Language." *SubStance #98/99* 31, no. 2–3 (2002): 94–108.

Finklepearl, Tom. *What We Made: Conversations on Art and Social Cooperation*. Durham, NC: Duke University Press, 2013.

Fischer-Lichte, Erika. *Semiotics of Theater*. Bloomington: Indiana University Press, 1992.

———. *The Transformative Power of Performance: A New Aesthetics*. Translated by Saskya Iris Jain. New York: Routledge, 2008.

Florida, Richard. *The Rise of the Creative Class*. New York: Basic Books, 2002.

Foster, Hal. *Design and Crime: and Other Diatribes*. London: Verso, 2002.

———. "The Archive without Museums." *October* 77 (Summer 1996): 104–6.

———. "The Crux of Minimalism." In Foster, *Return of the Real*, 35–70.

———. *The Return of the Real: The Avant-Garde at the End of the Century*. Cambridge, MA: MIT Press, 1996.

Foster, Sheila. "Race(ial) Matters: The Quest for Environmental Justice." *Ecology Law Quarterly* 20 (1993): 721–53.

Foucault, Michel. *Archaeology of Knowledge*. Translated by Alan Sheridan. New York: Pantheon, 1972.

———. *Discipline and Punish: The Birth of the Prison*. London: Verso, 1995.

———. *The History of Sexuality Volume 1*. Translated by Robert Hurley. New York: Random House, 1990.

———. *Language, Counter-Memory, Practice*. Edited by Donald Bouchard, translated by Donald Bouchard and Sherry Simon. Ithaca, NY: Cornell University Press, 1977.

Foulkes, Julia. "Learning from Chicago: Responses to *Dorchester Projects* from The New School Faculty." In *Entry Points: The Vera List Center Field Guide on Art and Social Justice No. 1*, ed. Carin Kuoni and Chelsea Haines, 253–71. Durham, NC: Duke University Press, 2015.

Fraser, Andrea. "From the Critique of Institutions to an Institution of Critique." *Artforum* 44 (2005): 100–106.

———. "Rethinking the Public Sphere: A Contribution to the Critique of Actually Existing Democracy." *Social Text* 25/26 (1990): 56–80.

Freire, Paolo. *The Pedagogy of the Oppressed*. New York: Penguin, 2017.

Fried, Michael. "Art and Objecthood." In *Art and Objecthood: Essays and Reviews*. Chicago: University of Chicago Press, 1998.

———. "Three American Painters, Kenneth Noland, Jules Olitski, Frank Stella: Fogg Art Museum, 21 April–30 May 1965." In *Art and Objecthood: Essays and Reviews*, 213–68. Chicago: University of Chicago Press, 1998.

Frye, Northrup. "The Mythos of Summer; Romance." In *Modern Genre Theory*, edited by David Duff, 98-117. New York: Longman, 2000.

Fuchs, Elinor. "Another Version of Pastoral." In *The Death of Character: Perspectives on Theater after Modernism*, 92–107. Bloomington: Indiana University Press, 1996.

Fuss, Diana. *Identification Papers: Readings on Psychoanalysis, Sexuality, and Culture*. New York: Routledge, 1995.

Garrett, Shawn-Marie. "The Awkward Age: New York's New Experimental Theater." *Theater* 31, no. 2 (May 2001): 45–46.

Gates, Theaster. *12 Ballads for Huguenot House*. Cologne: Walther König, 2012.

Geertz, Clifford. "Thick Description: Towards an Interpretive Theory of Culture." In *Interpretation of Cultures: Selected Essays*, 3–32. New York: Basic Books, [1973] 2000.

———. "Thinking as a Moral Act: Ethical Dimensions of Anthropological Fieldwork in the New States." In *Available Light: Anthropological Reflections on Philosophical Topics*, 21–41. Princeton, NJ: Princeton University Press, 2001.

Genette, Gerard. "The Architext." In *Modern Genre Theory*, edited by David Duff, 210–18. New York: Longman, 2000.

George-Graves, Nadine. *Urban Bush Women: Twenty Years of African American Dance Theater, Community Engagement, and Working it Out*. Madison: University of Wisconsin Press, 2010.

Gerlis, Melanie. "How Do Art Fairs Contribute to the Climate Crisis?" *Financial Times*, June 6, 2019. https://www.ft.com/content/c8f21a30-8386-11e9 -a7f0-77d3101896ec.

Giddens, Anthony. *The Third Way: The Renewal of Social Democracy*. Cambridge: Polity Press, 1999.

Gig Workers Collective. "Instacart Emergency Walk Off." March 27, 2020. https://gigworkerscollective.medium.com/instacart-emergency-walk-off -ebdf11b6995a.

Gillick, Liam. "Contingent Factors: A Response to Claire Bishop's 'Antagonism and Relational Aesthetics.'" *October* 115 (Winter 2006): 95–106.

Gilroy, Paul. *The Black Atlantic: Modernity and Double-Consciousness*. Cambridge, MA: Harvard University Press, 1995.

———. *Darker than Blue: On the Moral Economies of Black Atlantic Culture*. Cambridge: Cambridge University Press, 1997.

Glave, Dianne. "A Garden So Brilliant with Colors, So Original in Its Design: Rural African-American Women, Gardening, Progressive Reform, and the Foundation of an African American Environmental Perspective." *Environmental History* 8, no. 3 (2003): 395–411.

Goffman, Erving. *Forms of Talk*. Philadelphia: University of Pennsylvania Press, 1981.

———. *Frame Analysis: An Essay on the Organization of Experience*. New York: Harper and Row, 1974.

———. *The Presentation of Self in Everyday Life*. New York: Anchor Books, 1959.

Goldberg, Roselee, ed. *Performa 11: Staging Ideas*. New York: Performa Publications, 2013.

———. *Performance Art: From Futurism to the Present*. London: Thames and Hudson, 2001.

Gough, Maria. *The Artist as Producer: Russian Constructivism in Revolution*. Farmington Hills, MI: Thomson Gale, 2006.

Graff, Gerald. *Beyond the Culture Wars: How Teaching the Conflicts Can Revitalize American Education*. New York: Norton, 1992.

———. *Professing Literature: An Institutional History*. Chicago: University of Chicago Press, 1987.

Gramsci, Antonio. *The Prison Notebooks of Antonio Gramsci*. Edited and translated by Quintin Hoard and Geoffrey Nowell Smith. London: Lawrence and Wishart, 1971.

Green, Garth L., and Philip W. Scher. *Trinidad Carnival: The Cultural Politics of a Transnational Festival*. Bloomington: Indiana University Press, 2007.

Greenberg, Clement. "How Art Writing Earns Its Bad Name." *Second Coming Magazine* 1, no. 3 (March1962): 67–71.

———. "Modernist Painting." In *The New Art: A Critical Anthology*, edited by Gregory Battcock, 68–69. New York: E. P. Dutton, 1973.

Greenblatt, Stephen, and Giles B. Gunn. *Redrawing the Boundaries: The Transformation of English and American Literary Studies*. New York: Modern Language Association of America, 1992.

Groves, Jason. "A View from the Edge: The Peripatetic Perspective." In *The Best Things in Museums Are the Windows*. San Francisco: Exploratorium Museum, 2014.

Guattari, Félix. *Soft Subversions: Texts and Interviews 1977–1985*. Los Angeles: Semiotext(e), 2009.

Guillory, John. *Cultural Capital: The Problem of Literary Canon Formation*. Chicago: University of Chicago Press, 1993.

Guyote, Maura. "Theaster Gates' Dorchester Art + Housing Collaborative Offers Affordable Housing and Art Space in Chicago." *Creative Capital*, August 29, 2014. https://creative-capital.org/2014/08/29/theaster-gates -dorchester-arthousing-collaborative-offers-affordable-housing-community -space-chicago/.

Habermas, Jürgen. *The Structural Transformation of the Public Sphere: An Inquiry into a Category of Bourgeois Society*. Translated by Thomas Burger. Cambridge, MA: MIT Press, 1991.

———. *Democracy and the Public Sphere*. Translated by Luke Goode. Ann Arbor, MI: Pluto Press, 2005.

Hall, Stuart. "Encoding, Decoding." In *The Cultural Studies Reader*, edited by Simon During, 507–17. New York: Routledge, 1999.

Halperin, Julia. "It's Hard to Make Good Art about Climate Change: The Lithuanian Pavilion at the Venice Biennale Is a Powerful Exception." *Artnet*, May 10, 2019. https://news.artnet.com/exhibitions/lithuanian-pavilion-1543168.

Halttunen, Karen. *Confidence Men and Painted Women*. New Haven, CT: Yale University Press, 1982.

Hantelmann, Dorothea von. "The Experiential Turn." In *On Performativity*, edited by Elizabeth Carpenter. Vol. 1 of *Living Collections Catalogue*. Minneapolis: Walker Art Center, 2014. https://walkerart.org/collections /publications/performativity/experiential-turn/.

———. *How to Do Things with Art: The Meaning of Art's Performativity*. Zurich: JRP Ringier, 2010.

Haraway, Donna. "Situated Knowledges: The Science Question in Feminism and the Privilege of Partial Perspective." In *Simians, Cyborgs and Women: The Reinvention of Nature*, 183–202. New York: Routledge, 1991.

Hardt, Michael. "Affective Labor." *boundary 2* 26, no. 2. (1999): 89–100.

———. "Immaterial Labor and Artistic Production," *Rethinking Marxism: A Journal of Economics, Culture & Society* 17, no. 2 (2005): 175–77.

Hardt, Michael, and Antonio Negri. *Multitude: War and Democracy in the Age of Empire*. New York: Penguin Press, 2004.

Hare, Nathan. "Black Ecology." *Black Scholar* 1, no. 6 (April 1979): 2–8.

Hartman, Saidiya. *Lose Your Mother: A Journey along the Atlantic Slave Route*. New York: Farrar, Straus, and Giroux, 2007.

Heathfield, Adrian, ed. *Live: Art and Performance*. New York: Tate Publishing, 2004.

Heatwole, Joanna. "Media of Now: An Interview with David Hall." *Afterimage* 36, no. 1 (2008): 14–17.

Helguera, Pablo. *Education for Socially-Engaged Art*. New York: Jorge Pinto Books, 2011.

Helbo, André. *Les mots et les gestes*. Lille, France: Presses universitaires de Lille, 1983.

Hemenway, Robert E. *Zora Neale Hurston: A Literary Biography*. Champaign: University of Illinois Press, 1980.

Hochschild, Arlie R. *The Managed Heart: Commercialization of Human Feeling*. Berkeley: University of California Press, 1983.

Holmes, Brian. *Unleashing the Collective Phantoms: Essays in Reverse Imagineering*. New York: Autonomedia, 2008.

Holt, John. *How Children Fail*. New York: Pitman, 1964.

Horwitz, Andy. "Visual Art Performance vs. Contemporary Performance." *Culturebot*, November 25, 2011. http://www.culturebot.org/2011/11 /11663/visual-art-performance-vscontemporary-performance/.

Hull-House Maps and Papers. New York: Arno, 1970.

Inazu, John D. "The Forgotten Freedom of Assembly." *Tulane Law Review* 84 (2010): 565–612.

Jackson, Michael. *Paths Toward a Clearing: Radical Empiricism and Ethnographic Inquiry*. Bloomington: Indiana University Press, 1989.

Jackson, Shannon. *The Builders Association*. Cambridge, MA: MIT Press, 2015.

———. "Caravans Continued: In Memory of Dwight Conquergood." *TDR: The Drama Review* 50, no. 1 (Spring 2006): 28–32.

———. "Civic Play-Housekeeping: Gender, Theater, and American Reform." *Theater Journal* 48, no. 3 (1996): 337–61.

———. *Lines of Activity: Performance, Historiography, Hull-House Domesticity*. Ann Arbor: University of Michigan Press, 2000.

———. "Performing Show and Tell: Disciplines of Visual Culture and Performance Studies." In "Show and Tell: The State of Visual Culture Studies," edited by Martin Jay. Special issue, *Journal of Visual Culture* 4, no. 2 (2005): 163–77.

———. "Professing Performance: Disciplinary Genealogies." *TDR: The Drama Review* 45, no. 1 (Spring 2001): 84–95.

———. *Professing Performance: Theater in the Academy from Philology to Performativity*. Cambridge: Cambridge University Press, 2004.

———. "Social Turns: In Theory and Across the Arts." In *Routledge Companion to Art and Politics*, edited by Randy Martin, 104–13. New York: Routledge, 2014.

———. *Social Works: Performing Art, Supporting Publics*. New York and London: Routledge, 2011.

———. "Staging Institutions: Andrea Fraser and the 'Experiential' Museum.'" In *Andrea Fraser: A Retrospective*, edited by Sabine Breitwieser and Tina Teuffel, 21–29. Berlin: Hatje Cantz Verlag, 2015.

———. "What Is the 'Social' in Social Practice: Comparing Experiments in Performance." In *Cambridge Handbook of Performance Studies*, edited by Tracy Davis, 136–50. Cambridge: Cambridge University Press, 2008.

Jackson, Shannon, and Paula Marincola, eds. *In Terms of Performance*. Philadelphia: Pew Center for Arts and Heritage. http://www.intermsofperformance.site.

Jackson, Shannon, and Marianne Weems. *The Builders Association*. Cambridge, MA: MIT Press, 2015.

Jones, Amelia. *Body Art/Performing the Subject*. Minneapolis: University of Minnesota Press, 1998.

Jones, Bill T. "'Political' Work?" October 4, 2006. https://web.archive.org/web/20071209124832/http://www.billtjones.org/billsblog/2006/10/political_work.html, accessed November 23, 2021.

Jones, Caroline A. "Biennial Culture: A Longer History." In *The Biennial Reader*, edited by Elena Filipovic, Marieke van Hal, and Solveig Øvstebø, 66–87. Bergen, Norway: Bergen Kunsthall, 2010.

Jowitt, Deborah. "Walking Backward in Devotion." *DanceBeat*, March 3, 2012. http://www.artsjournal.com/dancebeat/2012/03/walking-backward-in-devotion/.

Judd, Donald. "Specific Objects." In *Donald Judd: Complete Writings 1959–1975*, 181–89. Halifax: Press of the Nova Scotia College of Art and Design, in association with New York University Press, 1975.

Kano, Betty Nobue. "Cultural Collisions for a New Public Space." *International Review of African American Art* 23, no. 2 (2010): 15–17.

Kant, Immanuel. "Succinct Exposition of Some Meditations on Fire" [1755]. In *Immanuel Kant: Natural Science*, edited by Eric Watkins, 309–26. Cambridge: Cambridge University Press, 2012.

Kaprow, Allan. "The Legacy of Jackson Pollock." *Art News* 57 (October 1958): 24–26, 55–57.

Kaye, Nick. *Site-Specific Art: Performance, Place, and Documentation*. London: Routledge, 2000.

Kelley, Jeff. *Childsplay: The Art of Allan Kaprow*. Berkeley: University of California Press, 2007.

Kershaw, Baz. *The Radical in Performance: Between Brecht and Baudrillard*. London: Routledge, 1999.

Kester, Grant. *Conversation Pieces*. Berkeley: University of California Press, 2004.

———. *The One and the Many: Contemporary Collaborative Art in a Global Context*. Durham, NC: Duke University Press, 2011.

Khong, En Liang. "How a Beach Opera at the 58th Venice Biennale Quietly Contends with Climate Change Catastrophe." *Frieze*, May 17, 2019. https://frieze.com/article/how-beach-opera-58th-venice-biennale-quietly-contends-climate-change-catastrophe.

Kiaer, Christina. *Imagine No Possessions: The Socialist Objects of Russian Constructivism*. Cambridge, MA: MIT Press, 2005.

Kimmelman, Michael. "Art Is Where the Home Is." *New York Times*, December 17, 2006. https://www.nytimes.com/2006/12/17/arts/design/in-houston-art-is-where-the-home-is.html.

Kinne, Wisner Payne. *George Pierce Baker and the American Theater*. Cambridge, MA: Harvard University Press, 1954.

Kirshenblatt-Gimblett, Barbara. "Objects of Ethnography." In *Exhibiting Cultures: The Poetics and Politics of Museum Display*, edited by Ivan Karp and Steven D. Lavine, 386–443. Washington, DC: Smithsonian Institution Press, 1991.

Kitamura, Katie. "Tino Sehgal." *Frieze* 131 (May 2010). https://www.frieze.com/article/tino-sehgal-2.

Knowles, Ric. *Reading the Material Theater*. Cambridge: Cambridge University Press, 2004.

Kohn, Hans. *American Nationalism: An Interpretive Essay*. New York: Macmillan, 1957.

Kourlas, Gia. "Do Not Feed or Annoy the Dancers." *New York Times*, April 1, 2012. http://www.nytimes.com/2012/04/02/arts/dance/michael-clarks-whos-zoo-at-whitney-biennial-2012.html.

Kozol, Jonathan. *Free Schools*. New York: Houghton Mifflin, 1972.

Kramer, Hilton. "The New American Painting." *Partisan Review* 20 (July–August 1953): 421–27.

Krauss, Rosalind E., and Marcel Broodthaers. *A Voyage on the North Sea: Art in the Age of the Post-Medium Condition*. New York: Thames and Hudson, 2000.

Kraut, Anthea. *Choreographing the Folk*. Minneapolis: University of Minnesota Press, 2008.

Kuoni, Carin, and Chelsea Haines, eds. *Entry Points: The Vera List Center Field Guide on Art and Social Justice No. 1*. Durham, NC: Duke University Press, 2015.

Kuoni, Carin. "Gates Gatherings." In Kuoni and Haines, *Entry Points*, 260–61.

Kwon, Miwon. *One Place after Another: Site-Specific Art and Locational Identity*. Cambridge, MA: MIT Press, 2002.

La Rocco, Claudia. "All Things Seen: Claudia La Rocco in Conversation with Marissa Perel." *Movement Research Critical Correspondence*, April 19, 2012. https://movementresearch.org/publications/critical-correspondence/all-things-seen-claudia-la-rocco-in-conversation-with-marissa-perel.

————. "Do a Little Dance, Make a Little Love." *Performance Club*, March 6, 2012. http://web.archive.org/web/20120309015731/http://theperformanceclub.org/2012/03/do-a-little-dance-make-a-little-love/.

————. "Mothers in Search of a Child." *New York Times*, May 18, 2012. http://theater.nytimes.com/2012/05/19/theater/reviews/there-we-will-be-buried-at-the-whitney-biennial.html.

————. "Ode to Sweat." *Performance Club*, March 15, 2012. https://claudialarocco.com/the-performance-club/.

————. "Yvonne Rainer Blasts Marina Abramovic at MOCA LA." *Performance Club*, November 11, 2011. http://web.archive.org/web/20120111103205/http://theperformanceclub.org/2011/11/yvonne-rainer-douglas-crimp-and-taisha-paggett-blast-marina-abramovic-and-moca-la/.

Lacan, Jacques. "The Meaning of the Phallus." In *Feminine Sexuality*, edited by Juliet Mitchell and Jacqueline Rose, 74–85. New York: W. W. Norton, 1986.

LaCapra, Dominick. *History and Criticism*. Ithaca, NY: Cornell University Press, 1985.

Laclau, Ernesto, and Chantal Mouffe. *Hegemony and Socialist Strategy: Towards a Radical Democratic Politics*. London: Verso, 1990.

Lacy, Suzanne, ed. *Mapping the Terrain: New Genre Public Art*. Seattle, WA: Bay Press, 1994.

Lambert-Beatty, Carrie. *Being Watched: Yvonne Rainer and the 1960s*. Cambridge, MA: MIT Press, 2008.

Land, Nick. *The Thirst for Annihilation: Georges Bataille and Virulent Nihilism*. New York: Routledge, 1990.

Landsman, Aaron, and Mallory Catlett. "Introduction to *City Council Meeting*." *Theater* 43, no. 3 (2013): 51–63.

Latour, Bruno. "From Realpolitik to Dingpolitik or How to Make Things Public in Making Things Public." In *Making Things Public: Atmospheres of Democracy*, edited by Bruno Latour and Peter Weibel, 14–41. Karlsruhe, Germany: ZKM Center for Art and Media, 2005.

Lave, Jean. *Situated Learning: Legitimate Peripheral Participation*. Cambridge: Cambridge University Press, 1991.

Lazzarrato, Maurizio. "Immaterial Labor." In *Radical Thought in Italy: A Potential Politics*, edited by Paul Virno and Michael Hardt, 133–50. Minneapolis: University of Minnesota Press, 1996.

Lepecki, André. "Choreopolice and Choreopolitics; or, The Task of the Dancer." *TDR: The Drama Review* 57, no. 4 (Winter 2013): 13–27.

———. *Exhausting Dance: Performance and the Politics of Movement*. New York: Routledge, 2006.

Lessing, Gotthold Ephraim. *Laocoön: An Essay on the Limits of Poetry and Painting*. Translated by Edward Allen McCormick (Baltimore and London: The Johns Hopkins University Press, 1984).

Levere, Jane. "MoMA Expands Again." *ARTnews* 105, no. 10 (2006): 67.

Levin, Laura. *Performing Ground: Space, Camouflage and the Art of Blending*. London: Palgrave Macmillan, 2014.

Levine, David. "Bad Art & Objecthood." *Art/US* no. 13, May/June 2006. Reprinted in *The Performance Club*, September 11, 2012. http://theperformanceclub.org/2012/09/reprint-bad-art-objecthood/.

Levine, David, Marsha Ginsberg, Jason Grote, and Amy Holzapfel. "The Habit of Realism (Interview)." *Theater* 42, no. 1 (2012): 95–107.

Linebaugh, Peter, and Marcus Rediker. *The Many-Headed Hydra: Sailors, Slaves, Commoners, and the Hidden History of the Revolutionary Atlantic*. Boston: Beacon Press, 2000.

Lippard, Lucy R. *Six Years: The Dematerialization of the Art Object from 1966 to 1972*. Berkeley: University of California Press, 1997.

Lissak, Rivka Shpak. *Pluralism and Progressives: Hull-House and the New Immigrant*. Chicago: University of Chicago Press, 1989.

Lyotard, Jean-François. *The Postmodern Condition: A Report on Knowledge*. Translated by Geoff Bennington and Brian Massumi. Minneapolis: University of Minneapolis Press, 1994.

———. *The Inhuman: Reflections on Time*. Translated by Geoffrey Bennington and Rachel Bowlby. Stanford, CA: Stanford University Press, 1992.

Mackay, Robin. "A Brief History of Geotrauma." In *Leper Creativity: Cyclonopedia Symposium*, edited by Ed Keller et al., 16–20. Brooklyn: Punctum, 2012.

MacKinnon, Catherine A. "Sexuality, Pornography, and Method: 'Pleasure under Patriarchy.'" *Ethics* 99, no. 2 (January 1989): 314–46.

Mackinnon-Little, Guy. "Interview: Lucia Pietroiusti." *TANK Magazine* 80 (2019). https://tankmagazine.com/issue-80/talks/lucia-pietroiusti/.

Madison, Soyini, and Judith Hamera, eds. *The SAGE Handbook of Performance Studies*. Thousand Oaks, CA: SAGE, 2006.

Marcuse, Herbert. *One-Dimensional Man: Studies in the Ideology of Advanced Industrial Society*. Boston: Beacon Press, [1964] 1991.

Marinis, Marco De. *The Semiotics of Performance*. Bloomington: Indiana University Press, 1993.

Marx, Karl. *Capital: A Critique of Political Economy, Vol. 1*. Translated by Ben Fowkes. New York: Vintage Books, 1977.

———. *Grundrisse: Foundations of the Critique of Political Economy*. Trans. Martin Nicolaus. London: Penguin Books, 1993.

Masten, Jeffrey. *Textual Intercourse: Collaboration, Authorship, and Sexualities in Renaissance Drama*. Cambridge: Cambridge University Press, 1997.

Masten, Jeffrey, Peter Stallybrass, and Nancy Vickers. *Language Machines: Technologies of Literary and Cultural Production, Essays from the English Institute*. New York: Routledge, 1997.

Matthews, Brander. *The Development of the Drama*. New York: C. Scribner's Sons, 1903.

Maxwell, Richard. "Richard Maxwell (Interview)." Interview by David Velasco. *Artforum*, April 25, 2012.

McDonough, Tom, ed. *The Situationists and the City*. London: Verso, 2010.

McGill, Meredith L. *American Literature and the Culture of Reprinting, 1834–1853*. Philadelphia: University of Pennsylvania Press, 2003.

McKenzie, Jon. *Perform or Else: From Discipline to Performance*. London: Routledge, 2001.

Menger, Pierre-Michel. *Les intermittents du spectacle*. Paris: Éditions de l'École des hautes études en sciences sociales, 2005.

Meyer, James. *Minimalism: Art and Polemics in the Sixties*. New Haven, CT: Yale University Press, 2001.

Mink, Louis O., Brian Fay, Eugene O. Golob, and Richard T. Vann. *Historical Understanding*. Ithaca, NY: Cornell University Press, 1987.

Mirzoeff, Nicholas. "The Subject of Visual Culture." In *The Visual Culture Reader*, edited by Nicholas Mirzoeff, 3–23. London: Routledge, 2002.

Mitchell, W. J. T. "Showing Seeing: A Critique of Visual Culture." In *The Visual Culture Reader*, edited by Nicholas Mirzoeff, 86–101. London: Routledge, 2002.

Morgan, Ted. *Reds: McCarthyism in Twentieth-Century America*. New York: Random House, 2003.

Morris, Robert. "Notes on Sculpture, Part II." *Artforum* 5 (October 1966). https://www.artforum.com/print/196608/notes-on-sculpture-part-2-36826.

Morton, Timothy. *The Ecological Thought*. Cambridge, MA: Harvard University Press, 2012.

Moten, Fred. *In the Break: The Aesthetics of the Black Radical Tradition.* Minneapolis: University of Minnesota Press, 2003.

Moten, Fred, and Stefano Harvey. *The Undercommons: Fugitive Planning and Black Study.* New York: Autonomedia, 2013.

Muñoz, José Esteban. *Cruising Utopia: The Then and There of Queer Futurity.* New York: New York University Press, 2009.

Nagler, A. M. *Theater Festivals of the Medici, 1539–1637.* Translated by George Hickenlooper. New Haven, CT: Yale University Press, 1964.

Neill, A. S. *Summerhill: A Radical Approach to Child Rearing.* New York: Hart Publishing, 1960.

Network of European Museum Organizations. "NEMO Publishes Initial Results of Survey on the Impact of the Corona Crisis on Museums in Europe." July 4, 2020. https://www.ne-mo.org/news/article/nemo /nemo-publishes-results-of-survey-on-the-impact-of-the-corona-crisis-on -museums-in-europe.html.

Oliver, Valerie Cassel. "Craft Out of Action." In *Hand + Made: The Performative Impulse in Art and Craft,* edited by Valerie Cassel Oliver, 11–20. Houston: Contemporary Art Museum Houston, 2010.

Olsen, Tillie. "One out of twelve: women who are writers in our century." *College English* 34, no. 1 (Oct. 1972): 6–17.

Ortiz, Paul. "C. L. R. James' Visionary Legacy." *Against the Current* 156 (Jan./ Feb. 2012). https://againstthecurrent.org/atc156/p3494/.

Paley, Grace. "Wants." In *You've Got to Read This: Contemporary American Writers Introduce Stories that Held Them in Awe,* edited by R. Hansen and J. Shepard, 469–71. 1st ed. New York: Harper Perennial, 1994.

Parker, Andrew, and Eve Kosofsky Sedgwick, eds. *Performativity and Performance.* New York: Routledge, 1995.

Patterson, Orland. *Slavery and Social Death.* Cambridge, MA: Harvard University Press, 1985.

Pavis, Patrice. *La mise en scène contemporaine: Origines, tendances, perspectives.* Paris: A. Colin, 2007.

———. *Languages of the Stage: Essays in the Semiology of the Theater.* New York: Performing Arts Journal Publications, 1982.

Phelan, Peggy. *Unmarked: The Politics of Performance.* London: Routledge, 1996.

Pinder, David. "Arts of Urban Exploration." *Cultural Geographies* 12 (2005): 383–41.

Pine II, B. Joseph, and James H. Gilmore. *The Experience Economy: Work Is Theater and Every Business a Stage.* Boston: Harvard Business Review Press, 1999.

Pink, Daniel H. *A Whole New Mind: Why Right-Brainers Will Rule the Future.* New York: Riverhead Books, 2006.

Poirier, Agnès. " How the Maverick Christiane Taubira is Transforming French Politics." *Guardian,* August 14, 2013. http://www.theguardian.com /commentisfree/2013/aug/14/christiane-taubira-french-politics.

Postlewait, Thomas, and Bruce A. McConachie, eds. *Interpreting the Theatrical Past: Essays in the Historiography of Performance.* Iowa City: University of Iowa Press, 1989.

Puar, Jasbir, Lauren Berlant, Judith Butler, Bojana Cvejić, Isabell Lorey, and Ana Vujanović. "Precarity Talk: A Virtual Roundtable with Lauren Berlant, Judith Butler, Bojana Cvejić, Isabell Lorey, Jasbir Puar, and Ana Vujanović." *TDR: The Drama Review* 56, no. 4 (2012): 163–177. muse.jhu.edu/article/491900.

Puchner, Martin. *Stage Fright: Modernism, Anti-Theatricality, and Drama.* Baltimore: Johns Hopkins University Press, 2011.

Purves, Ted, ed. *What We Want Is Free: Generosity and Exchange in Recent Art.* Albany: State University of New York Press, 2004.

Quinn, Michael. *The Semiotic Stage: Prague School Theater Theory.* New York: Peter Lang, 1995.

Rainer, Yvonne. "Some Retrospective Notes on a Dance for 10 People and 12 Mattresses . . ." *Tulane Drama Review* 10, no. 2 (1965): 168–78.

Rancière, Jacques. *Die Aufteilung des Sinnlichen: Die Politik der Kunst und ihre Paradoxien.* Translated by Maria Muhle, Susanne Leeb, and Jürgen Link. Berlin: b_books, 2006.

Raunig, Gerald. *Art and Revolution: Transversal Activism in the Long Twentieth Century.* Cambridge, MA: Semiotext(e), 2007.

Readings, Bill. *The University in Ruins.* Cambridge, MA: Harvard University Press, 1996.

Reynolds, Joshua. *Discourses on Art.* New Haven, CT: Yale University Press, 1975.

Ritchie, Abraham. "The Slant on Theaster Gates." *Artslant,* May 2010.

Rivière, Joan. "Womanliness as Masquerade." In *Formations of Fantasy,* edited by Victor Burgin, James Donald, and Cora Kaplan, 35–43. New York: Routledge, Chapman, and Hall, 1986.

Roach, Joseph. *Cities of the Dead: Circum-Atlantic Performance.* New York: Columbia University Press, 1996.

———. "Reconstructing Theater/History." *Theater Topics* 9, no. 1 (March 1999): 3–10.

Robb, Mary Margaret. "The Elocutionary Movement and Its Chief Figures." In *The History of Speech Education in America,* edited by K. R. Wallace, 178–201. New York: Appleton-Century-Crofts, 1954.

———. *Oral Interpretation of Literature in American Colleges and Universities: A Historical Study of Teaching Method.* New York: H. W. Wilson, 1941.

Rodenbeck, Judith. *Radical Prototypes.* Cambridge, MA: MIT Press, 2011.

Rosaldo, Renato. *Culture and Truth: The Remaking of Social Analysis.* Boston: Beacon, 1989.

Rosenberg, Harold. "The American Action Painters." *ARTnews* 52 (January 1952): 23–39.

Rosenthal, Mark. *Joseph Beuys: Actions, Vitrines, Environments.* New Haven, CT: Yale University Press, 2005.

Rosenthal, Nan. "Assisted Levitation: The Art of Yves Klein." *Yves Klein, 1928–1962: A Retrospective,* exhibition catalog, 90-135. Houston: Rice University Institute for the Arts, 1982.

Rosenzweig, Roy, and Barbara Melosh. "Government and the Arts: Voices from the New Deal Era." *Journal of American History* (September 1990): 596–608.

Rubin, Gayle. "The Traffic in Women: Notes on the Political Economy of Sex."
In *Toward an Anthropology of Women*, edited by Rayna Rapp, 157–210.
New York: Monthly Review Press, 1976.

Russeth, Andrew. "Whitney's 2012 Bucksbaum Prize Goes to Sarah Michelson." *Observer*, April 19, 2012. http://observer.com/2012/04/whitneys-2012
-bucksbaum-award-goes-to-sarah-michelson/.

Said, Edward. *Orientalism*. New York: Vintage Books, 1979.

Saltz, Jerry. "How I Made an Artwork Cry." *New York*, February 3, 2010.
http://nymag.com/arts/art/reviews/63638/.

Sapiro, Virginia. "Women, Citizenship, and Nationality: Immigration and
Naturalization Policies in the United States." *Politics and Society* 13, no. 1
(1984): 1–24.

Sayer, Andrew, and Richard Walker. *The New Social Economy: Reworking the
Division of Labor*. Cambridge, MA: Blackwell Publishers, 1992.

Sayre, Henry M. *The Object of Performance: The American Avant-Garde
since 1970*. Chicago: University of Chicago Press, 1989.

Schaefer, Brian. "Sarah Michelson and the Infiltration of Dance." *Out Magazine*, January 30, 2014. https://www.out.com/entertainment/theater-dance
/2014/01/30/sarah-michelson-whitney-museum.

Schechner, Richard. *Between Theater and Anthropology*. Philadelphia: University of Pennsylvania Press, 1985.

———. "A New Paradigm for Theater in the Academy." *TDR: The Drama
Review* 36, no. 4 (1992): 7–10.

———. "Performance Studies: The Broad Spectrum Approach." *TDR: The
Drama Review* 32, no. 3 (1988): 4–6.

———. "Theater Alive in the New Millennium." *TDR: The Drama Review*
44, no. 1 (2000): 5–6.

Scher, Philip W. *Carnival and the Formation of a Caribbean Transition*. Gainesville: University Press of Florida, 2003.

Schneider, Rebecca. *The Explicit Body in Performance*. London: Routledge,
1997.

———. *Performing Remains: Art and War in Times of Theatrical Reenactment*. New York: Routledge, 2011.

Schwab, Jim. *Deeper Shades of Green: The Rise of the Blue-Collar and Minority Environmentalism in American*. San Francisco: Sierra Club, 1994.

Scott, James C. *Domination and the Arts of Resistance: The Hidden Transcript*. New Haven, CT: Yale University Press, 1989.

Scott, Joan. *Gender and the Politics of History*. New York: Columbia University Press, 1988.

Sebaly, Abigail. "Cold Storage and New Brightness: The Cunningham Acquisition Moves in at the Walker." *Walker Art Online Magazine*, July 29,
2011. https://walkerart.org/magazine/cold-storage-and-new-brightness-the
-cunningham-acquisition-moves-in-at-the-walker.

———. "Cold Storage and New Brightness: The Merce Cunningham Acquisition at the Walker Art Center." *Brooklyn Rail*, December 10, 2010. http://
www.brooklynrail.org/2011/12/dance/cold-storage-and-new-brightness
-the-merce-cunningham-acquisition-at-the-walker-art-center.

Sedgwick, Eve Kosofsky. "Queer Performativity: Henry James's *The Art of the Novel.*" *GLQ: A Journal of Lesbian and Gay Studies* 1, no. 1 (1993): 1–16.

Sexton, Jared. *Amalgamation Schemes: Antiblackness and the Critique of Multiculturalism.* Minneapolis: University of Minnesota Press, 2008.

Sapiro, Virginia. "Women, Citizenship, and Nationality: Immigration and Naturalization Policies in the United States." *Politics and Society* 13, no. 1 (1984): 1–24.

Sholette, Greg. "Activism as Art: Shotgun Shacks Saved through Art-Based Revitalization: Interview with Rick Lowe." *Huffington Post*, November 22, 2010. Accessed January 2012.

———. *Dark Matter: Art and Politics in an Age of Enterprise Culture.* New York: Pluto Press, 2010.

Sholette, Gregory, and Blake Stimson. *Collectivism after Modernism: The Art of Social Imagination after 1945.* Minneapolis: University of Minnesota Press, 2007.

Silverman, Kaja. *World Spectators.* Stanford, CA: Stanford University Press, 2000.

Simone, AbdouMaliq. "People as Infrastructure: Intersecting Fragments in Johannesburg." *Public Culture* 16, no. 3 (Fall 2004): 407–29.

Slotoerdijk, Peter. *Foams, Spheres Volume III: Plural Spherology.* Cambridge, MA: MIT Press, 2016.

Smith, Dorothy E. *The Everyday World As Problematic: A Feminist Sociology.* Boston: Northeastern University Press, 1987.

———. "A Peculiar Eclipsing: Women's Exclusion From Man's Culture." *Women's Studies International Quarterly* 1 (1978): 281–95.

Smith, Marquard. "Visual Studies, or the Ossification of Thought." *Journal of Visual Culture* 4, no. 2 (August 2005): 237–56.

Smith, Roberta. "A Survey of a Different Color: 2012 Whitney Biennial." *New York Times*, March 1, 2012. https://www.nytimes.com/2012/03/02/arts/design/2012-whitney-biennial.html.

Smith, Rogers M. "The 'American Creed' and American Identity: The Limits of Liberal Citizenship in the United States." *Western Political Quarterly* 41, no. 2 (1988): 225–51.

Smith, Susan Harris. *American Drama: The Bastard Art.* Cambridge: Cambridge University Press, 1997.

Solnit, Rebecca. *Wanderlust: A History of Walking.* New York: Penguin Books, 2001.

Southern, Richard. *The Medieval Theater in the Round: A Study of the Staging of the Castle of Perseverance and Related Matters.* 2nd ed. London: Faber, 1975.

Spingarn, Joel Elias. *Creative Criticism and Other Essays.* New York: Harcourt, Brace, 1931.

Stengers, Isabelle. *Cosmopolitics I.* Minneapolis: University of Minnesota Press, 2010.

Stewart, Susan. *On Longing: Narratives of the Miniature, the Gigantic, the Souvenir, the Collection.* Durham, NC: Duke University Press, 1993.

Stocking, George. *Race, Culture, and Evolution: Essays in the History of Anthropology.* Chicago: University of Chicago Press, 1982.

Susman, Warren. *Culture as History: The Transformation of American Society in the Twentieth Century*. New York: Pantheon Books, 1984.

Tancons, Claire. "Curating Carnival: Performance in Contemporary Caribbean Art." In *Curating in the Caribbean*, edited by David A. Bailey, Alissandra Cummins, Axel Lapp, and Allison Thompson, 37–62. Berlin: Green Box, 2012.

Tang, Jeannine. "Biennialization and its Discontents?" *Red Hook Journal*, April 8, 2013.

Taussig, Michael. *The Nervous System*. New York: Routledge, 1992.

Taylor, Diana. *The Archive and the Repertoire: Performing Cultural Memory in the Americas*. Durham, NC: Duke University Press, 2003.

Taylor, Dorceta. "Green Power." *Crisis Magazine* 118, no. 2 (April 2011): 16–18.

Taylor, Richard A. "Do Environmentalists Care about Poor People." *US News and World Report*, April 2, 1983, 51–52.

Thacker, Eugene. *In The Dust of This Planet: Horror of Philosophy, Volume 1*. Winchester, UK: Zero Books, 2011.

Thompson, Nato. *Living as Form: Socially Engaged Art from 1991–2011*. Cambridge, MA: MIT Press, 2012.

Thornton, Sarah. *Seven Days in the Art World*. New York: W. W. Norton, 2008.

Tiampo, Ming. *Gutai: Decentering Modernism*. Chicago: University of Chicago Press, 2011.

Tolstoy, Leo. "The School at Yasnaya Polyana." In *Tolstoy as Teacher: Leo Tolstoy's Writings on Education*. New York: Teachers and Writers Collaborative, 2000.

United States Cybersecurity and Infrastructure Security Agency. "Guidance on the Essential Critical Infrastructure Workforce." https://www.cisa.gov /publication/guidance-essential-critical-infrastructure-workforce.

Vele, Ivanmaria. "Elmgreen & Dragset: Boiler's Choice." *Boiler* 1 (2003): 112–19.

Vince, Ronald W. *Renaissance Theater: A Historiographical Handbook*. Westport, CT: Greenwood Press, 1984.

Virno, Paolo. *A Grammar of the Multitude: For an Analysis of Contemporary Life Forms*. Cambridge, MA: Semiotext(e), 2004.

———. "Virtuosity and Revolution: The Political Theory of Exodus." In *Radical Thought in Italy: A Potential Politics*, edited by Paul Virno and Michael Hardt, 189–212. Minneapolis: University of Minnesota Press, 1996.

Vlach, John Michael. *By the Work of Their Hands: Studies in Afro-American Folklife*. Ann Arbor, MI: UMI Research Press, 1991.

———. "Shotgun Houses." *Natural History* 86, no. 2 (1977): 51–57.

Wallace, Michael. "Visiting the Past: History Museums in the United States." In Benson, Brier, and Rosensweig, *Presenting the Past*, 137–64.

Ward, Ossian. "Art Shows in Kassel and Munster." *TimeOut London*, June 27, 2007. www.timeout.com/london/art/features/3089/Art_shows_in_Kassell _and_Munster.html, accessed November 2010.

Wark, McKenzie. "What the Performative Can't Perform: On Judith Butler." *Public Seminar*, June 8, 2016. http://publicseminar.org/2016/06/butler/.

Warner, Michael. "Publics and Counterpublics." *Public Culture* 14, no. 1 (Winter 2002): 49–90.

Washburne, Marion Foster. "A Labor Museum." *The Craftsman* 6, no. 6 (Sept 1904): 570–80.

Waterman, Stanley. "Carnivals for Elites? The Cultural Politics of Arts Festivals." *Progress in Human Geography* 22, no. 1 (February 1998): 54–74.

Weeks, Kathi. "Life within and against Work: Affective Labor, Feminist Critique, and Post-Fordist Politics." *ephemera* 7, no. (2007): 233–49.

Weinstein, Tresca. "David Levine's 'Habit' at Mass Moca." *Times Union*, February 26, 2011. https://blog.timesunion.com/localarts/david-levine%E2%80%99s-%E2%80%9Chabit%E2%80%9D-mass-moca-22611/15156/.

White, Hayden. *The Content of the Form: Narrative Discourse and Historical Representation*. Baltimore: Johns Hopkins University Press, 1987.

———. *Tropics of Discourse*. Baltimore: Johns Hopkins University Press, 1978.

Whitney Museum of American Art. "Sarah Michelson Receives 2012 Bucksbaum Award." April 9, 2012. http://whitney.org/2012BucksbaumAwardToSarahMichelson.

Wilderson, Frank. *Incognegro: A Memoir of Exile and Apartheid*. Durham, NC: Duke University Press, 2015.

———. *Red, White, and Black: Cinema and the Structure of U.S. Antagonisms*. Durham, NC: Duke University Press, 2010.

Wilkinson, Chris. "Noises Off: What's the Difference between Performance Art and Theater?" *Guardian*, July 20, 2010. https://www.theguardian.com/stage/theaterblog/2010/jul/20/noises-off-performance-art-theater.

Williams, Raymond. "Criticism." In *Keywords: A Vocabulary of Culture and Society*, 84–86. New York: HarperCollins, 1983.

Wolf, Eric. *Europe and the People without History*. Berkeley: University of California Press, 1982.

Wolfe, George C. *The Colored Museum*. New York: Grove Press, 1988.

Yusoff, Kathryn. *A Billion Black Anthropocenes or None*. Minneapolis: University of Minnesota Press, 2019.

INDEX